California Sabers

California

James McLean

Sabers

THE 2ND MASSACHUSETTS CAVALRY IN THE CIVIL WAR

INDIANA UNIVERSITY PRESS

Bloomington • Indianapolis

This book is a publication of

Indiana University Press
601 North Morton Street
Bloomington, Indiana 47404-3797 USA

www.indiana.edu/~iupress

Telephone orders 800-842-6796
Fax orders 812-855-7931
Orders by email iuporder@indiana.edu

The paper used in this publication meets the minimum
requirements of American National Standard for
Information Sciences—Permanence of Paper for
Printed Library Materials, ANSI Z39.48-1984.

Manufactured in the United States of America

Library of Congress Cataloging-in-Publication Data

McLean, James, date
California sabers : the 2nd Massachusetts Cavalry in the Civil War / James McLean.
   p. cm.
Includes bibliographical references and index.
ISBN 0-253-33786-0 (alk. paper)
  1. United States. Army. Massachusetts Cavalry Regiment, 2nd (1862–1865) 2.
Massachusetts—History—Civil War, 1861–1865—Regimental Histories. 3. United
States—History—Civil War, 1861–1865—Regimental Histories. 4. United States—
History—Civil War, 1861–1865—Cavalry operations. 5. Soldiers—California—
History—19th century. 6. California—History—Civil War, 1861–1865. I. Title.

E513.6 2nd .M38 2000
973.7'444—dc21
                                       00-035040

1   2   3   4   5   05   04   03   02   01   00

A line in a long array where they wind betwixt green islands,
They take a serpentine course, their arms flash in the sun—
hark to the musical clank,
Behold the silvery river, in it the splashing horses loitering
stop to drink,
Behold the brown-faced men, each group, each person
a picture, the negligent rest on the saddles,
Some emerge on the opposite bank, others are just
entering the ford—while,
Scarlet and blue and snowy white,
The guidon flags flutter gaily in the wind.

—"Cavalry Crossing a Ford," Walt Whitman (1865)

Contents

Maps

Acknowledgments

Preparing a history like this takes a lot of help from lots of people. I owe many thanks to all of them. My old friend John Selby convinced me I should take on this project. Sadly, he did not get to see it completed.

Larry Rogers, the sergeant major of the California Hundred reenactment group, steered me to some of the sources available in the San Francisco Bay area.

Mrs. Geraldine Chase graciously provided me a copy of Valorus Dearborn's diary and permission to use it in the text. William Kooiman of the San Francisco Maritime National Historical Park provided information on the steamers that took Californians to the East Coast. Thaddeus George of Americus, Georgia, researched the files at Andersonville prison for the death records of the Californians interred there. John L. Huffer and Earl E. Meese of the Waynesborough, Virginia, Historical Society guided me through the little known battles at Waynesborough.

J. Michael Comeau of the Commonwealth of Massachusetts Archives Division provided a copy of the pages from the "Record of Massachusetts Men in the Civil War" pertaining to the 2nd Massachusetts—a task he performed twice because I misplaced some of the pages.

The Bancroft Library at the University of California gave me permission to quote from Sam Corbett's diary. The Massachusetts Historical Society gave permission to quote from Colonel Crowninshield's letters in the Magnus Crowninshield papers. On one journey to their library in Boston, I was able to hold the actual letters—a "time trip" experience. Eureka Cartography in Berkeley led me through the map making process and prepared the maps for the book.

Mike Fitzpatrick researched the National Archives and gave me his wealth of information on the Battle of Rockville. The account of that fight herein would not have been so complete without his tremendous input.

Richard Tibbals freely offered his expertise on the Civil War and provided encouragement and criticism. He offered copies from his large collection of photos to be used in the book without restriction and spent hours editing the manuscript, correcting my mistakes. His comments and assistance were invaluable and I am deeply indebted to him.

And to Marilee, who listened to all of my anecdotes about the war and tramped the battlefields with me—thank you.

California Sabers

I | Join the Cavalry!

The night before the duel, Senator David Broderick was restless. He spent the evening at a small farmhouse with his close friend Edward Baker. The two sat up until the early hours of September 13, 1859, discussing California politics and their hopes for the future. Just before sunrise, they arose and rode out to the dueling ground, a cold and damp field just over the San Francisco–San Mateo County line. There they found a small group of newspaper reporters and David Terry, Justice of the State Supreme Court, and his seconds. Duels were not uncommon in the turbulent California of the 1850s, and only occasionally were they fatal.[1] Even more rarely were they between two prominent state leaders like Broderick and Terry.

With Baker on the sideline, Broderick won the toss for position; he elected to stand with the rising sun to his back. Another coin was tossed and Terry's long-barreled French dueling pistols with odd-shaped stocks were selected. Unbeknownst to Broderick, these guns had a very delicate trigger. David Colton, one of Broderick's seconds, stepped forward, and the two duelists took their positions. Colton, chosen by coin toss to give the commands, waited and then turned toward Justice Terry. The judge wore his hat with the brim turned up and stood sideways so as to present a narrow silhouette. He was calm; the pistol in his right hand hung down with the muzzle pointing at the ground. Colton, satisfied the judge was ready, turned to Senator Broderick, who was standing twenty paces to the east. The senator's coat was buttoned to his chin and, although his back was to the rising sun, his hat was pulled down just short of his eyebrows. He stood with his body half-turned; he looked tired and ill at ease. The tail of his surcoat seemed to be in the way of his right arm; he brushed it away. Then he flexed his hand over the pistol grip, trying to find a comfortable position. After a few minutes Colton could wait no longer. Aware of the importance of his words, Colton asked, "Gentlemen are you ready?" Justice Terry immediately responded, "Yes."

There was a moment or two of hesitation as the senator made a last adjustment to his grip. At last, he indicated his readiness with a nod. A hush came over the witnesses. The seconds stepped back.

Colton drew a deep breath and said, "Fire!" Broderick fired first. His arm was only halfway raised when the pistol discharged. The ball buried itself in the ground about ten feet in front of him. "One!" Coulton called. As if in slow motion, Justice Terry raised his arm, aimed, and fired. A puff of lint erupted from the Senator's right chest. The two shots reverberated in the still morning. Colton shouted "Two!" —the signal that the duel was over.

Terry turned, disappointed, thinking he had only wounded his opponent. Broderick stood erect and extended his arms out in front trying to steady himself. The pistol was still in his right hand. Terry's seconds called for him to return to his position, because it appeared that the duel was not over. Broderick suddenly shuddered and his pistol fell to the ground. He turned and fell to his left knee, then his right knee buckled. He knelt as if praying, balanced by his outstretched arms. His seconds rushed to him and he apologized for not rising, saying, "The blood blinded me."

A spectator shouted, "This is murder!"

Terry was still in his place, holding his pistol. A friend, Samuel Brooks, who had been opposed to the duel, said to Terry, "Are you satisfied?"

Terry angrily retorted, "For the present."

Brooks, aghast, asked, "Why for the present?"

"Because Broderick's defamation still remains. He must retract it," Terry replied. Broderick's seconds lifted him and carried him to a waiting farm wagon. Terry mounted his horse and returned to Oakland, convinced he had not seriously wounded Broderick.[2]

Senator David C. Broderick died on September 16, 1859, after lingering in pain for three days. The newspapers covered his deteriorating condition on almost an hourly basis. Edward Baker delivered a fiery eulogy at the funeral on September 18. According to the papers and Baker, Broderick's last words were that he had been killed because he opposed slavery in California. The papers were filled with the story, some denouncing the practice of dueling but more reviling Justice Terry. Faced with growing public hostility and perhaps remembering the Vigilante Committees of a few years earlier, Terry fled to his ranch in Modesto in the San Joaquin Valley. He was charged, but never brought to trial because of machinations by Broderick's political enemies—including the district attorney and the judge, who was later impeached.[3]

Justice David Terry was a supporter of Broderick's real opponent—the aristocratic, Southern-born William Gwin. Gwin was a slave-owning Tennessee Democrat and a close friend of Andrew Jackson. With Jackson's help Gwin was appointed to several governmental posts where he tried to parlay his salary into wealth through land speculations. His schemes collapsed and, facing bankruptcy, he returned to Washington, D.C., as a congressman from Mississippi. He tried to recoup his fortune while in Congress through manipulation of Indian subsidies. He lost his House seat to a promising politician from Mississippi named Jefferson C. Davis. Still, his loyalty to the party was not forgotten, and he was appointed to the much sought after post of Commissioner of Public Works for the Port of New Orleans. The position was extremely lucrative, and in a short time his financial problems were finally behind him.

When Zachary Taylor's administration came to power Gwin lost the commissioner's post and left Washington for California. He told his friend Stephen Douglas that he would return as one of California's first senators.[4] Within a short time Gwin built a strong following among the state's Democrats and, true to his word, he was elected to the six-year term by the first state senate.[5] His fellow senator for four years would be John C. Frémont. The post of senator included control of the federal patronage, and Gwin quickly used his opportunities to secure his followers appointments to federal posts around the state. Because of his background, most of his supporters were Southerners, and the press nicknamed them "The Chivalry" because of their strong Southern sympathies.

David C. Broderick was from New York. In his early years he had worked as a mason, a bar tender, and a ward heeler for Tammany Hall. He came to San Francisco in 1849, and by 1850 he entered the state senate. He was a Northern Democrat, opposed to the expansion of slavery and, because of his plebeian background, a fierce advocate of workingman's rights. In his first years in San Francisco he made a fortune in real estate and from a private minting firm.[6] He also amassed enough power to control state patronage. In 1854 he tried to convince the state senate to appoint him to Gwin's senatorial seat before the term was up. He was unsuccessful and he earned the deep enmity of William Gwin. He tried again in 1855, but this time Gwin was ready and the two leaders created such a deadlock in the state senate that no one was appointed for two years.

In 1857 Gwin approached Broderick and offered to give him control of the federal patronage if Broderick would support his reappointment. Broderick had Gwin sign a secret protocol containing the details of the agreement. With the deadlock broken, the senate sent both men to Washington. Unfortunately for Broderick, the newly elected president, James Buchanan, was a Southern Democrat and a friend of Gwin who relied on Gwin for candidates for the federal jobs in California. Broderick was furious. He leaked the protocol to the newspapers and over the next two years took every opportunity to malign Gwin and his supporters.

Broderick's ally, Edward Dickinson Baker, was born in London in 1811. He came to the United States with his parents when he was four years old. He qualified to practice law at nineteen, and a year later married a widow with two children. He moved to Springfield, Illinois, where he met another attorney named Abraham Lincoln. They formed a friendship that would last a lifetime. In 1852 he took his family to San Francisco where he established a successful law practice. Isaac Wistar joined him as a partner in 1856. He switched to the new Republican Party in 1854.[7] In spite of the differences in their political allegiance he became a close friend of David Broderick because of a shared antipathy to The Chivalry.

One night in 1859 one of Justice Terry's friends overheard Broderick make a disparaging remark about Terry, who was an ardent supporter of The Chivalry, and reported the conversation to the hot-blooded judge. Terry demanded a retraction and, when Broderick equivocated, challenged him to a duel. Friends tried to mediate the dispute but the negotiations fell apart. An agreement for the conduct of a duel was prepared. On September 12, Broderick, Terry, and their seconds showed up at the agreed site, only to be met by the San Francisco sheriff and several deputies, who were there to enforce the "no dueling" law. To satisfy the sheriff and avoid arrest, both parties disavowed any intent of fighting a duel, only to return the next day to consummate the arrangement. For California, the two shots fired on that overcast morning in a little clearing in San Mateo County were the first shots in a cataclysm that soon would shake the state and the nation.

The Broderick–Terry duel marked the end of a bitter, ten-year-old struggle for the control of the California Democratic Party. Ironically it crippled the party and set the stage for Lincoln's narrow victory in California in 1860. In the fall of that year the presidential race included two Democrats—John Breckinridge and Stephen Douglas—and Republican Abraham Lincoln. California Republicans favored a strong federal government and opposed the extension of slavery into the territories. They supported granting legal rights to nonwhites, but stopped short of granting minorities the right to vote. One of the major planks of California Republicans, led by Leland Stanford, was the creation of federal subsidies to finance the construction of the transcontinental railroad. They had never elected a single candidate to office and were clearly the minority party.

To California's Democratic Party, which had controlled the state from the beginning, the election of one of the Democratic candidates seemed assured. Only six of the fifty-two newspapers in the state supported Lincoln, whereas twenty-two supported Breckinridge and twenty-four endorsed Douglas. The voters, still reeling from the death of Broderick, were split. Thousands of Democratic voters, shocked by the venality and violence in their party, were undecided.

Edward Baker, now a newly appointed senator from Oregon, stopped in San Francisco on his way to the East to take his seat in the new congress. The leaders of the local Republican Party persuaded him to speak on Lincoln's behalf. On Friday, October 26, 1860, Baker delivered what one writer called "the greatest speech ever delivered in California."

Later, at a meeting among his friends Baker made a statement that roused the listeners to a fever pitch by invoking the memory of the slain Broderick:

> . . . it was my fortune one week later to stand by the bedside of my slaughtered friend Broderick, who fell in your cause and on your behalf, and I cried "How long, oh how long shall the hopes of Freedom and her champion be thus crushed!" The tide has turned. I renew my hopes. I see better omens. The warrior rests. It is true he is in the embrace of that sleep that knows no earthly waking. Nor word nor wish nor prayer nor triumph can call him from that lone abode but his example lives among us. In San Francisco, I know, I speak to hundreds of men tonight—perhaps to thousands— who loved him in his life and will be true to his memory always.

The shorthand notes of the speech and his departing statement were quickly set to type. "The morrow's sun had not risen when copies of the pamphlet were ready for the outgoing steamboats and stage coaches that were to convey them to the uttermost parts of the state." His words became the rallying call of the Republican Party.

The election of 1860 was a closely run thing. In California, Baker's speech likely turned the tide, and the Broderick wing of the Democratic Party went for Lincoln.

The bulk of the Breckinridge votes came from the southern part of the state and the San Joaquin Valley. San Francisco, the Sacramento Valley towns, and the Mother Lode counties gave an edge to Lincoln, who carried the state by only 614 votes.[8]

When Lincoln was inaugurated in March 1861 the Southern states began their long-threatened dismemberment of the Union. For a while Gwin and his supporters pushed the idea of a Pacific Confederacy that would include Oregon, California, and the Nevada Territory. The concept was not popular in San Francisco and the Mother Lode. In San Francisco a group of pro-Union citizens decided to form a military committee to keep California in the Union. In May 1861, at a great mass meeting in San Francisco, twenty-five thousand Union supporters elected a "Committee of Thirty-Four." San Franciscans, with their recent history of Vigilante Committee violence, proclaimed that the purpose of this committee was "solely to aid the constituted authorities in the detection and suppression of any treasonable combinations." The committee included retired and active army officers and prominent businessmen. A former army lieutenant and member of the committee, Henry W. Halleck, involved in the Almaden quicksilver mine in Santa Clara County, was named head of the state militia by Gov. John G. Downey. The Committee of Thirty-Four established a type of secret police. Another member, De Witt C. Thompson, a wealthy banker and real estate owner, wrote: "So complete was the surveillance of the committee that no military book could be bought at the stores or drawn from the libraries without the person and the purpose being known."[9]

In 1861 a New York group decided to organize a regiment composed of men who had once lived in California and had returned to the East. They proposed to organize the regiment under federal, rather than state, sponsorship and call it the 1st California Infantry. In April, after enrolling a few hundred volunteers, they asked Sen. Edward Baker to serve as colonel. He agreed but said he was too busy in Washington to spend time organizing the regiment and recruiting volunteers, so his law partner, Isaac Wistar, did the work. Wistar was appointed lieutenant colonel as partial compensation for his recruiting efforts. Later, recalling his recruiting duty, he commented on "how many drinks of bad whiskey I was obliged to consume and bestow in the service of my country; but on the second night I took one hundred men to New York by the midnight emigrant train, at the fare of a dollar a head, which was my pecuniary tribute to the cause."[10]

One company came from Washington, D.C., another from New York, and the balance of the men were from the Philadelphia area. The regiment was the first of the three-year regiments to complete its organization and was the only federally sponsored regiment. Governor Andrew Curtin of Pennsylvania complained about "outsiders" enlisting men in Philadelphia, so the regiment was officially designated the 71st Pennsylvania Infantry and credited against Pennsylvania's quota to appease him. However, wartime reports often refer to the regiment as the 1st California Volunteers.

The regiment was decimated in a nasty action at Ball's Bluff, Virginia, on October 21, 1861. Colonel Baker, in charge of the invading troops, was shot through the brain. As he fell, in a strange twist of fate, his blood spattered the uniform of a young captain of the 20th Massachusetts standing beside him. The captain was Caspar Crowninshield, who, along with the brother of a fellow officer in his regiment, would become the commander of the only organized group of Californians to fight in the main theater of the war. Nicknamed the "Harvard Regiment" because many its officers were graduates of that college, the 20th Massachusetts also included in its ranks Lts. William Lowell Putnam and James Jackson Lowell; two grandsons of Paul Revere, one a major, the other a surgeon; and 1st Lt. Oliver Wendell Holmes.

The fight was a botched up affair; the Union troops were butchered. The Federals were driven into the Potomac, where many drowned. Captain Crowninshield escaped by swimming across the river. The 1st California was badly cut up, losing almost half the men who had been in the fight.

In July 1862, after Maj. Gen. George B. McClellan's failed Peninsula campaign, President Lincoln approved the Conscription Act and called for three hundred thousand men to be enrolled in the army for three years or unless discharged sooner. Though California and Oregon were exempt because of the expense of moving men to the East Coast, the Committee of Thirty-Four was seeking ways to affirm California's attachment to the Union. James Sewell Reed, a Massachusetts-born businessman, member of the committee, and officer in the 1st Light Dragoons, a local militia unit, wrote Ira Rankin, the collector of the Port of San Francisco and the highest federal officer in San Francisco. Reed proposed to raise a hundred men for service in the East with the contingency that the men would provide their own uniforms, horse tack, and pistols if others furnished their transportation. Rankin wrote to Gov. John Andrews of Massachusetts asking if a company would be acceptable under the proposed conditions. Governor Andrews in turn asked Secretary of War Edwin M. Stanton if the army would endorse this arrangement as it violated standard practice. Throughout the Civil War the basic unit was the regiment. With the exception of a select few regular army infantry and cavalry regiments and artillery batteries, regiments were sponsored by a state and credited against the quota required of it by the federal government. Stanton assented and plans were started to enroll volunteers. The city of Boston was persuaded to give the company $20,000 to defray the costs of transportation on the condition the men would be credited against that city's quota. The funds were raised by private subscription among the city's wealthiest families. John Forbes, a wealthy financier, contributed a major portion of the required funds.

Andrews sent his approval on October 22, 1862. J. Sewell Reed was named captain and a recruiting station was set up at the northwest corner of Kearny and Post Streets in Assembly Hall.[11] Archibald McKendry was appointed first lieutenant and John W. Sim was named second lieutenant. A selection committee was appointed to take charge of fitting out and reviewing the applicants. Acceptance would be based on the man's age, his ability to stand the rigors of active service, and his horsemanship.

The company was called the California Hundred, and recruitment proceeded over the next two months. Contemporary accounts vary as to how many men applied. One newspaper said five hundred, another two hundred, and another simply said recruits were "plentiful." By the end of October twenty-six men had been accepted. The last man was picked on December 10.

Other members of the committee proceeded to raise $5,000 to clothe and equip the company. An appeal was made to the San Francisco Board of Supervisors but they declined to help because they feared that the Californians' identity would be lost with their attachment to a Massachusetts regiment. One member, in a speech parroting a states' rights Southern governor and referring to the "California Column," a unit the state sent to the Arizona Territory to secure the Texas border but which wound up fighting Apaches, said: "We had already sent thousands of our men to Texas and elsewhere beyond the borders of this state, which regiments are deficient in numbers. We ought to relieve our own troops first."

Personal friends of the new cavalrymen made individual contributions. Captain Reed was given a brace of silver and ivory mounted pistols along with a saddle and full field gear. The pistols were engraved, "To Captain J. Sewell Reed, from the First Light Dragoons San Francisco Nov. 26, 1862." Lieutenant McKendry received a pair of gauntlets, a sash, and an engraved saber. Thomas Star King, a prominent minister, delivered a lecture in Platt's Hall that was well attended; proceeds from the event provided a major boost to the unit's fund. Additional benefit events and contributions from private donors brought in an additional $4,000 to $5,000. After all the expenses were deducted and the men clothed and equipped there was actually a surplus. It was given to Captain Reed to hold as a company fund.

Eighty-six men were mustered in by Lt. Col. George H. Ringgold at Platt's Hall on December 2. San Francisco's Mayor Henry F. Teschemacher presented the company with a silk guidon. The upper half was crimson with a gilt "US" and the lower half was white with a painted grizzly bear similar to that on the state flag.[12] On December 7 the recruits attended a religious service at Reverend King's Unitarian Church. Each man was presented with a Bible. Two days later a music festival was held at Platt's Hall to honor the recruits. The soon-to-depart soldiers were subjected to the usual long-winded patriotic speeches from those who were staying home.

The day before their departure another fourteen men were mustered. The next day, December 11, they assembled and marched to the Lick House, where they were served a hearty breakfast. The company fell in after breakfast and marched to Rincon Wharf, where the men embarked on the *Golden Age*, a Pacific Mail Steamship Company steamer. One man, Pvt. Patrick Kelly, failed to show up and was dropped from the rolls. A roar of cannon, bells, and music provided by a brass band accompanied the whole proceeding. The crew cast off the lines at noon and, while the band on shore played, the passengers lined the rail for their last glimpse of the city as the steamer slid between Telegraph Hill and Alcatraz Island. As the ship passed Fort Point at the entrance to the bay, Pvt. Sam Corbett felt an unpleasant queasiness in his stomach. A nearby sailor directed him to the leeward rail, "where your humble servant was forced to part with his breakfast, ditto several more in the same fix."[13]

On the fourteenth they ran into a severe tropical storm off Baja California. The storm proved to be a disaster for the enlisted men, who depended on the food provided by the Pacific Mail Steamship Company. The surging seas smashed the cattle pen on the main deck, and the cattle, which were to supply fresh meat for the recruits during the voyage, were washed into the ocean. On December 18, after four days of heavy weather, the battered steamer limped into Acapulco with its load of seasick would-be cavalrymen to repair the storm damage and replenish its coal bunkers. During the layover the men took advantage of the day ashore. Acapulco was a familiar stop for many of the Californians, who had passed through the city in the 1850s with family or friends on the way to the diggings in California. Local natives crowded around the dock selling fresh fruit. Some of the recruits went swimming along Acapulco's white sand beach while the ship took on provisions and coal. The layover was all too short. At 5 A.M. on the nineteenth they were again on the way south, and arrived at Panama City at 8 A.M. on the twentieth. There the troops disembarked and boarded a train to cross the isthmus. The trip took most of the day and, after a jolting, bumpy ride through the steamy jungle, they reached Aspinwall[14] on the Atlantic coast. At Aspinwall the sergeants took charge, formed a column of fours, and quickly marched the men to the docks, where the steamer *Ocean Queen*, a Vanderbilt Line ship, awaited them. The Vanderbilt Line was known for its less than sumptuous accommodations. The *Ocean Queen* lived up to her reputation.

They sailed for New York on the twenty-first. The officers and their wives were quartered in the staterooms, while the enlisted men were put into steerage. The food in steerage was primarily salt pork, hardtack, beans, and rice. After a few days of this diet the men became angry and a delegation asked to speak to Captain Reed, who met with them and heard their complaints about the food and accommodations. The meeting quickly grew acrimonious. The enlisted men accused Reed of misappropriation of the travel funds. Angered by the accusation, Reed called them "a damned set of scoundrels" and threatened to have them thrown in the brig. Cooler heads prevailed, however, and the meeting broke up without any repercussions except a lingering bitterness between the men and Captain Reed.

It was a dismal voyage. After a severe storm off Cape Hatteras they finally arrived at New York at 2 A.M. on January 3, 1863. The trip had taken just twenty-three days.[15] At sunrise they were led off the ship and marched to Battery Barracks, a hospice set up by patriotic New York ladies. The ladies served them a "soldier's breakfast" that one soldier reported as spartan fare. At noon, a committee from the Sons of Massachusetts headed by Col. Frank E. Howe marched the California Hundred to the New England Rooms, a hospitality hall set up for New England regiments. There they were served a sumptuous lunch. The lunch did not come free, however; they had to endure the congratulations and orations of a number of local dignitaries. In the evening they marched back to the New England Rooms and were served dinner. Once again oratory was the entertainment. Alas for the historical record, no one recorded any of these speeches. Escorted by two regiments of infantry and several bands, they marched back to City Hall, where Mayor George Updyke welcomed them to the city. When he was finished they tramped to the

docks and boarded another steamer on which they resumed their journey to Massachusetts. After a short cruise up the East Coast to Stonington, Connecticut,[16] they
boarded a waiting train for the night ride to Readville, Massachusetts. Finally, a
little before sunrise on January 5, they arrived at Camp Meigs, their home for the
next month.

The barracks at Readville were long, rectangular buildings of raw lumber construction with rough wooden floors and exposed-shingle roofs. The walls were
brushed with a coat of fresh whitewash. Coal-oil lanterns hung from the rafters
provided lighting. A small potbelly stove in the center of the room supposedly
served to heat the whole building during the cold New England nights. The ground
surrounding the barracks in January was frozen, but when the thaw came in the
spring it would turn into a sea of mud.

The conditions were not what the men of the Hundred expected. They were, in
their own minds at least, the select few of the four or five hundred men who had
volunteered to be there. The greeting they had received at Readville had been less
than effusive, and effusion is what they expected. They saw themselves as a distinguished group that had come east to represent California, and they expected to be
treated like heroes.

Some used their feet to express their disillusionment. Five men—William Ham-
merburg, Frank Knowles, Alfred Magary, E. Nellis, and H. Nelson—deserted in a
group on the night of January 26. The officers tightened security, but another man,
Charles S. Dewey, managed to slip away on February 27. The rest of the Hundred,
like all Americans new to the military, complained bitterly. Because they were from
a remote part of the country, they were out of touch with the grim and bitter reality
of the war in early 1863. In later months they would look back on the potbelly
stove, the wooden floor, and the shingle roof as the good times. But for now they
were angry and very disillusioned soldiers.

A few days after the arrival of the Hundred, the ladies of the Bunker Hill Association presented the company with a flag. On the fifteenth they were invited to a
reception at Faneuill Hall in Boston. Then, on the seventeenth, the men received
a ten-day furlough. Those with local relatives quickly spread throughout the area.
The company reassembled on February 1 and was issued horses and equipment.

The unit experienced some major organizational changes in February. Lieutenant McKendry was made commander of the nascent Company G; Company A's
first sergeant, Henry Burlinghan, became a second lieutenant; and Cpl. Darnly Bal-
com and H. F. Woodman were made sergeants and transferred to Company B. Captain Reed was promoted to squadron commander[17] and Lieutenant Sim took over
command of Company A. First Sergeant Hugh Armstrong was made a second lieutenant and Charles Ackerman was promoted to first sergeant. While these changes
were being made several noncommissioned officers were detailed to recruiting duty
to try to fill up the Massachusetts companies.[18]

The successful raising of the California Hundred prompted the Committee of
Thirty-Four to offer to raise a battalion under the same conditions. On January 15,
1863, Maj. De Witt C. Thompson of San Francisco was authorized by the War

Department to raise a full battalion of four companies. The new companies were initially designated A through D. Charles S. Eigenbrodt, an Alameda County supervisor who had been a major on the staff of the local militia, was appointed captain of Company A. On January 25, Zabdiel Adams, an officer in the California National Guard, was appointed captain of Company B.[19] The four companies, made up primarily of men recruited from the state's agricultural counties, later became known as the California Battalion but were initially given the fanciful name "California Cossacks." The *Daily Alta Californian* opined, "If the California Cossacks prove as troublesome to the rebels as the Russians Cossacks have to enemies of the great Empire, California will not regret sharing these four Companies from her peaceful pursuits."

Thompson moved the recruiting station from Assembly Hall, where the California Hundred was recruited, to the new and larger Platt's Music Hall on Montgomery Street. The main floor was reserved for drilling with galleries set aside for visitors. The basement had a "well-arranged kitchen" and storerooms. The officers were assigned sleeping quarters and offices on the second floor hall. The uppermost floor was set aside for sleeping quarters for the enlisted men.[20] By March 1, 150 men had been enrolled and were being drilled by Captain Van Voast of the 9th Infantry, a West Point graduate.[21] This time enough money was set aside for uniforms and transportation, and the remainder was offered to the enlistees as a bonus. The bonus was to be paid when the men arrived in Massachusetts. Additional money was raised through fund-raising benefits. The battalion's first appearance was on February 24, 1863, at a military parade and review. "The California Battalion turned out, about 140 men, under command of Major D. W. C. Thompson. They made a very showy and elegant appearance."[22]

Not everybody in the state was happy about California providing recruits to another state. An article in the Santa Cruz *Sentinel* read: "We have a letter from a person who signs himself J. Wing Oliver, Lieutenant, Company A, California Light Cavalry, asking us to do what we can to assist in raising the four companies for service in the Massachusetts regiments. We beg to decline for reasons heretofore expressed. The regiments of our own State want more men to take the place of those sick or disabled. There has been a call upon this state for one regiment of infantry and seven companies of cavalry, which has not been responded to. When California fills the requirements of the General Government, then we will have no objection to providing a few substitutes to Massachusetts."[23] In San Francisco rival recruiting stations for the 6th Infantry and 1st Cavalry offered men subsistence, clothing, blankets, and $25 of the $100 bounty payable at once. In spite of these inducements, the Massachusetts-bound companies rapidly enrolled cavalrymen.

The four companies of the battalion became Companies E, F, L and M of the 2nd Massachusetts Cavalry. At muster-in the company officers were:

Company A: (E)[24]   Capt. Charles S. Eigenbrodt
           1st Lt. John C. Norcross
           2nd Lt. Henry H. Crocker

Company B: (L)   **Capt. Zabdiel B. Adams**
                   1st Lt. William C. Manning
                   2nd Lt. Josiah A. Baldwin

Company C: (F)   **Capt. David A DeMerritt**
                   1st Lt. Rufus W. Smith
                   2nd Lt. Horace B. Welch

Company D: (M)   **Capt. George A. Manning**
                   1st Lt. Alvin W. Stone
                   2nd Lt. Hiram E. W. Clark

After being reviewed by Brig. Gen. George Wright, commander of the Department of the Pacific, the battalion left for New York on the steamer *Constitution* on March 21. Company M was not full; another fifty men were needed. The fifty men and Captain Manning would follow on April 23 aboard the steamer *Sonora*.[25]

Conditions were crowded aboard the *Constitution*. Three hundred fifty men aboard a paddle-wheel steamer made for a large passenger list. After the war, Major Thompson, who was traveling in a first-class cabin with his wife, wrote, "The high character and good habits of these soldiers were fully tested during the voyage." The trip was not without mishap, however. On March 25, somewhere between San Francisco and Panama, Hiram Townsend, a Company L recruit, fell overboard and was lost at sea.[26] The *Constitution* arrived at Panama a few weeks later. After crossing the isthmus the men boarded the steamer *Ocean Queen*, the same ship that had carried the California Hundred to New York.

The voyage from San Francisco to Panama had been reasonably pleasant. The rest of the trip was as bad as the California Hundred had experienced. "Of our trip from Aspinwall to New York, suffice to say that we were treated worse than dogs should be: crowded into steerage, the atmosphere of which was enough to kill ordinary men: the food consisted of decayed 'salt horse' salt pork ditto, and musty hard bread. It was unfit for human beings to eat, and would have turned the stomach of a starved Digger Indian."[27]

The battalion arrived at New York on April 14. Its reception was not what the troops had expected. In fact, no one knew who they were or that they were due to arrive. "Our reception at the wharf was as follows: a delegation of a dozen hack drivers, two newspaper boys, a few old apple women, whose pinched features and haggard looks plainly told that the wheels of time had not very lightly rolled o'er their heads—these and a Deputy Sheriff, with an order of Habeas Corpus which he served on Major Thompson awaited our arrival."

The Writ of Habeas Corpus required the release of Pvt. William Piquet of Company L. Piquet had listed his age as twenty-one at enlistment; the writ claimed he was not yet eighteen. He was immediately discharged and put in the care of local relatives.[28]

The battalion then marched to Park Barracks, where the men were served a good supper—something they had not seen for about a month. After dinner the whole battalion spent the evening at the New Bowery Theater as the guests of the manager. The gesture was greatly appreciated, and the troops enjoyed the show. The next morning the men formed in dress parade in a local park and were addressed by Gov. James W. Nye of the Nevada Territory. They then were marched around the equestrian statue of General Washington and down Battery to the northbound steamer. The next day they arrived at Readville, nine miles southwest of Boston on the Boston to Providence Railroad. It was a "rather pleasant place, surrounded by fine villages and country Villas. It had its limitations however, its boundaries are too limited for extensive cavalry drills."[29]

A training program was set up for the new cavalrymen. The day included dress parade at 8 A.M., four hours of mounted drill, and inspection of arms at six in the evening. There were musters at least twice a day and inspections once a day. They went through an additional medical examination and several men were discharged or assigned to detached duty. Some of the men who had relatives in the Massachusetts area were given short furloughs.

The horses furnished the battalion were "very inferior . . . not more than one in ten is really fit for the service required of them: many of them are wild and unmanageable, and some were never saddled before. We have had considerable sport in breaking these Massachusetts mustangs, as yet with few accidents. Serg't. Gilbert R. Merritt of Co. F had his leg broken by a kick while in the ranks, but is now doing well. Corporal Alfred A. McLean of Co. L was thrown off his horse and had his ankle dislocated also doing well."[30]

Sergeant Merritt eventually received a medical discharge; his broken leg never healed properly. Corporal McLean returned to limited duty as a regimental mailman. The extent of his injuries did not become apparent until long after the war, when X-rays, then a new invention, were taken of his shattered foot. Part of the problem the Californians had with the new horses may have been that the men were used to Mexican-style saddles. The Union cavalry adopted the McClellan saddle just before the war began. It was lightweight and strong, with wooden stirrups covered with leather hoods. It had a high front and an open back. There was no saddle horn.

In early May an order came out requiring every man in the battalion to sign a draft to the state treasurer for $50—the amount of the bounty paid to the men when they enlisted. Most of the men thought that the California bounty was to be paid to them and assumed the Massachusetts bounty would be sufficient for their other expenses. They were somewhat surprised when they learned that Major Thompson had pledged the money to Amos A. Lawrence of Boston, who had advanced money to help pay for their trip from San Francisco. When the majority of the men refused to sign the order, they were threatened with arrest. The camp was closed and no one could leave on furlough or a pass unless he had signed. The issue was reminiscent of the difficulties between the men of the Hundred and Captain Reed. Wiser heads prevailed, however, and the men reluctantly signed over their bonuses. One of the more vocal malcontents expressed his dissatisfaction: "We confess to being somewhat 'verdant,' but not sufficiently so to again come all the way from California to help Massachusetts out of her scrape, have to pay our passages with our bounty and when we arrive here, be put on a footing of equality, if not beneath, a negro."[31]

Like most Californians in 1863 the men were transplanted from the rest of the United States and immigrants from western Europe and Canada. One hundred four of the recruits were New York natives, and 39 men represented New Jersey and Pennsylvania. One hundred nine were New England–born, including 54 from Massachusetts. Ninety-nine came from the Midwest, 21 from the border states, and there were 8 Southerners. Forty-one came from Europe, including 31 Irishmen, 17 Germans, 10 Englishmen, and 4 Scots. One man, Frank Barrows of Company F, was from Iceland. Only one native Californian was included: Company A's James "Santiago" Watson from Monterey, the son of an early American immigrant who had married into one of the wealthy Mexican ranchero families.

After their arrival at Readville they were joined by seven companies of recruits primarily from Massachusetts but also from other states in New England, New York, and Canada. As the war went on, replacements recruited on the East Coast were assigned to the California companies and the distinction between the California Hundred, the California Battalion, and the Massachusetts companies would be blurred. Throughout the war, however, the Californians were the core of the 2nd Massachusetts, providing the leadership and ability that made the regiment one of the foremost cavalry units in the army.

2 | Gone for a Soldier

The 2nd Massachusetts Cavalry was part of the state's 19,080-man quota of the 300,000 three-year men called for by President Lincoln in July 1862. The government announced it would not accept any volunteer regiments after August 15 except those being raised to meet the July quota. After that date, if a state failed to meet its quota the governor would be required to institute a draft. The incentive to fill the regiments on time was built into the bonus system prescribed in the Conscription Act. Volunteers in the "quota" regiments or men enlisting in one of the regiments in the field were eligible for a $100 bonus plus one month's pay in advance when they were mustered into the army; draftees were ineligible for such inducements. Most of the governors pleaded for an extension as none wanted to require a draft, and they claimed they could provide the required numbers if enough time was allowed. The political pressure was overwhelming, and the Lincoln administration relented, granting each governor the right to set his own draft date.[1]

Governor Andrews and Maj. Gen. Nathaniel Banks were instrumental in getting the Boston city council to sponsor the new cavalry regiment. Banks, a former state legislator and Speaker of the House, had recently returned to the state after leading the Union army in the Shenandoah to a disastrous defeat at the hands of Maj. Gen. Thomas J. "Stonewall" Jackson. He was planning an expedition in Louisiana to repair his badly tarnished military image, and so lobbied the council diligently, assuming the new regiment would be part of his nascent army.[2] John Murray Forbes, a wealthy Boston industrialist, was in the forefront, raising funds and lobbying the city council and the state legislature to provide additional incentives to induce enlistments in the regiment.[3] One of Forbes's protégés was a scion of the Lowell family, Charles Russell Lowell.

Lowell was born January 2, 1835, in Boston, the son of Charles Russell Lowell and Anna Jackson Lowell. The Lowells, one of Boston's oldest families, had extensive interests in cotton, trade, and wool and iron mills. The family had been cultural, political, and economic leaders in Massachusetts for over two hundred years. Destined for Harvard, Charles prepared at Boston's prestigious Latin and English High Schools. He was admitted to Harvard in 1854 at the age of fifteen, the youngest member of his class. His course of study was general rather than specific. As the heir of a wealthy father, he could allow his training to be broad. At graduation, nineteen-year-old Charles, because of his near-perfect scholastic record, was selected as valedictorian. His commencement address was unabashedly entitled "The

Reverence Due from Old Men to Young." The address had allusions to Greek and Roman mythology, as befitted a speaker with a Harvard education. In retrospect, considering the enormous task to come, with its appalling sacrifices, it was surprisingly prophetic. One important passage expresses his theme: "No nation, of course, can view its young men with indifference: Young men have always been sought and never more than at the present—But for what are they sought? Because they are a power on the earth, because they bring zeal and vigor which the world is eager to use."[4]

Lowell's father had suffered some financial losses, so the extended Lowell family relieved him of managerial responsibilities in the family businesses. He was relegated to working in the private library of the Boston Athenaeum, a collection of one hundred thousand books maintained by the leaders of Boston society. Charles, lest he follow in his father's footsteps, embarked on a training program. His first job was in a counting house to learn bookkeeping and business ways. He worked there for six months before being sent to the Ames Company iron mill in Chicopee. "Studying all that went on around him—the processes and details of iron working—with keen interest; also the 'kick of the gun,' the reaction of the business on the human beings, workman, boss, or a member of the managing corporation, was no less a matter of thought for him."[5]

In 1855, Lowell took an office position at a rolling mill in Trenton, New Jersey, where "He met the workman simply and bravely and made himself acquainted, as far as he could, with this, to him, new type. He interested himself in them, neither sentimentally nor yet patronizingly, but had respect for them." While in New Jersey he was diagnosed as having tuberculosis. In the nineteenth century it was a sometimes controllable but always incurable disease. His great uncle, who was also his physician, prescribed travel and avoidance of any strenuous activity until 1865, when he would be thirty years old. He left the mill and went on a two-year tour in warmer climates, including the Mediterranean and the West Indies.

Lowell could not accept the role of invalid and set a regime for himself to regain his health, "doctors be damned." He exercised and spent hours on horseback. He took up fencing and the saber. He studied languages—French, some Italian, and Spanish. He took the opportunity to observe the maneuvers of the Austrian and French armies. Fortuitously during his travels he encountered John Murray Forbes. In spite of Lowell's youth, Forbes was impressed with him, and they became close friends. Lowell came home and was promptly given a job as treasurer of Forbes's Burlington and Missouri Railroad in Burlington, Iowa. He was in charge of the railroad's finances and the disposition of three hundred thousand acres of land it had acquired through land grants. A subordinate wrote: "He left his mark indelibly wherever he went; the affection with which he is remembered by the many, especially working men, with whom he was brought in contact with in his business, is remarkable."[6]

In 1861 Lowell returned to the East to take a job as ironmaster at a foundry in Mount Savage, Maryland. On April 19, a mob of rebel sympathizers in Baltimore attacked the 6th Massachusetts, a ninety-day militia regiment en route to Washington, as it was changing trains in the center of the city. Three Massachusetts men were killed and forty-one were wounded. Lowell immediately went to Washington and applied to Charles Sumner, a Massachusetts senator, for an appointment in the army. "I speak and write English, French and Italian and read German and Spanish. Knew once enough of mathematics to put me at the head of my class at Harvard, though now I may need a little rubbing up; am tolerable efficient with the small sword and single stick; and can ride a horse as far and bring him as fresh as any other man. I am 26 years of age, and believe that I possess more or less of that moral courage about taking responsibility which seems at present to be found only in Southern officers."[7]

There was little doubt that he would obtain a commission; his family connections were too strong. At first he had hoped for the artillery, but on May 16 Lowell accepted a captaincy in the 3rd (later the 6th) U.S. Cavalry, a regular army regiment, and subsequently participated in the 1862 Peninsula campaign. During this campaign his younger brother, Lt. James Jackson Lowell of the 20th Massachusetts Infantry and a survivor of the Ball's Bluff debacle, was killed. At the end of the campaign Lowell joined General McClellan's staff and served as a courier in McClellan's headquarters at Antietam, carrying orders all over the battlefield while under fire. Because of his bravery, McClellan selected him to carry the thirty-nine Confederate battle flags captured in the battle to Washington.[8]

In his photographs, Lowell appears as a slight young man with a pencil-thin mustache in an era when copious facial hair was the rule. At about 5-foot-6, he was shorter than most of his contemporaries. His cheeks have a hollow, cavernous look, perhaps because of his dormant tuberculosis. His dark hair is parted in the middle. His most arresting feature is his eyes: they have an intense and piercing look. He was an abolitionist, but not radical in his views. He enjoyed books and music. He was undoubtedly a patrician. Like most young Harvard graduates of the time, he had an overweening image of his own importance. He had little doubt he would succeed in anything he undertook and, to a certain extent, because of his self-confidence, he did. None of these traits would endear him to the independent, self-sufficient Californians.

From the war's outset Lowell's former employer, John Henry Forbes, used his immense wealth to help raise troops in Massachusetts. Earlier he had proposed raising a battalion of "gentlemen" for Lowell to command. In spite of the opportunity a battalion command would offer, Lowell quickly rebuffed the idea. "The battalion as an independent organization is not recognized by the War Department. If I get permission to take command of such an organization it would only be through improper influence and in defiance of General Orders—But with my own regiment (the Third Cavalry) as Captain I should now almost always have command of a battalion. Were I to accept [this] offer I would merely be exchanging active service for at least temporary inaction for the sake of getting rank and pay as a Major. I want to keep my military record clearer than that."[9]

While there is no direct evidence that Forbes used his influence to get the 2nd Massachusetts Cavalry command for Lowell, it is certain that Governor Andrews relied on him for advice. However it happened, Andrews wrote Secretary of War

Stanton in October and asked that Lowell be assigned to the new cavalry regiment. Lowell quickly returned to Boston and by the end of the month had set up a recruiting station at 21 Church Street.

During the winter of 1862–63 he was engaged to a longtime friend and sweetheart, nineteen-year-old Josephine Shaw. Josephine came from a wealthy Long Island family and was well educated for a mid-nineteenth-century woman. She spent four years in Rome during her teen years and shared Lowell's views on abolition. A tall, slender, and exceedingly attractive woman, Josephine, like Lowell, enjoyed books, poetry, and riding, and was very interested in politics.

Josephine's brother was Charles Shaw, a Harvard classmate of Lowell's and the colonel of the first regiment of black soldiers raised in a free state, the 54th Massachusetts. During the spring of 1863, as their regiments were undergoing training and organization at Readville, Colonels Lowell and Shaw lived in the same boardinghouse near the camp. In between his military duties Colonel Lowell courted Josephine, who was visiting friends in Boston.

Lowell started recruiting men about the end of November 1862.[10] "The fascination of cavalry service and the reputation of its young colonel appealed to young men of good physique and active spirit and soon applications came pouring in for commissions for their sons from mothers and fathers of young Harvard students and graduates, from ministers and Boston's dancing master, Papanti. It was an easy task to fill the list of officers. But the recruiting for the ranks was a different matter."[11]

The patriotic fire that had swept the North after the attack on Fort Sumter had burned out, doused by the blood shed at Antietam, Fredericksburg, and Shiloh. The country's best men were already in the army; all that was left were reluctant draftees. In order to raise the required troops, Governor Andrews appointed a committee of prominent citizens like Amos Lawrence as recruiting agents:

> Massachusetts had sent over fifty thousand into the army and navy drafts had been ordered, and "bounties" and "substitutes" were familiar words. The methods of recruiting in 1862 and 1863 were very business-like and uninspiring. Each town had its quota of men to fill. The recruiting agent, like Mr. Lawrence, would write to a town that he would supply them with men for their quota at the rate of $200 apiece. He would then send some officers of the regiment through the country or into Canada to raise men who for the bounty of from $100 to $175 would enlist—the remainder of the money going to the payment of expenses and the regimental fund. At the time of recruiting the Second Cavalry, the farms, shops and factories had been thoroughly ransacked, an army of bounty jumpers had developed, and even the jails had been called upon to open their gates to certain classes of prisoners, who on their promise to enlist were given their freedom. The result was that while there was a good body of patriotic young men in the ranks of the Second Cavalry, there was also a strong mixture of rough and mutinous elements.[12]

An unfortunate incident that occurred during the recruiting showed Lowell to be a strict disciplinarian in an age of harsh discipline. He stopped one morning at one of the recruiting stations and found it in turmoil. The sergeant in charge explained that he had ordered one of the new recruits to be handcuffed because of some infraction. The other recruits had refused to permit the handcuffing of the miscreant and were in a state of mutiny. Lowell told the men the order must be obeyed before he would listen to their grievances. He warned that he would shoot the first man who resisted. The sergeant then started to handcuff the prisoner and the recruits surged forward. Lowell shot the leader dead. The rest of the men surrendered. Lowell left the recruiting station and went directly to the governor's office, where he reported the incident. Lowell was never charged; a later investigation showed that the victim had been in the regular army and had a "bad record," reason enough, in nineteenth-century Boston, to exonerate someone of Lowell's stature.[13]

Henry S. Russell, a close friend of Lowell's, was assigned as lieutenant colonel. Russell had served as a captain in the 2nd Massachusetts Infantry and was captured during Banks's Shenandoah Valley campaign. He spent some months in Libby Prison in Richmond before being exchanged. The imprisonment had affected his health but it was hoped that the transfer to the newly formed 2nd Massachusetts Cavalry would give him the opportunity to fully recover.

Caspar Crowninshield, a Harvard crew stroke, swimmer, witness to Edward Baker's death, and survivor of Ball's Bluff, joined the regiment as a major. He had transferred to the 1st Massachusetts Cavalry after Ball's Bluff. His departure from the 20th Massachusetts was not altogether amicable. He made some disparaging remarks to friends in Boston concerning the conduct of an unnamed officer during the Ball's Bluff debacle. In addition, he claimed to be the last man to leave the field. A fellow officer from the 20th, Henry Livermore Abbott, denied Crowninshield's claim and called him "base and dishonorable." Crowninshield was quickly judged as being ambitious and egocentric: "he is perfectly selfish & indifferent to everybody else, though ordinarily too shrewd & well bred to show it. This power of concealing his feelings, joined to his deuced pleasant address is what has made him so popular."[14]

The recruiting in Massachusetts went slowly because many men, despite the threat of an impending draft, were loath to enroll. In December Company B enlisted just 58 men, and 32 of those deserted after receiving the federal and state bonuses. Company C and D enlisted 102 men, of whom 56 were gone after the muster-in—along with an additional 14 from Company B. The record for a single day was set on December 22, 1862, when 22 men from Companies B and C left camp. The authorities were at a loss. Few, if any, of the deserters were ever caught.[15] The Conscription Act created a whole new industry in the United States: bounty jumping. Men joined a regiment, were mustered in, and then deserted, only to repeat the process in another area or state. Desertion continued at a high rate in the Massachusetts companies throughout the war. An average of 42 percent deserted within sixty days. Surprisingly, if they were assigned to a California company as replacements, the rate fell to just 12 percent.[16]

The 2nd Massachusetts Cavalry Regiment was clearly an anomaly. The city, county, and state levels of government in California did not support the men of the

Hundred and the battalion. Under the president's call of 1862, California provided troops to man the western forts and protect the Overland Trail. There was not to be a draft in the state, and there was no intent to send troops to the East Coast. Unlike the 1861 volunteers in the eastern states, westerners did not have to deal with the peer pressure of neighbors who were recruits. At this distance in time it is hard to fathom their reasons for enlisting. For some it may have been the adventure; others may have been true patriots determined to help save the Union. We know that a handful of the California recruits saw it as an easy way to get to the East, where they then deserted.[17] Whatever their individual motivation, two things are clear: (1) they were not pressured by the draft, and (2) they had given up healthy bonuses for the privilege to fight. By contrast, their Massachusetts counterparts, even if they did not desert, were in the army because of the threat of a draft or because of the bounties offered by the state and federal governments. The differences between the two groups would take training and the crucible of combat to be forgotten.

The training started immediately. Most states had set up permanent Camps of Instruction for cavalry and infantry regiments.[18] The 2nd Massachusetts went through training at Camp Meigs in Readville. Infantry regiments often went into combat after only a few weeks of drill and tactical training. Cavalry regiments, particularly in the North, were given several months of instruction before they were sent to the front. The training stressed fundamentals, including riding, controlling, and caring for a horse. Training in tactical formations came later. Many of the Massachusetts recruits were from the Boston area, where horses were dray animals, so they had little experience with horsemanship. Riding came easier to the Californians because horses were still a principle form of transportation in the Far West.

In mid-February Colonel Lowell decided that five companies—Company A (the California Hundred), and Companies B, C, D, and K—were ready for active operations and should gain some experience in the field. Under the command of Major Crowninshield, the battalion, numbering about 325 men, was issued pistols and sabers and ordered to proceed to Fortress Monroe, a relatively quiet post on the James Peninsula.[19] They left Readville by train on February 12 and arrived at Baltimore on February 15, after a slow and uncomfortable trip. There was a five-day layover in Baltimore because of a shortage of shipping. Crowninshield used the time to rest the horses and men. The Massachusetts recruits were a continual problem.

> From the time we left the station at Readville until the present moment desertions have been going on at a sufficiently rapid a rate. Quite a large part of the Battalion are at the present moment scattered along the road between this place & Boston. [It] was impossible to prevent it in the loading and unloading the horses. The men got away & when I posted a guard the guard generally deserted—with the exception of the Californians.
>
> The men are a disgrace to the state which sent them. They get beastly drunk & fight among themselves draw their sabres & pistols & cut and slash each other. Two men have already been severely hurt. We have been detained here for some time

owing to a want of transportation & the men have been quartered in a store house. There was a guard of some 15 infantrymen put over them & I left Lieut. Payson also to look out for them. While he was gone to get his supper the men attacked the guard disarmed them & went out of the building & were drunk & fighting all night long around town during that night & the next day. Most all of them were arrested & brought back but some have still remained absent & have I suppose deserted.

Yesterday I sent most all of them down on two transports to Fortress Monroe. The Californians & about twenty men of Co. B still remain here & I shall probably get off with them tomorrow but there is a scarcity of boats here & I may be left (a) while longer. . . . When I get the men in camp down at the Fortress I hope to be able to make something like soldiers out of them. Though like enough many will desert to the enemy and as they are a most expert set of thieves perhaps they will be more serviceable to us in that capacity than they could possibly be as soldiers. It would give me real pleasure to see 100 of them, whom I could pick out, hanged all in a row. Well enough of this I hope I shall be able to give better accounts of them when next I write; but just to illustrate what a class of men they are two of them had a dispute & one of them drew his saber & stabbed the other in the stomach. The sword glanced & only a slight wound was inflicted I happened to be near by & I ran up & knocked the man who had the saber down & had him secured.[20]

The Californians and Major Crowninshield left Baltimore on February 20 and were taken by steamer to Fortress Monroe and then to Gloucester Point, Virginia, arriving the next day. The battalion was made part of the division commanded by Maj. Gen. Erasmus Keyes. The division was part of the Department of Virginia, which included Yorktown, Williamsburg, and Fortress Monroe, commanded by Maj. Gen. John A. Dix. Brigadier General Richard J. Busteed, a reactionary Republican judge and political appointee from New York, commanded the post at Gloucester Point. He was once mentioned in Confederate congressional resolutions as an example of the kind of judge Southerners might expect to rule them if they lost the war.[21] Crowninshield was not impressed with General Busteed: "He is a vulgar man, a very vulgar looking man, no pretensions toward being a gentleman, and has about as much military knowledge and ability as you would expect a pettifogging lawyer to have. . . . He is the sort of man that I utterly hate and despise, but he is one of the class of men that rule this country."[22]

Throughout March the battalion was continually engaged in picket duty and scouting. On March 28, some unseen rebels fired twice at the pickets, arousing the whole camp. It was the first hostile fire the regiment heard.[23]

The camp at Gloucester Point was reasonably comfortable. The men were housed in conical-shaped Sibley tents. On March 30 a group from Companies B and C asked permission to ride beyond the lines to commandeer a pile of planking several men had spotted on an earlier scouting expedition. The planking would be used to build a floor inside the Sibley tents. Major Crowninshield agreed. Captains Francis Washburn of Company B and George S. Holman of Company C prepared to move out with a working party and two wagons. An armed escort of twelve men led by Lt. Charles Payson accompanied them. It was a sunny afternoon and, at the last moment, Major Crowninshield decided to go along. After leaving the working party to load the planking, Crowninshield and the two captains decided to ride farther out. Lieutenant Payson and his twelve men were ordered to follow a hundred yards behind. About two miles from the working party the three officers spotted a lone rebel on the road ahead of them and gave chase.

I suppose he was a scout and that there were probably no others near him so we, the Capts. and I started after him and he ran like smoke. We chased him until we came to where the woods came close up to the road an the left hand side of the road and then we lost sight of him. . . . All of a sudden Capt. Washburn called to me and said "hold on I hear noise in the woods here' and he called out, 'take care Major here come the Rebels through the woods." . . . We turned toward Lt. Payson and digging our spurs into our horses we just got by the Rebs. They must have been within twenty feet of us. They all fired at us but wonderful to state they did not hit us. I don't see how they could possibly have missed us but they did. They started after us in hot haste but by this time we had got a good start. When we got well clear of the woods and within support of Lt. Payson's men we halted and faced the Rebs. Payson's men, hearing the firing and seeing us come out of the woods were thrown into confusion and three or four turned tail and fled for dear life. The rest galloped up and joined us. We hastily formed across the road. All this was done in a very short time. The Rebs rather turned and then like good fellows we gave them a parting howl. . . . I was much pleased with [our men] for an unsuspected ambush of that kind is rather oft to shake a fellows nerves particularly if he has never been under fire before.[24]

The comment about ambushes would prove to be prophetic in subsequent months. In his official report Crowninshield called the expedition a reconnaissance and reported that Union troopers "only escaped capture by running a gauntlet of fire."[25]

The first important raid the battalion joined started on April 7, 1863.[26] It was commanded by Col. A. H. Grimshaw of the 4th Delaware Infantry. Grimshaw left Gloucester Point at 7 A.M. on April 7 with a detail from his own regiment, three companies of the 169th Pennsylvania Drafted Militia, Crowninshield's battalion, and a squadron of the 6th New York Cavalry. Major William P. Hall of the 6th New York commanded the cavalry. The party moved out on the main road to Gloucester Courthouse. Grimshaw left a company from the 169th Pennsylvania at Abington Meetinghouse to prevent any communications with the enemy's pickets. Major Hall was ordered to proceed to the right with the cavalry beyond Hickory Ford after destroying any grain he might find; he was then ordered to rejoin the column at or near Gloucester Courthouse. Grimshaw returned the next day.

After the raid, Companies A and B were sent to Fort Magruder near Williamsburg under the command of Captain Reed because of reports of an impending attack by the rebels. They were assigned to a cavalry brigade commanded by Colonel R. M. West.[27] On April 29, while Private J. W. Owen "was standing on picket night, three rebels crawled upon him and the cowardly scoundrels fired upon him, killing his horse at the first shot but not injuring him in any way. Finding they had not killed him they advanced upon him, and he broke for a fence, from behind which he delivered three shots at them from his revolver, when they sloped (ran), one spunky man proving too much for three dastardly cowards. So much for their brag of one of them being equal to three of us."[28]

The remainder of the battalion—Companies C, D and K at Gloucester Point—participated in another raid later in the month. The raiders "destroyed a large amount of stores of the rebel army, consisting of grain, cotton, bacon, flour, salt, coffee, sulphur, powder, flints, percussion caps, and quinine: also collected and drove within the lines 57 head of horned cattle, 260 sheep, and 8 horses and mules."[29]

Companies A and B were issued Burnside breech-loading carbines during the last week of April. "[W]e are now thoroughly armed as cavalrymen. The carbines are neatly made, light and serviceable, and capable of throwing a ball five hundred yards with force enough to kill a man, and with great accuracy. When mounted, with all our arms on, we are pretty well loaded; and I expect we will all get round-shouldered, [with] so much weight resting on our shoulders."[30]

Reed's squadron returned to Gloucester Point in mid-May, joining the battalion's other three companies. While the battalion was stationed there, the animus toward Captain Reed that started during the passage from San Francisco took an ugly turn. A letter from a member of Company A dated May 28, 1863, describing the problems appeared in the *Daily Alta Californian*. It reported that in the latter part of May a delegation selected by the men of the California Hundred went to Captain Reed and asked for an accounting of the company funds. According to the writer there had been about $20,000, and, after deducting transportation costs, there should have been about $8,000 to $10,000 remaining—a considerable sum in 1863. The correspondent claimed that Reed refused to tell the delegation anything about the status of the money because they had nothing to do with it. "Capt. Reed's conduct to the men in other respects is no less reprehensible—it is really that of a supercilious tyrant." Moreover, according to the writer, Pvt. E. Henry Allen had been ordered to groom the orderly sergeant's horse. Private Allen decided that this was "menial labor," which, according to army regulations, he could not be required to perform. The orderly sergeant did not agree. Punishment came quickly. Private Allen was suspended from the nearest tree by his thumbs. The men of the company were outraged and as a body went to the captain and told him that if he did not cut Allen down, they would. Reed ordered Allen cut down and the men, grumbling, returned to their campsite.

Then, on May 23, "Ross, Beach, Hill, Campbell, Rone, Quant, Ackerman and Powers were detailed to police duty. After all police duty was over they were ordered to clear away the manure and filth around the rear of the officers' quarters that had been accumulating for months. The said officers had plenty of negro servants and hostlers lying around doing nothing. The men, deciding this was menial work, refused to obey the order. They were immediately arrested and placed in a former slave pen already overstocked with filth and vermin of all kinds." Captain Reed suggested to the guard that the men be chained. The men were charged with mutiny, disobedience, and conduct unbecoming a soldier. Reed refused to let the company send over their blankets, and so for "four nights they slept on the bare floor without any covering."

There were mutterings in the camp that night that must have reached Captain Reed, who went to Major General Keyes in the morning and reported that the company was about to mutiny. Six companies of infantry, two companies of cavalry, and two pieces of artillery surrounded the camp at midnight. The men were then awakened, placed under arrest, and marched to Fort Monroe and into prison. Most of them were released after thirty hours of close confinement. Four men were named as ringleaders and kept in prison to await trial for treason. Private Charles W. Hill of San Francisco was singled out and, after a speedy court-martial, discharged on June 27, 1863.[31] The remainder of the company returned to duty.

Not all the men in Company A agreed with the majority. A letter from Lieutenant Sim appeared in the June 29, 1863, *San Francisco Bulletin* refuting the charges. Reed, he said, had intended to use the money to buy uniforms and to equip the company but had been dissuaded from doing so by his superiors. In the end, according to Sim, Reed decided to keep the money in a company fund for the benefit of the sick and wounded, and to divide the balance among the surviving men at the end of the war.

Sim also offered a different account of the thumb-hanging incident involving Private Allen: "Capt. Reed was absent at the time this occurred. When he returned he had him taken down, incurring the displeasure of the commanding officer, for interfering with another officer [whose horse Allen had refused to groom] when punishing a private for disobedience." As for the rancor over "menial duties," Sim reported that, having been quoted the army regulations, "These same men now do the work they refused to do then, and do it willingly, because they are now satisfied that it is their duty, and it is not menial."[32] In addition to Lieutenant Sim, all of the company's sergeants, six corporals, and three privates endorsed the letter.

This published exchange of letters had little impact on the regiment. Months later, Colonel Lowell declared: "Reed is a very good officer, and since the trouble, has done well by them; his fellows have been under fire since those letters were written and I feel sure now the feeling is changed. I think the men in all the battalions are beginning to feel that their officers know more than the officers of any regiments they are thrown with; and this feeling, of course, has a healthy effect on their morale."[33]

On June 19 Company A participated in a raid commanded by Lt. Col. Hasbrouck Davis of the 12th Illinois Cavalry. The raiders went up the north side of the Pamunkey River to King and Queen Courthouse, where they captured eight rebels, "100 good horses and mules thirty new blockade-run Colt revolvers, three mails from Richmond, a number of wagons, &C." In all they covered 130 miles in three days, arriving back in camp on June 21.[34]

Earlier, on June 14, General Dix was ordered to concentrate his troops and attack the bridges over the North Anna and South Anna Rivers and the Little River on the Richmond, Fredericksburg, and Potomac (RF&P) and Virginia Central

Railroad lines between Ashland and Taylorsville Station, about twenty-five miles
north of Richmond. The RF&P was the main route running north-northeast to
Fredericksburg. The Virginia Central was the route to the Shenandoah Valley. The
two railroads, which crossed at Hanover Junction, were crucial to the Confederate
war effort. The RF&P was the main supply route for Gen. Robert E. Lee's Army of
Northern Virginia, with seven to eight trains passing north each day. The Virginia
Central supplied the small Confederate force in the Shenandoah Valley and carried the rich agricultural harvests from the Valley to Richmond. Two redoubts had
been built at the Virginia Central bridge on the South Anna. A larger fortification
was in place at the RF&P bridge stretching between the South Anna and Little
Rivers. In order for a raid to be successful, both bridges across the South Anna had
to be destroyed. If only one bridge was burned, goods could be transported over the
remaining bridge and then switched at Hanover Junction to either of the two
routes.

The Confederate command was aware that a raid was being planned. Major
General D. H. Hill, with about eighty-five hundred men to defend Richmond and
the two railroads, accurately anticipated the raid in a letter to Secretary of War
James Seddon: "In regard to an advance on the capitol, we have but two things to
apprehend. A direct advance will not be made. They will either move upon Hanover, and cut the railroad and canal, or they will land at City Point, and isolate
Petersburg, crossing the Appomattox between its mouth and this city. The former
movement can be met by an attack in flank and rear. The latter would be a very
serious one for us."[35]

The cavalry force that General Dix gathered was commanded by Col. Samuel P.
Spear of the 11th Pennsylvania Cavalry and included about eight hundred Pennsylvanians, a scratch detachment of 250 commanded by Lt. Col. Davis made up of
troopers from the 12th Illinois Cavalry, and Crowninshield's battalion from the
2nd Massachusetts Cavalry.[36] Dix's plan was to move up the Pamunkey by steamer
to White House, then cross the river and move up the north side toward Hanover
Courthouse and the bridges. The bridges were reportedly guarded by a brigade from
Maj. Gen. George E. Pickett's division, but, unknown to Dix, only a single regiment—the 44th North Carolina Infantry commanded by Lt. Col. T. L. Hargrove—
protected the bridges. Hargrove had two companies at Hanover Junction and one
at each of the other four bridges in the area.[37] A company from the Holcombe
Legion (the 15th Virginia Cavalry) commanded by Capt. Edward W. Capp had
been sent to White House on June 16 to picket the landing. On June 24 the picket
alerted Richmond headquarters that "there are seven gunboats and transports at
West Point, and apparently they are about to effect a landing."[38]

The Union troops landed at White House between seven and eight o'clock in
the morning on June 25. There was a brief skirmish and the twelve Confederate
pickets from Capp's company quickly withdrew. Spears sent out a detachment to
Tunstall's Station on the Richmond and York Railroad, about three and a half miles
southwest along the south bank of the Pamunkey. They captured one unnamed
rebel and Confederate cavalry general, Brig. Gen. W. H. F. "Rooney" Lee, son of

Robert E. Lee, who was recovering at home from a wound received June 8 at the Battle of Brandy Station. They cut the telegraph wire, burned the sutler's store and "other Confederate buildings,"[39] and destroyed some Confederate earthworks.[40]

Dix, along with the infantry from Yorktown, arrived at White House on the twenty-sixth. He joined Spear at Tunstall's Station later that morning and the column moved on through New Castle and on to Hanover Courthouse, where Spear and his cavalry found a large quartermaster's depot with a train of thirty-five six-mule wagons complete and "ready for the road." In addition, they captured a hundred good mules and burned the wagons, three hundred sets of harness, stables, blacksmiths and wheelwright shops, an office, books and papers, and "everything pertaining to the depot at this point." They also tried to open a large Confederate safe but failed.

Companies B, D, and K of the 2nd Massachusetts were detailed to guard the captures, cover Littlepage's Bridge across the Pamunkey, and keep the road back to White House clear. The balance of the command cautiously moved on to the South Anna bridges. A few rebel pickets contested the approach, and at each turning of the road there was a brief flurry of carbine fire. By late afternoon the first of the bridges, the Virginia Central bridge on the South Anna, was in sight. The advance guard reported that there were entrenchments guarding the span, with an unknown number of rebel infantry in position and waiting. Spear sent out a skirmish line to push back the last of the rebel pickets and reconnoiter the bridge defenses. Lieutenant Colonel Hargrove and the forty men of his company fell back across the bridge and took cover behind the trees on the north side. At the same time he sent a courier on foot for reinforcements.[41]

Spear probed the defenses and, seeing that he could not fire the bridge unless the Confederates were driven off, decided to flank the rebels. The California Hundred and Company C, commanded by Captain Reed with Lieutenants Sim, William Rumery, and John T. Richards, were sent to cross the river at a ford below the bridge. They would work their way around to the Confederate rear using the woods on the other side as cover. The 11th Pennsylvania opened fire to distract the rebels. While the movement was underway, Company G of the 44th North Carolina arrived on the scene after making a hurried march from one of the other bridges. Hargrove moved it into a small breastwork about three hundred yards north of the river and in the rear of his position.

After crossing the river on several logs while under direct fire, Captain Reed's squadron moved through the trees to a position behind the rebel trenches. A bugle sounded and the men rose from cover, charging the breastwork newly occupied by Company G. The 11th Pennsylvania charged the rebels in front at the same time. The Confederates put up a determined resistance but there were just too many Union troopers. After a fierce fight, Hargrove was forced to surrender. Two Californians fell; Pvt. Joseph Burdick was killed instantly and Richard Ellet was wounded.[42] The other cavalry units lost two killed and two wounded.[43]

Spear later wrote: "I completely destroyed the bridge, and burned it till it fell into the river. It was fired above and below and nothing is left. Lt. Col. Hargrove

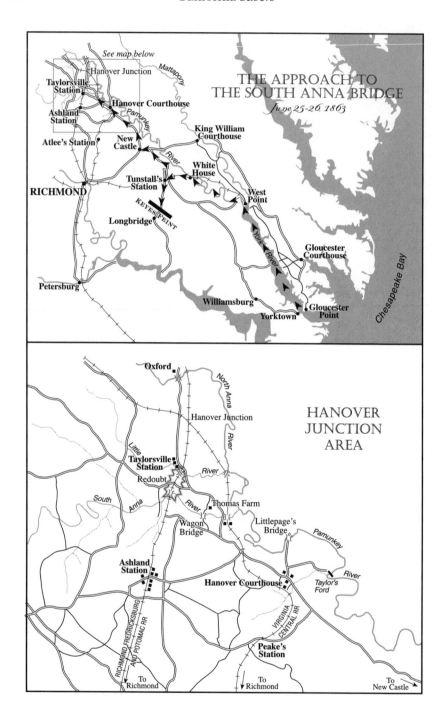

THE APPROACH TO
THE SOUTH ANNA BRIDGE
June 25-26, 1863

HANOVER
JUNCTION
AREA

had sent to Hanover Junction for reinforcements, and when they arrived, too late to support the attack, they at once went to the other crossing, Richmond and Fredericksburg Railroad, which rendered it impossible with the loss of ammunition, and my fatigued command, to attempt to carry this bridge with prudence or safety."

Spear, thirty miles behind enemy lines and all alone, perhaps overwhelmed with his sudden success, lost his nerve and ordered a retreat. He based his decision on "Information reliable as any in the country [that] told me a strong force of infantry and artillery would oppose me there [the RF&P bridge], arriving on Colonel Hargrove's requisition." Spear's command fell back to Hanover Ferry and crossed over to the north side of the Pamunkey, returning via King William Courthouse to White House on the twenty-seventh, where he reported to Dix. In addition to General Lee and Lieutenant Colonel Hargrove, Spear captured a Confederate naval officer, two captains, five lieutenants, ninety-four enlisted men, thirty-five wagons, five hundred mules, and two hundred horses.

The 2nd Massachusetts suffered another casualty during this expedition. Sometime during the return march, John (also shown as Joseph) Nixon of Company B (who had enlisted in Company A), was killed by bushwhackers, although one source says he was taken prisoner while straggling.[44] There is no further record regarding Nixon, so it is probable that he was a victim of guerrillas.

Only one of the bridges had been destroyed, and now the Confederates had been alerted. A second, more ambitious, expedition was necessary. Dix decided to move immediately. This time the raiding force, under the command of Maj. Gen. George W. Getty, would include the cavalry, augmented by Getty's division, Brig. Gen. Robert S. Foster's brigade from Brig. Gen. Michael Corcoran's division, and an independent brigade led by Col. David W. Wardrop of the 99th New York Volunteers. The infantry totaled about eighty-five hundred men. An additional force was ordered to move down the Richmond Road toward Bottom's Bridge on the Chickahominy River southwest of White House, creating a demonstration to divert Confederate forces from Getty's expedition. This force, commanded by General Keyes, included three brigades. Keyes was selected because he had fought over the same ground during McClellan's 1862 Peninsula campaign. He had about six thousand infantry and fourteen artillery pieces.

Getty moved his artillery and wagons across to the north side of the Pamunkey on the night of June 30. The infantry and cavalry stayed on the south side and camped around White House that night. They spent the evening making final preparations for the next day. No one doubted that this time the Confederates would be ready and waiting. The men rose at 4 A.M., and, after a quick breakfast of hardtack and coffee, moved out at six over the railroad bridge. The wagons and artillery let the cavalry soldiers and infantry regiments move past the road before they swung into line.

The infantry marched about nine miles that day through the hot and dusty bottomlands along the Pamunkey to the small Virginia village of King William Courthouse. The cavalry led the way with pickets out on the farm roads and in front of the main column. The infantry arrived at 3 P.M.; the rest of the force—including stragglers, the wagons, and artillery—wandered in during the night. The cavalry, still under Colonel Spear, continued up the north bank of the river to cover any fords or bridges across the Pamunkey. Their orders were "to destroy bridges, ferries, boats and other means of crossing," as far as Hanovertown, about twenty miles up-river from White House. They also covered the left flank of the infantry column. That night they camped about three or four miles upriver from the main column.

The pickets were pulled in early the next morning and the main column moved out at six, marching to Brandywine, ten miles away. The cavalry moved up along the Pamunkey by way of Taylor's Ferry, then on to Littlepage's Bridge. They camped that night a few miles north of Hanover Courthouse. Colonel Spear reported lat-er that during the march his troopers captured two enemy soldiers and two detec-tives from the Richmond police department. The cavalrymen set fire to Littlepage's Bridge and destroyed five ferryboats and a "70 yard long bridge at the Widow Nel-sons" the next day. A Confederate commissary lieutenant and seven privates were captured and sent to the rear.

The infantry reached Taylorsville on July 3 at about 10 P.M. "[T]he heat and dust were intolerable, and the troops suffered exceedingly. There were numerous cases of sunstroke, and many men fell out from exhaustion. In addition to these there were great numbers of stragglers, chiefly from the [165th] and [166th] Regiments Pennsylvania Militia."[45]

The next day Getty ordered Col. Griffin Steadman's 2nd Brigade, Capt. John Simpson's 1st Pennsylvania Light Battery A, the California Hundred, and two of the three artillery batteries accompanying the expedition, along with the wagons and baggage and "the sick, exhausted, and foot sore from the other commands" to stay at Taylorsville. The Californians went out on picket at Taylor's plantation.[46] The main force marched to Littlepage's Bridge, where Col. Michael T. Donohoe's brigade was left to cover the river crossing and the ruins of the bridge. The three remaining brigades then marched on to Hanover Courthouse, where they encoun-tered a group of rebel pickets. The rebels were soon driven away, and Col. Samuel M. Alford's 1st Brigade was left at Hanover Courthouse to cover the advance. Getty's force was now reduced to two infantry brigades, Spear's cavalry, and an artillery battery. The extra ammunition had been left with the wagon train at Tay-lorsville, so the troops had only forty rounds each.

The balance of the force, about a third of the troops that had left White House on July 1, went forward to the bridges on the South Anna. General Foster took over command of the advance party. He had five infantry regiments, including the straggling Pennsylvania militia regiments, Wardrop's provisional brigade with two newly formed infantry regiments, Davis's Massachusetts battery, and Spear's cav-alry, which included Companies B, C, D, and K from the 2nd Massachusetts.[47] The cavalry led the march to the bridge. It was late afternoon when they started, some-what cooler than midday, but still the infantry was quickly left behind.

Spear reported encountering picket stations every two or three miles along the way, which they charged and drove off. Reaching the river about 6 P.M., Spear found the railroad bridge well guarded. Scouts located a wooden bridge about four hundred yards farther upstream. When he learned that General Foster had not yet arrived, Spear advanced to within a hundred yards of the bridge accompanied by Capt. P. A. Davis of the 7th Massachusetts Battery. The advancing force was fired on by riflemen and a twelve-pounder howitzer. Spear ordered his men to halt and deploy. He then directed Captain Davis's battery to set up in an adjoining field. While the battery was moving into place, General Foster rode up, took command, and ordered the guns to move to another position.

Spear, emboldened by the presence of the infantry, felt that the attack on the bridge should have proceeded and resented Foster's decision to move Davis's battery: "Had not General Foster come up as he did, I should have opened fire in ten minutes."

General Foster later wrote: "The command arrived at the place indicated about 7:30 PM. I immediately acquainted myself, so far as possible, with the adjacent country, and placed my command in a position to resist any onward movement or to make an aggressive movement, as I might under the contingency conclude to do."[48]

One cannot help but wonder what was going through Foster's mind when he arrived on the scene and assumed a defensive posture. After all, the whole purpose of moving fourteen thousand men through the countryside that hot July day was to make an aggressive move, such as burning the South Anna bridge.

Foster later tried to justify his decision as being prudent in light of information gleaned from a nearby resident who reported that

> the enemy had been busy during the three previous days in replenishing the garrison at the earthworks commanding the bridge. He told me that the trains, two to four a day, had come loaded with soldiers, and that one train contained artillery exclusively, viz. eight pieces, and also that his son was over the river that morning and saw six pieces of artillery mounted and in position.
>
> The position I occupied was a very precarious one, as I was liable to an attack on all sides and there was only one feasible position for the artillery, and that on a hill on a small compass of ground, with woods on one side and the railroad on the other. This position was liable to a concentrated fire from the enemy's artillery from three points, noticed particularly by Captain Davis, this would have been the result.[49]

After dark Foster sent out pickets and then advanced two companies of the 118th New York and one company of the 99th New York from Wardrop's brigade, as skirmishers. Both regiments were under fire for the first time. A small party of volunteers charged one redoubt and captured ten prisoners, who told Foster three regiments from Fredericksburg plus regiments from Richmond held the fortifications. A small firefight ensued with the green infantry firing at the flashes of the Confederate rifles. Wardrop's brigade lost two killed, ten wounded, and four missing.

The Confederate prisoners were wrong. The South Anna bridge was defended by two regiments of convalescents from Richmond under the command of Brig. Gen. John R. Cooke. Cooke had twelve guns but he was short of ammunition. The convalescents had been sent up from Richmond to man the defenses constructed after the earlier attack.

Foster decided to retreat before daybreak without attempting anything further. One company of infantry was ordered to destroy as much track as it could during the remaining hours of darkness. Foster returned to Hanover Courthouse, arriving there at 4 A.M. The skirmishers were withdrawn at 2:30 A.M. and fell back to Taylor's Farm, arriving there at 1 P.M. on July 5.[50]

Earlier, two companies of the 11th Pennsylvania Cavalry under the command of Maj. Franklin A. Stratton had been ordered to proceed to Ashland Station, where they burned the station, a small bridge, and about a half-mile of track. They also destroyed the telegraph line so that there was no communication between Richmond and the bridge's defenders. An eyewitness to the burning described the raid:

> About one o'clock I was awakened by E. leaning over me, and saying in a low tremulous tone, "Mother, get up, the Yankees are come." We sprang up, and there they were at the telegraph office, immediately opposite. In an instant the door was broken down with a crash, and the battery and other things thrown out. Axes were at work cutting down the telegraph poles, while busy hands were tearing up the railroad. A sentinel sat on his horse at our gate as motionless as if both man and horse had been cut from a block of Yankee granite. We expected every moment that they would come to the house, or at least go into the hotel opposite to us; but they went off to the depot. There was a dead silence, except an occasional order. "Be quick," "Keep a sharp look-out" etc. etc. The night was moonlight, but we dressed ourselves and sat in the dark; we were afraid to open the window shutters or light a lamp, lest they might be attracted to the house. We remained in this way perhaps two hours, when the flames suddenly burst from the depot. All parts of the building seemed to be burning at once; also immense piles of wood and of plank. The conflagration was brilliant. As soon as the whole was fairly blazing the pickets were called in, and the whole party dashed off, with demoniac yells.[51]

The Confederate losses were very small: one killed and six wounded; the number of captured was not reported. Cooke reported capturing ten Union soldiers.

Foster retreated back to White House by way of King William Courthouse, arriving on July 7.

Keyes's demonstration against Bottom's Bridge was an even greater fiasco than Foster's expedition against the South Anna bridge. His approach was so cautious and poorly handled that the Confederates quickly perceived the movement was only a demonstration. Keyes's failure had little effect on the final results.

Secretary of War Stanton was furious. "Sir," he wrote to General Dix, "we feel a good deal chagrined at the slight results of the late operations in your department. General Getty in all probability multiplied the enemy's force two or three times, for his representations do not accord with the conditions of things shown in Davis's letter to Lee [a captured dispatch from Davis to Lee]. The great murmuring in every quarter at the waste of force in your command will probably be a good deal aggravated by this last disappointment."[52]

Dix, stung by Stanton's rebuke, preferred charges against Keyes and relieved him of his command.[53] He spent the next year serving on boards and commissions. Dix's command was dispersed and he was sent to New York where, two weeks later, he commanded the troops that put down the July 1863 draft riots in that city. Foster went on to command a department in the Carolinas. Getty, who had the best chance to accomplish something important, returned to his divisional command without censure. He later commanded a division in Sheridan's Army of the Shenandoah, where he fought alongside the 2nd Massachusetts.

One of the best opportunities to seriously disrupt the Confederate's fragile communications and supply network in Virginia was lost. The Confederates rebuilt the Virginia Central bridge, and the RF&P and Virginia Central Railroads continued to supply Lee throughout the rest of 1863.

The bridges survived an 1864 attack by Sheridan largely because of the extensive entrenchments built after the July 1863 attacks. They were finally destroyed in 1865 when Sheridan crossed Virginia to join the armies in the trenches at Petersburg. Ironically, the 2nd Massachusetts was the unit that would burn them. But by then the bridges were no longer militarily important.

3 | Gettysburg and Guerrillas

On April 28, 1862, the Confederate Congress passed a bill popularly called the Partisan Act. The bill authorized Southerners not already in line regiments to operate as guerrillas and make a profit from their endeavors. They were to be paid "full value in such manner as the Secretary of War may prescribe" for "any arms and munitions of war captured from the enemy" and allowed to dispose of all other captured goods as they saw fit. As an additional incentive, a recruit in a properly authorized and enrolled unit was considered to be part of the Confederate army and therefore not subject to conscription.[1]

In the spring of 1863, without the formal approval required by the Partisan Act but with the approbation of Maj. Gen. J. E. B. "Jeb" Stuart, John Singleton Mosby organized a small band of fifteen men for guerrilla activities.[2]

Mosby was born near Richmond in 1833. While attending the University of Virginia he shot an unarmed fellow student, supposedly in self-defense. He was subsequently tried and sentenced to prison, where he took up the study of law. His family's connections and political influence got him a pardon after he served only seven months. Upon release he married the daughter of a former congressman and opened a law practice in Bristol, a small town in the southwest corner of Virginia. Mosby enlisted in the 1st Virginia Cavalry when the Civil War began and was with his regiment at First Bull Run but did not see combat. He was promoted to first lieutenant on April 2, 1862, and appointed to serve as regimental adjutant. Mosby promptly took advantage of his status as an officer and resigned from the regiment just three weeks after being commissioned. Befriended by Stuart, he performed and led several scouting missions behind Union lines, including Stuart's ride around McClellan's army in June 1862. He was included among the privates noted for special commendation in Lee's order announcing Stuart's feat.[3]

With the inducements included in the Partisan Act, he had little trouble finding recruits. His band of fifteen quickly grew to three full companies by the end of the year. Mosby's guerrillas were armed with a variety of weapons provided by the men themselves or captured from Union troops. Most of Mosby's men carried three or four revolvers of varying makes. Captured Union carbines were much in demand, particularly the single-shot, breech-loading, Sharps carbines. Sabers were rarely employed; Mosby believed that a pistol was the best weapon for his men.[4]

In March 1863, moving at night over back roads and bypassing Union picket posts, Mosby captured Brig. Gen. Edwin Henry Stoughton in bed at his headquarters at Fairfax Courthouse. An unverified story was that a young woman made sure Stoughton was drunk before Mosby arrived. She then guided Mosby to the headquarters, where the general was found surrounded by empty champagne bottles. The guerrillas hustled Stoughton to the south along with thirty-nine other prisoners and fifty-eight horses.[5]

The raid made Mosby and his band famous throughout the North. General Lee was so impressed with Mosby's feat that he commissioned him a captain and authorized him to form a company to be mustered into Confederate service. Northern newspapers used the incident to attack the administration. Pro-Lincoln papers called for more troops to be detached to protect the capitol. Lincoln aptly and succinctly expressed the military importance of the incident. When told about the raid the president reportedly said "that he did not mind the loss of the Brigadier as much as he did the horses; for said he 'I can make a much better Brigadier in five minutes, but the horses cost a hundred and twenty-five dollars apiece.'"[6] Stoughton was released in May but the notoriety ruined his career.[7]

Northern and Southern newspapers alike dubbed Virginia's Loudoun and Fairfax Counties "Mosby's Confederacy." Bounded by the Potomac River to the north and east, the Occoquan River to the south, and the Blue Ridge Mountains to the west, the two counties were a sort of no-man's-land throughout the war. East of the Blue Ridge, but parallel, are the Bull Run Mountains. The fertile Loudoun Valley lies between the two ridges.

Three turnpikes crossed the area.[8] The most northerly was the Leesburg and Georgetown Turnpike. It ran from Washington through Dranesville and Leesburg, then west through the Blue Ridge Mountains to Harper's Ferry in the Shenandoah Valley. The second was Little River Turnpike, which ran from Alexandria to Fairfax Courthouse through Chantilly and Aldie's Gap. The road split at Aldie's Gap with one branch, the Snicker's Gap Turnpike, running northwest to Snicker'sville then on to Berryville and Winchester in the Shenandoah Valley. The second branch, the Ashby Gap Turnpike, headed southwest to Middleburg and Paris. It crossed the Blue Ridge at Ashby's Gap and continued on to Winchester.

Two railroads traversed the country. The most important in 1863 was the Orange and Alexandria, which ran southwest to Rappahannock Station on the north fork of the Rappahannock River. Throughout most of 1863 and 1864 it was the main supply line to Maj. Gen. George G. Meade's Army of the Potomac. A second railroad, the Loudoun Hampshire Railroad, ran from Alexandria, about two miles south of the Leesburg and Georgetown Turnpike, to Leesburg. It had been heavily damaged during the first two years of the war and was no longer operable.

The terrain is largely low, open, rolling hills with numerous country lanes meandering between the turnpikes. Fairfax County, to the east, was more wooded than Loudoun County. The largest stream in the area is Goose Creek, which rises in the hills south of Leesburg and flows north to the Potomac at Edwards Ferry. Little River joins Goose Creek about three miles north of Aldie. Farther east, Broad Run flows north from Gum Springs on the Little River Pike into the Potomac about three miles below Goose Creek.

The inhabitants were small independent farmers growing wheat, corn, and milk

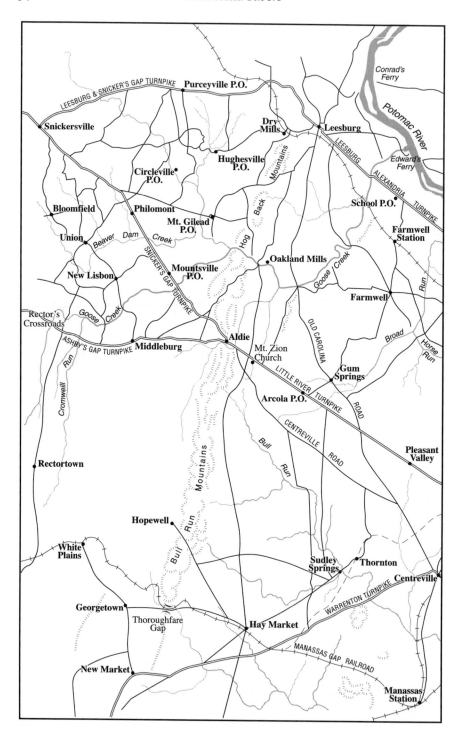

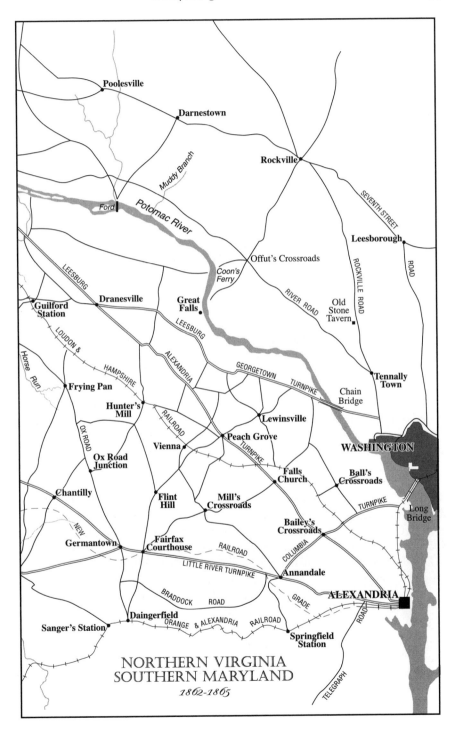

NORTHERN VIRGINIA
SOUTHERN MARYLAND
1862-1865

cows. Few owned slaves except for an occasional house servant. Alexandria and Leesburg were the principal regional centers; most of the villages were little more than two or three houses, a post office, a church, and perhaps a tavern if the village was on one of the turnpikes. Every creek and run had a gristmill. There were toll-gates along the turnpikes but during the war no one dared to collect tolls.

The allegiance of the population was mixed. Generally the townspeople and farmers living west of the Bull Run Mountains were pro-Confederate. Most of the farmers in the northern and eastern reaches were Union sympathizers. A number of Dunker families from Maryland had settled along the Potomac in the north. At first the Dunkers were neutral—until their rich barns became a favorite target of Confederate guerrillas.

On May 1, 1863, Maj. Gen. Joseph "Fighting Joe" Hooker moved most of the Army of the Potomac around the left flank of Lee's Army of Northern Virginia at Petersburg and crossed the Rapidan River. In a brilliant move, Lee sent Stonewall Jackson around Hooker's right flank and drove the Union army back across the river.

Hooker's defeat at Chancellorsville frightened Washington and calls were sent out to each of the states to send any available troops to the capital. Among the available regiments was the 2nd Massachusetts Cavalry at Readville. On May 12, 1863, five companies left Readville for the defenses of Washington. Three of the companies were made up of Californians: Capt. Charles Eigenbrodt's Company E, Capt. David DeMerritt's Company F, and Capt. Zabdiel Adams's Company L. The two other companies were from Massachusetts: Capt. Archibald McKendry's Company G, and Capt. Charles Rice's Company I. Captain William Forbes was promoted to major on May 12 and seconded Colonel Lowell during the movement. Lieutenant Colonel Russell remained at Readville with Company H, awaiting the arrival of Company M from San Francisco.

Lowell described the three-day trip to Washington via Stonington, Connecticut; Jersey City and Camden, New Jersey; and Baltimore in a note intended to give Russell guidance when he took the remaining two companies south. He said that the trip was plagued with confusion as a result of delays loading the steamer in Stonington and trains along the route. He advised Russell to "start loading earlier and feed on the pier" in order to avoid similar problems. He further advised Russell to keep a close eye on his men as they had lost ten men while watering and loading the horses onto a train in Jersey City. Despite the problems, which included the loss of eleven deserters and one dead horse, Lowell reported the gain of six horses, and concluded, "On the whole I recommend this route highly."

During the trip Lowell wrote a letter to his fiancée, Josephine Shaw. Their courtship had included long rides through the countryside and she knew each of Lowell's horses. "We are just passing Schuyler and it is only 7½ o'clock so we shall be at the Jersey dock before nine,—that I call very good luck. I wonder whether Bertold looks at it in that light; I think he'll be glad to leave the steamboat at all events; he is wedged in tight between Ruksh and Nig, wanting to kick both, but unable to raise a foot, without human sympathy (lumps of sugar), for even Robbins has not been able to get near him since he came on board."[9]

The regiment arrived at East Capitol Hill on May 16,[10] and the troops were quartered in Sibley tents laid out by squadrons. The officers' quarters overlooked the camp. One balmy Sunday afternoon while sitting at his camp table, Colonel Lowell, with his attachment for order, described the encampment in a letter to Miss Shaw: "the ground slopes gently off and at fifty yards distance commence the company lines,—from here you look down into these so entirely that not a man can swear or a horse switch his tail in anger without our knowing it. The tents are in three rows, the two companies of a squadron being on a line, the horses of each squadron to the right of the tents."[11]

Lowell set up a rigid training schedule to prepare the men for the contest that would inevitably come. Each day started with reveille at 5 A.M., morning muster, and then a break for breakfast. This was followed by individual drill and company drill. Three afternoons a week were spent in squadron drill. On alternating days, including Sunday mornings, the troops had regimental drill. The day's work ended with evening muster. After evening muster the men were free to cook dinner, smoke their pipes, and relax. Taps sounded at 9 P.M. as men wearily crawled into their tents. The only time the troopers had to themselves was on Sunday afternoons. That time was spent washing clothes, writing letters, and resting.

The purpose of continual drill was to train the men and horses to move together as a cohesive group through the various formations and movements required in battle. Changes from column to line of battle and flank and wheeling movements were practiced almost every day. Usually the commands were passed orally, but sometimes bugle calls were used. Lowell, pleased with the progress of the training, wrote to Josephine: "I should wish you were here to see one [of our regimental drills], only to the outsider there is little visible but a cloud of dust. The men are getting on so well in squadron drill that tomorrow I shall commence the 'individual drill' for the morning, squadron drill three afternoons, and regimental drill two afternoons and Sunday morning. The training of the horse, and the teaching of the trooper to ride, you see which ought to come first, come last in our method of raising cavalry,—we must do the best we can, however."[12]

Sometime during the last week in May, Lowell, taking advantage of his political connections, visited with Secretary of War Stanton, who "commenced by asking after the regiment, and why I had not been to see him,—told me that he expected a great deal from it; that he would do anything and everything I wanted to make it an 'Ironsides' regiment (I do not know what that means, but I told him I would do all I could to make it a good regiment). He said he knew it, and added that he was away from Washington when that affair in Boston occurred, or he should have written me a personal note of thanks. I spoke of bringing up my companies from Gloucester Point,—he said it should be done, that I should drill them here, should have all my requisitions filled by preference, and when I said I was ready, he would send the regiment where it should meet the enemy, and would give it the post of honor."[13]

Lowell was skeptical but said that was all he wanted. He noted that Stanton seemed pleased. Lowell's skepticism was well founded. In spite of Stanton's promise that he would determine when the regiment was ready, army headquarters had other plans. On May 29, Maj. Gen. Silas Casey, commander of the Washington defenses, directed Lowell to report at once how much time he would need to take the regiment into the field. "Two hours," Lowell responded. Two days later the 2nd Massachusetts was ordered to Camp Brightwood. Lowell said the new camp, located "about four miles north of Washington, on rough ground thickly studded with oak stumps" was "not so pretty a site as our last, but much healthier; we do not present so attractive an outside to visitors, but in reality are probably better off. I have two companies and a half on picket fifteen miles apart, and am expecting some night alarms, knowing it to be all play and got up for drill purposes. I would much prefer to drill my men for the present in my own way not General Heintzelman's way."[14]

Two days later he continued on the same theme: "The change from the camp to the field (we are now, so far as work and life go, to be counted in the field, though there seems to me a good deal of 'sham' about it) is a very critical one for a regiment, it is so important to start picket duty aright, so hard to make men understand that the only way to keep tolerably clean is to keep perfectly clean, so hard to get new officers to keep the proper line between their men and themselves."[15]

By now the usual bounty jumpers among the Massachusetts men and the few Californians who had enlisted just to get to the East were gone. The regiment was disciplined and fit and the Massachusetts volunteers were learning to ride and care for their horses. As soldiers they could hold their own with the picked California contingent "except in horsemanship in which the latter excelled."

Lowell, pleased with the results of his rigid regimen, decided to relax discipline slightly: "I am going to try the experiment, too, of taking off my camp guard and giving my 'pet lambs' a chance to wander where they please,—punishing them, of course, if found outside of camp. I am not sure how it will work."[16]

The war came to the regiment in early June. At daybreak on June 10, John Mosby crossed the Potomac at Muddy Branch with about 250 men and attacked the camp of Company I, 6th Michigan Cavalry, at Seneca Mills, Maryland. Most of the men were out on picket duty and the guerrillas drove the few who remained from their camp, then moved up the line, picking up sixteen pickets at isolated posts between Seneca Mills and Muddy Branch. Mosby claimed the rebels killed seven and captured seventeen against the loss of only four men. Union losses were actually four killed, one wounded, and sixteen captured.[17]

Lowell was ordered to take every available man and move up the north bank toward Poolesville. A cavalry force commanded by Maj. Gen. Julius Stahel, part of the Washington defenses south of the Potomac, was alerted and ordered to cooperate with Lowell. Stahel arrived at Fairfax Courthouse "with 400 good men, under command of good officers, who know the country, in pursuit of the rebels." Another 450 men from the 1st West Virginia Cavalry and 5th New York under Maj. John Hammond were sent from the Harper's Ferry area to sweep through Aldie and

Middleburg to try to catch the guerrillas as they returned through the Bull Run Mountains.[18]

Lowell was directed "to pursue, and destroy, if possible, the party of Confederates which crossed the river this morning. Major General Stahel has been notified of the situation, and probably before this time has sent parties to operate on the right bank of the Potomac against the same people."[19] Headquarters gave Lowell the responsibility of determining the route of the search: "Consult your own discretion in your direction. Go where you please in pursuit of Mosby. A squadron from Winchester will probably pass Middleburg or Aldie today. It has been notified to be on the lookout for Mosby."[20]

At 3 A.M. on June 12 most of two squadrons from the 2nd Massachusetts crossed the Potomac at Edwards Ford on Mosby's trail. The battalion passed through Leesburg and marched south to Carter's Ford across Goose Creek. It reached Aldie in the afternoon and, as Lowell was preparing to move on to Middleburg, Major Hammond and his troopers met him. Hammond reported all quiet at Middleburg and told Lowell that Mosby had arrived at two o'clock the day before and had immediately disbanded. Realizing there was no possibility of capturing any of the raiders, Lowell returned by way of the Leesburg and Georgetown Pike to the Chain Bridge and back to Camp Brightwood. The return route was somewhat circuitous but it gave Lowell and the officers an opportunity to become familiar with the northern parts of Fairfax County.

After the war the North learned how close it had come to capturing the partisan leader. Mosby joined his wife in Salem (present-day Marshall), about ten miles south of Middleburg on the Manassas Gap Railroad, after the guerrillas dispersed at Middleburg. During the night, a detachment from the 1st New York Cavalry commanded by Capt. William C. Boyd passed through Salem on a sweep from Berryville in the Shenandoah Valley. As the troopers moved through the countryside they searched every farmhouse for rebels. Informants told them that Mosby was at the Hathaway home. Three Union troopers, including a lieutenant, were ordered to search the house from top to bottom. Before they reached the upstairs bedroom where Mosby and his wife were staying, the guerrilla chieftain slipped out a window and clambered onto a nearby tree. He stayed there, concealed by the foliage, while the three troopers questioned his wife. When the patrol moved on he climbed back into the house.[21]

In early June General Lee decided to make another invasion of the North in an attempt to bring the war home to the Northern states. Both armies lay along the river at Fredericksburg, warily watching each other. Hooker made two demonstrations on June 5 and 6, but Lee recognized they were only feints. A major cavalry fight at Brandy Station almost upset his plans but he proceeded anyway, sending Lt. Gen. Richard S. Ewell's corps marching toward the Valley.

By the fifteenth Lee had concentrated his army in the Shenandoah. The Army of the Potomac was moving north and generally concentrated around Centreville, on the Orange and Alexandria Railroad. Major General Alfred Pleasanton sent three cavalry brigades toward Aldie Gap to try to determine the location of Lee's army. They arrived at Aldie on June 17, just as Brig. Gen. Fitzhugh Lee's Confederate brigade, temporarily commanded by Col. Thomas Munford, was setting up camp for the night. The rebels withdrew, but not before inflicting heavy losses on the Union troopers.

Orders came sending Lowell on a reconnaissance from Centreville through Wolf Run, Brentsville, and Manassas Junction in an attempt to intercept any Confederates moving south from the Aldie fight. The patrol returned with eight captured rebels including a lieutenant colonel. Lowell reported all was quiet.

Hooker's cavalry was attempting to cover the gaps through the Bull Run Mountains but there were not enough troopers. Standing orders permitted an army commander to take over local troops, so Hooker took command of Stahel's cavalry. Stahel reported to Washington that Hooker had ordered him to concentrate his force and wait for orders. Headquarters in Washington soon realized that this meant the picket line along the Potomac, which Stahel's cavalry manned, was being withdrawn. Another wire was sent to Stahel: "Gen.: the major general commanding [Halleck] desires that you comply with the desires of Gen. Hooker. Your pickets, as far as possible, must be left out."

Stahel answered: "I was ordered by Gen. Hooker to withdraw the whole picket, as his corps are in front of my line, all over, and he will protect me. This leaves my picket unnecessary." The next day Hooker sent Stahel on a sweep along the Rappahannock to determine the location of Lt. Gen. A. P. Hill's corps on the left flank of Lee's army. Hooker, like McClellan before him, failed to grasp the importance of shielding Washington and the Potomac crossings. The only troops covering the approaches to Washington were a small party at Monocacy commanded by Capt. Samuel McKee, and a detachment at Poolesville. The next day Hooker ordered McKee's company to report to General Pleasonton at Aldie. Then, exacerbating the problem, he ordered the troops at Poolesville to march to Harper's Ferry. With these moves the fords across the Potomac from Monocacy to the Chain Bridge were wide open, leaving Washington vulnerable to a quick dash by guerrillas or regular Confederate cavalry from the relatively undefended Maryland side.

By the twenty-fifth Hooker's army was closed up on the Potomac and ready to move across the river at Edwards Ferry near Leesburg the next day. Army headquarters and I Corps at Hunter's Mill would cross first and march to Poolesville. The tail end of the army, VI Corps at Centreville and Fairfax, would march at 3 A.M. through Chantilly Church, Frying Pan, Herndon Station, and Dranesville to Edwards Ferry, and, after covering the withdrawal of the pontoon bridges, would follow II Corps.[22] Sometime during the day (or perhaps on the twenty-fourth), Colonel Lowell was ordered to patrol the fords below Edwards Ferry. Lowell went to Poolesville on the pretext of clarifying the order but, as he later privately admitted, to attempt to get the regiment included in the march north. He was not pleased with the assignment of fighting guerrillas and the army's move north presented him with a golden opportunity to present his case to friends on Hooker's staff, who got him an audience with the commanding general.

Lowell met briefly with Hooker and asked that the regiment be assigned to the Army of the Potomac. He was an ambitious young man who recognized that the road to promotion was with the Army of the Potomac, not on detached duty fighting bushwhackers. By appealing directly to Hooker he had let his ambitions take control. At 8 P.M. on the twenty-sixth General Hooker ordered Lowell and the 2nd Massachusetts to join Maj. Gen. Henry W. Slocum's corps at Knoxville, Virginia, near Harper's Ferry. The orders were changed a half-hour later to report instead to Maj. Gen. William H. French at Harper's Ferry. Lowell notified Washington in a dispatch that was sent close enough to the regiment's 9 A.M. departure on the twenty-seventh to avoid having Hooker's order countermanded.[23]

During the night Lowell called in all his pickets and prepared to march. At 8:30 in the morning Lowell's command was on the road toward Knoxville and the Army of the Potomac and away from the lower fords. That same day, VI Corps moved up from Centreville to Dranesville, continued west along the Little River Pike to Edwards Ferry, and then across the Potomac. Unknown to Washington headquarters or General Hooker, Jeb Stuart was moving north behind VI Corps with the bulk of Lee's cavalry.

Earlier Stuart had asked Major Mosby to scout ahead with some picked men to find a suitable crossing site in the vicinity of Dranesville.[24] When he did not hear from Mosby, Stuart decided to simply follow Hooker north. When he ordered a rest halt at an abandoned Union camp, his command "regaled itself on the stores left by the enemy in the place." The Confederate cavalry finally reached Dranesville late in the afternoon on the twenty-seventh. They could still see VI Corps's campfires burning west of the town, and they captured several Union stragglers. Brigadier General Wade Hampton's brigade approached the river, and, after learning from a local citizen who had just forded it that there were no pickets on the other side crossed over early that night. Once on the other side, Hampton reported to Stuart that the water was two feet higher than usual and that "it would be utterly impossible to cross the artillery at that ford. In this the residents were also very positive, that vehicles could not cross. A ford lower down was examined, and found quite as impracticable from quicksand, rocks, and rugged banks. I, however, determined not to give it up without trial, and before 12 o'clock that night, in spite of the difficulties, to all appearances insuperable, indomitable energy and resolute determination triumphed; every piece was brought safely over, and the entire command in bivouac on Maryland soil."[25]

After wrecking a few locks on the Baltimore and Ohio canal and bagging a small Union wagon train, Stuart moved north and in a day or so discovered that he was actually between Hooker and Washington, D.C. There was no way out except to continue north and try to get around the Army of the Potomac. With Stuart off on another ride around the Union army instead of scouting to the front, Lee and the Army of Northern Virginia blundered northward.

Communications between General Halleck and the Army of the Potomac became disrupted. Stuart's movements through eastern Maryland badly frightened Halleck, who feared the Confederate cavalry would try to cut the railroad between

Washington and Baltimore, isolating the capital.[26] His fear quickly turned to anger and he began searching for a scapegoat. He was incensed with Hooker's orders to the 2nd Massachusetts and with Stahel, for permitting his force to become integrated with the Army of the Potomac. The axe fell quickly in a strongly worded dispatch sent at midnight: "Major General Stahel is relieved from duty with the Army of the Potomac, and will report to General Couch, at Harrisburg, to organize and command the cavalry in the Department of the Susquehanna. Lowell's cavalry is the only force for scouts in this department, and cannot be taken from General Heintzelman."[27]

Next on the list was Colonel Lowell. A wire from Washington sent at 10:45 A.M. on June 27, went to Lowell in care of Col. Albert B. Jewett at Poolesville: "You will not obey any order from Maj.-Gen. Hooker ordering you to move until you have instructions from these headquarters."

And another to Colonel Jewett: "If Colonel Lowell is not at Poolesville, this must be sent to him immediately."

The next wire, from Maj. Gen. Samuel P. Heintzelman to General French at Harper's Ferry, was very clear: "The commanding general directs that Col. Lowell, Second Massachusetts Cavalry, at once comply with the order he has received from the Gen.-in-Chief. He wishes you to advise Col. Lowell accordingly, and to inform him that it devolves upon him to watch the fords from Poolesville to Harper's Ferry."[28]

Lowell, caught in an acrimonious exchange between generals and faced with conflicting orders, found the whole affair "embarrassing, but I decided with much reluctance to obey Heintzelman, as he was backed by Halleck, though I was sorely tempted to stay with Hooker in the Army of the Potomac. So I moved down the Potomac about fifty seven miles, and when I reached the mouth of the Monocacy, met some of my wagons with the news that the rebels in strong force had crossed the Potomac at the *very ford* I was especially to watch; that there had been no picket there at all, and no notice had gone either to Washington or Hooker until nearly twelve hours after the crossing."[29]

The 2nd Massachusetts belatedly pursued Stuart's force for two days. They captured a lieutenant and four privates and kept Heintzelman informed of Stuart's progress. Lowell feared that when the chase was over he would be arrested for leaving his post without proper authority. He expressed his guilt in a letter home: "I was only to blame for having been unmilitary enough to express a wish to General Hooker to serve in a more active place and to leave the 'all quiet along the Potomac' to some poorer regiment."[30]

Lowell led the regiment back to Poolesville on June 29 and the next day moved to a camp near Langley on the Georgetown Turnpike, west of and outside the Washington defenses.[31] The regiment was met by welcome reinforcements: Captain DeMerritt and Lieutenant Stone, who had remained in San Francisco to fill out Company M, had arrived with a full hundred-man company.

Hooker was relieved late in the evening on June 28 and Maj. Gen. George G. Meade was appointed commander of the Army of the Potomac. On July 1 one of

Lee's divisions made a flank march to a small Pennsylvania crossroads town named Gettysburg in search of shoes. Cavalry would normally have screened this type of movement, but Stuart was somewhere to the east. The rebels got caught up in a firefight with two brigades of Union cavalry and both sides kept sending in more troops. The skirmish escalated into a bloody battle that changed the course of the war. Three days later Lee's army was forced to retreat after having suffered a major defeat.

While the Battle of Gettysburg was raging to the north, Lowell and the 2nd Massachusetts had the ignominious task of escorting canal boats from Harper's Ferry to Washington along the Baltimore and Ohio canal.[32] As it turned out, Lowell's part in the uncovering of the Potomac fords was overlooked by Washington in the glow of the Gettysburg victory. Lowell was relieved when a dispatch arrived stating that Washington was "gratified with my activity."

The defeated Army of Northern Virginia crossed the Potomac at fords at the lower end of the Shenandoah Valley above Harper's Ferry. Meade, after some delay, slowly followed it into Loudoun County. With the Army of the Potomac back in his territory, Mosby decided to set up a fixed base to keep his band concentrated and better able to take advantage of any opportunities for raiding. From the base, located in the trackless Bull Run Mountains, he could raid east into Loudoun and Fairfax Counties and, in a day or two, be safely back in the mountains. In mid-July he captured three heavily laden sutler wagons near Goose Creek, then two days later hit nine wagons on a foraging expedition near Circleville. A couple of days after that he captured a large number of mules and a half a dozen Union cavalrymen near Salem. With no effective patrols to hinder his guerrilla activities, Mosby had a free hand.

The authorities in Washington decided to take action. The 2nd Massachusetts and a company from Col. Percy Wyndham's 1st New Jersey Cavalry were the only cavalry forces available. The 2nd Massachusetts had six companies at Camp Brightwood. Lowell was ordered to make a sweep to Aldie through Ashby's Gap to clear the area of guerrillas and gather intelligence on Lee's position. The regiment crossed the river at Chain Bridge on July 10 with 304 men from the California Battalion (Companies E, F, L, and M) and a company of Massachusetts's men (Company G). Lowell picked up his orders from Wyndham that evening. The next morning the column left Alexandria with an additional sixty men from the 1st New Jersey Cavalry.

The patrol reached the village of Aldie at about 6 P.M. and stopped to question the few local Union sympathizers in the neighborhood before pushing on to Middleburg, the objective for the evening. Wyndham had instructed Lowell to detach a hundred men at Aldie and send them south through Thoroughfare Gap to cover his left as he approached Ashby's Gap. The patrol's outriders reported that the column had been observed by scouts from Mosby's band throughout the day's ride and that the locals had reported that a portion of Brig. Gen. William E. Jones's brigade was at Middleburg. Based on this intelligence Lowell wisely decided not to divide his force and canceled the swing through Thoroughfare Gap. With Middleburg in Confederate hands, an evening approach would not be prudent. Lowell stopped about a mile west on the Snicker's Gap road and camped for the night.

Early the next morning the patrol moved out. The van was reinforced and flankers were sent out on each side of the road. Finding Middleburg empty of rebels they moved on to Upperville where, according to the locals, the only Confederates in the vicinity were two companies from Brig. Gen. B. H. Robertson's North Carolina cavalry brigade at Ashby's Gap, some of the 6th and 12th Virginia Regiments and a portion of Jones's brigade at Snicker's Gap. They arrived at Paris, just below Ashby's Gap, at noon. The vanguard, composed mostly of men from Captain Eigenbrodt's company and led by Lieutenant Norcross, surprised a body of rebel troops. Norcross attacked and drove the rebels up to the gap. The Confederates fell back, skirmishing with Norcross's troopers and drawing them on. At the top of the gap, through the smoke and haze, Norcross saw three platoons of rebels astride the road. He drew his saber and ordered his little band to charge. As they bore down on the guerrillas another platoon of rebels, concealed behind a low stone wall on the side of the road, rose and fired. The smoke from the volley obscured the road and, for a moment, Norcross's men fell back. However, as the rest of the advance guard came up, they charged again. A second blast hit the charging troopers, felling nine men. Three men, including Lieutenant Norcross, had their horses shot down and were taken prisoner; the survivors turned and ran.

Lowell, in front of the main body, stopped and took stock of the rebel position. He ordered two of the California companies, L and M, to charge before the enemy had time to regroup. Companies F and G, the rest of Company E, and the 1st New Jersey troopers followed in reserve. With a shout, the Californians charged the rebels. The Union troopers were green; this was their first glimpse of "the elephant." The Confederates stood and fought for a few minutes, but the momentum and ferocity of the charge pushed them back; they could only retreat or be taken.

Lowell ordered the second line to stop and secure the prisoners and pick up the wounded while Companies L and M followed the retreating Confederates. The prisoners included a lieutenant from the 6th Virginia Cavalry, six privates from the North Carolina cavalry regiments, one man acknowledged to belong to Mosby's band, and two citizens accompanying the rebel party.

Led by Colonel Lowell, the Californians followed the Confederates to the Shenandoah. When they reached the river a Confederate picket force of about twenty to twenty-five men fired on them from the west bank, but no one was hit. The fleeing guerrillas crossed the river farther downstream and set up a skirmish line. As the Union troops moved down the river to the rebel position, a heavy firefight started. The two parties were now only two hundred yards apart. Six guerrillas were killed and the rest retreated, leaving the field in control of the Californians.

The California Battalion had fought well. Company E, in the van, had most of the casualties, although one man from Company M was wounded and another was captured during Lowell's attack. Private Harry Irving of Company E[33] was shot in the chest in the first attack. As he lay on the ground near death, a rebel approached to take his weapons. Irving tried to raise his pistol to shoot the Confederate but before he could pull back the hammer, the guerrilla shot him dead. He was buried in the town of Paris, more than two thousand miles from his farm at Half Moon Bay, California. Walter Barnes was hit in the shoulder by a bullet that passed completely through his body. He was conscious until his death in an ambulance wagon four hours later. Eight others were wounded. Five Californians, including Lieutenant Norcross, were captured and sent to Richmond. Norcross, a resident of Placer County in the California gold country, spent most of the war in Libby Prison, escaping in March 1865 while he was being moved south to Salisbury. Two of the enlisted men died in prison; the others were exchanged. The two other companies in the fight, Companies F and G, escaped unscathed.[34]

Lowell reported that the Confederates apparently had a small depot of stores and a skiff for crossing the river. The battalion continued on for about three miles along the river to Chester Gap. There, Lowell had a view of the whole of the lower Valley: "The day was so hazy that I could see nothing of camps or trains in the Shenandoah Valley. The river at Berry's Ford is entirely too deep for fording, and, from what I could learn from inhabitants, will scarcely run out for ten days."

They returned to Ashby's Gap in the afternoon, then left the gap at about 4 P.M. and marched through Union to Leesburg and then Dranesville on the Little River Turnpike, where they stopped for the night near Philomont.[35] As they passed through Leesburg they arrested Capt. A. M. Chichester of the Confederate Engineers Corps, an aide-de-camp to Maj. Gen. Robert E. Rodes; his orderly; and Alfred Leigh, a private in the 6th Virginia Cavalry, who was "said to be a notorious bushwhacker."

The Federals learned from the prisoners that the party at Ashby's Gap was made up of a portion of Robertson's brigade under Capt. Lewis A. Johnson, with dismounted men from various regiments and some of Mosby's scouts. Lowell reported his losses as "2 killed; 1 severely wounded, cannot live;[36] 4 slightly wounded; 1 lieutenant and 3 privates captured." (See Appendix for a correct listing of the losses.)

The next day they marched through Leesburg and camped near Dranesville. On July 14 they crossed the Potomac at Chain Bridge and arrived at Camp Brightwood about noon.[37] Four stragglers were missing.[38]

In mid-July Colonel Lowell was directed to take command of all XXII Corps's cavalry south of the Potomac. The command included the 2nd Massachusetts, a company from the 11th New York, detachments from the 2nd and 13th New York, a detachment from the 12th Illinois, and two companies of the 6th New York. Then, on July 15, the newly constituted brigade was assigned to Brig. Gen. Rufus King, who took command of a new division that included the famed Irish Legion commanded by Brig. Gen. Michael Corcoran. King's new division was given the task of repairing the Orange and Alexandria Railroad to Manassas Station.

As the Army of the Potomac moved south to the Rappahannock, the Orange and Alexandria Railroad and the Manassas Gap line would become the armies' principal supply route. Both lines had suffered while the armies were north of the Potomac and needed considerable work before they would be in operating condition.[39] King was ordered to move along the Orange and Alexandria line to Manassas Station, guarding it and repairing any damaged bridges. Brigadier General Herman Haupt supervised the repairs. In order to screen the infantry Lowell moved the main camp to Centreville.[40]

At sunset on the nineteenth Lowell wrote Miss Shaw, telling her about his new command:

> I was ordered on Wednesday to take command of all the available cavalry in the district (about 650 only). . . . Yesterday word came that Lee was again 'conscripting' along the Occoquan, and the conscripts (all men under 45) were to be at Bentsville; so down I started with three squadrons, found no conscripts, but arrested the Lieut. Colonel who had ordered the draft, and brought him in with quite a number of other prisoners,—much to the delight, I believe, of the neighborhood. To-morrow I don't know where I shall go, but to-night I wish you could see our bivouac; it is on the slopes of Centreville facing west, one of the most commanding positions in Virginia; now, just at dusk, it commands a lovely, indistinct view stretching quite out to the Blue Ridge.[41]

King's infantry provided security and the labor force for the work on the railroad. Lowell's cavalry was ordered to patrol the gaps to prevent Lee's cavalry from suddenly appearing from Loudoun Valley and interrupt the work. On the twentieth Lowell led a detachment on a long patrol. They left early in the morning and went over the Bull Run battlefield, site of two disastrous Union defeats, then down to the Bull Run Mountains and Thoroughfare Gap. From Thoroughfare Gap they marched to Warrenton, where they were fired upon by a band of rebels. Lowell ordered a charge through the town. They drove the rebels out, but lost one man captured and one wounded.[42] After the skirmish they marched back to Manassas Junction. The trip totaled fifty-four miles, all on a "scorching" July day. A few days later Lowell wrote Miss Shaw: "I picked a morning glory (a white one) for you on the battlefield of Bull Run, the other day, but crushed it up and threw it away, on second thought,—the association was not pleasant; and yet it was pleasant to see that morning glories could bloom on, right in the midst of our worries and disgraces."[43]

In addition to picketing the lower Potomac fords, Lowell was responsible for covering the Orange and Alexandria Railroad from Alexandria to Centreville. The task was enormous. Meade's divisions were settling in along the Rappahannock. With the sweeps to Thoroughfare and Ashby's Gaps, most of the officers and men of the 2nd Massachusetts had become acquainted with the area. For Mosby, the conditions in Fairfax and Loudoun Counties were changing. With the appearance of large Union patrols moving through the countryside he prudently decided that an organized guerrilla force with a fixed base would attract too much attention. Setting a pattern he would follow for the rest of the war, he dispersed his men among the various "safe" houses in the Loudoun Valley.

The scattering of the guerrillas created several major problems for the guerrilla leader. Henceforth he would be unable to concentrate his men quickly enough to attack the patrols that would crisscross "Mosby's Confederacy" in ever-increasing numbers over the next two years. In effect, dispersal meant giving up control of Loudoun and Fairfax Counties to the enemy. Another difficulty was that when a rendezvous was called, Mosby could never be sure how many men would show up. Unlike most soldiers, Mosby's guerrillas could decide whether they wanted to go on a raid or not, and frequently they stayed home. General Lee pressed Mosby several times to increase the number of men he took on raids, but to no avail.

By August 1 the rail line was open all the way to Front Royal, and trains were running regularly to the Rappahannock.[44] Hardtack, desiccated vegetables, bacon, salt pork, and coffee—the standard government rations—came by way of the railroad. It carried forage for the thousands of horses in the army, ammunition, medical supplies, recruits, and men returning from leave. Hundreds of boxcars had to be moved each day just to supply the necessities.

A secondary supply line, but equally important to the common soldier, was the sutlers' supplies carried by mule teams and wagons over the local roads. During the war the few comforts a soldier might be able to enjoy while in camp were supplied by a group of independent but licensed sutlers. They followed the army wherever it went, providing the things that made army life bearable. Sutlers had fresh fruit, baked pies, pickles, canned peaches, hams, and even whiskey when they could slip it past the Provost Marshal. They had essentials like writing materials, warm socks, newspapers, books, paper, pencils, stamps, and envelopes. The sutlers also had photography studios where a soldier could get his picture taken for the folks at home. The Civil War sutler was equivalent to the modern-day post exchange. Although the high command recognized the sutlers' importance to the well-being and morale of the troops (the officers welcomed the whiskey), it only occasionally provided guards or escorts for their wagon trains.

In the late summer of 1863, with the Army of the Potomac in position along the Rappahannock River, the sutlers' trek to the army took two days. The wagons went from Washington to Alexandria and then down the Little River Turnpike to Germantown and on to the junction with the Warrenton Pike. The leg took most of a day to travel. The area around Germantown and Fairfax Courthouse was a favorite layover location. From there it was another day's haul to Warrenton through Manassas Junction and then to the thousands of ready buyers down along the Rappahannock. The route ran through the eastern limits of Mosby's Confederacy.

The Stoughton raid earlier in the year had been forgotten by the high command. Mosby was not considered to be a threat in the eastern part of Fairfax County. The lack of concern gave the guerrillas a once-in-a-lifetime opportunity. The goods sutlers carried had been in short supply in the Confederacy since the beginning of the war. A single wagon could fetch exorbitant prices and make a daring guerrilla a rich man on the other side of the mountains.

John Singleton Mosby was not a man to let opportunity slip through his fingers. At the end of July he sent out orders for a rendezvous. Surprisingly, the response was small. According to the rebels who were there, only twenty-six partisans appeared. Mosby may have been disappointed but, with this small body, he moved down the Little River Turnpike to Germantown. There was no fixed objective; the guerrillas were simply looking for plunder. Mosby timed his arrival at Germantown at dusk on the night of July 30. Just beyond the junction the guerrillas came upon a single wagon. They quickly seized it and sent it back to Germantown. They continued down the pike to Fairfax Courthouse, where they took a pair of wagons guarded by seven men from a Pennsylvania cavalry regiment. One of the wagons was filled with cavalry boots that were quickly passed around among the raiders. The second wagon was carrying ice cream. It was a hot, humid Virginia evening and most of the guerrillas were barely out of their teens. It takes only a small stretch of the imagination to picture the scene that must have occurred around that wagon. For a few moments the war was forgotten. In later years the men-boys who were there and survived the killings that came later fondly remembered that night's work as "the ice cream raid."

When the ice cream was gone, the captured wagons and prisoners were moved west toward Germantown. The guerrillas, resplendent in their new cavalry boots, moved east toward the Federal camps around Fairfax Courthouse. It was pitch dark. Using the darkness as their cover, they followed the road about a mile to the low side of a small rise. Two scouts, Bush Underwood and Welt Hatcher, crept up over the rise to reconnoiter the ground ahead. There, camped by the road unguarded, were twenty-nine fully loaded sutlers' wagons. The drivers, save one insomniac, were all asleep around two or three dying campfires. Creeping up silently, the partisans secured the sleeping sutlers one by one. It was reported later that the insomniac, "a Dutchman, was treated in a very uncivil manner" by Hatcher. The wagons were quickly started down the road toward Aldie with partisan guards. Joe Calvert, one of Mosby's most trusted men, was sent up front to act as an advance guard. Mosby and the main body stayed with the slow-moving, heavily laden wagons.

General King, at Centreville, got word of Mosby's seizure of the first pair of wagons almost immediately. He sent a telegram to Lowell ordering him to intercept the guerrillas and recapture the wagons. Lowell reacted without delay. The 2nd Massachusetts's camp was nearer to Aldie than was the captured train; quick action could thwart the rebel's plans. The first troops ready and mounted were from Capt. George Manning's Company M. Lowell sent them trotting down the Old Centreville Road, a back road running parallel to the Little River Turnpike. Their goal was to reach Aldie before the guerrillas. Another twenty men under the command of Lt. Goodrich Stone were detailed to catch up with an ambulance train that was moving west on the Little River Turnpike. The rest of the command, about 150 men, started off at 8:30 P.M. and followed Captain Manning's detachment. About two miles out of Centreville a road branches off to Gum Springs and crosses over to the north side of the turnpike. Lieutenant William Manning, Captain Manning's brother, took twenty men from Company L and picketed this road from Gum Springs to the turnpike. His orders were to attempt to stop any escape to the north. Meanwhile, Captain Manning reached Aldie and sent pickets out to the east along the turnpike. The rest of the regiment, led by Lowell, reached Aldie at 1

A.M. and set up camp about a mile east of town. A courier established communication with Captain Manning and Lieutenant Stone. The trap was in place.

As the sun rose the captured wagon train, moving slowly up the pike, neared Matt Lee's farm. The guerrilla van led by Joe Calvert spotted the white canvas tops of an ambulance train moving over a small rise a mile or so ahead. Word went back to Mosby. Ambulance trains carried medical supplies, commodities not easily available in the Confederacy. The guard force accompanying an ambulance train was usually small because Union commanders put more emphasis on the safe delivery of rations and ammunition. It was a prize that the partisans could not resist. Mosby decided to capture the ambulances.[45] Unbeknownst to Calvert and Mosby, the train, hurried along by Lieutenant Stone, was already within Captain Manning's concealed skirmish line at Mount Zion Church.

Earlier in the predawn hours, Lieutenant Manning decided to take eight men from his detachment down the road from Gum Springs to Matt Lee's farm on the turnpike to find if the wagon train had passed the intersection during the night. They arrived at the turnpike about the same time as Joe Calvert's advance guard. Manning drew his saber and ordered his men to charge. The little band of Union troopers surprised the guerrillas. Joe Calvert ran, and Bush Underwood was severely slashed by a saber wielded by Pvt. Thomas McFarland. A quarter of a mile behind, Mosby was leading the main body forward to take a look at the ambulances. When the action broke out to his front, Mosby and his men were behind a small hillock in the pike. As they topped the hill, Mosby was surprised to see the melee. He quickly ordered the guerrillas with him to charge. The partisan band galloped down the hill with Mosby in the lead. Overwhelmed and outnumbered, the little band of California troopers was decimated. Privates Peter Raymond and Hazen Little were killed outright; Amos Howard, Chauncey Hull, and James Bard were wounded; and Edward Seagrave was captured when his horse was killed. The rest turned and ran. Only Lieutenant Manning, McFarland, and another Company L trooper were unscathed when the survivors reached Captain Manning's picket line at Mount Zion Church.

Lowell, alerted by the firing, ordered the main body to mount and charge down the road toward Mount Zion Church. As the guerrillas came up the low hill at the church they suddenly faced a hundred charging cavalrymen in line of battle, sabers flashing. They panicked and scattered into the nearby fields. Four or five went back down the road. Lowell sent a group after the scattering rebels. The balance of the detachment went down the road to the wagon train. When the Federals topped a rise in front of the train, the remaining guerrillas guarding the wagons made off at a gallop, taking fifteen prisoners with them.

Lowell started the train back to Centreville under guard and moved west along the turnpike with the rest of the troops, following Mosby's trail toward the Bull Run Mountains. On the west side of the ridge he came upon all the prisoners, including Private Seagrave from Manning's company and seven noncommissioned officers from the Pennsylvania cavalry regiment that had been guarding the boots.

He also captured twenty saddled horses left by their riders, who had fled on foot into the thick undergrowth alongside the road.

Privates Raymond and Little were "buried in the door yard of a large brick house near the scene of the conflict, and there may they in peace 'sleep the sleep that knows no waking.'"[46]

It was only a partial victory. Mosby had refused to fight. He later claimed Lowell had a whole regiment at Mount Zion Church. His band keenly felt the loss of the rich sutlers' wagons. One member wrote after the war: "If the boys could only have got home safely with those twenty-nine loaded wagons we could have opened a big department store in Mosby's Confederacy."[47]

Lowell led the tired troopers back to Centreville that afternoon.[48] A few days later he wrote about the men he lost: "I dislike to have men killed in such an 'inglorious warfare' as Cousin John calls it,—but it's not a warfare of my choosing, and it's all in the day's work."[49]

General Lee forwarded Mosby's report to the Confederate War Department on August 18. Lee, known for rarely castigating others, wrote a stinging criticism: "Respectfully forwarded for information of the War Department. I greatly commend Major Mosby for his boldness and good management. I fear he exercises but little control over his men. He has latterly carried but too few on his expeditions, apparently, and his attention has been more directed toward the capture of wagons than military damage to the enemy. His attention has been called to this."[50]

The last episode of this affair occurred at Gooding's Tavern, about halfway between Annandale and Fairfax Courthouse. James Coyle, the tavern's proprietor and a Confederate sympathizer, had taunted the drivers of the passing wagons the night before as they passed by. His bullet-riddled body was found in a pool of blood on the floor of his tavern the next day. The murderers were never caught.[51]

4 | Inglorious Warfare

On July 27 companies A, B, C, D, and K, under the temporary command of Captain Reed, left Yorktown for Washington. They boarded the steamer *Juniata* in the evening and arrived in the capital the next day. Major Crowninshield, who was in the city on business, met them there. Later that evening, the battalion marched across the Long Bridge to Camp Wyndham on the south side of the Potomac. On August 6 Crowninshield took the battalion to Centreville. There, for the first time, the 2nd Massachusetts was united as a single command.

The regiment's role had been greatly expanded and Crowninshield's battalion was a welcome reinforcement. With Lowell in command of all Union cavalry south of the Potomac and Lieutenant Colonel Russell still at Reedville, Major Crowninshield assumed temporary command of the 2nd Massachusetts. He was not impressed with what he saw. He found the regiment's drill proficiency and discipline to be less than satisfactory and complained about the divisiveness and dissatisfaction he encountered in the ranks. Still, he wrote, "As a fighting regiment I don't believe that there is a better one in the service and if it has a chance I am sure it will distinguish itself."[1]

After it was reunited, the regiment was split into three battalions. The 1st Battalion, commanded by Capt. J. Sewall Reed, was made up of Massachusetts Companies B and D and California Companies E and M. The 2nd Battalion, under Maj. William Forbes, had California Companies A and L, with H and K from Massachusetts. The 3rd Battalion, commanded by Maj. De Witt Thompson, had only one company of Californians—Company F. Companies C, G, and I made up the rest of the battalion.

The breakup of the California Battalion was not popular with the men. "We complain not of Massachusetts as a state," wrote Quartermaster Sgt. Thomas Merry of Company L, ". . . but we do complain of her officers who have treated us in a most niggardly and contemptible manner. We have just reason to complain of the colonel that the State chose to command this regiment, Col. Lowell, has done all in his power to spite us, both officers and men; he has divided and broken up our battalion, putting one Massachusetts and one California company to form a squadron, when it was specially agreed our battalion should remain intact, under the command of our own Major [Thompson]."[2]

Merry, identifying himself by his initials only, was a lawyer by trade and, like many of his ilk, had a vitriolic pen. He misstated the facts. None of the advertisements or recruiting posters in San Francisco stated that the battalion would remain together as a unit. The decision to split the California companies among the three battalions was a military decision based on the fact that they had the largest number of men and, in the summer of 1863, were the best riders and potentially the best fighters. The California Battalion still contained more than half the men in the regiment; maintaining it as a unit would leave the other two battalions precariously under strength.

About the same time, the rest of the companies from the 13th and 16th New York Cavalry joined Lowell's cavalry force south of the Potomac. The three regiments and the detachment from the 12th Illinois, numbering about 1,200 officers and men in July 1863, were designated the "Cavalry Forces, Department of Washington." The 2nd Massachusetts was the largest single unit. During July the regiment collected convalescents, new recruits, and detailed men, boosting its return for August 10 to 45 officers and 869 men present and available for duty—an increase of about 100 men from the previous month.[3]

In early August, despite Lee's earlier admonitions, Major Mosby launched a series of attacks on the host of sutler trains heading south. Moses Sweeter, a storekeeper, reported that Fairfax Courthouse had been surrounded by a band of about two hundred of Mosby's guerrillas. He said they had captured every wagon entering or leaving the area and then headed for the mountains with their booty.

General King ordered a detachment of infantry and a detachment from the 2nd Massachusetts under Maj. William Forbes sent out to try to capture the guerrillas. The infantry returned the next day with some wagons and mules they had recaptured from the raiders. Major Forbes and his detachment returned to camp at noon after failing to locate any of the rebels.[4]

Two days later, August 6, a party of about forty to fifty guerrillas captured a number of wagons two to three miles from Fairfax Courthouse. This time the infantry stayed in camp. Lowell sent the 12th Illinois detachment and Company F of the 2nd Massachusetts after the guerrillas and succeeded in recapturing nearly all of the wagons, prisoners, and stolen property. Unfortunately, Lowell reported, they "didn't take Mosby, who is an old rat and has a great many holes."[5]

On Monday, August 10, Lowell received a report from Brig. Gen. G. A. De Russy, commander of the Union defenses south of the Potomac, that a picket post near Falls Church had been fired on the night before and that a local informant named "Reed" claimed Mosby was headquartered about five miles from town with about forty men. The problem, Lowell reported, was that "My own cavalry force is not sufficient to send out a large enough party to verify this information and keep up the regular nightly patrols."[6]

Lowell may have not trusted De Russy's intelligence, but he was obliged to act because the information came from higher headquarters. He decided to set up a net to trap Mosby. Pickets were placed at Ox Road, Fairfax Courthouse, Flint Hill, and on all the crossroads between there and Vienna. The pickets were ordered to start for Fairfax Courthouse at noon on Tuesday the eleventh. A group of thirty men was sent to Vienna and another seventy-five were ordered to take position at Freedom Hill. These detachments were ordered to move toward Falls Church from the west early and scout all the crossroads along the way. Lowell led another party of thirty men to scour the country around Chichester Mills. If Mosby was at Falls Church he would be caught.[7]

The whole effort was useless; Mosby was not at Falls Church. The guerrilla chieftain and about 140 of his men moved down the Little River Turnpike to the vicinity of Gum Springs and spent the night of the tenth there. Before dawn they were up and moving east on the pike, then followed the back roads near Ox Road Junction to the fortified picket post at Flint Hill. After reconnoitering the position from a screen of trees, the guerrillas marched through Vienna after the Union detachment there had started its sweep toward Falls Church. They then moved south by way of Mills's Crossroads, slipped around the flank of Lowell's picket line, and reached the Little River Turnpike at Gooding's Tavern, *east* of the line of picket posts between Fairfax Courthouse and Vienna and south of the men moving toward Falls Church. Perhaps it was luck, but it seems more likely that Mosby's informants were aware of Lowell's plans. It is even possible that the informant "Reed," who had reported Mosby's presence, may have been a party to the deception.

Mosby, accompanied by Harry Sweating, Jack Barnes, and one other guerrilla, captured three teamsters "lying in the shade with their pistol-belts unbuckled" near Gooding's Tavern. The prisoners informed Mosby that twelve unguarded wagons were nearby. He and his companions rode to the train and, with pistols drawn, ordered the teamsters to mount up and start moving west on the turnpike. Jack Barnes led the procession.[8] In the meantime, farther back the pike, the main body of Mosby's force had captured seven more wagons. When Mosby and his group reached the main body, he decided to "cut and run."

This time Mosby, recognizing the countryside was filled with Union troopers, ordered his men to loot the wagons. The guerrillas gathered up the mules and harnesses but made no attempt to take the still heavily laden wagons. None were burned because a column of smoke would alert the enemy. Only the mules, horses, twenty-five disgruntled sutlers, harness sets, and as much loot as the guerrillas could carry on horseback started back toward Hunter's Mill.[9] About a mile from the mill they split into two groups, half going through Dranesville and the other half through Hunter's Mill to Chantilly and on to Gum Springs.

A rider brought the news of the capture of the sutler train to Captain McKendry, who was investigating the purported liquor traffic at Fairfax Courthouse. He started out toward the Little River Turnpike at once with about forty men. At the same time Lowell telegraphed Captain Reed at Fort Ethan Allen to take eighty men west on the Leesburg-Georgetown Turnpike to Dranesville.

A seventy-man patrol commanded by Major William P. Hall of the 6th New York Cavalry was on a scout near Gum Springs and Aldie but it missed the guerrillas. Mosby's luck held; all of the pursuers were too late. Mosby and his men had a couple of hours' head start and, unencumbered with wagons, made their escape. Both groups quickly disappeared behind the Bull Run Mountains.

Lowell reported that Captain McKendry had identified the route taken by Mosby on Tuesday but that he had yet to hear from Captain Reed. He further advised Washington headquarters that he had sent back 116 horses, some of which were recaptured U.S. horses and some belonging to guerrillas.[10]

With so much Union cavalry about, the abandoned wagons were plundered several times. One Californian wrote: "Two days ago we captured forty wagons, which he [Mosby] had taken only the day before within four miles of Alexandria, and our boys have had plenty of everything good. Some of the wagons were sutler's, and we have had lots of can fruit, boots, etc. I captured some five cans condensed milk, four cans turkey, two of peaches and four strawberries; these are all worth $2.50 per can out in the front—so you see for these few days, we have pretty good living and our boys enjoy themselves and are contented as long as their appetites are satisfied."[11]

Army headquarters was becoming concerned with the depredations. The sutlers were licensed and supposedly under the army's protection. The threat of claims against the government prompted several proposals to protect the trains. Lowell offered a solution in his report of the affair: "With your approbation I propose to establish a regular escort of 30 to 50 men over the pike from Centreville to some point near Alexandria, once each way at irregular hours, all sutlers and stray wagons to be halted and compelled to come with escort. This will be less fatiguing to my horses, and will I think, with the detachments going to the front, afford all necessary protection to the sutler's."

His suggestion was incorporated in General Orders No. 79, Army of the Potomac, which directed that a regiment of cavalry from the Cavalry Corps leave Warrenton Junction each Thursday at 9 A.M. for Washington and return the following Monday. The order also required sutlers to submit an invoice of the goods they carried. Sutlers attempting to transport goods to the army without an invoice could expect their goods to be confiscated. This last requirement was an attempt to stop the flow of illegal whiskey to the troops in the field.

On August 15 Lt. Col. J. H. Taylor, Halleck's chief of staff, wired Lowell that Col. Elijah V. White and his 35th Virginia Cavalry Battalion[12] was in the vicinity of Dranesville with a body of 350 men. Taylor asked Lowell to send an expedition to the area with sufficient force to attack him.[13]

Lowell led two hundred men from Centreville north toward the Alexandria-Leesburg Turnpike. They spent the night near Dranesville and scouted that area the next day. Lowell reported that White had probably been in the area but with only about forty men. Lowell next decided to move west to Aldie, scouting the country south of Goose Creek. After questioning local residents he concluded that White's main camp was probably somewhere in the vicinity of Leesburg. He sent a courier back with orders to have fifty men meet him at Ball's Mill near Leesburg. There was a misunderstanding and three hundred men were dispatched. Lowell's force was now too large to move around during the day and expect to surprise an enemy. He split the group into five columns. One column of a hundred men from the 16th New York was sent to check an enemy camp reported near Lewinsville. The remaining four hundred were sent by four different routes through Leesburg,

Waterford, and Hughsville. The four columns met at Mount Gilead after sunset and marched to Mountville, where they stopped to feed and water the horses.

During the stop Lowell learned from a scout that White was camped about two miles north of Middleburg on Goose Creek. The command moved out at 2:30 the next morning in the hope of achieving surprise,

> but he had word of my approach from Mount Gilead, and had changed camp during the night. I sent out small scouting parties, who found about 100 of his men still in the immediate neighborhood, but they were on the alert, and ran when a company was sent to engage them. Lost several hours trying to get near them, but the country is very open there and they were determined to keep out of the way. Gave up the attempt; sent a party down across Bull Run Mountains, and another back by Carter's Mills, and passed through Aldie myself. Found nowhere any force. Returned to camp with 10 prisoners—White's and Mosby's.
>
> White is very rarely with his battalion. He passes about the country with an escort of from 30 to 40 men. The battalion generally numbers about 250 strong, being left under the command of Major Ferneyhough. White is looking up recruits and desert-ers, many of his men having been at home since the army went into Maryland. He now has six companies, with over 700 men on his rolls, and prisoners say that he expects to take that number with him when he leaves the country.[14]

In spite of the hard marching, Lowell wrote an upbeat letter to Miss Shaw the next day: "I came in about ten last evening after four days' vain endeavor to get a fight out of White's battalion, four very pleasant days in one of the loveliest coun-tries in the world, south and west of Leesburg."[15]

On August 24 Mosby led a party of guerrillas in an attack on a group of Califor-nians near Fairfax Courthouse. A member of the California Battalion described the ensuing fight. He wrote that a party of twenty-six men from the 2nd Massachu-setts led by 2nd Lt. Hollis C. Pinkham of Company G, the acting regimental quar-termaster, went to Washington leading a herd of used up horses. The horses were taken to the remount camp at Giesboro. After procuring 102 new horses, Pinkham ordered Commissary Sgt. Joseph B. Varnum of Company M to take command and return to Centreville. The horses were only half-trained, so it was necessary for each man to lead three of the animals. There was no escort. As they approached Fairfax Courthouse, "one of the men at the head of the column suddenly exclaimed, 'There's some rebs,' and just at that moment about sixty of them left their ambush and charged on our men. You may well imagine the confusion that ensued; the horses green and untrained, became frightened at the pistol shots, and also unman-ageable, and stampeded down the road; but another party of rebels attacked our men from the rear. The confusion that followed may better be imagined than de-scribed. Some of the men had three horses tied to their saddles, were dragged off and dismounted; but our boys though laboring under great disadvantages, fought like heroes."[16]

Sergeant Varnum was in the act of holding a rebel by the throat and beating him over the head with an empty pistol when he was killed. John McCarty of Company

A was killed in the first rush and John Mickey and George W. Vierick were knocked off their horses and wounded. Vierick died of his wounds a week later.

Unbeknownst to the Californians, Mosby was shot and seriously wounded by Sgt. William H. Short of Company F during the fighting.[17] Mosby, staggering in the saddle, turned and rode away followed by his surgeon. A rebel officer was killed and another wounded by John A. Cain and Levi Turner from Company E during the hand-to-hand fighting.

Most of the horses were recaptured when Mosby withdrew, but Lowell ordered a pursuit of the fleeing guerrillas. A disgruntled Californian wrote that Lowell took every available man but failed, "as usual." The cynical writer added that "he succeeded, however, in using up both men and horses to his satisfaction."[18]

Although Lowell did not submit a formal report to headquarters, he described the action in a letter to Miss Shaw in which his concern is apparent:

> I told you last week that Stanton had ordered a Court of Inquiry about some horses taken from us by Mosby, his order said 'horses taken from Thirteenth New York Cavalry.' I wrote at once that the horses were lost by Second Massachusetts Cavalry, my regiment, and that I wished to take the blame, if there was any, until the court settled where it belonged. He made General Stoneman, President of the Court, and that vexed me, for all such courts hurt a fellow's chances, and Stoneman had intimated he was likely to give me command of one of his three Cavalry Depots, which would have been very pleasant winter quarters. Now whatever the court may find, I do not consider myself at all to blame, and I am ashamed to say that last week my pride was somewhat hurt and I felt a good deal annoyed, although Heintzelman had told me he was more than satisfied, was gratified at what had been done.[19]

The regiment lost two men killed, two wounded—one mortally—and seven captured. All but one would survive imprisonment. For the Californians, this fight was just another item contributing to their antipathy toward the Massachusetts officers:

> we can never catch them [the guerrillas] by traveling over the turnpikes, while perhaps at the very time the guerrillas are hid in the woods by the roadside laughing at our folly. Let Major Thompson have absolute command of his California battalion and of the California Hundred . . . and they will soon make short work of the guerrillas; but Col. Lowell will never do it, for all the knowledge that he possesses of fighting indians or guerrillas has been acquired by reading Sylvanus Cobb's stories in the New York Ledger while burning the midnight oil at Harvard, but what he is deficient in his knowledge in this, he more than makes up in his knowledge of dress parades and policing camp.[20]

Captain David A. DeMerritt of Company F led one of the groups pursuing Mosby. DeMerritt had suffered a broken leg on June 10 but was well enough to ride. As the column moved down the pike he suddenly rode off at a gallop. Several men pursued him and brought him back. He was no sooner back than once again he galloped away, and once again was brought back. He disappeared for a third time after dark and managed to escape his pursuers. The next morning he rode into camp alone and completely broken down. The medical officer sent him to the insane asylum in Washington. In retrospect it seems likely that DeMerritt suffered a nervous breakdown; he was popular with the men and would be missed in the ensuing months.[21]

The August raids were failures in terms of enrichment for the guerrillas and damage to the Union side. All Mosby accomplished was the capture of a few mules and sutlers; the supplies his men were able to carry on horseback were negligible. The recaptured horses and captured guerrilla mounts more than balanced the loss in stock. The threat of the appearance of the 2nd Massachusetts had thwarted any real gains. General Lee was not pleased. After receiving Mosby's report he wrote of his displeasure with Mosby's command in a dispatch to General Stuart:

> I have heard that [Major Mosby] has now with him a large number of men, yet his expeditions are undertaken with very few, and his attention seems more directed to the capture of sutler's wagons, &c. than to the injury of the enemy's communications and outposts. The capture and destruction of wagon trains is advantageous, but the supply of the Federal Army is carried by the railroad. If that should be injured, it would cause him to detach largely for its security, and thus weaken his main army. . . .
>
> I do not know the cause for undertaking his expeditions with so few men, whether it is from policy or the difficulty of collecting them. I have heard of his men, among them officers, being in rear of this army selling captured goods, sutler's stores &c. This had better be attended to by others. It has also been reported to me that many deserters from this army have joined him. Among them have been seen members of the Eighth Virginia Regiment. If this is true, I am sure it must be without the knowledge of Major Mosby, but I desire you to call his attention to this matter, to prevent his being imposed on.[22]

In an attempt to gain Lee's approbation, Mosby's report on September 30 tried to put a positive slant on his activities:

> On the 27th and 28th instant, I made a reconnaissance in the vicinity of Alexandria, capturing Colonel Dulany, aide to the bogus Governor Peirpoint,[23] several horses, and burning the railroad bridge across Cameron's Run, which was immediately under cover of the guns of two forts.
>
> The military value of the species of warfare I have waged is not measured by the number of prisoners and material of war captured from the enemy, but by the heavy detail it has already compelled him to make, and which I hope to make him increase, in order to guard his communications, and to that extent diminishing his aggressive strength.[24]

Stuart forwarded Mosby's report with the recommendation that Major Mosby be promoted another grade "in recognition of his valuable services." Once again Lee was not impressed. In his endorsement he wrote: "Major Mosby is entitled to great credit for his boldness and skill in his operations against the enemy. He keeps them in constant apprehension and inflicts repeated injuries. I have hoped that he would have been able to raise his command sufficiently for the command of a lieutenant colonel, and to have it regularly mustered into service. I am not aware that it numbers over four companies."[25]

Mosby's estimate of his worth was somewhat overblown. The August returns for the Army of the Potomac show 76,219 effectives, the Department of Washington had 21,506 officers and men present, and the Middle Department, which included Baltimore and Delaware, had 3,989 effectives. The Valley Department could add another 15,000. Only Colonel Lowell's three regiments of cavalry and Maj. Henry A. Cole's Marylanders were assigned the full-time duty of pursuing Mosby. This disposition had little effect on the "aggressive strength" of the Federal armies; only occasionally were troops from the Army of the Potomac or the Shenandoah assigned to anti-guerrilla work.

In spite of Mosby's claim, his bridge-burning efforts had failed. In a report to General Halleck in response to a letter from Col. D. C. McCallum, military director of railroads, General Heintzelman listed three bridges damaged in the past month, including the Cameron Run Bridge, which Mosby had reported on September 30 as burned. However, according to Heintzelman, the Cameron Run Bridge fire was "discovered and extinguished without interruption to the trains."[26]

Elijah White was actively gathering recruits and deserters in Fairfax and Loudoun Counties during August. On Friday, August 28, General King sent an infantry force under Col. McMahon and a party from the 2nd Massachusetts under Major Thompson to sweep the countryside from Centreville to Dranesville.[27] White was reportedly near Broad Run enforcing the Confederate conscription supported by a body of two hundred to three hundred infantry between Leesburg and Snickers Gap. Both parties returned to Centreville on Sunday. McMahon reported that Mosby had been severely wounded the previous Monday and had been taken beyond the mountains. Lowell was ordered to send another scouting party out toward Leesburg. Major Thompson had all the available horses, however, and Lowell sought permission to rest both men and animals before sending them out again. Permission was granted and Col. Thomas C. Devin's cavalry brigade from the Army of the Potomac was sent to Leesburg instead, arriving there on the thirty-first. Devin reported that White had been there the day before with about three hundred men but had retired to Upperville. Devin also confirmed that Mosby had received two serious wounds and had been taken to his father's house at Amherst.[28]

Lowell sent scouting parties through Maryland via Leesburg and Point of Rocks September 2–4, toward Bull Run and Sandy Springs on September 8, and to Leesburg, Aldie, and Gum Springs on September 18. Seven guerrillas were taken prisoner and brought back to Vienna by the latter patrol.

The toll on the men was heavy. One of Captain Adam's men wrote in Company L's monthly returns: "Detachments out constantly patrolling this vicinity. The company has daily furnished large details for picket and scouting, making the duty very arduous. The men have but one night in bed, out of four."[29]

With the Army of the Potomac now converging on the triangle between the

Rapidan and Rappahannock Rivers, and the repair of the Orange and Alexandria Railroad complete, headquarters decided to concentrate Lowell's brigade at Vienna to cover the Potomac fords and upper Loudoun and Fairfax Counties. On September 15 Major Thompson took the 3rd Battalion to Washington, where the men exchanged their horses. The next day they marched a short distance beyond Tennallytown where they camped for the night. In the morning they marched through Rockville and Dawsonville where they camped. They broke camp on the twenty-first and marched back to Rockville, then along the towpath of the canal to White's Ford, White's Island, and Seneca. Pickets were set out to covering the Potomac crossings up to Falling Waters. Thompson moved the camp to Edwards Ferry on the twenty-seventh and extended the picket posts to include the river between the mouth of the Monocacy and the Great Falls.[30] The rest of Lowell's brigade moved to Vienna in early October. The troops at Vienna included eight companies of the 2nd Massachusetts commanded by Major Crowninshield, seven companies of the 13th New York commanded by Maj. Douglas Frazer, and the four remaining companies of the 16th New York commanded by Maj. Morris Hazard. There were thirty-two officers and 514 men present for duty.[31]

The guerrillas' lack of success with wagon trains may have prompted a change in tactics. In early October they started a series of attacks on picket posts. The first attack occurred on October 8 at Vienna. A group of guerrillas under cover of darkness crept up to one of the new picket posts surrounding the camp. When challenged they responded with "friend" and then suddenly charged the post, wounding Luman Washburn of Company L. They grabbed the post's horses and fled into the night. Washburn died of his wounds in mid-November.

Four days later Lowell took two hundred men on a scout down the Little River Pike to Gum Springs, Captain Rumery led a party of sixty to Ball's Mill, and the rest of the men spent the night in camp at Gum Springs. Informants told Lowell that Mosby had gone toward Fairfax Courthouse a few days earlier. Lowell's party returned to Vienna the next day. Meanwhile, Captain Rumery's detachment ran into a party of White's men on the Little River Turnpike and killed one of the guerrillas and captured three horses.[32]

On October 9 Lee's Army of Northern Virginia marched out of its camps on the south side of the Rapidan and started west behind Cedar Mountain. Turning north through Culpepper, it crossed the Rappahannock at Jefferson and headed around the right flank of Meade's Army of the Potomac toward Manassas Junction in a reprise of Jackson's advance during the summer of 1862. Ever cautious, Meade retreated up the Orange and Alexandria Railroad, ordering the larger railroad bridges destroyed as the army withdrew. It was a close race and Meade barely won. At Bristoe Station a trap set up by Brig. Gen. Gouverneur K. Warren dealt Lee's advancing army, led by Lt. Gen. A. P. Hill's corps, a nasty blow, killing or capturing almost two thousand Confederates for a loss of about three hundred bluecoats.

Meade entrenched along the Centreville–Chantilly ridge. Although Lowell's brigade was not part of the Army of the Potomac, he was asked to keep Meade informed of any enemy movements on the right rear flank.[33] During the October maneuvering General Corcoran replaced General King, who was appointed minister to Rome. Corcoran was responsible for protecting the line of communications to Alexandria. Lowell's role was to maintain heavy patrols throughout Loudoun and Fairfax Counties and keep the guerrillas away from the supplies flowing to Meade.

Lee was confident he could turn Meade's position and drive him back to Washington. However, with the Orange and Alexandria Railroad shut down and the rainy season imminent, any further advance seemed risky. On October 16 the skies opened up and the streams and rivers began filling; the decision was obvious. The next morning Lee ordered a retreat back down the line of the railroad. As they fell back, his troops completed the destruction started by Meade.

Durign the withdrawal Stuart and Fitz Lee laid a trap at Buckland Mills for Brig. Gen. Judson Kilpatrick's cavalry. Led by Brig. Gen. George A. Custer's brigade, the Union cavalry crossed Broad Run and moved confidently in pursuit of a supposedly fleeing Stuart. At Buckland Mills Custer was hit in front and flank. His brigade collapsed and his men ran as fast as they could for the safety of Broad Run, five miles away. The rout was later called the "Buckland Races." Kilpatrick lost about thirteen hundred killed and captured. Stuart's losses were about four hundred, mostly wounded.[34]

With the advent of the October rains, the roads in Northern Virginia became almost impassable. Furthermore, the destruction of the Orange and Alexandria Railroad prevented any buildup of men and material until it could be rebuilt, a time-consuming process. Meade fended off demands for an advance on the grounds that the weather made offensive operations impractical.

Although the Army of the Potomac's campaigning season may have been over, the "inglorious war" continued. Mosby returned to Fairfax on October 15 and engaged in several skirmishes with Union troops. He reported the capture of a hundred horses and mules, several wagons, and seventy-five to a hundred prisoners—including five captains and one lieutenant—with no loss. In spite of the magnitude of the purported Union losses there are no reports from Union officers corroborating Mosby's account. It is probable that his prisoners came from isolated groups rather than organized Union formations.[35]

On October 18 Col. Lafayette Baker led a detachment of his 1st District of Columbia Cavalry and a detachment of the California Battalion commanded by Captain Eigenbrodt on a sweep that encountered a squad of Mosby's men near Annandale.[36] In the ensuing skirmish the guerrilla leader, Lt. Franklin Williams, was wounded, one guerrilla was killed, and three were captured.[37] The prisoners admitted they were looking for government horses and sutlers' wagons. Lowell reported to Corcoran that one of the prisoners claimed Mosby and 275 men were prowling around the area south of Vienna in search of Union supply trains. Lowell suggested that all wagon train traffic without a strong escort be delayed until Mosby's movements could be determined.[38]

A little over a week later, Mosby attacked a large train of supply wagons between New Baltimore and Warrenton. Mosby hit the center of the train, which had a heavy guard at the front and rear. He succeeded in unhitching the teams from forty to fifty wagons and, after sending them off, prepared to burn the wagons. Before any wagons were fired, however, a Federal cavalry force appeared and drove Mosby and his men off. Mosby reported "bringing off 145 horses and mules and upwards of 30 negroes and Yankees (among them 1 captain), to a place of safety. Many of the captured animals were lost on the night march but I have sent out a party which I am in hopes will succeed in recovering some of them."

Stuart once again lauded his favorite guerrilla despite the lack of evidence of positive results: "This is but another instance of Major Mosby's skill and daring in addition to those forwarded almost daily."[39]

General Meade's report of the incident noted that about a hundred animals were lost but made no mention of any Union soldiers being captured.[40]

On the last day of October 1863 Colonel Lowell obtained a short leave to marry Josephine Shaw at her parents' home on Staten Island. They returned shortly after the wedding and moved into a small house near Vienna. Colonel Lowell continued in active command of the brigade despite the obvious domestic distractions. His only concession was to have others lead the sweeps that continued during the winter.

Lowell at Vienna and Corcoran at Fairfax Courthouse continued patrols to the west. Because of the constant activity, Lowell asked Corcoran on November 17 to keep him informed when he sent parties out so as to avoid clashes between different groups meeting at night. Advanced picket posts were particularly vulnerable on the long November nights, and guerrilla raids on isolated picket posts continued. On the sixteenth fifty guerrillas attacked the picket post at Germantown, two miles from Fairfax Courthouse. A sergeant and two men of the 13th New York Cavalry were captured and one man was wounded during the attack. Three parties of fifty men each were sent out but failed to capture any Confederates.[41]

Like the guerrillas, Lowell regularly used local disaffected citizens to counter the partisans. In November he was presented with a rare opportunity.[42] Charles Binns, a deserter from Mosby's command, reported to Colonel Lowell and agreed to lead the Federals on a sweep through Mosby country. An expedition guided by Binns was set for November 18. There was a shortage of mounts in the command because an epidemic of hoof-and-mouth disease had decimated the reserves of cavalry horses. During October and November Lowell's command only got a hundred new horses as replacements—not enough to mount troopers lacking horses. Thus, when the expedition was organized, Lowell decided to include dismounted cavalry.

Captain Rumery led a scouting party consisting of twenty-five mounted and seventy-five dismounted 2nd Massachusetts troopers from Vienna on the eighteenth. There was some heavy grumbling among the dismounted "cavaliers," who had to suffer the indignity of marching like common infantry. Binns and Yankee Davis, a Union scout, guided the group. The party moved toward the Blue Ridge using back roads. Rumery was ordered to march chiefly at night and to conceal the presence of the dismounted troopers as much as possible.[43]

The party passed near Frying Pan and Gum Springs, crossed Goose Creek to

Mountsville, then headed up the north side of Goose Creek to Rector's Crossroads. Lowell joined Rumery early on Sunday morning the twenty-second at a point between Middleburg and Rector's Crossroads with a hundred mounted men from the 2nd Massachusetts and fifty men from the 13th and 16th New York. Rumery gave Lowell all the information he had obtained during his march and Lowell planned the rest of the sweep. Forty mounted men under Lieutenant Sim were sent north through Philomont. Rumery led another forty mounted men southward through White Plains, across the Manassas Gap Railroad, and back across the Bull Run Mountains through Hopewell Gap. Lieutenant Manning led fifty dismounted men back down the pike to a point south of Aldie, where Mosby was said to have a rendezvous. Lowell led the remainder of the force down the pike to Mount Zion Church at Aldie to await the three patrols. The last party reached the church at about midnight Monday. The patrols captured eighteen uniformed soldiers claiming to belong to Mosby's command and seven smugglers and "horse thieves." One Confederate was killed and one prisoner escaped. They also took thirty horses and thirteen sets of horse equipment, all without a loss to the command. Lowell was pleased with Binns and recommended that he be allowed the same pay as other government scouts in his employ.

Meanwhile, Colonel Lowell, "having a newly-wedded wife at camp concluded to see her that night and taking the advance guard as an escort, started at a hard gallop, and kept it up the whole distance some thirty miles, making it in three and a half hours."[44]

The main body returned to camp the next day with the prisoners. It was here that the only casualty occurred. Private Frederick Wilson of Company L was assigned as one of the guards to watch the prisoners at the log guardhouse. "Standing in the doorway of the log house and leaning his breast upon the muzzle the carbine suddenly slipped from the sill striking the hammer as it went which exploded the cap, and the charge entered his breast, just over the heart, coming out under the shoulder on the back causing his death in a few minutes."[45]

While Lowell was sweeping through Mosby's usual haunts, Mosby and seventy-five men were on a raid near Bealetown, below Manassas on the Orange and Alexandria Railroad. The purpose of the raid was to attack the railroad, but when a small train of five wagons escorted by thirty Rhode Island cavalrymen approached, the guerrillas changed objectives. They charged the wagons, routing the Federal soldiers. As a party of Union cavalry from Bealetown approached several guerrillas gathered some of the stores[46] from the wagons as the rest fled, breaking into small parties.[47] Brigadier General David McM. Gregg sent a party in pursuit. It captured two of the guerrillas.[48]

Twice before the end of the year Mosby raided encampments at Brandy Station, southwest of Bealetown, with little success. Both times the guerrillas were driven off by Union troops with no booty to show for their efforts.

Lowell continued to run patrols through the upper reaches of Fairfax County. A patrol sent out on December 8 rode through Frying Pan and Dranesville and returned late in the evening on the ninth after encountering only small and scattering parties of guerrillas. The patrol leader reported they had pursued the rebels but that they had failed to capture any.[49]

About midnight on the ninth, twenty to thirty guerrillas attacked the picket post at the junction of the Lewinsville road and Leesburg Pike. A corporal and five men defended the post. The guard challenged the advancing guerrillas, who replied that they were "friends with the countersign." In an instant the whole party of guerrillas charged the post as the pickets mounted their horses. They captured two Union troopers and killed one horse against the loss of one man wounded.

While this attack was underway, thirty guerrillas led by Capt. William Smith and Lt. Thomas Turner[50] attacked the Lewinsville Station. Fortunately for the picket post there a local Union man misled them and they charged a vedette post instead of the picket reserve. The officer in charge of the picket line, who was visiting the post at the time, was thrown from his horse. The reserve turned out dismounted and captured one guerrilla but failed to mount up and pursue the fleeing rebels. Later, a force of forty men from the 13th New York went in pursuit but failed to capture any of the rebels, who quickly dispersed into the countryside.[51] Private Cyrus Jones of Company L was wounded in the attack on the picket post. He died at the regimental hospital in Vienna on February 5, 1864.[52]

The next night another group of rebels attacked the picket at Langley, capturing Pvt. James Randall of Company L. Randall was from San Francisco and had been an assistant U.S. Marshal there. Ironically, Randall's brother published a pro-Confederate newspaper called *The Dixie* in the Mother Lode town of Sonora. Randall never returned to California; he died July 7, 1864, at Andersonville Prison.[53]

Lowell sent another party out in an attempt to counter these attacks. The men patrolled dismounted in the direction of Dranesville. When they returned they reported that Mosby had passed through Dranesville after the fight on the tenth. They also reported that the rebels had admitted to local citizens that they had been badly whipped at Lewinsville, losing three men badly wounded.

The guerrillas exacted revenge for the Lewinsville defeat a few days later when a force about twenty strong crawled up unseen on a picket post at Germantown and fired without warning, mortally wounding two men and capturing five horses.[54] The Californians's attitude in the aftermath of these bushwhacking attacks was expressed by one of them in a letter: "It is the worst kind of murder to kill a man stationed on picket, and none but the most cowardly, pusillanimous rebels would attempt such a thing. The step from a traitor to a murderer seems to be easily taken, and quite natural; and all rebels caught lurking around picket stations, with arms upon them, ought to be hung to the nearest tree. Woe be to the one that should be caught by us!"[55]

Between 6 and 7 P.M. on December 17, a large party of Confederate cavalry commanded by Brig. Gen. Thomas L. Rosser at Sangster's Station attacked a detachment of about fifty men from Corcoran's Irish Brigade. Word of the attack did not reach headquarters at Fairfax Courthouse until about 8 P.M. because the telegraph operator was too drunk to receive the dispatch. Corcoran sent a few troops out, including a squadron from one of the New York cavalry regiments. The Confederates routed the cavalry, who were acting as the advance guard, because, according to Corcoran, "the most efficient officer with the squadron could not make himself understood by the men from the fact that he did not speak German, and they did not understand commands given in English."[56]

Lowell sent an officer to Fairfax Courthouse to get information about the attack. General Corcoran was unable say which way the attackers were headed, so Lowell decided to move up the Little River Turnpike. He crossed their trail at Chantilly and learned that the force consisted of Rosser's three regiments of cavalry—about 1,300 strong—and White's battalion with 300 to 400 men. They were on their way to the Shenandoah Valley to go into winter quarters, and the attack was only a diversion. Mosby and his men were acting as guides for the movement. Lowell divided his force on the return march. The group returning by way of Dranesville captured twelve horses but missed capturing two of Mosby's men.

Two days later, December 22, the guerrillas attacked the picket post at Hunter's Mill. The post was manned by six Californians from Company E. At first the Californians stood and fought. However, seeing they were badly outnumbered, they retreated, leaving Oscar Burnap and Seth Cooper wounded on the field. Cooper had been shot in the head and appeared dead. The picket reserve, hearing the firing, quickly mounted and raced toward the sound of the guns. The rebels fled, taking Burnap with them. About a quarter of a mile away, Burnap's guerrilla captor stopped briefly, turned, and shot him in the chest, then fled, leaving him for dead. Cooper and Burnap were found, miraculously still alive, and brought into camp.[57] Lowell sent out mounted and dismounted parties but the rebels had disappeared. The two wounded men survived but were discharged "because of disability." Cooper was crippled for life, and Burnap barely escaped death. The ball fired at him by the fleeing rebel missed his heart by just one inch.[58]

In the minds of the men of the 2nd Massachusetts, particularly the Californians, Burnap's wounding and the attacks on picket posts constituted a long bill of indictment against the guerrillas. At least one correspondent, writing about the shooting of Cooper and Burnap, blamed Colonel Lowell. He accused Lowell of having "no regard for the lives and liberties of our men; sending five men to stand picket three and four miles from camp, where no assistance can reach them until it is too late. When the news of the disaster reaches camp he sends out a party of men and marches them around over the turnpikes and returns to camp."

A party from the 13th New York went out on Christmas Day with Binns as guide. They scouted as far as Leesburg, where they searched a number of houses. Binns pointed out several suspicious citizens who reported that Mosby had been at Guilford Station with eighty men the day before. The patrol also encountered a small mounted party, which scattered through the woods after a brief exchange of shots.[59]

The last patrol of the year was somewhat more successful. Word came that a large group of rebels was at Middleburg and adjacent towns on furlough and gathering horses. A dispatch from army headquarters said that clothing would be issued to Mosby's men at Rector's Crossroads on Monday and they were to gather again on

Tuesday the twenty-ninth. On the twenty-eighth Lowell led Companies A, E, L, and M, one company of Massachusetts men, and detachments from the two New York regiments out Little River Pike to Mount Zion Church. He sent parties out in several directions and reported: "One of the parties had a skirmish on Tuesday night with a squad of Mosby's men killing 1 and capturing several."[60]

The skirmish was described in more detail in a letter to a San Francisco newspaper: "Thomas McFarlan[d], a resident of the Mount Diablo Coal Mines, was wounded in a hand to hand encounter with a guerrilla. The rebel fired ten shots at M, two of which took effect on his horse, and one pierced his thigh; but after this, still undaunted, he drew his sabre, having fired all the shots in his pistol, and ran the rebel through the body, and hit him a cut on the head, which finished him. A spring wagon was captured and our wounded comrade brought to camp, and he has now well nigh recovered from his wound."[61] The raiders brought in a captain, a lieutenant, seventeen privates (ten from Mosby's battalion), ten citizens, and a rebel forage contractor. They also took twenty-five horses and ten to fifteen sets of arms and equipment.[62]

In spite of the success, one participant complained:

Captain Adams with his company [Company L] and a few New Yorkers were ordered to take a side road and go to Upperville. Shortly afterwards Captain Eigenbrodt was ordered to take his company [Company E] and a few others, and go to meet Captain Adams at Middleburg: but on approaching the town he saw rebels here and there in squads; a courier was sent to Colonel Lowell to inform him of this, but he was captured by the rebels.[63] Captain Eigenbrodt found it impossible to go further, for the rebels largely outnumbered him, and was reluctantly forced to return to the main column. The valiant Captain wanted to charge through the town at the head of his brave company but the guide would not listen to it. When Colonel Lowell was informed of this, he, instead of taking his whole command and going up there to fight the rebels, and reinforce Captain Adams got his column in line and after considering a moment remarked, "I guess I'll let Adams wait." . . . [and] made for camp with all speed.[64]

5 | The Killing Ground

On January 1, 1864, Pvt. Valorus Dearborn of Company A, the California Hundred, 2nd Regiment Massachusetts Cavalry, sat down and opened a new diary. On the first page, he wrote,

> January 1, Friday
> Rec. Of Capt. Reed 10.00
> Again has another year commenced to join its ages with the past and the record of the old year is written with all its joys and sorrows. Who can read its record and not feel a sickening pang run through his veins to learn the deed of death that has been perpetrated in our once happy land, Many a brave and noble heart has been erased from the book of time and now stands before its maker—there to wait its final sentence. May God be merciful to such and may their faith shine forth like a star in the final day. May He speed the day when traitors and secessionists shall be crushed and our noble union be again restored to its once peaceful position.
> The Reg't has been mustered for pay.
> To work for the Captain, his wife came to camp.[1]

The regiment moved into winter quarters at Camp Ayr, located near Vienna, about fifteen miles outside of Washington. Chaplain Charles Humphreys, who had joined the regiment in August, said the camp

> was surrounded with a heavy abatis of felled trees branching outwards to guard against sudden attacks of guerrillas. Here we spent the winter of '63 to '64, and made ourselves as comfortable as we could, with board floors in our wall-tents, and with brick fireplaces, and with chimneys made of mud and sticks. Our chimneys were of necessity so shallow that on windy days the smoke would be forced in gusts down the flue into our tents, and I have often been driven out into the storm for self-preservation—though doubtless if I had stayed in I would have been preserved, but only as a smoked and dried specimen of suffering humanity. Still we had a great deal of satisfaction in our fireplaces, and when the nights were cold and clear, and the logs blazed brightly, our tents often resounded with laughter and song, and all went merry as a marriage-bell.[2]

The enlisted men were housed in Sibley tents with an iron stove in the center. The horses were sheltered in stables with canvas tarps laid on wood frames. The officers lived in wall tents at the perimeter of the area.

Chaplain Humphreys regularly visited the men in their tents and encouraged them to visit his tent. He maintained a personal library of two hundred volumes, which "kept both officers and men in reading matter, and lightened the tedium of many a dull winter's day." Several of Humphreys's lady friends in Massachusetts, led by Mrs. John M. Forbes of Milton, knit several hundred pairs of cavalry mittens that were specially adapted for holding the bridle rein. Humphreys distributed them through the regiment. The mittens likely prevented many men from developing frostbite. The women also made knit caps that Humphreys distributed to every officer in the regiment, and Mrs. Forbes ensured a steady supply "of delicacies for the sick in our brigade hospital."

Humphreys also collected and sent money home for the soldiers, and when paydays were delayed, men would often seek him out for a small loan. "I used to have several hundred dollars thus floating round in the regiment," wrote Humphreys, "and, though much of it got water-logged and sunk never to return, I felt that it had done good service. There were so many Californians in my regiment who had a great admiration for Rev. Thomas Starr King and attributed to his patriotic devotion and eloquent appeals the keeping of California in the Union, that I ordered from Black—the best Boston photographer in the sixties—several dozen copies from his negative of King, and distributed them through the companies from California."[3]

Colonel Lowell and his new bride lived in a house on a hill overlooking the camp. While Lowell attended to the brigade's business, Josephine fulfilled her role as the commanding officer's wife. She visited patients in the camp hospital, delighting "the Frenchmen, Italians, and Germans by conversing with them in their own languages, that so vividly recalled their early homes." In addition, her presence in the camp "had a refining influence upon officers and men, and in the hospital, by her tender sympathies and beautiful bearing and sweet simplicity, she was like an angel visitant."[4]

The regiment's first casualty in 1864 was Pvt. George Barnes of Company M. Barnes, a carpenter from Marysville, California, was shot while on picket duty near Difficult Creek on January 3 and died twelve days later.

The first snow fell on January 4.[5] Guerrillas attacked the post at Flint Hill on the sixth but failed to cause any damage.[6] A company of cavalry sent in pursuit failed to intercept the rebels. Scouting continued through much of the month despite the cold weather. A scouting party sent out on January 12 returned with four prisoners. On the fourteenth guerrillas boldly slipped by the stable guard and got away with fifteen horses. The losses were made up on the twenty-fourth when a hundred horses were brought in from the remount camp at Giesboro accompanied by seventy-two recruits.[7]

Two detachments of Lowell's cavalry went on sweeps in the middle of the month, one to Wolf Run Shoals and Dumfries, the other to Leesburg and Snickersville, returning via Upperville. Both groups picked up only a single rebel each. Lowell reported that the area was "all quiet."[8]

On January 27 a large group of rebel cavalry was reported in the neighborhood of Sangster's Station. Brigadier General Robert O. Tyler ordered Lowell to send a squadron of cavalry to scour the country from Vienna through Centreville to Bull Run Bridge. Before Lowell's party departed, however, a report came in that a group of guerrillas had captured two four-horse teams near Annandale and that several other parties had been seen between Fairfax Station and Devereux. Armed with this new intelligence, Lowell sent an additional scouting party toward Annandale. Both parties returned on the twenty-ninth. The Bull Run group reported that Mosby had passed through the area with about sixty men the day before. They found a few Confederates in the vicinity of Centreville, but otherwise everything was quiet.

Part of the reason for the lull was that affairs in Richmond demanded Mosby's attention.[9] By the late summer of 1863 most Confederate leaders agreed that the Partisan Act needed to be amended or repealed. In his November 1863 annual report Secretary of War Seddon recommended disbanding the partisan units and incorporating them into the regular army. However, he noted that some partisan leaders had "distinguished themselves and their corps by services as eminent as their achievements have been daring and brilliant," and left the decision to disband partisan groups to department commanders.[10]

In Virginia, Brig. Gen. Tom Rosser, the Confederate cavalry commander in the Shenandoah Valley, wrote a scathing appraisal of partisan bands to General Lee on January 11, 1864:

> Without discipline, order, or organization, they roam broadcast over the country, a band of thieves, stealing, pillaging, plundering, and doing every manner of mischief and crime. They are a terror to the citizens and an injury to the cause. They never fight; can't be made to fight. Their leaders are generally brave, but few of them are brave soldiers, and have engaged in this business for the sake of gain. They cause great dissatisfaction in the ranks from the fact that these irregular troops are allowed so much latitude, so many privileges. They sleep in houses and turn out in the cold only when it is announced by their chief that they are to go upon a plundering expedition.
>
> Major Mosby is of inestimable service to the Yankee army in keeping their men from straggling. He is a gallant officer, and is one I have great respect for; yet the interest I feel in my own command and the good of the service coerces me to bring this matter before you, in order that this partisan system, which I think is a bad one, can be corrected.

General Stuart, in his endorsement to Rosser's letter, acknowledged that while Mosby's command was "the only efficient band of rangers I know of, . . . Such organizations, as a rule are detrimental to the best interests of the service."[11]

After reviewing Rosser's letter and Stuart's endorsement, Lee forwarded the documents to the War Department with a recommendation that the partisan corps be abolished. The War Department passed the correspondence on to the Congressional Military Committee, which was considering repealing the Partisan Act.

Mosby somehow got word of Rosser's letter and Lee's recommendation and in late January went to Richmond to confer with Seddon. His appeals must have worked, because when the Confederate Congress repealed the partisan law on February 17, 1864,[12] the bill included a clause allowing the secretary of war to exempt such companies, as he deemed proper for operations behind enemy lines. The remainder were to be mustered into regular line units. Only Mosby's battalion and Capt. John McNeill's West Virginia partisans were exempted. Mosby's lobbying efforts were successful and he would continue the guerrilla warfare in Northern Virginia to the end of the war.[13]

While Mosby was in Richmond an event occurred that shook the 2nd Massachusetts. On February 4 a small scouting party led by Captain Reed was passing through Aldie when it was savagely attacked by about eight of Mosby's men. During the fight they recognized the leader of the guerrilla band as William E. Ormsby, who had deserted from Company E on January 24, taking two pistols and two horses with him. Reed ordered his men to charge, and they captured the guerrilla leader. The party returned to camp the next day with the Ormsby under close guard.

Colonel Lowell convened a court-martial that evening. At the prisoner's request, Chaplain Humphreys acted as defense counsel. The judge advocate was Lt. Lewis Dabney, an attorney who became one of the leaders of the Boston Bar Association after the war. The court-martial convicted Ormsby and sentenced him to be shot the next day.

Ormsby was taken from the guardhouse at noon February 6 and escorted to the place of execution. The regimental band led the procession playing a funeral dirge. Four pallbearers bearing a coffin followed the band. Ormsby marched immediately to the rear of the coffin followed by a firing party of twelve men. Chaplain Humphreys marched beside Ormsby, who leaned on his arm as they walked.

The brigade was formed in a three-sided square with the 2nd Massachusetts and the 13th and 16th New York regiments on either side. Companies C, F, G, and J were at the Muddy Branch camp. Major Crowninshield granted Ormsby's request to speak to Captain Eigenbrodt and the men of Company E. Chaplain Humphreys recorded Ormsby's words: "Comrades! I want to acknowledge that I am guilty and that my punishment is just. But I want also that you should know that I did not desert because I lost faith in our cause. I believe we are on the right side, and I think it will succeed. But take warning from my example, and whatever comes do not desert the old flag for which I am proud to die"[14]

After speaking to his former comrades, Ormsby stepped up before the firing party and said, "Boys I hope you fire well."[15] He was then seated upon his coffin and Chaplain Humphreys bound a handkerchief over his eyes, shook his hand in farewell, and said, "Now die like a man."[16] The members of the firing party raised their muskets on command, aimed, "and William E. Ormsby was in Eternity."[17] The regiments were marched off after the execution, each passing the corpse on their way back to camp.

There were some mitigating circumstances for Ormsby's actions, according to one witness. Sometime before he had single-handedly captured two rebels. One of them managed to escape but he took the other back to camp. When they reached camp Ormsby was accused of accepting a bribe to let the first prisoner escape. He was arrested and confined in the guardhouse for a month without charges being

preferred. The witness insisted the accusations were false and that Ormsby naturally resented his "unfair" treatment. There were also rumors that Ormsby "had
contracted an intimacy with a young lady of the rebel persuasion."[18] These circumstances apparently prompted Ormsby to desert.[19] Chaplain Humphreys, knowing
these facts, pleaded in vain that Ormsby's life be spared.[20]

Ironically, it is possible that a regularly constituted court-martial tribunal might
have ordered a lesser sentence. Legislation in 1862 required that the president review all death sentences except during an extreme emergency or when the conven-
ing officer was unable to communicate with his superiors.[21] Although neither condition applied in Ormsby's case, President Lincoln was not given an opportunity to
review his sentence.

When Lowell reported the execution to Washington that afternoon he must
have been aware that he had ignored regulations. Yet there was never even a reprimand. Years later Lowell's wife reported that "General Auger and Mr. Stanton,
who would naturally be consulted in such a case, were both pleased at Colonel
Lowell's action for if the case had been referred to Washington, the President would
have probably pardoned the man, who was young and infatuated of a Southern
girl; but they could not commend Colonel Lowell for going beyond the authority
of the regulations, therefore deemed silence the best means of expressing their
approval."[22]

Lowell's political connections guaranteed that there would be no reprisal and, as
further sign of the government's approval, he was temporarily detached from the
brigade on February 13, ostensibly to take command of the Giesboro remount camp
but actually to enjoy a brief honeymoon with his new bride. Colonel Henry M.
Lazelle of the 16th New York took over command of the brigade in his absence.

On the night of February 20 Mosby decided to celebrate his promotion to lieutenant colonel, which he received shortly after his Richmond trip. Unfortunately
for the celebrants, Major Cole, commander of the Loudoun Rangers, got word of
the affair and decided to crash the party. Cole and his men raided Upperville the
day after the celebration, capturing eleven guerrillas. A rebel named McCobb
leaped on his horse and attempted to flee but was thrown and died of a broken neck
when the animal jumped a fence.[23] Mosby gathered the remaining guerrillas in the
area and a nasty running fight ensued. Cole lost one officer and one man killed and
captured eighteen rebels. However, Mosby again escaped. Another party from Cole's
cavalry captured eight guerrillas near Front Royal. Mosby later admitted to losing
only three men wounded, perhaps because of the embarrassment of being caught
unaware.

On February 21[24] Captain Reed led a column of fifty men from Company B and
seventy-five men from Companies E and M of the 1st Battalion, 2nd Massachusetts, and twenty-five men of the 16th New York[25] on a sweep from Vienna up the
Leesburg Turnpike though Middleburg and back to Vienna. Charles Binns, the
Confederate deserter who had led the November raid through the same area, served
as guide for the expedition. They encamped on the Kephert family farm about six
miles beyond Leesburg at 2 A.M. on the twenty-second.[26]

By chance, about three hundred of Mosby's men were gathered in Piedmont for McCobb's funeral when a scout rode in with word of Reed's expedition. For once Mosby was not confronted with the time-consuming task of rounding up his men. He ordered the main body to move to Guilford Station, three miles southwest of Dranesville on the Loudoun and Hampshire Railroad. Meanwhile, Mosby and two or three others reconnoitered Reed's camp sometime before sunrise and returned to Guilford Station after determining the size of his force. He left two scouts behind to watch and report what direction the Federals marched after they broke camp.[27]

Sitting around an early morning campfire, Mosby concluded that the Federals would move east down the turnpike toward Vienna. He was so confident he was correct that he decided to set up an ambush without waiting for word from the scouts he had left behind. He selected a site about two miles from Dranesville at Anker's blacksmith shop. Across from the smithy, on the south side of the pike, was a small stand of pines that would conceal the waiting guerrillas. Mosby ordered twenty-five dismounted men armed with carbines to take a position at the center of the stand of trees facing the turnpike. Two companies, one on the right and one on the left, were hidden in the trees. Three men were stationed on the pike to serve as bait for the Federal party.

The bluecoats rode into sight at about 11 A.M. The two groups in the pines mounted their horses and waited for the signal to attack. The twenty-five dismounted men along the pike cocked their carbines and did their best to find cover. The approaching Federals were in a typical "cautious approach" formation with four roving men at the point followed by fourteen men led by a sergeant about a hundred paces to their rear. The main body was in column formation, four abreast across the turnpike, about three hundred paces farther back. Captain Reed rode at the head of the main body.

The four point men spotted the three guerrillas in the middle of the road and, after a brief exchange of shots, the guerrilla trio turned and raced down the turnpike. The Federals shouted and spurred their mounts to a gallop. The fourteen troopers in the van quickly followed. Captain Reed ordered the main body forward in support. When the troopers in the van reached the center of the stand of woods, a blast of carbine fire erupted from the trees and emptied a half dozen saddles. The two mounted groups of guerrillas waiting behind the trees quickly moved to the road, then turned and charged the trapped Federals. It was a brilliantly conceived and executed ambush.

The Californians were tough, seasoned fighters inured to the hand-to-hand fighting of guerrilla warfare, and at first it looked like they would hold. However, the fight quickly turned into a swirling melee that spread beyond the limits of the road into the adjacent fields behind Anker's smithy.

Although Mosby later said that the Federals had put up "but feeble resistance," John Munson, one of his men who was badly wounded that day, said they "were standing up to the rack like men, dealing out to us the best they had."[28]

A German adventurer fighting with Mosby, Baron Robert von Massow, charged Captain Reed with his saber. According to von Massow, Reed made a gesture that he interpreted as surrender. He signaled for Reed to go to the rear and continued forward. As he passed, Reed turned and shot him. One of the guerrilla officers, Capt. William Chapman, then shot Reed, killing him instantly. Reed, who had organized and commanded the California Hundred, was the first California officer to be killed in combat. Von Massow recovered but his guerrilla days were over.[29]

The confusion created by the attack of the mounted guerrillas, coupled with the deadly fire of the dismounted riflemen, soon overwhelmed the Union troopers, who broke and scattered across the adjacent fields. Charles Binns, the Confederate turncoat, disappeared at the first shots. Companies B and M were devastated. In addition to losing Captain Reed, the regiment lost nine enlisted men killed—most of them in the initial volley. Four men were wounded, one of whom later died, and fifty-six were captured. The prisoners included Capt. George Manning and his brother, Lt. William Manning of Company L. The worst loss came afterward in Georgia: sixteen Californians and nineteen Massachusetts men died in the Confederate prisons at Andersonville and Savannah.

Losses among the New Yorkers were also heavy: one man killed, three wounded, and eight captured. Mosby claimed to have lost only one killed and five wounded.[30] However, an account by one of his men puts Mosby's losses at two killed and four wounded.[31]

When word of the defeat reached Camp Ayr, Major Crowninshield moved out in pursuit with 250 men. They found Reed's body on the battleground, stripped to his underwear.[32] One of his ivory-handled revolvers lay nearby, but his horse, saddle, and second revolver were gone.[33] Crowninshield returned to Vienna on the twenty-third after following the guerrillas as far as Goose Creek. They brought back Reed's body, seven of the enlisted dead, and seven wounded.[34] Reed's wife was visiting him at the time of his death, and Chaplain Humphreys had to inform her of his loss. The members of the California Hundred contributed money to have the body embalmed by a Washington mortician. His widow received two grim reminders of her husband: the remaining presentation revolver and the bullet that had killed him. Accompanied by Chaplain Humphreys, she took his remains to her home in Dorchester, Massachusetts, where he was buried.[35]

Caspar Crowninshield mourned Reed's loss: "I miss poor Capt. Reed very much. He was honest & brave & a great friend of mine. His wife was in camp at the time & a brave woman she proved herself to be. Capt. Reed died possessed of no property & I understand that Mrs. Reed's family are not well off. If you should ever meet her say a kind word for my sake."[36]

A group of about fifty men from Companies A and E was sent toward Dranesville on February 24 to gather any stragglers and stray horses that remained in the area. Charley Binns, who fled the fight at Anker's blacksmith shop, had returned and once again acted as scout.[37] The party discovered a strong rebel picket above Dranesville and learned that about six hundred Confederates were camped at Goose Creek. General Tyler ordered Lowell's entire brigade, 530 men strong and still temporarily commanded by Major Crowninshield, out the next day in an effort to intercept the enemy. At the same time he asked headquarters if Meade's cavalry could be sent out to move on the Goose Creek force from the west.[38] Crowninshield returned to Vienna on the twenty-sixth after sweeping the area through Dranesville to Centreville and back to Vienna. He reported finding no sign of any of Mosby's guerrillas west of Middleburg; they apparently had dispersed back through the mountains.

Following Captain Reed's death, the men of the California Hundred were anxious to get the issue of the company fund settled once and for all. On the twenty-sixth, Lieutenant Sim called a meeting to discuss the issue. Sim proposed that the fund be turned over to Mrs. Reed, but some of the men opposed this idea. The principal objection was that some men had drawn out a lot of money while others had taken very little. The meeting broke up without arriving at any conclusions.

The defeat at Anker's smithy did not change the routine of regular patrols. At the end of the month informants reported that Mosby was at Falls Church with four of his men. A new tactic was tried. A force consisting of Companies A and B set out on foot with a mounted detachment from the 16th New York, all under the command of Capt. Zabdiel Adams, and set up an ambush near Union Church on the Alexandria-Leesburg Turnpike. About 10 P.M. a light snow started falling and the men were soon covered with a white powder. At 5 A.M. Adams decided to move them to a grove of trees about three hundred yards away from the pike for shelter. The snow continued throughout the day. Finally, at 5 P.M., Adams gave up on the ambush and allowed his men to move into the old church. They piled dirt on the wood floor and built small fires to warm up. In time the interior of the old church was warm and cheery and all thoughts of an ambush were soon forgotten as they waited out the storm. The next morning, March 2, was crisp and clear so they set out for camp, arriving that night at 11 P.M.[39]

In early March Ulysses S. Grant was promoted to lieutenant general and given command of all the armies in the United States. Grant decided early to prepare for a coordinated campaign scheduled to start on May 1. By April, the Union armies in the eastern theater were organized into:

(1) The Army of the Potomac with about 102,000 men commanded by Maj. Gen. George Meade. Meade's army was assigned the formidable task of following and destroying General Lee's Army of Northern Virginia. Richmond was no longer an objective.

(2) The IX Corps with about 19,000 men commanded by Maj. Gen. Ambrose E. Burnside. Originally operating under Grant's direction, IX Corps was eventually placed under Meade's command.

(3) The Departments of Virginia and North Carolina with 52,000 men, including Maj. Gen. Benjamin F. Butler's XIX Corps. Butler was to hold a beachhead in North Carolina and move up the James River to tie up the movement of reinforcements to Lee's army as Meade moved south.

(4) The Department of West Virginia with 32,110 men commanded by Maj. Gen. Franz Sigel. Sigel's force was ordered to move up the Shenandoah Valley.

(5) The Department of Washington, designated XXII Corps, with 30,231 men commanded by Maj. Gen. Christopher C. Auger. The department was a static command that included the fortifications surrounding Washington and the forts on the Virginia side of the Potomac around Alexandria.

(6) The Middle Department, headquartered in Baltimore, with 6,426 men commanded by Maj. Gen. Lewis Wallace (who later wrote *Ben Hur*). Wallace's troops were mostly home guards and Veteran Reserve Corps regiments. Their mission was to guard the railroads to the north.

(7) The Department of the East, headquartered in New York City, with about 3,000 men commanded by Maj. Gen. John Dix guarding the city and manning the harbor forts. In addition, Maj. Gen. Darius Couch had 846 men in the Department of the Susquehanna headquartered in Philadelphia.

Throughout the reorganization and reinforcing of the field armies, Lowell's independent cavalry brigade remained with XXII Corps. Charged with the mission of suppressing guerrilla activities in Loudoun and Fairfax Counties, the brigade continued its constant patrolling. Lowell made one change during this period, sending the 1st Battalion to Muddy Branch, replacing the 3rd Battalion. The 1st Battalion, which had been badly mauled in the fight at Anker's smithy, needed time to recuperate. The relatively easy duty on the north side of the Potomac would give the men a welcome respite.[40]

Major Crowninshield was promoted to lieutenant colonel on March 1, a rank more befitting the commander of a regiment.[41] Most of the month was quiet in Loudoun and Fairfax Counties. Mosby later observed that "During the months of March and April but few opportunities were offered for making any successful attacks on the enemy, the continual annoyances to which they had been subjected during the winter causing them to exert great vigilance in guarding against surprises and interruptions of their communications."[42]

A patrol that included most of the 2nd Massachusetts went out on March 12 but accomplished little.[43] A sweep toward Leesburg on the nineteenth netted two prisoners from Stuart's command and eleven supposed guerrillas.[44]

On April 1 1st Lt. Rufus Smith, who succeeded Captain Reed as commander of Company A,[45] called the California Hundred together and informed the men that Mrs. Reed had authorized him to settle the company account. He presented her accounting of the fund and after some discussion the company voted to accept her report. They next drew up a paper authorizing an amount of money to be withdrawn from each man's account, as each saw fit, and given to Walter Reed, the captain's crippled son. With this selfless gesture the men of the Hundred forgave Reed and generously settled their dispute with the dead captain.

Several heavy spring storms passed through the area in early April but Colonel Lazelle continued to send out large patrols. A patrol made up of two hundred troopers from the 2nd Massachusetts and 16th New York regiments left camp at 2 P.M. on April 4 led by Major Frazer of the 16th New York. After a six-hour march the column reached Chantilly. Frazer left the men of the 2nd Massachusetts there and proceeded on to Centreville with the New Yorkers. Private Dearborn, who went along on the mission, recalled that the night was cold and wet, "the worst night I have experienced for a long time. No fires to sit by and no chance to sleep."[46]

The rain continued the next day and at noon the men from the 2nd Massachusetts, with the exception of ten men left behind to wait for dispatches from camp, were ordered to join the rest of the patrol in Centreville. When they arrived, they made themselves "as comfortable as possible in the Old Tavern (horses and all), a desperate nightmare."[47] The scouting party returned to camp the next day, drenched and empty-handed.

Colonel Lowell returned to take over command on April 4 and during the next several weeks sent out several expeditions.

A group of fifty troopers went out on the ninth to capture a Mark Roderick, who was wanted by the authorities in Washington. Although they failed to find Roderick, the party returned with nine prisoners, including three civilians.[48]

Twenty-five men were sent out on foot the night of April 13 to scout through the area from Vienna to Dranesville. On the fourteenth Major Forbes led a scouting party consisting of about a hundred men from the 2nd Massachusetts 16th New York regiments. They left camp at 1 P.M. and marched to Hunter's Mill, then headed west over back roads to Middleburg, arriving there at 1 A.M. on the fifteenth. At Middleburg they turned around and marched through Aldie to Mount Zion Church. At 3 A.M. they stopped to cook breakfast and feed the horses. Forbes then led them back through Centreville along a back road south of the Little River Turnpike. Along the way they captured six of Mosby's guerrillas, [49] including some who had been in the fight at Anker's blacksmith shop.[50]

On April 18, after receiving reports that Mosby was in the vicinity of Hamilton with about four hundred men,[51] Lowell led a scouting party through Loudoun County and on toward Rectortown to drive off the guerrillas. Accompanying this raid was Herman Melville, author of *Moby Dick*. He later described the raid in an epic poem entitled "Scout to Aldie."

The Confederates fired on the van as it approached Leesburg that evening. Colonel Lowell, without waiting to ascertain their numbers, ordered his men to charge. The column raced forward, the men in the lead squadron with drawn sabers and the rest holding their carbines at the ready. The Confederates in the tree line to their front fired a few shots and then scattered.[52] Charles Goodwin of Company H was wounded in the attack and died two days later in a nearby farmhouse.

The troopers remained just outside the town without campfires. The next morning patrols were sent out in three directions and one soon returned with a Confederate officer and ten enlisted men. At ten o'clock they moved back to Goose Creek and stopped to rest the horses. While they were eating dinner a man came into camp and reported that Mosby had just passed through a field not two miles away. The troopers mounted up and three men and an officer set out to find Mosby's trail while the main body rode cross-country to strike the Little River Turnpike near Rectortown and cut the fugitives off. When they reached Rectortown they found, to their chagrin, that Mosby had passed through about forty-five minutes earlier. A chase in this part of the country was impossible, so the column returned to Ball's Mill and camped there for the night. At sunset Colonel Lowell sent a dismounted party of seventy-five men toward Leesburg because he had learned earlier from a captured letter that there was to be a wedding between a local beauty and a rebel soldier. The raiders arrived half an hour after the ceremony but met several members of the wedding party on the streets and engaged in a brief skirmish. The regiment lost one man killed and three wounded, none seriously. No Confederate casualties were reported, and the officer in charge said he believed that his own men, "firing without orders in the rear, did at least half the mischief."[53]

The dead and wounded were left in the house where the wedding had taken place. The next morning a sad and chastised column returned to Vienna.

On the twenty-eighth, Lowell, acting on a tip from a Union sympathizer, led another large patrol toward Upperville. Later, in a somewhat sardonic and humorous report, Lowell wrote:

> I have the honor to report return of the cavalry scout sent out on Thursday after visiting Leesburg, Upperville, Paris, Bloomfield, Union, and Rectortown. No force but Mosby was found there. We searched most of the houses designated by Gen. Augur, and have brought in quite a number of arms and contraband goods; also 21 of Mosby's men and 2 blockade-runners (besides 1 of Mosby's men and 1 blockade-runner turned over by Col. McMahon), and from 20 to 25 horses. A report in full from the provost-marshal will be forwarded to-morrow. We brought off a portion of the wool indicated in the letter to Gen. Augur, and supplied the command pretty well with tobacco. It was impossible to get teams to haul the remainder of the wool. . . . We lost 1 sergeant killed, 1 prisoner, and 2 wounded of Second Massachusetts Cavalry,[54] 2 privates killed and 3 prisoners Sixteenth New York Cavalry; 1 of the killed and all of these prisoners were straggling away from the command improperly. We killed one of Mosby's battalion and 1 of Sixth Virginia Cavalry, serving with Mosby; wounded two, besides two wounded brought in. All has been quiet in this vicinity during the last twenty-four hours.[55]

During the expedition, Captain DeMerritt accidentally shot himself in the foot. He had returned to the regiment in August 1863 after a long rest at the Washington insane asylum and commanded a squadron between August 15 and September 15, when he suffered another breakdown. He was sent back to the asylum for three months. When he returned in December, he was appointed acting inspector of cavalry, a post that hopefully would be easier on him. The wound eventually brought an end to his military service and he was discharged for medical reasons on September 2, 1864.[56]

General Auger's endorsement to Lowell's report summarized the regiment's achievements during the month and gave high praise to Colonel Lowell: "This is the third successful operation of Col. Lowell within the last month, embracing in all a capture of about 50 of Mosby's men, between 30 and 40 horses and equipments, and a good deal of other property. I desire to commend in strong terms the zeal and ability displayed by Col. Lowell in these various expeditions."

Horses, particularly cavalry mounts, were in short supply that spring. More than two thousand dismounted troopers from Maj. Gen. Philip H. Sheridan's cavalry were awaiting mounts at the dismount camp at Giesboro. According to the inspector general's evaluation, because of heavy service during the winter, the horses in a number of cavalry regiments were not fit for duty and needed rest. In an effort to legalize the impressment of stray horses and reduce the number of mounts available for use by the guerrillas, the Department of Washington published an order permitting the seizure of livestock in "un-fenced" fields.

The effect of this order was obvious to Union soldiers. Fence rails were a readily available and convenient source of firewood, and a Union column could "un-fence" a considerable area in a short period of time. Now stock inside an "un-fenced" area—including horses, sheep, and cattle—were fair game.[57]

Mosby's command continued its attacks on isolated picket posts and countersweeps by Lowell's cavalry became commonplace. On April 23, at about 4 A.M., the picket post manned by the 16th New York at Hunter's Mills was attacked by a dismounted party with a loss of nine horses, three men captured, and one wounded. The pickets were surprised and fired only three shots at the partisans. Lowell sent a scouting party out at reveille when news of the attack reached his camp. The troopers quickly picked up the guerrillas' trail. The raiders were about fifty strong and operating under Colonel Mosby's personal command. The Union troopers came within sight of them about ten miles from Aldie and the pursuit became an all-out "fox" chase. The guerrillas swept through Aldie's main street at a gallop, closely followed by the bluecoats. Outside town the guerrillas scattered in all directions. Only Lt. W. H. Hunter of Mosby's command was captured during the chase and brought back to Vienna.[58] One Union trooper, William Bumgardner, was wounded in the arm during the melee.[59] Mosby claimed eighteen horses and five men were captured, although he admits six of the horses were later recaptured.[60]

The guerrillas accomplished nothing of importance throughout the winter and spring of 1864. They managed to capture a few horses, enriching some of the guerrillas, but equal numbers were taken from them. Combat losses were perhaps heavier on the Union side but large numbers of guerrillas had been captured in their beds during the numerous sweeps made by the Union cavalry. Tactically, Lowell and Mosby were at a stalemate. Strategically, however, the victory belonged to Lowell and his brigade. The fact is, Mosby, in spite of what he and his supporters wrote after the war, had become merely a nuisance. The Army of the Potomac's supply routes running through Fairfax County remained intact. The Baltimore and Ohio Railroad ran on schedule, and communications with the west were secure. The buildup of the Army of the Potomac and Sigel's army in the Shenandoah had been completed without interruption.

On May 4, 1864, preparations for Grant's coordinated campaign intended to end the war were completed and the Army of the Potomac began crossing the

Rapidan. The movement of the armies seemed to cause a let-up in guerrilla activities in northern Virginia. The weather turned wet and miserable during the first two weeks of May and there were heavy storms in the Blue Ridge Mountains. The pontoon bridge at Harper's Ferry was washed away and part of the wooden trestle was lost. Passage across the Potomac was reduced to one lifeboat manned by Federal engineers. The pontoons were later recovered by Major Thompson's troops as they swept down the Potomac and returned to the army's Engineer Department.[61] There was an influx of convalescents and new recruits at Camp Ayr, and by the end of May Lowell had seventy-four officers and 1,354 men present for duty.

In the middle of the month, Lowell was ordered to send a regiment to Fairfax Courthouse, where it would be joined by a battalion of Pennsylvania infantry. He elected to send the 16th New York under the command of Colonel Lazelle. Lazelle was ordered to send a scouting party toward the Rappahannock the same day. Captain P. H. Mickles Jr. of the 16th New York reported he had met Mosby's force in considerable numbers on the afternoon of the seventeenth near Stafford Courthouse.

Lowell discounted Mickles's report: "We have on the best account that Mosby was in Loudoun County on Monday. It was reported in Dranesville that he was killed in the fight with [Brig. Gen. Benjamin F.] Kelly."[62]

Lowell was referring to an account by W. A. Duncan, a U.S. Deputy Marshal who had reported from Point of Rocks that Mosby was in Loudoun County and had been in a fight with the Loudoun County Rangers. Duncan reported that three of Mosby's officers were to be married in Leesburg the night of May 17, an affair that promised to be "A great frolic. There are about 300 of them. A good chance to catch them."[63]

The message was received in Alexandria at 5:40 P.M., too late to take any action. Lowell sent Major Forbes and three hundred men out early the next morning to scout Loudoun County through Rectortown and then work their way up to Leesburg in the hopes of catching the guerrillas there and intercepting members of Colonel White's battalion who had been reported in the area.[64] This time Lowell was wrong. Mosby had been at Belle Plain that day and Mickles came close to catching him.[65]

John C. Spalding, a deserter from Mosby's Rangers, served as Forbes's guide. He first led the Federal troopers to a home near Rectortown that was reputed to be one of Mosby's favorite stopping places. The party went into a nearby wood and half the men dismounted. Under cover of darkness they surrounded the house. A small group crept up to the entrance, broke the door down, and charged inside. They searched the house from top to bottom and seized three unfortunate Rangers found inside. The party then raided another house in the vicinity, capturing six more sleeping rebels. They gathered up the prisoners and marched back to Upperville and then to Middleburg the next day. They made camp at about 7 P.M. on the Little River Turnpike and the next morning returned to Vienna.[66] One of the ironies of guerrilla warfare was that Spalding had been a guest in the second house just a few days earlier.[67]

On May 23 the 2nd Massachusetts turned in its single-shot Sharps carbines and was issued lever-action, seven-shot Spencer repeaters. The Spencers were undoubtedly the best cavalry weapon of the war, and would play a decisive role later that summer.

In early June Lowell's brigade was covering the eastern part of Fairfax County from Alexandria to Fairfax Courthouse. The 16th New York was at Fairfax Courthouse and the 13th New York was at Vienna. The 2nd and 3rd Battalions of the 2nd Massachusetts moved from Vienna to Falls Church on May 24. The new camp was five miles closer to Alexandria and the railroad supplying the Army of the Potomac. The 1st Battalion remained at Muddy Branch, Maryland.[68]

A scouting party left camp on May 29 to scour the country between Dranesville, Chantilly, and Centreville. It returned to camp on June 1 with just one prisoner.[69] Two more scout parties left the next day. The first, a dismounted patrol, left at 9 A.M. under the command of Lieutenant Stone. At 2 P.M. Major Forbes led a mounted patrol out. They met near Snicker's Gap, where they arrested a rebel sympathizer, then returned by way of Middleburg and Aldie Gap, arriving at Vienna on June 4. Major Forbes reported they did not see a single guerrilla.[70]

On June 8 Companies A and G and Chaplain Humphreys were sent on what must have been one of the most unpleasant duties they experienced during the war. Just over the Rapidan, the Virginia countryside becomes a brush filled wasteland covered with second-growth scrub trees. Not surprisingly, the area is called the Wilderness. Other than some asphalt paving on a couple of the main roads, the area remains much like it was then.

The 1864 campaign opened with a brutal, grinding battle in the Wilderness. Grant had hoped to get through the timberland before Lee could react. Superior numbers and better artillery counted for naught in the matted brush of the Wilderness. The fight was Grant's first encounter with Robert E. Lee and his Army of Northern Virginia. The rugged gray columns hit the Union army hard, staggering the bluecoats. The seesaw battle raged for three days, until Grant finally broke it off and moved south, hoping to outflank Lee and catch him in open country.

The discharge of countless black powder rifle loads and cannon fire set the dry scrub ablaze and many of the wounded from both sides were burned to death in the flames that swept through the underbrush. More than twenty thousand soldiers were killed or wounded during the three-day battle in the smoke-filled woodland. The wounded that could be rescued were gathered into makeshift field hospitals. Many of the survivors lay out in the open for days awaiting succor.

The two 2nd Massachusetts companies were ordered to escort an ambulance train sent to gather wounded from the Wilderness battlefield. Fifty ambulances from Alexandria joined them. On June 9 the train marched to Occoquan Creek, then continued the next day to United States Ford and into the Wilderness.

As the column passed through Chancellorsville and into the Wilderness, Valorus Dearborn recalled: "The roadside is strewn with decayed bodies. If any doubt the bravery of our boys let them visit this place."[71]

The train reached the military hospital at Locust Grove in the early afternoon.

There they loaded the ambulances with all the wounded they could carry. The column took two days to return to Alexandria. One loaded ambulance overturned at United States Ford but no one was hurt. One of the wounded died during the second night and was buried by the roadside the next morning. The wagons reached Fairfax Courthouse after dark. After a brief stop, the train continued to Alexandria and the hospitals around Washington and the two cavalry companies went on to the camp at Falls Church.

Meanwhile, the bushwhacker war continued in Fairfax County. A four-man patrol from the 16th New York was hit by a party of about ten partisans between the Little River Turnpike and the Orange and Alexandria Railroad at about 11 P.M. on June 23.[72] Two members of the patrol were captured. Colonel Lazelle sent out a party of forty men from the 16th New York under the command of Lt. Matthew Tuck to search for the guerrillas. Tuck halted his party about a mile and half from Centreville to feed the horses. At that moment a party of about sixty rebels led by Mosby ambushed them. The New Yorkers panicked and scattered in all directions. Lieutenant Tuck reached camp at 6 P.M. on the twenty-fourth, the only survivor of the expedition. His command lost six men killed or wounded and thirty-one were captured. Lazelle sent out two parties in pursuit but they returned empty-handed.

Lowell reported that local citizens saw the cavalrymen's horses wandering around without their bits and that some of the men were sleeping in cherry trees on the other side of the road. Only one man was observed on picket, and he was sitting on a fence in a poorly chosen position. The 2nd Massachusetts commander concluded that it would be useless to pursue Mosby, who had a six-hour, fourteen-mile head start. Furthermore, the roads were very dusty, which meant that a pursuing party could be seen for miles, thus giving the enemy ample time to hide or escape.[73]

Lieutenant Tuck was not punished for his apparent lapse. He was a valuable scout and later led a number of patrols that earned him Colonel Lazelle's approbation.

By June, Grant's campaign in central Virginia had bogged down in the trenches around Cold Harbor, where a disastrous frontal assault had cost thousands of Union lives. In order to increase the pressure on Lee, Grant ordered Maj. Gen. David Hunter, who replaced Sigel after the Battle of New Market, to move up the Shenandoah Valley through Staunton to Lynchburg. Destroying the railroad terminus there would cut Lee's army off from its main source of supplies.

Hunter fought Brig. Gen. William "Grumble" Jones's little force at Piedmont and drove it off, killing Jones in the process, then began a campaign of destruction in the upper Valley. The Union troops marched on Staunton, destroying miles of railroad track, mills, depots, and factories. On June 11 they entered Lexington and torched the city. They looted Washington College and the Virginia Military Institute, then burned the military school and the home of Virginia's governor. The next day, with Lynchburg in jeopardy, Lee detached Lt. Gen. Jubal Early and his corps to counter the threat.[74]

Hunter reached Lynchburg on the seventeenth and was met by Early's hastily organized command, which soundly defeated Hunter's troops in two fights. Hunter subsequently retreated through the Cumberland Mountains into West Virginia, effectively putting himself out of the campaign for the rest of the summer.

After disposing of Hunter's force, Early moved down the Valley toward the Potomac, threatening Washington. The Union forces around Washington, Baltimore, and West Virginia were in disarray. Grant, at the urging of Charles Dana, the assistant secretary of war and a friend from the western theater, ordered Meade to send VI Corps to Washington and told Halleck to keep XIX Corps, which was en route from New Orleans, in the vicinity of the capital.

On the afternoon of July 2 John Mosby encountered Hugh Swartz, who was employed by Early's quartermaster department, in Rectortown. Swartz told Mosby that Early was marching toward Maryland and would camp in Winchester that night. Mosby, who was never part of Early's plans because Early had little regard for partisan troops, decided to take advantage of the confusion created by Early's movements. He ordered his command to rendezvous and about 250 guerrillas, each with a large sack in which to carry plunder, met at Upperville.[75]

Mosby wrote; "As I supposed it to be General Early's intention to invest Maryland Heights (at Harper's Ferry),[76] I thought the best service I could render would be to sever all communications both by railroad and telegraph between that point and Washington, which I did, keeping it suspended for two days."[77]

From Upperville, Mosby led his guerrillas to a shallow ford about a mile up river from Point of Rocks. There, accompanied by the guide, Mosby entered the water. He had made it about halfway across when he was fired on by sharpshooters concealed on the other side. After retreating to safety, Mosby positioned a twelve-pounder Napoleon on a hill overlooking the Maryland shore and sent a detachment of men armed with carbines to a small island in the river to provide covering fire. When all was ready, the riflemen opened fire and the little gun banged away as Capt. Adolphus E. "Dolly" Richards led a detachment across the river. The defenders, outnumbered and outgunned, fell back.[78]

Once they were safely across, Richards moved down the Baltimore canal towpath toward Point of Rocks. They overtook a steam packet on the canal loaded with government clerks on their way to Harper's Ferry to celebrate the national anniversary. Mosby's guerrillas had no qualms about shooting unarmed civilians, and as the clerks joined the retreating defenders, they opened fire. "When a poor fellow, overtaken by a bullet, would roll back down the cliff, whether in blue or in summer jeans, it aroused the same sort of stir in the blood as that which the ardent sportsmen sees the flying game fall to his shot."[79] The rebels ransacked the boat before moving on to Point of Rocks, a small village located at a curve on the Baltimore and Ohio Railroad. East of town the railroad ran northeast to Monocacy Junction and a spur connecting the main line to Frederick. West of town the track paralleled the Baltimore and Ohio Canal along the Potomac. Two companies of militia and a detachment of Loudoun Rangers defended the village.

After driving off the defenders, the guerrillas plundered the five stores in the small village. A train was sighted approaching the village but the engineer headed back to Harper's Ferry when the rebels fired on it with the Napoleon. Mosby later claimed to have taken fifty prisoners. The guerrillas, intent on personal gain, filled their sacks and loaded what they could not carry into several wagons, completely ignoring the opportunity to destroy railroad track. They then moved back across the river and spent part of the night looking for more wagons in which to transport their loot.[80]

Sometime that night Mosby sent a scouting party led by Wat Bowie across the river at Noland's Ferry. They cut telegraph wires and proceeded to attack a 2nd Massachusetts picket post guarding a number of canal boats at the mouth of the Monocacy. Bowie claimed he drove the Union troops away, killing two and taking four prisoners. The partisans then robbed a local store where "they procured greenbacks enough to give each man a dividend of five dollars."[81]

At headquarters, the first indication that raids were underway was when the telegraph between Washington and Harper's Ferry went dead. J. H. Taylor, General Auger's assistant adjutant general at XXII Corps, which manned the Washington defenses, sent a dispatch to Lt. Col. David R. Clendenin of the 8th Illinois Cavalry at the Giesboro remount camp. The dispatch informed Clendenin that telegraphic communication between Washington and Harper's Ferry had been cut and that it was necessary to find out why and by whom. Clendenin was ordered to leave one company behind and proceed immediately to Point of Rocks to ascertain the composition and disposition of enemy forces there. He was to remain in the vicinity and report to Brig Gen. Albion Howe, who would proceed by rail to the same point on July 5.

The dispatch added that Maj. De Witt Thompson, commanding cavalry forces on the upper Potomac, would communicate with him when he arrived.[82]

Clendenin left Washington at 7 P.M. on July 4 with 230 officers and men. At the same time, Major Thompson was ordered to send a squadron to meet Clendenin at the mouth of the Monocacy River. Thompson dispatched Capt. Charles Eigenbrodt with his two companies of Californians, Companies E and M. Clendenin reached the Monocacy early in the morning on the fifth and found Eigenbrodt ready to join him.

At about 2 P.M. the combined command moved to the ransacked village. Mosby got word of the approaching cavalry and moved back to the south side of the river opposite the Federals. He brought along his cannon and fired six shots, making a lot of noise and frightening no one. Skirmishing went on for about an hour and a half. Mosby pulled part of his force back in a half-hearted attempt to flank the Federals at Noland's Ferry. Clendenin countered by moving a detachment to the ferry that forced the guerrillas back across the river. During the flanking movement Mosby learned that a large cavalry force was in Leesburg. Having sent the wagonloads of loot in that direction the night before, Mosby withdrew his whole force and moved to Waterford, a small town northwest of Leesburg.[83]

Clendenin's cavalry and Companies E and M camped that night at Noland's Ford. The next morning, after determining that Mosby had withdrawn, Captain Eigenbrodt took Company E back to the fords at the mouth of the Monocacy and set up a picket line. He ordered Lt. Henry Crocker, in command of Company M, to move to the Frederick-Washington road to watch for rebels advancing toward Washington. Clendenin continued on toward Harper's Ferry.

Colonel Lowell sent out the cavalry force at Leesburg that had prompted Mosby's withdrawal. Major Forbes led a hundred men from the 2nd Battalion of the 2nd Massachusetts and fifty men from the 13th New York toward the Bull Run Mountains and the Potomac crossings near Leesburg.[84] The expedition passed through Aldie on Tuesday morning and found everything quiet in the mountain gaps. In the afternoon Forbes turned north toward Leesburg, moving down the Ball's Mill road. At Leesburg the patrol learned of Mosby's raid at Point of Rocks. Local Union people reported that four or five wagons of plunder had passed through the town that morning escorted by about sixty guerrillas. Forbes moved his command back across Goose Creek that night and encamped on the south side.

Mosby sent two scouts to Leesburg at daylight. Forbes retraced his route to Leesburg in the morning but obtained no additional information about guerrilla movements. The two scouts sent out by Mosby sped back to Waterford and reported that Forbes was in Leesburg. Mosby moved his troops out in pursuit and arrived at Leesburg as Forbes was leaving. Assuming Forbes would follow the same route as the day before, he moved toward Ball's Mill to set up an ambush.

But Forbes changed his route, thus avoiding Mosby's ambush. Instead of coming through Ball's Mill, he moved his force through Centre's Mill to Aldie and turned east on the Little River Turnpike, stopping to rest and feed his horses about a mile and a half out of town. When Mosby learned of Forbes's change of route he shifted his force to the south, striking the turnpike about a mile and a quarter east of Forbes's position.

After a couple of hour's rest Forbes ordered his troops to mount up and move east down the turnpike. His advance guard spotted the guerrillas at Mount Zion Church and the Federals moved toward the enemy, crossing from the north to the open fields on the south side of the road.

Mosby deployed his twelve-pounder and fired it once without doing any damage. However, the advancing Federals fell back along the north side of the road, dismounted, and took up an enfilading position on the Confederate flank. The main column deployed into line of battle as the reserve company came up behind it. All appeared to be under control without any confusion or hesitation.

Mosby's men reached the corner of a fence on the north side of road about 225 yards away and several men dismounted and began removing two panels from the fence so the rebels could move down the field on the south of the pike. At this point they were bunched up and started taking flanking fire from the Federal advance guard. As soon as the fence was down, the guerrillas advanced about seventy-five yards toward the Federals at a walk. They halted for a minute or so and waited, still under fire from the troopers in the van.

The forces were roughly equal, although Mosby had an edge of perhaps fifty men. The Federals were in a battle line, where their superior firepower would be effective. Mosby had a cannon. The Californians had only been under cannon fire once before—at the South Anna Bridge in 1863—but so far the Napoleon's fire had proven ineffective.

Just when everything was about ready, someone—perhaps an officer or a nervous sergeant, no one knows for sure—ordered Forbes's forward rank to open fire. The men in the line started shooting, causing some of the horses, which were new to the cavalry and not used to massed movements and gunfire, to become skittish. Pistol shots fired from the rear ranks added to the disarray. Forbes ordered the lead company to move to the right to calm the horses and extend his line of battle. At that point, seeing the confusion in the Federal ranks, the guerrillas charged, catching the troopers off guard as they were trying to execute a flanking movement on the right with unruly mounts.[85]

Unlike an attack by a disciplined cavalry force, the guerrillas came on in a sudden torrent, galloping toward the Union line and screaming the eerie rebel yell. For a few minutes Forbes's advance guard stood firm. But the men in the van were outnumbered more than two to one and were forced to fall back on the main body, which retreated about six hundred yards to a point near the church, where a high fence stopped it. A party of about twenty-five troopers turned on the partisans and fought "with determined but useless valor, in a hand-to-hand combat, for in a little while half of this gallant band were either killed, wounded or dragged to the ground by their wounded horses."[86]

The fence finally gave way and the Union retreat became a rout. Captain Goodrich Stone, who had been promoted and given command of Company L on May 5, was wounded at this point and all of the noncoms present from Companies A and L were wounded or killed. A bullet had lodged against Stone's spine, and, although partially paralyzed, he managed to muster enough strength to stay in the saddle and gallop away with Chaplain Humphreys by his side. When he saw there was no opportunity to rally his troops, he dashed onto a side road and his horse carried him another fourteen miles toward camp. The next day, ambulances headed for the field picked him up.

Chaplain Humphreys caught up with a party of about fifteen men who had rallied at Sudley Mills but were soon overwhelmed and forced to flee. Humphreys immediately "dashed along behind the rest of our men, to put myself and horse into the lightest running order. I pulled off my gauntlets, unstrapped my overcoat and oatbag from the saddle, and threw them away. In a few moments I came upon one of our men whose horse had been urged beyond his strength and had broken a blood vessel and in falling had pinned his rider under him. Not recognizing me as I galloped along, he took me for one of the enemy, and shouted, 'I surrender.' And I heard the shout repeated behind me as the guerrillas came up, and I saw one of them - regardless of the Union soldier's defenseless condition - shoot at him as he passed."[87]

After the war Humphreys learned that Colonel Mosby and a dozen select men had chased him because his horse was the same color as the one belonging to Yankee Davis, the Union sympathizer acting as a guide for the Federals. If he had been taken, Mosby undoubtedly would have hanged him. Fortunately he managed to elude Mosby by turning into a wooded area. During the night the chaplain found the soldier who had been pinned under his horse and managed to get him to a nearby farmhouse. The soldier, Owen Fox of Braintree, Massachusetts, had been shot and mortally wounded by the passing guerrillas. Aided by a local farmer with a lantern, Humphreys located one other wounded soldier and brought him back to the farmhouse. He stayed with the two men until about 4 A.M., then decided to go out to find his hat, which he had lost during the chase. Outside he discovered that his horse had been stolen. Humphreys headed toward the battlefield on foot and had gone only a short way when a rebel riding the stolen horse stopped him. At first he was able to convince the rebel to let him go his way, but the rider later returned and took Humphreys prisoner.[88]

About forty men had returned to camp by Friday. Mosby reportedly took forty-four prisoners. The rest of the men were missing but would probably show up sometime later. More than a hundred horses and accouterments were taken.

Lowell arrived at the battle site at about 11:30 A.M. on July 7. His party searched the woods, picking up a half dozen survivors, then he moved on to Centreville. The men reported that Major Forbes remained on the field until every man had left, emptying his revolver and disabling one guerrilla with a saber thrust—even lunging through Mosby's coat in a duel with the guerrilla leader. He was forced to surrender when his horse was killed, fell on his leg, and pinned him to the ground.

Losses in the detachment were high. The dead included two Californians, Cpl. Samuel Hanscom of Company A and Cpl. James McDonald of Company F. Massachusetts troopers killed were Charles Oeldrather of Company G; John Johnson, Patrick Riordin, Charles Rollins, and Cornelius Tobin from Company I; and William Dumaresq of Company K. The eight dead were buried in the Mount Zion Church graveyard.[89] Owen Fox of Company H was buried nearby. Corporal William Bumgardner was carried to a nearby farmhouse, where he died on July 22. Captain Stone was carried back to camp and died there on July 18. Nine men were wounded, including eight Californians. Twenty-six more—including Major Forbes, Chaplain Humphreys, and 2nd Lt. Charles Armory—were taken prisoner. Four of them died in the Confederate prisons at Andersonville and Danville. The 13th New York lost one man killed, three wounded, and eleven captured. Lowell did not make any excuses for his friend after the defeat: "Major Forbes' first platoon was ordered to fire. Here was the first mistake. . . . Had the order been given to draw sabers and charge, the rebels would have never got their gun off, I think, Major Forbes, seeing how uneasy his horses were at the firing must have intended to dismount some of his men."[90]

Any blame for the disaster has to be charged to Major Forbes. By moving through the same area twice, he gave the guerrillas time to concentrate and select the ground for the fight. Forbes could have turned his blunder into success if he had ordered a charge when his advance guard came upon the guerrillas. Instead he hesitated, always a fatal mistake. Mosby took the initiative and charged, throwing the Union troopers into confusion and winning the battle. It was the best opportu-

nity the regiment ever had to deal the guerrillas a punishing blow but Major Forbes
failed to meet the challenge.

Mosby admitted to losing only one man killed and six wounded,[91] while claiming the Federals lost eighty killed and wounded and fifty-seven captured—about
double the actual casualties. He also boasted that "After this affair the enemy never
ventured, in two months after, the experiment of another raid through that portion
of our district."

Mosby's boast was true, but not for the reasons he states. On July 9 the 2nd
Massachusetts, his principal foe in Loudoun and Fairfax Counties, was caught up in
the affairs across the river.

6 | Old Jube Invades

On July 4, 1864, the advance elements of newly promoted Lt. Gen. Jubal Early's Army of the Valley, waded across the Potomac River at Shepardstown and Williamsport, eight and twenty miles, respectively, above Harper's Ferry. By the sixth the whole rebel army, about fifteen thousand strong, was in western Maryland and moving toward Washington.

General Lew Wallace commanded VIII Corps in the Middle Department, which included Delaware and Maryland as far as the Monocacy River. His headquarters was in Baltimore. On July 2, John Garrett, president of the Baltimore and Ohio Railroad, told him telegraph operators farther up the line had reported Confederate troops in the area. Wallace decided to move his headquarters to Monocacy Junction to cover the crucial iron railroad bridge there and a small covered wooden bridge nearby.[1]

Wallace had about twenty-five hundred militia and Maryland Home Guards but lacked reliable cavalry until July 6, when Colonel Clendenin rode into Monocacy on his way to Harper's Ferry after the clash with Mosby at Point of Rocks. Wallace quickly attached him to his forces and ordered him to proceed the next day to the gaps in the Catoctin Mountains.[2] Clendenin started toward Middletown at daybreak with a section of artillery on the Hagerstown-Frederick road. He met Early's advance guard about five miles beyond Frederick and immediately sent back word that the enemy force included infantry, cavalry, and artillery. This information, forwarded to Halleck in Washington, established that the rebel forces were not just a raiding party but a full-scale invasion.[3]

Clendenin's report, forwarded from Halleck, convinced Grant that Early's movement was a real attack on Washington, not just a raid. He ordered Maj. Gen. James B. Ricketts's 3rd Division of VI Corps and all of the dismounted cavalry at City Point sent to Baltimore. As the soon as the reinforcements arrived, they were loaded on railcars and sent west. This welcome addition arrived at Monocacy about noon on July 8, giving Wallace about fifty-eight hundred men to hold back Early's fifteen thousand veterans.

Skirmishing broke out west of Frederick as Ricketts's division unloaded at Monocacy and continued all day without any advances by the Confederates.[4] That night Wallace withdrew his troops to the bluff overlooking the river at Monocacy Junction. The next day, at about 4 P.M., Brig. Gen. John McCausland's cavalry

forded the river and attacked Wallace's left, held by Ricketts's veterans. After the
Federals severely punished McCausland's dismounted troopers, Maj. Gen. John B.
Gordon's Confederate infantry charged. The rebels were repulsed twice with heavy
losses but reinforcements were brought up and the Union line finally gave way.
When the left flank collapsed, the rest of Wallace's little force was compelled to
retreat. A stubborn rear guard action by Ricketts's division covered the withdrawal.

It was one of the most important battles of the war. Wallace's troops, outnumbered, outgunned, and outflanked, held out for six hours, delaying Early's march at
least one day and arguably more. Another day was spent gathering the wounded
and the battlefield spoils. Late that evening General Wallace sent a dispatch to
Washington advising General Halleck that he was retreating from Monocacy Junction after making an all-day stand against a force numbering at least twenty thousand. "They do not seem to be pursuing. You will have to use every exertion to save
Baltimore and Washington."

Halleck received Wallace's wire at 11:50 P.M. and seven minutes later responded
with one of the more superfluous and inane orders of his military career: "I am
directed by the President to say that you will rally your forces and make every effort
to retard the enemy's march on Baltimore."[5]

While Wallace was waging his desperate struggle along the Monocacy, the 2nd
Massachusetts was covering the lower approaches to the Potomac. Major Thompson was ordered to gradually draw in his pickets and shadow Early's advancing column, being sure to keep his advance guard ahead of it, and provide periodic reports
on the enemy's movements. Thompson promptly ordered the pickets above Edwards Ferry to withdraw and sent Captain Eigenbrodt with Companies E and B to
establish a new line on the road from Edwards Ferry to Rockville. Lieutenant Crocker took Companies M and D and set up a line of posts at Gaithersburg covering the
Frederick-Rockville road. Patrols scoured the Potomac as far as the mouth of the
Monocacy. The camp at Muddy Branch was dismantled and all surplus government
property was placed on a canal boat. Thompson organized fatigue parties to fell
trees along the roads to Washington in an effort to delay a rebel advance in that
direction.

Eigenbrodt brought his troops back in the early afternoon and reported that
Union troops and rebels had been fighting for several hours at Buckeystown on the
Monocacy. The cannonading had started about 11 A.M. and was clearly heard at
Muddy Branch. Scouts from Company E reported that seven thousand enemy cavalry had passed through Adamstown and that Ricketts's division from VI Corps
had arrived at the battlefield. Major Thompson reported all of this to Washington
and added that a large cloud of smoke could be seen to the northeast. He thought it
was probably from the bridge across the Monocacy.[6] Captain Eigenbrodt's squadron
escorted the camp equipment back to Tennallytown and camped there that night,
weary and worried about what the morning would bring. The next morning Major
Thompson ordered the two companies to picket the River Road.

Lieutenant Crocker's squadron retreated down the Washington road toward Leesburg hoping to join reinforcements coming up from Washington. They camped

along the road for a few hours but got up long before sunrise and began moving back toward Washington. Beyond Leesburg the Washington road became Seventh Street. Like an arrow, Seventh Street led directly into the heart the nation's capital. At the boundary between Maryland and the District of Columbia, Fort Stevens, a formidable earthwork, covered the road. But on July 9 the fort was empty save for a handful of caretakers and sentries. For most of the day, 1st Lt. Henry H. Crocker, a former bartender from Oakland, California, and a handful of men from Company M of the California Battalion and Company D of the 2nd Massachusetts were the only troops between the rebels and the heart of the capital.

Help came that afternoon. General Auger, recognizing there was a gap in his screen and unaware of Lieutenant Crocker's movements, ordered the last available company of the 8th Illinois Cavalry commanded by Capt. Henry Hotopp, to cover Seventh Street. They were quickly on their way and would arrive before dark. The only other cavalrymen available north of the Potomac were those awaiting remounts at the Giesboro cavalry depot. Colonel William Gamble of the 8th Illinois Cavalry was in command there. Gamble had commanded one of the two cavalry brigades that had fought so heroically on the first day at Gettysburg the year before. He was a veteran cavalry commander but had recently been in poor health.

Orders were sent out to send all available cavalry mounts in the Washington area to Giesboro. In a short time five hundred troopers from every cavalry regiment in the Army of the Potomac were hurriedly equipped, mounted, and made ready for operations. Major William Fry of the 16th Pennsylvania Cavalry was placed in command. Gamble instructed Fry to take the newly formed battalion toward Leesburg and Rockville and cautiously reconnoiter the area. Fry was to avoid becoming decisively engaged and Gamble ordered him to fall back to Fort Stevens if he ran into a large enemy force.

Fry led his command out of the cavalry camp in the early evening. They marched through Tennallytown and camped at Falls Run, a small stream west of town.

The next morning, July 10, Fry organized the command into five squadrons and assigned one officer to each squadron.[7] A detachment under Maj. Coe Durland of the 16th Pennsylvania Cavalry took the Brooksville Road to the Seventh Street road. The rest of the command followed Major Fry out the Rockville Pike. Fry moved forward very cautiously, with a heavy advance guard and flankers on each side. When they were two miles beyond Fort Reno he sent back a courier with the message that there were no rebels in sight.[8]

The command reached Rockville at about 11 A.M., where Fry encountered Capt. Levi Wells, who was leading a squadron that consisted of Companies C and I of the 8th Illinois Cavalry. Wells and his troopers had been cut off from Clendenin's command the day before during the battle at the Monocacy River and they were trying to reach the Baltimore and Ohio Railroad.[9] Fry ordered him to turn around and reinforce his command. Wells protested, claiming he was ill and that his men and horses were used up. Fry allowed him to send a courier back to General Auger in Washington but insisted the Illinois troopers join his force.

Fry's column passed through Rockville in the midafternoon and continued toward Gerradsville. A burst of carbine fire announced the presence of the rebel advance guard. Skirmishing started immediately. Fry rode to the front and could see a brigade of enemy cavalry moving down the road toward his position. Leaving several small parties to ambush and delay the advancing Confederates, he ordered his troops to withdraw gradually to Rockville. There was some confusion as the troopers passed through Rockville because the makeshift command was short of officers to direct the movement. Fry left a rear guard on the west side of town to try to slow the Confederates, then halted the rest of his retreating troopers in the center of town to attempt regain control of his force. While the few officers and noncoms were shaking the column out and reorganizing, rebel sympathizers slipped around the rear guard and informed the advancing Confederates of the situation in the village. The rebels charged the rear guard without waiting to form a battle line. The Union troopers got off one ragged volley then fled toward the main column in Rockville with the Confederates in hot pursuit.

Fry quickly moved his command to a small knoll about a mile east of Rockville and ordered the troopers to dismount and form a skirmish line. The position had a stand of trees to the rear to shelter the horses and the ground in front was open.[10] He sent a courier back with a report of his actions and a recommendation "that the forts in the vicinity of Tennallytown be strongly guarded as the enemy's column is a mile long."[11]

Fry held the rebels for about an hour but was forced to retreat when the Confederates brought up a small battery of guns. He moved his men back to the woods, where they mounted their horses and moved down the pike. At every little hill or knoll they came to the Union troopers would halt and form a skirmish line in an effort to delay the Confederate advance. At nightfall Fry finally let his men dismount and rest at the picket line at Tennallytown. The horses remained saddled and the men lay on the ground and slept a few hours with the reins tied around their wrists. The ailing Wells and his Illinois troopers were released and sent back to Fort Reno, arriving about 10 P.M.[12]

Major Durland, who had left Fry near Tennallytown that morning to scout the Seventh Street road, reported that he had reached Leesborough at 9 P.M. He said a citizen who had just come from Rockville reported that 5,000 enemy cavalry had taken possession of the town.[13] The report was correct. That night General McCausland, commanding Early's van, dined with his staff at a local hotel, the Montgomery House, while the 14th Virginia Cavalry's band serenaded him.

During the afternoon, as the reports came in from Major Fry, General Auger considered his options. Fry's hastily organized command had performed bravely. Outnumbered, with only temporary company officers and unknown comrades, the recently remounted casuals had contested the rebel advance over nine hot and dusty miles from Rockville to Tennallytown. Their horses were worn out and the rebels had pummeled them without relief all day. The July sun had taken its toll on both men and horses. Behind the weary troopers was Fort Reno, garrisoned by raw militia and the invalids from the Veterans Reserve Corps. Behind Fort Reno lay Washington, wide open to a quick thrust by a mounted column.

Auger decided to move part of Lowell's brigade, his only remaining organized cavalry force, to the north side of the river. In the late afternoon he sent a telegram to Colonel Lowell at Falls Church instructing him to send a regiment to Washington. Then, perhaps concerned that Lowell might decide to send one of the weak New York regiments, Auger sent another dispatch. This time he ordered Lowell to personally bring the 2nd Massachusetts across the river and report to his headquarters for further instructions.[14]

When the orders arrived at Falls Church at 1 P.M., pickets and details were immediately called in. Lowell turned command of the remainder of the brigade over to Colonel Lazelle of the 16th New York and the 2nd Massachusetts hurriedly broke camp. A detail stayed behind to load the regimental wagons. There was no time to cook rations; the men simply gathered up what they could and swung into their saddles. By sundown the regiment had crossed the Potomac at the Chain Bridge. They marched to Tennallytown and at 10 P.M. arrived at Battery Rossell, seven miles from Washington. While the regiment set up camp near Brig. Gen. Martin Hardin's headquarters, Lowell reported to Hardin and received orders for the next day.[15]

During the war, whenever a regiment marched by, bystanders would call out, "What regiment?" The passing troops would then proudly shout out their regiment's number and state. After the war, one Californian said that at the beginning of their service they would respond with "the California Hundred" or the "California Battalion"; only rarely did they identify themselves as being from the 2nd Massachusetts. By the summer of 1864, however, the men were veterans and the regiment had earned a reputation for being tough fighters after a year of being Mosby's main antagonists in Fairfax and Loudoun Counties. This night, as the weary troopers marched through the beleaguered capital on the way to Fort Reno they answered with pride, "Second Massachusetts Cavalry."[16]

At daybreak the next morning, Major Fry started his weary command down the Rockville Road but before he reached Old Tavern Colonel Lowell and the 2nd Massachusetts overtook him. Lowell, as the senior officer present, took command and told Fry to fall in behind his regiment.

Lieutenant Henry Crocker sent a dispatch to Lowell at 6 A.M. reporting that he was at Leesborough with Company M. He informed Lowell that the 1st New Jersey Cavalry[17] was pulling back toward Brooksville and that the enemy was in Rockville. Lowell forwarded the dispatch on to General Auger in Washington along with word that he had reached Old Tavern.

Just beyond Old Tavern, at about 6:40 A.M., the advance guard encountered a rebel skirmish line. Lowell reported firing on his left along the River Road. He sent a courier back with the news and reported he could hold his position if required. The skirmishing went on all morning as both sides tried to find a weak point to exploit. Lowell sent a stream of reports back to General Hardin at Fort Reno. At about 11 A.M. the Union infantry pickets on the River Road were driven back. At 1:15 P.M. General Hardin wired Washington headquarters that the enemy was clearly moving to his right in an effort to get to Seventh Street and move against Fort

Stevens. Headquarters ordered Hardin to move all of his reserves to the right. The heavy guns opened up as the fighting spread toward Fort Stevens. By 3 P.M. the fighting in front of Fort Reno was easing, so Hardin ordered the cavalry back to the picket line.[18]

On Seventh Street, Maj. Gen. Alexander McD. McCook had abandoned his earlier plan to set up a reserve camp behind the fortifications. The gunfire from the cavalry skirmishing on the left could be heard clearly at Fort Stevens. McCook ordered every arriving unit into the rifle pits in front of the forts. During the morning several units from the Veterans Reserve Corps and some detachments of dismounted cavalry arrived and were guided to the rifle pits.

At noon a large Confederate skirmish line appeared in front of Fort Stevens. McCook ordered the picket line to fall back to the rifle pits. Several of the retreating pickets succumbed to heat prostration in the sweltering heat and humidity. The Confederates were held in check, but the pressure was steadily increasing. Finally, the long awaited troops from the Army of the Potomac began to arrive at Fort Stevens. The first unit was the detachment of six hundred dismounted men from the 2nd Division of the Cavalry Corps, commanded by Maj. George G. Briggs of the 7th Michigan Cavalry. The troopers passed through the line of the rifle pits and were joined by Companies M and D of the 2nd Massachusetts as they attacked the Confederate skirmishers.[19] The Confederates fell back as the bluecoats reestablished the original picket line in front of the fort.

The first VI Corps infantry units arrived in Washington from City Point at noon. They quickly disembarked from the ships that had carried them there and marched out Sixth Street, then Pennsylvania Avenue, and then Sixteenth Street to Camp Brightwood. The red Greek crosses on their hats identified them to the citizens crowding the streets as veterans of the Army of the Potomac. When they arrived at Fort Stevens they were formed into a battle line behind the fort. Additional troops came up and the line was extended. They remained in line until 6 P.M. and then the 2nd Rhode Island Infantry and 37th Massachusetts Infantry passed through the gates of the fort. Captain Elisha Rhodes, commanding the 2nd Rhode Island, wrote in his diary later that night: "Fort Stevens was firing shell into the Rebel lines while Fort Slocum was sending its shots with fearful screams after Early's men. Our column passed through the gate of Fort Stevens, and on the parapet I saw President Lincoln standing looking at the troops. Mrs. Lincoln and other ladies were sitting in a carriage behind the earthworks. We marched in line of battle into a peach orchard in front of Fort Stevens and here the fight began. For a short time it was warm work, but as the President and many ladies were looking at us every man tried to do his best."[20]

The line of battle followed and the firing in the front became heavy. When VI Corps passed through the fortifications toward the front, the 2nd Massachusetts's band serenaded them. A band member wrote: "They gave us three cheers and went in with a will."[21] The fighting continued until about ten that evening.

Over on the left, Lowell's tired troopers camped along the picket line in front of Fort Reno. That night they received the sad news that Capt. Goodrich Stone of

Company L died of the wounds he had received during the July 6 fight. Adding to the evening gloom, Confederate campfires could be seen forming a menacing ring from the River Road to the right of Fort Stevens on Seventh Street.[22]

Before he crawled into his blankets, Charles Lowell wrote a reassuring letter to his bride who was trapped in Washington by Early's invasion:

> There is no end of confusion out here, and very little known of the enemy. I took over our 1st squadron with a miscellaneous assortment from the Dismounted Camp to within two miles of Rockville this morning, met a superior force of Rebels (nothing very fierce, however) and fell gradually back towards Tennallytown, they following with a gun and a gradually diminishing column. They are reported approaching similarly on the 7th St. road—it looks at present more like a move to mask heavier movements than like a serious effort against this part of the fortifications. I gather from what I hear that you are cut off from Baltimore[23] and cannot do otherwise than stay.
>
> We had only two men wounded this morning, neither seriously—several horses, among others Ruksh, very slightly, just across the back behind the saddle, injuring an overcoat for me as once before on the Peninsula.[24]

Late in the evening on July 11, the 2nd Massachusetts was spread between the Potomac and Fort Stevens. Colonel Lowell was at Fort Reno with the 2nd and 3rd Battalions. The 1st Battalion was split, with Companies B and E posted along the River Road and Companies D and M and the regimental band at Fort Stevens.

At sunset, Brig. Gen. Montgomery C. Meigs, the quartermaster general of the army, reported to Fort Stevens with fifteen hundred armed, organized, and equipped quartermaster employees. They were ordered in the rifle pits at Fort Slocum. Another two thousand convalescents came in a little later. At about midnight the command of the line of fortifications was divided from left to right among General Hardin, General Meigs, and Maj. Gen. Quincy A. Gillmore. General McCook was confirmed in charge of the whole.

At dawn on July 12, Confederate sharpshooters opened up on the cavalrymen, including Companies D and M manning the Union skirmish line in front of Fort Stevens. The Confederates and about five hundred stragglers were occupying a line about eleven hundred yards from Fort Stevens. McCook decided to try to disperse them with cannon fire. The first round exploded prematurely and killed a Union soldier in the trenches in front of the fort, but the guns continued to fire at targets all along the front throughout the day. A body of cavalry was dispersed with four twenty-four-pounders, and four rounds fired at an enemy column twenty-two hundred yards away caused it to turn and deploy into line of battle. However, the explosions from two thirty-pounder shells caused the rebels to reconsider the maneuver and they began to fall back.

At about 6 P.M. a brigade was sent to force the Confederates back. It succeeded in pushing the rebels back until it encountered a second Confederate line at the Carbery house, about eleven hundred yards in front of Fort Stevens. McCook ordered every gun in the fort to concentrate on the house in an effort to dislodge the

Confederates who were holding up the Union skirmish line. The guns finally set the house afire and the Confederates fell back. The artillery continued firing until after dark as the VI Corps veterans dug rough trenches to protect their gains. One of General Meigs's men, a civilian clerk, was killed during the skirmishing. Major General Horatio G. Wright's VI Corps suffered about thirty casualties. Two 2nd Massachusetts men, Pvt. John Dolan of Company D and Pvt. James McGrath of Company K, were killed during the day's fighting.[25]

The story was much the same at Fort Slocum. The enemy took cover in outlying buildings that were then pulverized by the big guns. Any body of troops in the open was hit with percussion shells, causing the men to head for cover. Most of the firing was at targets three thousand yards away. The infantry in the trenches never fired a shot.

At the cavalry camp near Tennallytown, things began to stir early in the predawn hours. A few small fires were kindled and the men boiled coffee before the horses came up. When they arrived, the troopers mounted and the sergeants rode down the column moving the men into position. The officers took their posts at the front of each company. The advance party and the scouts went out in front along the road and the column quietly moved forward into the early morning gloom.

Just beyond Tennallytown the road splits. The left-hand road leads to Offut's Crossroads, and the right fork goes to Rockville. Lowell took the 2nd Battalion down the left fork and directed Crowninshield to move up the right-hand fork with the 3rd Battalion. The rising sun, promising another hot day, appeared on the horizon behind them as the two commands parted.

Lieutenant Colonel Crowninshield ordered the Californians of Company F to form a skirmish line across the road and then move forward. They moved down the road cautiously for about a mile before they struck the enemy picket line. The remainder of the battalion formed into line of battle across the road and started moving toward the Confederates. The Californians in the skirmish line fired a volley from their Spencers and then fell back to join the main body.

Meanwhile, Lowell sent a company ahead on the River Road to scout out Offut's Crossroads. It returned a short time later to report there was no Confederate movement on the north-south road. Another company went up the Aqueduct Road along the river and scouts were sent north toward the Rockville Pike in an effort to find the left flank of the rebel line. The scouts located the flank a short way from Tennallytown just about the time Crowninshield's battalion began firing on the Confederates along the Rockville Pike. Lowell quickly moved his remaining three companies about a half-mile north and dismounted. The number fours[26] took the horses to the rear. At Lowell's command the three companies charged the Confederate flank just as Crowninshield's battalion hit them in the front. The Confederates, reeling under the weight of the combined attack, fell back about a mile toward Rockville.

Lowell stopped the advance to regroup. He ordered Crowninshield to hold the position for two hours and then occupy the old infantry picket line a little ways to the rear. Lowell sent a courier back with a report that the cavalry picket was at Cabin John's, two and a half miles ahead of the infantry picket line. Everything was quiet to his front but there was sporadic firing throughout day.[27]

General Meigs was up at 2 A.M. on July 13, the second day of his first combat command. If there was to be a final thrust on the U.S. capital, he reasoned that it would start at sunrise. "I rode to Fort Stevens and took position on the parapet to watch the breaking day," Meigs wrote a few days later. "The gray dawn spread over the landscape widely extended in sight. An occasional shot from a suspicious picket and the low of a cow or the bray of a mule alone broke the stillness of the morning, and at last the sun arose and all remained quiet."

General Meigs never again had the opportunity to command troops in combat. Instead, President Lincoln appointed him a brevet major general that day. It was a richly deserved honor, not because of his activities on July 12, but because of his capable service as the Union quartermaster general.

Cavalry pickets commanded by Captain Hotopp of the 8th Illinois were sent out. They reported that the rebel positions of the night before had been abandoned. Postmaster General Montgomery Blair's house had been burned to the ground, and Francis Blair's house was "turned topsy-turvy, all his liquors consumed, and his papers ransacked."[28]

Lowell moved out on the Rockville Pike in pursuit of the retreating Confederates with nearly the entire 2nd Massachusetts plus Major Fry's makeshift battalion. Company's B and E moved up the River Road to cover Lowell's left flank. At about 9:15 A.M. Lowell's advance guard came upon the Confederate rear guard four and a half miles from Rockville. The regiment formed up and skirmishing started as the Confederates slowly pulled back. In a dispatch written at about 10:40 A.M. Lowell was able to report:

> There seems to be no force within a quarter and a half mile from Rockville. They have been passing on the old city road certainly ever since daybreak. . . . Citizens here report their trains moving on that road when they went to bed last night and columns of dust seen and noise heard all this morning. The rebels talked to the citizens as if they were going to cross the river the first opportunity. . . . Any serious attempt against them with infantry must, I think, be made soon. Three prisoners taken from Early's old division of Early's present corps confirm the above. . . . They say they have been run to death.[29]

Lowell slowed the march, hoping for infantry reinforcements to attack the Confederate column and perhaps cut off a portion of Early's army, but no Union infantry was forthcoming. The last of the Confederates passed through Rockville a little after noon. As the dust from the retreating Confederates settled, the 2nd Massachusetts moved forward. They reached Rockville at about 2 P.M., but not before Lowell posted Major Fry and his weary men at the intersection of the Brooksville Road and the Georgetown Pike near Saint Mary's Church. As a further precaution, Lowell ordered Lieutenant Colonel Crowninshield to lead the advance to the west side of Rockville.

Unbeknownst to Lowell or Crowninshield the Confederates had set a trap for them. Earlier that morning General Early had given Brig. Gen. Bradley Johnson, commander of the Confederate rear guard, a tongue lashing for permitting the Federals to get so close to the army's rear. Johnson's troops were known as the "Maryland Line," a brigade of Marylanders that combined infantry, cavalry, and artillery into a single unit. Johnson later admitted that "The Second Massachusetts Cavalry hung on our rear and made it very uncomfortable for us generally."[30] Johnson decided to set a trap for the Union cavalry. He ordered Col. William Jackson to set up a screen at Watt's Branch just outside Rockville and wait for the enemy to advance. Behind Watt's Branch the Darnestown Road ran though a shallow valley then angled behind a low hill. Johnson formed the 1st Maryland Cavalry into an assault column just out of sight behind the hill, where they waited for the Federals to advance.

Crowninshield encountered Jackson's skirmish line and, perhaps recalling Lowell's criticism of Major Forbes, ordered his men into line and had them draw sabers and prepare to charge. As the Union troopers moved toward the Confederate line, Johnson ordered the Maryland cavalry hiding behind the knoll to attack. The charging rebels swung into view, surprising Crowninshield's badly outnumbered squadron. The bluecoats halted their horses, fired one ragged volley, and then turned and ran. Some found themselves racing side by side with their attackers toward Rockville. A dense cloud of dust hung over the area and the sound of firing told Lowell what had happened. One trooper with Lowell's column wrote:

> When the riderless horses of our advance guard came dashing pell mell through our closed columns, communicating their panic stricken spirit to many a sober man and beast, and giving rise I think to questionable orders which soon turned our courses backwards. Some of us who were disposed to go slowly soon found ourselves in the retreating rear rank and while passing the Court House over a triangle block which broke the main street of the town our attention was attracted by the clattering hoofs of a horse. And upon looking around we saw our capless Colonel following in haste. The magical effect of his voice when he neared and said "Boys, will you dismount and check them" was all that could be desired in any emergency.[31]

The troopers had enough combat experience to know that a dismounted man without a held horse nearby had a good chance of becoming a prisoner. In spite of this, they obeyed without reservation. They swung from their saddles with carbines in hand, and slapped their mounts on the haunch, sending the animals trotting to the rear. The dismounted troopers then ran for cover.[32] Some men found shelter behind fences and trees while others took position behind several sturdy brick buildings. They did not have to wait long for the attack they knew was coming. Within a few minutes, a howling pack of rebels poured out of the mouth of the street to their front "enveloped in a cloud of dust, only to be startled, bewildered and driven back by the prompt rapid fire of our repeating carbines."[33]

The Confederates were forced back to the edge of town by the withering fire.

The Union troopers followed them for "about a quarter of a mile where we met and repulsed a better organized and more formidable charge in an engagement so close that pistols were freely used. And the pitiful sight of a wounded foeman clutching for dear life to the neck of his horse, with such apparent helplessness, impressed my mind deeply."[34]

When the Confederate cavalry fell back, Johnson, frustrated by the stubborn Union defense, decided to attack once more. This time he ordered his infantry to attack in front while a cavalry brigade swept around Lowell's left. Lowell ordered a handful of men to take position in a grove of trees on his flank in an effort to stem the flanking Confederates but to no avail. The 2nd Massachusetts was steadily forced back and in danger of being encircled by the thrusting cavalry. As the weight of the rebels' overwhelming numbers began to make the position untenable, Lowell ordered his troopers to fall back to Major Fry's position outside of town.

The horses were quickly rounded up and the battalion fell back. On the other side of Rockville the Confederates regrouped and moved forward again. The firing

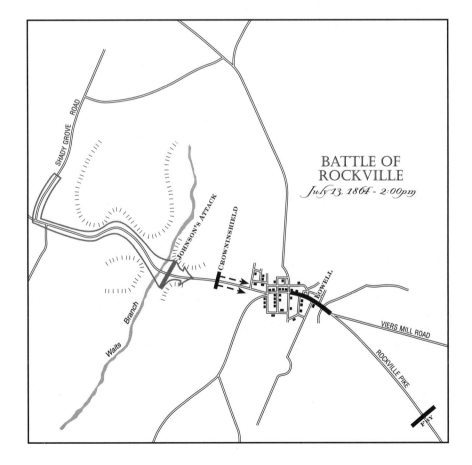

BATTLE OF
ROCKVILLE
July 13, 1864 - 2:00pm

became steady. Small parties would charge forward, fire, and then fall back. Fry had dismounted his men, who were able to deliver deliberate and effective fire. They were armed with Burnside carbines and had been resupplied with ammunition the night before. The two brigades stubbornly fell back about two miles to a knoll on the Rockville Pike. With Lowell's men covering the flanks, the line held for the rest of the day.[35]

The regiment lost three killed or mortally wounded and twenty-six wounded. Charles Backus of Company K, a native of Nantucket Island, was killed outright. The mortally wounded included Colonel Lowell's orderly, Henry Allen of Company A, and George Carr of Company L, who did not die until October. A total of thirty-eight men were captured as a result of Lowell's order for the men to leave their horses. Three Californians escaped. Samuel Rhodes and Luman Manchester, both from Company E, slipped away at Staunton and made it back to the regiment. Warren Cochran of Company F later escaped from Danville Prison and made the harrowing walk all the way to Union lines in Tennessee.[36]

When word of the Rockville fight reached Washington, Secretary of War Stanton sent a wire to General Hardin at Fort Reno asking: "What number of cavalry regiments did Lowell have? He says his regiment left in Rockville was badly whipped. What is the extent of his loss?"

Stanton, assuming Lowell had more than one regiment at his disposal must have been surprised by Hardin's reply: "Colonel Lowell had, I think, four companies of his own regiment, Second Massachusetts, and several detachments from other regiments. His loss is something over 100 as near as I can learn."[37]

While Lowell and Crowninshield were battling the Confederates at Rockville, Companies B and D, commanded by Capt. George S. Holman, were holding the skirmish line in front of Fort Sumner against several assaults. At 2:20 P.M. Holman reported that his squadron had three wounded troopers and was out of forage and ammunition. One of the wounded, John Gillespie of Company D, died in Washington on July 20. Gillespie was thirty-two years old and was one of the first Bay Staters to join the regiment. A simple peddler before the war, he is buried in Arlington National Cemetery.[38]

Reinforcements from the Army of the Potomac continued to arrive throughout the afternoon, including 1,689 men from VI Corps and 3,500 from XIX Corps. That brought the total from XIX Corps up to 4,300, with two more divisions due to arrive shortly.

Late in the afternoon General Wright sent two of his VI Corps divisions past Fort Reno toward Rockville. General Ricketts was en route from Baltimore with his 3rd Division.

During the night, Lieutenant Colonel Crowninshield held the forward skirmish line behind Rockville, supported by Major Fry a few miles back. Lowell was ordered to report to General Wright at Fort Reno. He brought thirty-eight enemy prisoners with him. Near sunset Crowninshield sent a dispatch advising General Hardin that the rebels continued to occupy the town in strength and that there were reports of another brigade on the other side of the town. He informed Hardin that he

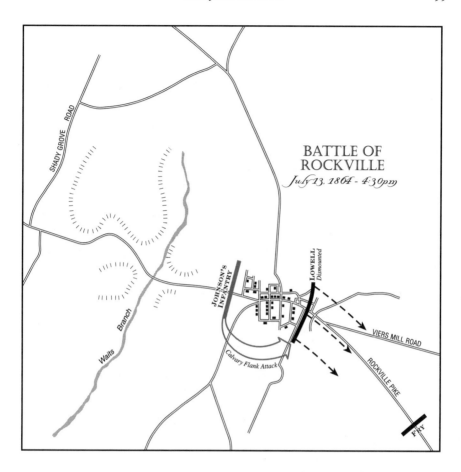

BATTLE OF
ROCKVILLE
July 13, 1864 - 4:30pm

had sent a scouting party out and that he would update Hardin as soon as the scouts reported in.

A little later he sent a second dispatch advising Hardin that "The rebels are still in Rockville. Shall I advance in the morning or not? Men and horses are quite tired. Horses have (many of them) had no water or forage to-day."[39]

Meanwhile, Lowell met with General Wright, who put him in charge of the cavalry force that would lead the pursuit of the rebels at daybreak.[40] He rode back to the skirmish line at Rockville that night with the new orders.

Thursday July 14 promised to be another hot day. Shortly after sunrise Lowell sent Companies B, D, and M down the River Road to the old camp at Muddy Branch. Their mission was to cover the Potomac crossings. Lowell led the remaining nine companies and Fry's cavalry through Rockville toward Poolesville, in advance of Wright's infantry. At 11:30 A.M. they reached Dawsonville, ten miles west of Rockville. Lowell reported that the rebel infantry had crossed the Potomac at White's or Conrad's Fords or the ford near the Monocacy. He estimated that the

Confederate rear guard was about an hour or two in front of him. According to a loyal citizen, the trains and stolen property had passed through Poolesville early in the morning and were probably across the river.[41]

In the afternoon Lowell marched to Poolesville, where he found the rebels in force. They opened on the Union troopers with two guns and, after a sharp skirmish, fell back in the direction of Edwards Ferry.

Wright's infantry reached the outskirts of Poolesville at about 6 P.M., completing a thirty-mile march in twenty-four hours on dusty roads and through excessive heat. The trains were scattered along the road and the last of them did not arrive until midnight. That night Wright tried to communicate with General Hunter at Harper's Ferry but to no avail. Now in his first independent command, Wright suddenly found reasons to delay. He wrote Halleck that he had only ten thousand men from his own corps plus five hundred from XIX Corps, "which, unless I overrate the enemy's strength, is wholly insufficient to justify the following up of the enemy on the other side of the Potomac. I presume this will not be the policy of the War Department, and I shall, therefore, wait instructions before proceeding farther, which I hope to receive by the time the 19th Corps arrives."[42]

While Wright awaited instructions, the Confederates completed their crossing of the Potomac unhindered. The wagonloads of loot and booty, as well as the distraught prisoners, were sent south while Early's main body camped near Leesburg for the night, covered by McCausland's cavalry brigade and the stragglers still operating north of the Potomac.

With Wright halted at Poolesville, Washington was trying to find out where Early was headed. Colonel Lazelle, commanding the remainder of Lowell's old cavalry brigade at Falls Church, was ordered to send a scouting party toward the Manassas Mountains to find the enemy's advance guard. The scouts returned and reported that all was quiet.

During the fighting at Rockville ten companies of the 2nd Massachusetts had taken on an entire Confederate brigade and held for three hours. The regiment proved it was capable of standing up to the best in the Confederate army. The experience the men gained would not be wasted during the trials of the coming months.

7 | Hard Marching

Instead of vigorously pursuing the retreating rebels, General Wright kept his column near Poolesville all day Friday, July 15, trying to establish communications with General Hunter, who had about forty-five hundred men in garrisons from Harper's Ferry to the Kanawha Valley covering the vital Baltimore and Ohio Railroad. His mobile force, commanded by Maj. Gen. George Crook, included two divisions of infantry and two small cavalry divisions totaling about eleven thousand officers and men present for duty.[1] Half of this force, commanded by Brig. Gen. Jeremiah Cutler Sullivan, was at Harper's Ferry. The rest, accompanied by General Crook, were en route from the rugged mountains west of Harper's Ferry.

General Hunter ordered Sullivan to take the troops at Harper's Ferry—about four thousand infantry and eighteen hundred cavalry—and link up with Wright. Sullivan marched out that afternoon. Hunter assured Washington that the remainder of Crook's forces would follow as soon as they arrived. Crook arrived at midnight, so Hunter ordered him to immediately overtake Sullivan and take command.

In Washington, Undersecretary of War Dana summed up the situation with remarkable accuracy in a wire to Grant at 11:30 that morning: "Our latest advises indicate that the head of the retreating rebel column has reached Ashby's Gap. Wright is not yet at Edwards Ferry. The enemy will doubtless escape with all his plunder and recruits, leaving us nothing but the deepest shame that has yet befallen us."

At 4 P.M. he wired Grant: "A signal officer at Point of Rocks says enemy crossed large wagon train at Noland's Ferry, yesterday morning, followed by the mass of their cavalry and infantry. Another signal officer, at Sugar Loaf Mountain, says they crossed 400 wagons at White's Ford, three miles below mouth of Monocacy, yesterday morning, moving in direction of Snicker's Gap. They were still crossing at 11 a. m."[2]

Toward evening two of Wright's couriers made it back from General Hunter's headquarters at Harper's Ferry. Another showed up after reaching Brig. Gen. Albion P. Howe on Loudoun Heights overlooking Harper's Ferry.[3] Wright learned from them that Sullivan's command had crossed the Potomac at Knoxville and was moving on Leesburg.

Wright, in command of the pursuit, was now in danger of being eclipsed by a more aggressive commander who was supposed to be under his command. He quickly wrote orders sending his troops across the Potomac at White's Ford and toward Leesburg the next morning.[4] At daybreak on the sixteenth, supported by two infantry regiments and the 1st New York Independent Battery, Lowell led the 2nd Massachusetts toward the river. Major Fry's command was left behind to await the arrival of the supply wagons and Ricketts's division, which were moving up the River Road from Washington.

As the troops passed through the village common at Poolesville, they were greeted by the sight of a man hanging by the neck at the end of a rope. The unfortunate soul was a soldier named Hymes from the 65th New York Infantry caught spying for the Confederates. He had been quickly tried by court-martial, found guilty, and hanged.[5] The sight served as a grim reminder of the fate of William Ormsby for the cavalrymen of the 2nd Massachusetts.[6]

Lowell's column crossed the Potomac at Whites Ford about noon.[7] The 2nd Massachusetts, leading the advance, struck Early's rear guard a few miles out of Leesburg in the afternoon but the rebels retreated before infantry supports could be brought up. After a desultory exchange of carbine fire, the rebels fell back into the cover of the wooded mountains at sunset. There was no sense of urgency. The Federal troopers dismounted and started setting up camp. Pickets were sent up the road ahead and down the country lanes on each side. Accompanied by a small escort, Colonel Lowell rode back to General Wright's headquarters for the next day's orders.

Wright's column marched out of Poolesville at 5 A.M. and waded across the Potomac behind the cavalry. It reached Leesburg in the late afternoon after a tiring march on a hot, humid day. The populace, who had welcomed Early's troops a few days before, watched glumly from behind curtained windows as the blue-clad column tramped through town. Wright halted the column at Clark's Gap a few miles to the southwest and his troops were all in roadside campgrounds by early evening.

Sometime during the day on the fourteenth, Colonel Mosby led a raiding party across the Potomac at the ford at Muddy Branch. The next day they rode on to Poolesville, arriving shortly after Wright's main body departed. For once Mosby's scouts failed him. They were unaware of the presence of Major Fry's command or the nearness of Wright's supply train. After a brief halt in Poolesville, Mosby and his men moved out of town a few miles and camped for the night. The next day the guerrillas rode to the cavalry post at Muddy Branch where, perhaps out of revenge, they burned the little blockhouse built the preceding spring by the men of the 2nd Massachusetts and scavenged the campsite, destroying whatever goods Major Thompson had left behind earlier in the week.[8]

A few miles away, during the late afternoon, the supply wagons and Ricketts's division joined Fry's cavalry, still undetected by the marauding guerrillas. Major Fry led the advance to Young's Island at Goose Creek, arriving after dark on the fifteenth. He reported that he was "saluted with a few shells from a battery near the mouth of Goose Creek." The next morning Fry's cavalry moved to the Virginia shore and cleared the area for Ricketts's division, which crossed during the day and went into camp.[9]

General Sullivan's command left Harper's Ferry, crossed the Potomac near Berlin, and marched toward Hillsborough.[10] Crook arrived about 11:30 A.M. He immediately sent out cavalry scouting parties and ordered Brig. Gen. Alfred Duffie to send fifteen hundred troopers toward Aldie.

Two regiments under Col. William Tibbits of the 21st New York Cavalry hit the rebel supply train at the junction of the Purcellville Road and the Leesburg Pike, capturing two hundred wagons and 150 prisoners before being overwhelmed by a large force of counterattacking Confederates. Tibbits retreated, losing all but fifty-four of the prisoners and eighty of the wagons. His command lost three men killed, six wounded, and eleven missing and presumably captured.[11]

Crook had begun moving his infantry down the Purcellville Road when Duffie sent word that Tibbits was engaged. At about 9 P.M. the advance guard hit the Confederate rear guard and there was a brief skirmish in the dark. After driving the Confederates back, Crook moved on to Purcellville and camped for the night. A courier sent to General Wright's headquarters at Clark's Gap returned with orders to attack the enemy rear guard with cavalry and infantry the next morning.

Crook ordered General Duffie to take the rest of his division and Col. James A. Mulligan's infantry brigade to Snicker's Gap. Duffie reached the gap about noon without meeting any opposition. He then moved down to Snicker's Ford on the Shenandoah River, where he found the Confederates strongly posted on the other side. He dismounted his cavalry and skirmished with the Confederates until nightfall. In time the firing became heavy as some of the Union skirmishers tried to force a crossing but were driven back.

For some unknown reason, instead of pursuing the retreating rebels, Wright, content with letting Crook chase the enemy, let his infantry spend the day in camp at Clark's Gap. He incorrectly assumed Early was retreating and wrote a hopeful dispatch to Washington early that evening: "I have no doubt that the enemy is in full retreat for Richmond, but the cavalry reports, which can hardly fail to be received to-night, will settle the matter. He is represented as much demoralized, though this is doubtful, as regards his old infantry force."[12]

Ricketts's division arrived at Clarksville at 6 P.M., so now Wright had his full force at hand. During the night, word came back from Crook that instead of an enemy force "in full retreat for Richmond," Wright faced an entrenched enemy who was still full of fight.

Crook moved out at 4 A.M. on the Snickersville Pike and headed through Snicker's Gap to the river. Ricketts and the rest of VI Corps would follow Crook through the gap. Brigadier General William H. Emory, who was at Leesburg with the XIX Corps's 1st Division and a brigade from VI Corps, was ordered to march through Clark's Gap and then through Snicker's Gap behind VI Corps. Lowell's cavalry was ordered to cover both flanks and the rear of the infantry until they had passed through the gaps. When the infantry column cleared the gap he was directed to leave a covering force and report to headquarters with the remainder of his troops.[13]

Crook sent General Duffie south through Ashby's Gap in order to come up on the left flank of the Confederate position at Snicker's Ford. Crook led his infantry through Snicker's Gap without encountering any Confederates. The best information available to General Crook indicated that the Confederates ahead at the Shenandoah were only a cavalry rear guard. He ordered Col. Joseph Thoburn to take three brigades and cross at Island Ford, two miles downriver. When Thoburn's men reached the far shore they were attacked by a large force of Confederate infantry. Hunkered down behind a stone wall and with a wide river at their backs, Thoburn's veterans fought with desperation. In a short time the action started to take on the appearance of an impending disaster.

Ricketts's division, marching at the head of VI Corps, arrived early in the evening. He looked over Thoburn's position along the River Road and decided it would not be prudent to cross. Without reinforcements the lodgment on the west bank could not hold, so Crook ordered Thoburn to retreat to the east bank. Thoburn lost 65 killed, 301 wounded, and 56 missing.[14] The rest of VI Corps arrived later that evening and followed Ricketts's division. Wright ordered XIX Corps to hold Snicker's Ford.

While Thoburn was engaged, General Hunter at Harper's Ferry sent orders to Col. Rutherford B. Hayes, commanding a reinforced brigade from Crook's division at Key's Ford on the Shenandoah, to move downriver and hit the Confederates at Snicker's Ford from behind. Hayes delayed but reported he could hear the firing from Thoburn's desperate defense. Hunter then ordered him to try to establish contact with Crook for further orders. Fortunately for Hayes's future political career, Thoburn managed to escape total annihilation. If he had been caught in the middle of the river like the Union force routed at Ball's Bluff, it is very likely that Hayes, because of his inaction that afternoon, would have been blamed.

Wright decided to send VI Corps downriver, combine with Hayes's force, and cross the river at Key's Ford, flanking the Confederates at Snicker's Ford. Lowell was ordered to send a small force to guard the supply train moving toward Key's Ford.

Upriver, Duffie and the cavalry fared only a little better than Thoburn. Duffie left the Shenandoah at 1 P.M. and marched toward Ashby's Gap. They camped that night near Upperville. The next morning, July 19, they moved through the gap, attacking and driving out a small body of rebels. They pushed on to the ford, where the command was met by heavy Confederate rifle and artillery fire. The cavalrymen made several charges across the river in the face of the Confederate fire, but each time they were beaten back with heavy casualties. Duffie pulled back to the gap that evening short of rations, forage, and ammunition. He lost twelve men killed, forty-four wounded, and sixty-eight missing.

When Wright learned that Duffie and Thoburn had met strong resistance at their attempted crossings, he decided that the Confederates must be thinly spread and that a crossing could be effected at Snicker's Ford. He sent out a dispatch canceling the move toward Key's Ford and instead directed his forces to remain in their positions.[15] Lowell was ordered to hold his cavalry, with the exception of the detachment at Snicker's Gap, and be ready to move across the river.[16]

At about 10 A.M. the main body of infantry moved down toward the river. Emory was a short distance south of the ford with XIX Corps. Ricketts, with VI Corps, was on the main road. Crook took up a position behind Emory, ready to cover both crossings. During the night some artillery had been positioned to cover the crossings. At sunrise the skirmish line was pushed to the edge of the covering brush and trees. A battle line moved into place behind the skirmishers to provide cover when they moved across. The only sound came from a few birds and the moving water. The order was quietly given for the skirmishers to begin crossing the river. They moved warily from the protection of the trees, first in small groups, then in a continuous line. At Island Ford, two regiments, the 37th Massachusetts and the 2nd Rhode Island, made the initial crossing. The men dashed into the stream and gained the opposite bank, only to find it was an island. They took to the water again and soon reached the rebel side, unopposed except for a handful of chickens in front of the Rhode Islanders. The fowl were quickly vanquished. When it became clear that the rebels had retreated, the supporting troops were formed into columns and moved down to the ford. The first regiments hurried across without stopping and then spent the rest of the day with wet shoes and socks. The men at the rear of the column were luckier, there was time for them to stop and remove their socks and shoes, which they draped over their shoulders.

The 2nd Massachusetts crossed over at about 11 A.M. and moved out toward Berryville, covering the front. Pickets were sent down the small country lanes on either side of the main road. As soon as General Wright was across he sent a wire to General Hunter at Harper's Ferry advising him that he was sending a wagon train to Harper's Ferry to gather rations and ammunition. Other events shaped the next movements. As Wright was pushing his troops across the Shenandoah, Brig. Gen. William Averell commanding Crook's other cavalry division, encountered a large Confederate force near Winchester. A fierce firefight developed, but the rebels retreated when Averell sent in the last of his reserves. Averell decided not to pursue. The next morning Averell discovered the Confederates had abandoned their positions during the night, so he moved on to Winchester.

Word of Averell's success reached Wright during the morning as the Union cavalry occupied Winchester. In addition, Wright's scouts reported that Early was moving toward Front Royal and Strasburg. Wright, mindful of his orders to return to the Army of the Potomac as soon as possible, concluded that the object of his expedition had been accomplished. In the afternoon he ordered the VI and XIX Corps to turn around and move toward Washington. He ordered General Crook to move toward Winchester by way of Berryville and join General Averell. In Wright's mind the pursuit was over.

General Duffie, still at Ashby's Gap, was ordered to return to Snicker's Gap. A relief train of ten wagons moved out with needed rations and ammunition and five ambulances to carry Duffie's wounded. On the way back the next day Duffie reported that his troops had succeeded in capturing six of Mosby's guerrillas while "breaking up their den at what is called 'The Trap.'"

Wright proved to more efficient in retreat than in the advance. The movement of Wright's command almost took on the appearance of a rout. The VI and XIX

Corps marched most of the night, passing through Leesburg on the Leesburg-Alex-andria Pike. The only losses during the retreat occurred in the early evening, when a group of guerrillas struck a portion of the VI Corps train near Leesburg, capturing a number of sick and wounded men. [17]

The next day the troops passed through Dranesville, the site of Captain Reed's defeat earlier in the year. The Leesburg-Georgetown Turnpike branched off to the left just beyond Dranesville, leading directly to the Chain Bridge, but Wright de-cided to turn north at the Peach Grove post office rather than follow the road to Georgetown. The army camped that night near Battery Vermont on the north side of the Potomac.

As the VI and XIX Corps troops moved into camp, preparations were made to muster and pay the men and issue them new uniforms and shoes. Wright antici-pated this would take two days, after which VI Corps would be sent back to City Point and XIX Corps assigned to the Washington defenses.

The 2nd Massachusetts returned to Camp Ayr at Vienna, where the men spent the day washing and repairing clothes and the regimental blacksmiths and farriers replaced worn horseshoes and equipment. Some time was spent getting the camp in order because it had "been occupied by the 16th New York while were gone and they have turned everything upside down in regular Dutch style. The more such Regts. Uncle Sam has in his service the poorer he is."[18]

That evening Charles Dana summed up the past twelve days in a dispatch to John Rawlins, Grant's chief of staff:

> The pursuit of Early, on the whole, has proved an egregious blunder, relieved only by Averell's success at Winchester, in which he captured 4 guns and some prisoners. Wright and Crook accomplished nothing, and Wright started back as soon as he got where he might have done something worthwhile. As it is, Early has got off with the whole of his plunder, and Hunter will hardly be able to break up the railroad beyond what can be repaired in a short time. Had Wright remained in the Valley the com-bined forces might have made a sure campaign, at least against the railroad and the crops.[19]

At about the same time Dana's wire was being dispatched to City Point, anoth-er, more ominous, telegram came in to Grant's headquarters from General Hunter at Harper's Ferry. Hunter's wire, sent at 8:45 P.M., advised Grant that officers and men returning from the front claimed Crook had met with disaster and that one of his brigades had been captured.

Two hours later Hunter sent a second wire reporting that Crook's "Second Bri-gade of cavalry has stampeded. I shall do all I can to check it. I have no official information from the front. All agree in saying that the rebel cavalry flanked our position. Will send you all the news I get."[20]

The next morning, when the extent of Crook's defeat became apparent, the XIX Corps and Lowell's cavalry were ordered to report to General Wright. Colonel Gamble was ordered to send all available cavalry at the Giesboro remount camp.

The reports from Crook and Hunter suggested that the defeat was the result of cowardice on the part of Averell's cavalry. Secretary of War Edwin M. Stanton and General Halleck, instead of offering useful advice or ordering up help, told Hunter that "Summary punishment, by drum head court martial, should be imposed upon those of your command who are guilty of cowardice in the face of the enemy."[21]

Wright ordered the VI and XIX Corps and all the available cavalry, commanded by Lowell, to immediately begin preparing for movement. Each man was to carry four days' rations and an additional eight days' rations were to be loaded in the wagons. The men were ordered to carry fifty rounds of ammunition and an additional sixty rounds per man were to be loaded into the wagons. The cavalry was ordered to load three days' forage. All of this had to be completed before sunrise on July 26.

A heavy rain began falling early in the morning on the twenty-fifth and lasted most of the day, hampering Wright's preparations. General Hunter reported that skirmishing along the Harper's Ferry picket line started at sunrise. When General Crook reported that infantry and cavalry were pursuing him, Hunter ordered him to cross the Potomac and fall back on Maryland Heights. As a further precaution, trains on the Baltimore and Ohio Railroad were stopped at Harper's Ferry and Camden Station in Maryland.

During the afternoon it seemed likely that another devastating raid was on the way. In less than a month, the Union army had failed to stop the Confederates. The next morning, General Wright moved out on the Rockville road toward the Monocacy. The VI Corps had a little over eleven thousand men, and XIX Corps was on the way from Washington with an additional eight thousand troops. Halleck sent a wire to Grant at 11 A.M. overestimating the size of the rebel force and pleading for Grant to send additional reinforcements.

Halleck, the archetypal bureaucrat seeking to avoid responsibility, only acted as a reporter. That had been his role in the raid earlier in the month. This time Grant tried to get Halleck to assume a responsible role. In a 12:30 P.M. telegram that may have crossed wires with Halleck's, he wrote:

> General Crook's dispatches indicate the probability of another raid north by the enemy. It takes a long time for dispatches to come here and go back, during which conditions may change; consequently it is absolutely necessary that some one in Washington should give orders and make dispositions of all the forces within reach of the line of the Potomac. No force has gone from here to re-enforce Early unless it may be odd regiments. Deserters come in every day, enabling us to keep track of every change the enemy makes.[22]

Meanwhile, Wright had moved out on the Rockville road seeking to link up with General Hunter at Point of Rocks, South Mountain, or Harper's Ferry. The next morning, July 27, the 2nd Massachusetts led the way, moving out at 3 A.M., followed by the main body an hour later. The XIX Corps trailed Lowell's cavalry, then came VI Corps, and then the wagon train. The route was along the Frederick

Pike through Gaithersburg, Middlebrook, Nealsville, Clarksburg, and Hyattstown, where they would camp that night.

Lowell was ordered to take the cavalry to the banks of the Monocacy River. For the men, who had just completed two weeks of hard duty, the march was unreasonable. "Still on the march destination unknown." wrote one of the men. "We camp tonight within one mile of Rockville Md. Our rations gave out yesterday, beging is now the order of the day. Hard tack and salt pork is held at a premium."[23]

Cavalry reinforcements were on the way. Halleck's headquarters informed General Wright that three battalions, totaling 1,363 men, from the Army of the Potomac had landed in Washington and were on their way to join the 2nd Massachusetts. Marching orders for Wright's infantry went out before sunrise. Secretary of War Stanton wired Grant that the troops would march to the Monocacy River and halt on the eastern side to await orders.[24] He followed that message with a dispatch to Halleck that gave him sole command of all Union forces in Maryland, West Virginia, northern Virginia, and southern Pennsylvania—and sole responsibility for the defense of the nation's capital.[25]

This was a bureaucrat's worst nightmare come alive, and Halleck was the consummate bureaucrat. Only two other dispatches were issued from Halleck's headquarters that fateful evening. The first, sent at 8:45 P.M., advised Grant about the bridges on the Rapidan and that Crook would join up with Wright at the Monocacy or Harper's Ferry. The other dispatch, generated by Halleck's staff, was to General Auger and dealt with the disposition of certain batteries in the Washington defenses. Forced to take command, Halleck disappeared for the rest of the night, perhaps suffering from a mild case of shock. In spite of his fears, the Union troops now under his command were well placed to defend against any raid on the North. All that was needed was a single coordinating leader.

General Averell, commanding Crook's 2nd Cavalry Division, was at Hagerstown, Maryland. His troops were covering the upper Potomac fords. Forewarning what would subsequently occur, he asked Crook for reinforcements: "If the enemy move up on my right, as they seem likely to do, Chambersburg will be entirely exposed, unless I can get some cavalry to operate in that direction."[26]

Skirmishing continued all day along Averell's line. The rebels made several attempts to cross but retreated each time Union troops came up.

Wright's force was on the road at sunrise on July 28 and reached the Monocacy near Frederick at 9 A.M. He advised General Halleck that all was quiet north of the Potomac and that he was awaiting orders from General Hunter as previously instructed. At about noon Hunter sent orders directing Wright to march to Harper's Ferry immediately. The VI Corps was ordered to take the shortest route through Frederick and Harper's Ferry, march to Jefferson, a small village on the western side of the Catoctin Mountains, and camp there for the night. The XIX Corps and the wagon train were to follow. Lowell's cavalry was ordered to continue screening the front and left flank of the column.

Reports came in throughout the day that the rebels were running threshing machines, harvesting the crops in the Shenandoah that would provide Lee's army with bread for at least a few more months.[27] The next morning Wright passed through Harper's Ferry and joined Crook's command at Halltown. This was the first time the Californians had been through Harper's Ferry, and the beauty of the area had an impact on Sam Corbett, who recorded in his diary: "Marching along with dust by the wholesale and have enough [heat] to pop corn. Passed through Harper's Ferry at 10 AM. This must have been quite a pretty place before the war, the scenery is very romantic."[28]

Although there were no Confederates north of the Potomac, Mosby was reported to be in Leesburg on the twenty-eighth, and Halleck feared that he might attempt a crossing at Edwards Ferry and attack Wright's supply wagons.[29]

The only troops in position to intercept Mosby were the Union cavalry at Muddy Branch, where the command confusion that gripped Washington in the last days of July was being repeated. On July 26, Maj. John M. Waite of the 8th Illinois Cavalry was ordered to Muddy Branch to relieve the 1st Battalion, 2nd Massachusetts. The orders relieved Major Thompson and the battalion "from the duty of picketing the fords of the Potomac from the mouth of the Monocacy to Great Falls." When Waite arrived at Muddy Branch, Major Thompson, supposedly in command of the "Cavalry Forces, Upper Potomac," found himself in a difficult position: Waite's commission was dated earlier than Thompson's, thus making Waite his superior.

Waite wasted no time taking charge. He sent a detachment of 8th Illinois troopers under Lt. John W. DeLaney to scout the Potomac fords. The patrol crossed the river at Conrad's Ferry and proceeded to within a mile and a half of Leesburg. They learned from prisoners that Mosby and White were moving into Leesburg with about four hundred men and that Early was in Upperville with ten thousand troops. While the patrol was out, Waite set up pickets along the river from Monocacy to the Great Falls.

At noon on July 29 General Wright was spread out on the road to Harper's Ferry. Halleck, fearing that Mosby would attack Wright's wagon train, ordered Waite to "collect your cavalry and afford such protection as you are able to any trains which may be on the road between the enemy and Washington."

In response to this order Thompson and Waite moved their force to Poolesville. At the same time Mosby moved his command toward the Potomac. He sent three companies across the river at Cheek's and Noland's Fords. The remainder of his force, including his artillery, remained on the south bank. One company remained at the fords on the north bank while the other two companies, commanded by Lt. Joseph Nelson, marched toward Adamstown on the Baltimore and Ohio Railroad. Nelson was ordered to attempt to capture a train and try to disrupt communications with Baltimore but he was too late to capture the Baltimore train. The raiders reached Adamstown early in the morning. There they "found the store open and the shops running and the citizens enjoying an Arcadia of peace. Our sudden and totally unexpected incursion gave them their first taste of war; and if it was not altogether agreeable, you may be sure we made it sufficiently pungent to them. Our first care was to cut down a telegraph pole and snap the wire. After which we proceeded to provide for our families, and appropriated to our own use, with liberal hand and joyous hearts 'sundry goods, wares and merchandises' with which we found the shelves of the only store well laden."

Unfortunately for the enterprising guerrillas, the storeowner convinced Lieutenant Nelson "that in spite of his surroundings, he was an original, unadulterated secessionist and entitled to our protection and admiration. I cannot do justice to the feelings of disappointment and disgust with which we relinquished our booty. Much of it, however was of such a character that it could not be restored, and many of the boys moved away with their heads as light as their hands, if their hearts were heavier." From Adamstown, the guerrillas skirted eastward around Sugar Loaf Mountain, then toward the river. On the way, they were a little bit luckier. "Alongside the road we came to a country store over which the owner did not succeed in raising the 'secesh flag' in time to save himself. His stock consisted for the most part of 'wet goods', which were clearly contraband of war; and the work of confiscation proceeded promptly and without interruption."

The revelry was cut short when word came that Waite and Thompson were moving up the canal towpath to try to cut them off from the river. The raiders began moving toward the ford, but their pace was slowed because the column was forced to stop twice to settle altercations between inebriated guerrillas. Two of the rebels were left by the roadside to fight it out and the advancing Union cavalry picked them up. Lieutenant DeLaney, back from the south side of the river, was picketing the mouth of the Monocacy with only eighteen men when the disorganized rebels rode up. Encouraged by the "wet goods" they had consumed earlier, the guerrillas joyfully and recklessly attacked DeLaney's little band. While one group engaged the Union troopers in front, "[Lt.] Harry Hatcher and Major Hibbs with Ned Rector and several others had gotten around in the rear of the pickets and, charging upon them unexpectedly killed or captured the whole party."[30]

Captains Eigenbrodt and Manning, approaching with two companies of Californians, heard the gunfire ahead and galloped up. The rebels escaped across the river at Noland's Ford, taking Pvt. Samuel Maddox of Company F, who was scouting ahead of the column. The Union troopers opened fire on the fleeing guerrillas but with only slight effect. Later Majors Thompson and Waite sent almost identical dispatches to Washington stating: "I am here with 600 cavalry. My scouting parties are in all directions toward the river. One has just come in from Conrad's Ferry and below. No enemy has crossed or is known to be near the river at those places. Mosby was in Leesburg yesterday with 400 men and three cannons, and has probably moved up or down."

The only difference in the dispatches was that Thompson closed with: "I will let you know if anything of importance occurs below the Monocacy."

Waite's dispatch closed with his losses: "DeLaney [of the 8th Illinois] wounded; 2 men killed, 3 wounded, 7 or 8 prisoners and about 25 horses and equipments captured."

The time it was sent was not noted; however, it was received at 6 P.M.[31] The next

day Major Waite charged that Thompson had failed to support Lieutenant Delaney's command in the fight with Mosby: "When eighteen of my men were fighting
Mosby's whole command yesterday, I am informed Major Thompson was within
supporting distance."[32]

J. H. Taylor, Auger's chief of staff, wrote back: "The major general commanding
desires that you ascertain the truth of this report, and in your communication state
specifically the distance of Major Thompson or his command from the scene of the
skirmish, and the means within his control of knowing the true state of affairs."

The rest of the story is not recorded in the *Official Records*. It was too minor an
incident to be the subject of a Court of Inquiry. However, the next day, August 2,
Major Waite, not Thompson, was reinforced with a detachment of cavalry "to enable you more satisfactorily to keep this side of the river clear of guerrillas." This
last was clearly a slap at Major Thompson.

De Witt Clinton Thompson was a prominent and highly respected San Franciscan. He had been a member of the Vigilante Committee of 1856. He was a land-
owner, a prominent agricultural developer, a banker, and a former deputy sheriff of
San Francisco County. In 1864 he was thirty-eight years old, ten years or so older
than most of the other officers in the 2nd Massachusetts.

Major Thompson had a unique position. Nominally he was in command of the
"Cavalry Forces, Upper Potomac." The title was somewhat of a sham, but while
Colonel Lowell was away commanding the cavalry around Washington, no one
questioned Thompson's authority. Lowell used the camp at Muddy Branch as sort
of a "rest and recreation" post for the 2nd Massachusetts while it was engaged in
the arduous work of fighting Mosby. Throughout the previous year the battalions
had rotated through Muddy Branch, and Thompson was always in command of
whatever battalion was assigned to the camp. He lived reasonably comfortably
there until July 8, when he was forced to leave because of Early's advance. He
returned to the post with the 1st Battalion after the regiment broke off its pursuit of
Early.

The order sending Major Waite to Muddy Branch in effect relieved Thompson
without the offer of a comparable position elsewhere. The charges that he had
failed to support DeLaney and the subsequent dispatches from Washington left
Thompson with no choice. Unsupported by Colonel Lowell and in an untenable
position because of Waite's orders, he submitted his resignation to General Sheridan. The resignation was accepted on August 9.

Thompson returned to California and after the war was active in veterans' affairs. He wrote a brief history of the California Hundred and Battalion for the state
Adjutant General and was generally accepted as the leader of the veterans of the
California Hundred and Battalion. He prospered in real estate and was responsible
for the development of much of Oakland. He died in Santa Rosa on May 13, 1919.[33]

While Thompson and Waite were off chasing Mosby's guerrillas, other Confederates were crossing with considerable force at Falling Waters and Hagerstown.
General Averell, whose headquarters was in Hagerstown, moved his division back

from the river to cover the approaches to Baltimore. As the afternoon wore on, it was clear that a rebel force was across the Potomac, its size and exact location unknown. Even more ominous, no one knew exactly where the rebels were going.

General McCausland led the twenty-eight-hundred-man rebel force, which had crossed the river at McCoy's Ford on July 29. It quickly brushed away a thirty-five-man cavalry picket led by Lt. Hancock McLean. Averell, moving north on parallel roads, kept his division between the rebels and the approaches to Baltimore and Washington. He camped that night at Greencastle, about nine miles from Chambersburg. He remained there even after receiving several dispatches warning him that McCausland was heading for Chambersburg. After brushing Averell's pickets aside, McCausland continued north after dark, arriving outside Chambersburg at about 11:30 P.M. The rebels fired a couple of cannon shots into the town, then moved into the business district at about 3:30 A.M. on July 30. He demanded $500,000 in ransom from the city fathers. The wily Pennsylvanians, knowing Averell was nearby, stalled for time. To their chagrin, Averell failed to make a move to save the city. Within a few hours, downtown Chambersburg was in flames and McCausland was headed south.

A total of 527 private and public buildings were destroyed. The loss in personal property was put at $915,137.24, a staggering loss for any community. One elderly citizen died of a heart attack. Three rebels were killed, including Capt. Caulder A. Bailey of the 8th Virginia Cavalry, who was left behind in a state of drunkenness. As the town burned around them, angry citizens beat Bailey to death.[34]

General Halleck, true to character, was slow to react. By 10 A.M. on the thirtieth, Washington had concluded the Confederates were heading north toward Pennsylvania.[35] Instead of issuing immediate orders to counter the threat, Halleck instructed General Hunter at Harper's Ferry to "Please report where your forces are and by what routes they will move. This information is absolutely necessary here in order to direct the march of General Emory's force."

Hunter advised Halleck that Wright's troops at Halltown were so fatigued and scattered that they would not be able to move that morning. He then described his dilemma: "If I go toward the fords over which he has passed to cut off his retreat to the Valley, he turns to the right and escapes by the lower fords of the Potomac. If I push on toward Frederick and Gettysburg, I give him a chance to return down the Valley unmolested."

He concluded the wire with a plea for Halleck to take command: "Please with your superior chances for information with regard to the whole position of affairs, direct me what is best to be done."[36]

After pleading his case to Halleck Hunter ordered Wright to start his infantry moving toward Frederick. The cavalry backtracked through Harper's Ferry, then moved to South Mountain Pass to cover the approaches from the east. On July 31, Sam Corbett wrote: "Passed through Harper's Ferry last night and tried to ford the Shenandoa river but could not do it. Everything at the town was a complete jam. Our Regt. managed to get through one at a time and went into camp at South Mountain Pass three o'clock this morning. The Rebels are supposed to be in Pensa.

There is quite a little settlement here, the ladies all go barefoot and Rye coffee without sugar is the principal beverage."[37]

The march proved to be one of the most difficult Wright's troops ever made. In three days they had gone from the Monocacy River through Harper's Ferry to Hall-town, where they stopped one night. They then marched back through Harper's Ferry to Frederick, all in the heat of a Virginia July. One wit wrote that "Some stragglers that fell out near here and remained until we came back saved them-selves three days' rest and cheated the government out of about thirty miles' march-ing. During the past week so many thirsty men had passed through the area the wells around Frederick and along the way were pumped dry."[38]

Averell finally caught up with McCausland on August 7 at Moorefield, Virginia. At dawn the Union cavalry charged into the sleeping Confederate camp, capturing or killing almost all of the men in one of McCausland's two brigades. Confederate losses "were 150 killed, wounded, or missing, 420 taken prisoner, three battle flags and all of the command's artillery lost, 678 horses killed or captured, and untold amounts of equipment lost.[39]

The burning of Chambersburg shocked the North. The press clamored for an end to rebel raids north of the Potomac. With 1864 a presidential election year, the administration faced a very real crisis of public confidence. General-in-Chief Grant would have to take immediate action.

8 | Sheridan Takes Command

The burning of Chambersburg set Grant in motion. He suspended a proposed attack on the Weldon Railroad south of Petersburg and ordered one of the cavalry divisions that was to make the attack back to Washington. In addition. the remainder of XIX Corps at Bermuda Hundred was directed to move to Washington. He decided to combine the various divisions and departments in northern Virginia into a single command called the Middle Military Division. After the War Department rejected Maj. Gen. William Franklin as its commander, he proposed giving the job to his old friend David Hunter, with Maj. Gen. Philip Sheridan commanding the forces in the field. Halleck and Stanton objected to both men.[1] They blamed Hunter for the success of Early's July invasion and thought Sheridan was too young. Grant insisted they were the best choice. Knowing that Grant had the president's ear, Stanton and Halleck finally relented.

Grant made his desires clear in a dispatch to Halleck:

> I am sending General Sheridan for temporary duty whilst the enemy is being expelled from the border. Unless General Hunter is in the field in person, I want Sheridan put in command of all the troops in the field, with instructions to put himself south of the enemy and follow him to the death. Wherever the enemy goes let our troops go also. Once started up the valley they ought to be followed until we get possession of the Virginia Central Railroad. If General Hunter is in the field give Sheridan direct command of the Sixth Corps and Cavalry division. All the cavalry will reach Washington in the course of to-morrow.[2]

Phillip Henry Sheridan was born in Albany, New York, on March 6, 1832, the son of Irish immigrants. When he was very young, the family settled in Somerset, Ohio. He entered West Point in 1848. He was suspended during his senior year for leaving a formation in a fit of anger and chasing a cadet officer with a bayonet. After a time in his father's store, he returned to "the Point" and graduated in 1853, thirty-fourth in a class of forty-nine. He was sent to the Rio Grande as a brevet second lieutenant, then to the Pacific Northwest. At the outbreak of the war he was assigned to the 13th Infantry and then as quartermaster and commissary to Halleck's troops during the Corinth campaign. In May 1862 he managed to obtain an appointment as colonel of the 2nd Michigan Cavalry. From that point on, his military star rose quickly. Sheridan served with distinction at Booneville and Stone's River, where he commanded a brigade and was instrumental in saving Maj. Gen. William Rosecrans's army. He was promoted to major general and given command of XX Corps. He fought at Chickamauga, Chattanooga, and Missionary Ridge, where his troops were in the forefront of the attack that wrecked Lt. Gen. Braxton Bragg's Army of the Tennessee. Grant appointed him commander of the Army of the Potomac's Cavalry Corps in the spring of 1864, and the Union cavalry became a potent force under his command during the summer campaign.

He was a small, black-haired, bullet-headed man. He covered his odd-shaped head with a flat, nonregulation black hat. Pugnacious and combative, he rode a large black horse and it was said that "he rolled and bounced upon the back of his steed much as an old salt does when walking up the aisle of a church after a four years' cruise at sea."[3]

He had an appeal to his soldiers that transcended his physical appearance, and he would need every bit of his personal charisma to weld his new command into an army. He inherited a fragmented, dispirited, worn out, mixed bag of Union soldiers from divergent commands. His troops came from the Army of the Potomac, the Washington defenses, West Virginia, the garrison at Harper's Ferry, and the Baltimore defenses.

Sheridan arrived in Washington on August 4 and, accompanied by Secretary of War Stanton, went to meet President Lincoln.[4] The president candidly told him that Stanton had objected to his assignment. Lincoln said that he had agreed with Stanton, but now that Grant had worked his way through the politics of the situation, he felt satisfied with what had been done and "hoped for the best."[5]

In Washington and at City Point there was a determination to ensure that the Shenandoah Valley would no longer be allowed to supply the Confederate troops around Petersburg or serve as a highway for invading Confederate forces. The North, with its overwhelming manpower advantage, simply could not permit another debacle like Early's July raid to occur again. After Lincoln saw Grant's dispatch to Halleck outlining Sheridan's orders,[6] he sent Grant a wire identifying the problem he had with Halleck and the rest of the commanders in the Washington area:

> I have seen your dispatch in which you say "put himself south of the enemy and follow him to the death. Wherever the enemy goes let our troops go also." This I think is exactly right as to how our forces should move. But please look over the dispatches you may have received from here even since you made that order, and discover, if you can, that there is any idea in the head of any one here, of "putting our army south of the enemy" or of "following him to the death" in any direction. I repeat to you it will neither be done nor attempted unless you watch it every day, and hour, and force it.[7]

Grant replied that he "would start in two hours for Washington" to meet with Hunter and Sheridan to be certain the command situation was clear to both. Bypassing the capital, he took a steamer north and then a train to General Hunter's headquarters on the Monocacy. Arriving there the next day, he found Hunter camped with the portion of XIX Corps that had moved up from City Point and "many hundreds of cars and locomotives belonging to the Baltimore and Ohio Railroad" near Harper's Ferry.

When Grant asked Hunter where the enemy was, he replied that he did not know. Hunter told Grant "that he was so embarrassed with orders from Washington moving him first to the right and then to the left that he had lost all traces of the enemy."

Grant said he would find the Confederates for Hunter and immediately ordered the locomotives and cars made ready to transport the infantry back to Halltown. He reasoned that the Shenandoah Valley was so important to the Confederates that they would "in a very short time be found in front of our troops moving south." The cavalry and wagon trains were ordered to start by road as soon as possible.[8]

Grant then wrote out instructions for Hunter explaining that he would be the administrative department head and Sheridan would command the troops in the field. Hunter demurred, saying that Halleck seemed to distrust him so much it would be better to relieve him. Knowing that Halleck wanted Hunter out, Grant reluctantly agreed. He sent a wire to Sheridan ordering him to report to the Monocacy immediately. Sheridan took a special train but did not arrive until after the troops had started moving toward Halltown. Grant told him what had occurred and gave him the instructions that he had prepared for General Hunter. Sheridan was now in command of about thirty thousand men, including eight thousand cavalrymen. The mobile force, called the Army of the Shenandoah, was made up of General Wright's VI Corps with three divisions, a division from XIX Corps commanded by General Emory, and Crook's two small divisions from the Army of West Virginia. By Union reckoning, the army was about the same size as Early's army.[9]

The troops were unaware of the command changes, although one old soldier got a glimpse of Grant at Monocacy and commented that he hated "to see that old cuss. Whenever he's around there's sure to be a big fight on hand."[10]

The 2nd Massachusetts marched to Point of Rocks and camped there on the night of August 4. The Baltimore and Ohio railroad passes through a gap in the mountains at Point of Rocks and the regiment covered the gap and the railroad while the trains carried the infantry to Harper's Ferry.[11]

Sheridan arrived at Harper's Ferry at 7:30 P.M. on August 6. He sent a wire to Grant in Washington advising that things were "somewhat confused" but that he would quickly straighten them out.[12] He ordered Colonel Lowell to make a reconnaissance on the south side of the Potomac toward Martinsburg. The rest of the troops in the newly created Middle Military Division were ordered to concentrate on Harper's Ferry and Halltown.

Lowell and his men moved out at midnight and followed the canal towpath upriver.[13] The column arrived at Harper's Ferry in the early morning and stopped for five hours before moving on to Boonsboro and Petersville, arriving at the latter about noon. After a brief halt they returned to Harper's Ferry and Sandy Hook, about two miles away.[14]

The stay at Sandy Hook was very short. The regiment was again in the saddle and on the way through Harper's Ferry at 3:30 A.M. en route to a camp two miles beyond Halltown, where it at last settled down to await the arrival of the rest of the cavalry force.[15]

As the 2nd Massachusetts established the army's front at Halltown, Sheridan reorganized his cavalry. One cavalry division, the Army of the Potomac's 1st Cavalry Division, was available. It had been commanded by Brig. Gen. Alfred T. A. Torbert. Eventually Sheridan would have four divisions of cavalry, so Torbert, who was the senior cavalry officer, was given command of the force. Crook's two cavalry divisions, commanded by Generals Averell and Duffie, were at Pleasant Valley, and Brig. Gen. James H. Wilson's 3rd Cavalry Division was en route from City Point.[16]

Brigadier General Wesley Merritt was given command of the 1st Division. The division included Brig. Gen. George Custer's 1st Brigade, Brig. Gen. Thomas Devin's 2nd Brigade, and the Reserve Brigade, sometimes called the Regular Brigade because it was made up of Regular Army regiments, commanded by Col. Alfred Gibbs.[17]

Lowell was given command of a scratch brigade designated the 3rd Brigade. At first it included the 2nd Massachusetts, the 14th and 22nd Pennsylvania cavalry regiments, and detachments from the 5th New York and 3rd New Jersey cavalry regiments, plus Major Cole's battalion of Marylanders. The 14th and 22nd Pennsylvania regiments were detached from Averell's division. The 5th New York and 3rd New Jersey troops were part of Wilson's division, which was still en route. The 3rd Brigade was nominally part of General Merritt's division but operated independently during the opening days of the campaign.[18]

On August 9, the only units present were Merritt's 1st Cavalry Division and Lowell's semi-independent brigade. Sheridan's army thus began the campaign with about 21,500 effectives, including the cavalry.

Early's army in early August was unchanged from the force that had beaten Generals Hunter and Wallace and threatened Washington. It included his II Corps made up of three divisions commanded by Maj. Gen. Stephen D. Ramseur, Gordon, and Rodes, Maj. Gen. John C. Breckinridge's division, and Maj. Gen. Lunsford L. Lomax's cavalry division with four brigades. Brigadier Generals John D. McCausland, Bradley T. Johnson, and W. L. "Mudball" Jackson commanded the cavalry brigades. In mid-August Lee sent Maj. Gen. Joseph B. Kershaw's infantry division and Fitzhugh Lee's cavalry division. Before Kershaw's arrival, Early had approximately twenty thousand men.[19]

Confederate partisan forces, while not involved with the regular Confederate army, nevertheless made a small contribution by forcing Sheridan to use ninety-day militia units and the garrison at Harper's Ferry as guards for couriers and wagon trains. Any count of these irregulars is only speculation because most able-bodied Virginians in the area not enrolled in the army became guerrillas and bushwhackers whenever the opportunity arose.

Lowell's brigade was camped on the left of Sheridan's line, near the Shenandoah River. The rest of the army was camped in an arc curving to the right and covering the approaches to Harper's Ferry. The remainder of Merritt's division was on the extreme right near the crucial Baltimore and Ohio Railroad. General Early's forces were concentrated at Bunker Hill on the Valley Turnpike about halfway between Martinsburg and Winchester. Rebel scouting parties ventured as far as Charlestown, only two miles away from the Union forces at Halltown.

Within a week after Sheridan's arrival every man knew that something special was occurring; an army was being organized and a real leader was in charge. Even the more sophisticated and educated were not immune. One evening before the campaign started, Charles Lowell wrote his wife:

> I've been ever so busy lately; I've hardly had time to sleep or think, except Sunday, when I slept all day, having been up all the night before. I am to have the 3rd Brigade, 1st Division in the New Cavalry Corps, nothing very stunning, I fear but good enough for a beginner. General Merritt has the Division. Everything is chaos here, but under Sheridan is rapidly assuming shape. It was a lucky inspiration of Grant's or Lincoln's to make a Middle Military Division and put him in command of it; it redeems Lincoln's character and secures him my vote, if I have one. It is *exhilarating* to see so many cavalry about and to see things going *right* again.[20]

The campaign would determine control of the Shenandoah Valley and have a major effect on the outcome of the war. For the South, defeat would mean the war could not continue much longer. Lee was dependent on the food supplies that came from the Valley's rich farms. Without this source of supply it would only be a matter of time before he would be forced to surrender. In the war-weary North, 1864 was an election year. Another disastrous defeat in the Valley coupled with Grant's Pyrrhic victories in the spring campaign and Sherman's seemingly interminable flanking movements in Georgia could be enough to elect the Peace Democrats and cause the sundering of the Union. At no other time in the Civil War was battlefield victory so crucial. The war would be lost or won in the next six months.

Sheridan sent for Lt. John Meigs of the Engineer Corps. The son of General Meigs, he was an expert on the topography of the Valley. Sheridan said later that he even knew the details of each farmhouse. They spent several days closeted together while Lieutenant Meigs instructed the general on the Shenandoah's terrain. The payoff for the lessons would come as the campaign developed.

The Shenandoah Valley is about 150 miles long, extending in a southwesterly direction from the Potomac River in the north to Purgatory Mountain south of Lexington. It is bounded on the west by the Alleghenies and on the east by the Blue Ridge Mountains. The Alleghenies are rugged, mountainous, and sparsely settled, with only a few passes leading into the Valley. The Blue Ridge Mountains have numerous gaps located at convenient intervals, all capable of providing easy access for troops moving into and from the Valley. These gaps were a threat because they provided easy access to the left flank or rear of any army moving up the Valley. The upper gaps from Front Royal south were even more threatening because they offered direct access to railroads running southwest along the base of the mountains.

A peculiar feature at Strasburg and Front Royal compounded the tactical prob-

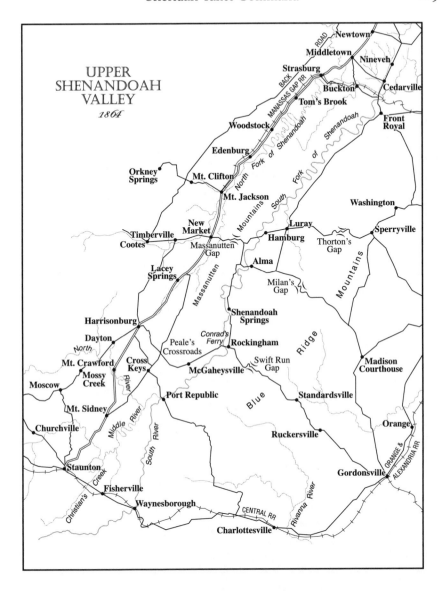

**UPPER
SHENANDOAH
VALLEY**
1864

lems. At this point the Valley is split into two parts by an isolated range paralleling the Blue Ridge called the Massanutten Mountain. The valley to the east of Massanutten Mountain is called the Luray Valley. With no roads crossing the mountain, it provided a "covered way" concealed from the valley on the west side. Front Royal is at the northern end of the Valley and Port Republic on the south.

At the northern end, the Shenandoah Valley is about fifty miles wide. The two main towns, both on the Baltimore and Ohio Railroad, are Martinsburg to the west and Harper's Ferry to the east. A macadamized road called the Valley Turnpike,

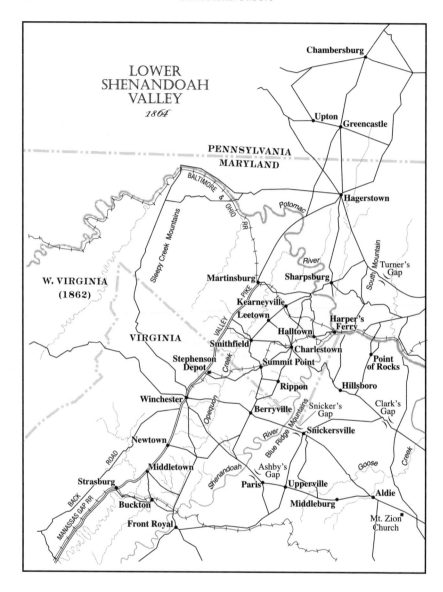

LOWER
SHENANDOAH
VALLEY
1864

starting at the Potomac, intersects the Baltimore and Ohio at Martinsburg. The turnpike continues to Winchester, about twenty miles below Martinsburg, and then runs southwest to Strasburg. From Strasburg it passes through Woodstock, Mount Jackson, New Market, Harrisonburg, and ends at Staunton.

Four railroads connect or run through the valley. In 1864 one of these, the Winchester Potomac Railroad, which ran between Harper's Ferry and Winchester, was inoperable. "Stonewall" Jackson had taken up most of its track in 1862.

The most northerly line running through the mountains, the Manassas Gap Railroad, left the Orange and Alexandria at Manassas Junction and passed through Thoroughfare Gap to Front Royal and Strasburg. At Strasburg it turned south to a terminus at Mount Jackson, about ten miles below Woodstock. The Orange and Alexandria left Manassas Station and ran south along the east side of the Blue Ridge, through Gordonsville and then to Charlottesville, where it turned west and passed through the Blue Ridge at Rockfish Gap before moving on to the upper Valley towns of Waynesboro and Staunton. At Staunton it turned south and passed through the Alleghenies, terminating at Covington, Virginia (now West Virginia). Another railroad, the Virginia Central, left the Orange and Alexandria at Gordonsville and ran east across the state to Richmond.

The last railroad, the Tennessee and Virginia, started at Charlottesville, ran south to Lynchburg, turned west through the Blue Ridge at Buford's Gap, and continued on to Knoxville, Tennessee.

The terrain between the Blue Ridge and the Alleghenies is made up of low, rolling hills ideally suited for cavalry operations. The road system, in addition to the Valley Turnpike, was adequate for the rapid movement of Civil War troops. In portions of the Valley, two smaller roads known as the Back Road and the Middle Road paralleled the turnpike. Numerous farm roads crossing the Valley tied the three north-south roads together. The Shenandoah River, fed by numerous east-west creeks, divides into two forks at Front Royal. The north fork, running along the western side of Massanutten Mountain, becomes a set of meandering creeks at Harrisonburg. The headwaters of the south fork, passing through the Luray Valley, are just below Port Republic.

By the end of the first week in August, Sheridan was ready to move up the Valley. In preparation for the move, the supply train was moved to Bolivar Heights near Harper's Ferry. Brig. Gen. John R. Kenly's brigade from XIX Corps was ordered to remain at Halltown. It would later be used to guard the wagon train.[21] On August 9 the remainder of the troops were furnished with three days' rations. The cavalry was issued two days' forage and told it would have to last five days.[22]

Sheridan sent a dispatch to Wilson in Washington urging him to hurry. "If you can get the whole of your division ready within three days, join me via Leesburg, Snickers Gap and Berryville."[23]

If the maneuver was to be a success, capturing the fords across the Opequon was crucial. Lowell's brigade was ordered to push the enemy picket line back so the movement would be concealed. Reveille sounded in the cavalry camps at 2:30 A.M. on August 10.[24] The 2nd Massachusetts and the rest of Lowell's brigade broke camp before sunrise and marched through Charlestown at about 10 A.M. following the Charlestown-Winchester Pike to the southwest. The pike first crosses the defunct Winchester Potomac Railroad at Summit Point Station. Just before reaching Summit Point, the advance guard reported that a Confederate picket line was ahead. The brigade formed into line of battle and Lowell sent skirmishers forward. The rattle of carbines soon sounded across the fields. The Confederates fell back and the brigade followed, moving slowly toward the Valley Turnpike. Thirteen prisoners were taken during the fighting before nightfall brought an end to the advance. Although the skirmishing was bloodless, the day's activities were not with out loss: Pvt. Alexander Forbes of Company A was killed when his pistol accidentally discharged, and Sgt. John Fletcher, also of Company A, was taken prisoner. That night the brigade camped about halfway between Summit Station and Winchester.[25]

General Torbert crossed the Winchester road at Summit Point with the rest of Merritt's division after Lowell moved through. They moved by back roads to a position near Berryville, providing a screen for the slower moving infantry columns and seizing the fords across Opequon Creek. The march went according to plan and by the end of the day the crossings over the Opequon were in Union hands. The infantry formed an arc northeast of Winchester with VI Corps across the Clifton-Winchester road, XIX Corps south of Clifton on the road to Berryville, and Crook's Army of West Virginia on the left at Berryville. Lowell covered the right flank below Summit Point and Torbert was on Crook's left.

On August 11 Lowell's brigade moved out toward Winchester covering VI Corps's right flank. Torbert's cavalry moved forward on the Millwood-Winchester road. As they neared the Valley Turnpike they found the rebels retreating up the Valley. When Sheridan received this intelligence he immediately ordered Torbert to drive for Newtown, about three miles south of Winchester, to cut off Early's retreat. Lowell was ordered to move his brigade through Winchester in pursuit.[26]

Valorus Dearborn, an A Company trooper, wrote of the march and skirmish: "Moved out at sunrise on an empty stomach, the boys are not too pleased at this. Co. A takes the advance and is in on the skirmish line, Captured one prisoner. Col. Lowell came up with the rest of the brigade. He changed direction to our left. Afternoon, joined the command and camped on the Ashby Pike, (White Post) Our forces advanced and engaged the enemy near Newton and were repulsed with a loss of 200 K W and M Water at Kamdan Springs. (Mineral water)."[27]

The three infantry corps moved south toward Newtown and went into camp for the night. Torbert skirmished with the rebels, but when Gordon's infantry division moved out from Newtown as rear guard, he was forced to fall back. Lowell's brigade went into camp with Torbert's cavalry about two miles north of Newtown.[28]

The 2nd Massachusetts led the 3rd Brigade's move to Newtown the next morning. At Newtown Devin's 2nd Brigade headed west toward Fawcett's Gap and then toward Cedar Creek on the back road running along the base of the Alleghenies. Lowell's brigade, followed by Custer's and Gibbs's brigades, moved down the Valley Turnpike toward Strasburg. Just beyond Middletown, on the heights above Cedar Creek, they came upon a rebel skirmish line. Lowell's brigade drove the rebels across Cedar Creek and reformed on Hupp's Hill.

The brigade held its position until a large infantry skirmish line arrived to relieve it in the late afternoon. The infantry camped along the north side of Cedar Creek. Lowell's brigade withdrew across the creek and camped with the Reserve Brigade west of the turnpike along Cedar Creek, covering the infantry's right flank.

The 1st Brigade covered the army's left flank east of the pike along the Shenandoah River.

Part of Wilson's cavalry division started out from Washington late that same afternoon. With Sheridan's force below Winchester, they could safely go through Snicker's Gap.

On the morning of the thirteenth, Sheridan sent Gibbs's Reserve Brigade on a reconnaissance toward Strasburg by way of the Valley Turnpike. Gibbs reported that the rebels were posted on Fisher's Hill, a strong position south of Strasburg overlooking the turnpike. Meanwhile, mail arrived in the 2nd Massachusetts camp, and the men took the opportunity to write home while the infantry advanced across Cedar Creek.[29]

The brigade was reorganized during the rest stop at Cedar Creek. The 14th Pennsylvania was ordered to report back to General Averell's division and the 5th New York and 3rd New Jersey troops were sent off to rejoin Wilson's division. The brigade now consisted of the 2nd Massachusetts, 22nd Pennsylvania, and Cole's Marylanders. During the day Duffie's small cavalry division arrived and went into camp along the Valley Turnpike.

Rumors began to reach Sheridan that Confederate reinforcements were on the way to Front Royal. One report said Lt. Gen. James Longstreet was on the march with thirty thousand men, and Fitz Lee was moving to reinforce Early with an additional ten thousand men.[30] Sheridan ordered Torbert to send a brigade out to determine the truth of the reports.

The next day, Col. N. P. Chipman arrived at Sheridan's headquarters with a dispatch Grant sent to Halleck on August 12. The message confirmed that "it is now certain two divisions of infantry have gone to Early and some cavalry and twenty pieces of artillery. This movement commenced last Saturday night. He [Sheridan] must be cautious and act now on the defensive until movements here force them to detach to send this way. Early's force, with this increase, cannot exceed 40,000, but this is too much for Sheridan to attack."[31]

Sheridan replied that

At the time the Sixth Army Corps was occupying the heights of Strasburg the enemy had taken position about three miles beyond and near the base of Signal Mountain. It did not appear that there was more there than their rear guard, with about twelve pieces of artillery. I was making preparations to attack them when your dispatch arrived. It did not appear as though they would make a stand, and looked more like an invitation for me to follow them up. I did not think it best to do so, and I have taken position on the south side of Cedar Creek. All the reports I hear, and have been hearing for some days, confirm your telegram that Longstreet is in the Valley, and that Fitz Lee's cavalry is making its way up the country and when last heard of was at Orange Courthouse. So far as I have been able to see there is not a military position in this Valley south of the Potomac. The position here is a very bad one, as I cannot cover the numerous roads that lead in on both of my flanks. . . . Mosby attacked the rear of my train this morning, enroute from Harper's Ferry, and burned six wagons.[32]

Sheridan's reference to the attack on his wagon train assumed much larger proportions after the war when members of Mosby's band tried to justify their role in the conflict. This relatively minor incident later became a subject of controversy and legend because the guerrillas claimed the attack forced Sheridan to retreat down the valley.

Mosby did not even report the attack to Lee until September 12, almost a month after the event and long after Sheridan had retreated. His report claimed that he had completely routed the eight-hundred-man guard force, taking more than two hundred prisoners, including three lieutenants, and killing or wounding several more Union troops. He also reported the capture or destruction of seventy-five loaded wagons and the capture of between seven hundred and eight hundred beef cattle, horses, and mules, as well as many other valuable stores. He listed his own losses as two men killed and three wounded from a force numbering more than three hundred men.[33]

Major John Scott, one of Mosby's guerrillas, said in his 1867 memoir that the train consisted of 150 wagons guarded by 250 cavalrymen and a brigade of infantry. According to Scott, all the wagons were burned and the attackers secured three hundred prisoners and more than nine hundred cattle, horses, and mules. In his mind, though, "the chief advantage derived from the blow which had been struck was, that Sheridan's army was compelled to fall back from Strasburg to Winchester, and subsist on short rations for a week."[34]

Sheridan convened a court of inquiry immediately after the affair. The court records include testimony and documents covering the raid. Unless the Union authorities were able to concoct a massive cover-up, which is inconceivable, the facts are clear.

Mosby attacked the rear of the wagon train around sunrise on August 13, setting fire to about twenty-five wagons and running off the teams for about forty wagons. The rear of the train was composed of the wagons of the cavalry Reserve Brigade and included "a few wagons carrying forage, ten wagons carrying subsistence stores and the various regimental and headquarters wagons."

Contrary to orders, the Reserve Brigade teams had been unhitched and were not ready to move when the wagons were attacked. After the guerrillas set fire to more than two dozen of the wagons the guard force extinguished the fires in all but six. Although the mule teams were captured, General Kenly was able to supply extra teams to bring most of the wagons to Winchester. The army's train included 525 wagons, of which fifty came from Gibbs's Reserve Brigade.[35] The members of the board concluded that the guard was insufficient for the number of wagons and the brigade quartermaster received a mild reprimand because they determined that he had "failed to look after his train personally."[36]

The board further concluded:

> 1) Only six wagons were destroyed, six others were badly burned, and thirteen were damaged. The teams for about twenty-five of the wagons were captured. There is no record of any beef cattle being taken.

2) The rear guard, consisting of two companies—sixty-seven officers and men—of the 144th Ohio, a hundred-day militia unit, put up a creditable fight but was outnumbered and outgunned and lost five men killed, five wounded, sixty captured, and seven missing.[37]

The conclusions of the court of inquiry and Grant's correspondence with Sheridan show that there could scarcely have been three hundred prisoners given the size of the force. Moreover, Sheridan had already decided to go back to Halltown before he knew about this attack. Even if he had advance notice of the impending attack, the minuscule damage would not have caused him to retreat.[38]

One Californian, Charles L. Speaight of Company A, was taken prisoner during the raid. Another, Cpl. Alfred McLean of Company M, was wounded. Speaight died at Danville Prison February 25, 1865. McLean, a printer from San Francisco on limited duty as company mailman because of an ankle injury he had suffered at Camp Meigs, was shot in the thigh. He spent the rest of the war as a hospital orderly in Washington. His injuries continued to bother him until his death in 1931.[39] The record is not clear as to why Speaight was there, but returning convalescents and remounted men commonly accompanied the supply trains.

The attack on the wagon train had no effect on Sheridan's planning. He had decided before the Berryville attack to move the army to a more defensible position.[40] After reviewing the terrain between Strasburg and Harper's Ferry with Lieutenant Meigs, Sheridan determined that Halltown was the only position where a smaller force could be reasonably strong and still cover Washington and the vital Baltimore and Ohio Railroad. The wagon train was ordered to issue three days' rations, which were supposed to last four days, and the wounded and sick were loaded and the wagons ordered back to Harper's Ferry.

At 7:15 P.M. on August 15 General Emory was instructed to begin moving XIX Corps to Winchester that night and wait there for further orders.[41] The VI Corps and Crook's divisions were ordered to move the next day. Torbert was ordered to reinforce the 2nd Brigade, then fall back toward Winchester along the Front Royal–Winchester Turnpike, covering the army's left flank. Wilson, who was nearer to Harper's Ferry, was ordered to Stony Point. Lowell's brigade was directed to move back along the Back Road on the army's right flank.

The retreat took on a new dimension when Sheridan ordered the cavalry covering the army's rear to destroy "all the wheat and hay south of a line from Millwood to Winchester and Petticoat Gap. You will seize all horses, mules and cattle that may be useful to our army. Loyal citizens can bring in their claims against the Government for this necessary destruction. No houses will be burned."[42]

Sheridan was acting on instructions Grant had given Hunter earlier in the month and which Hunter in turn passed on to Sheridan. The orders read in part:

> In pushing up the Shenandoah Valley, as it is expected you will have to go, first or last, it is desirable that nothing should be left to invite the enemy to return. Take all provisions, forage and stock wanted for the use of your command; such as cannot be consumed destroy. It is not desirable that the buildings be destroyed; they should

rather be protected; but the people should be informed that so long as an army can subsist among them recurrences of these raids must be expected, and we are determined to stop them at all hazards.[43]

After the war, Sheridan justified his orders in his memoirs by saying that he did

not hold war to mean simply lines of men shall engage each other in battle, and material interests be ignored. . . . Those who rest at home in peace and plenty see but little of the horrors attending such a duel and even grow indifferent to them as the struggle goes on, contenting themselves with encouraging all who are able-bodied to enlist in the cause, to fill up the shattered ranks as death thins them out. It is another matter, however, when deprivation and suffering are brought to their own doors. Then the case appears much graver, for the loss of property weighs heavy with the most of mankind; heavier often, than the sacrifices made on the field of battle. Death is popularly considered the maximum of punishment in war, but it is not; reduction to poverty (that) brings prayers for peace more surely and more quickly than does the destruction of human life, as the selfishness of man has demonstrated in more than one great conflict.[44]

Sheridan's views would have shocked most Northerners had they been widely known at the time. He, Grant, and Sherman shared a different vision of warfare than did most nineteenth-century commanders. That vision is less shocking today after two global conflicts and a half-century of living with the threat of nuclear war.

Lowell's brigade began moving at 7 A.M. on August 16. The cavalrymen covered the five miles to Old Forge, where the Back Road crosses Cedar Creek, then scouted the Back Road and the Grade Road to Strasburg before setting up camp at Mammoth Springs.[45]

At about 2 P.M. on the sixteenth Devin's pickets along the north fork of the Shenandoah at Front Royal were driven back by two brigades of Confederate cavalry. The two Union brigades were quickly formed into line of battle. The Confederates charged Devin's line but were repulsed, and Custer's brigade routed a Confederate cavalry brigade with a spirited countercharge. Merritt reported discovering a brigade of infantry moving on the opposite side of the river toward the defenders' left flank and attacked and drove the Confederates back across the river. Afterward he reported that two brigades of cavalry and Kershaw's infantry division had attacked him. Sheridan was convinced more than ever that the rearward movement was justified.[46]

Another wire from Grant announced that the Army of the Potomac had taken prisoners from Fitz Lee's cavalry, which meant he was not in the Valley. However, the message confirmed that Kershaw's infantry and perhaps two other brigades had been sent to Early. Grant concluded with an admonition that Sheridan not attempt to attack Early in an entrenched position.

Sheridan replied that Kershaw was indeed present, as were Brig. Gen. Williams C. Wickham's and Lomax's brigades from Fitz Lee's cavalry division. He added that

Merritt's 1st Cavalry Division captured three hundred rebels, most of whom belonged to Kershaw's division. "The cavalry engagement in front of Front Royal was splendid; it was on open ground; the saber was freely used by our men," he added. "Great credit is due to Generals Merritt and Custer and Colonel Devin. My impression is that troops are still arriving. Kershaw's and Fitz Lee's divisions came through Culpepper."

Sheridan also mentioned the attack on the wagons again: "Mosby has annoyed me and captured a few wagons. We hung one and shot six of his men yesterday. I have burned off all stock, sheep, cattle, horses &c., south of Winchester."[47]

Sheridan was probably mistaken about the seven executed men. There is nothing in the records confirming that they were members of Mosby's band. The Valley was infested with deserters who took every safe opportunity to rob the Union troops. In addition, the local citizens were often guerrillas at night and farmers by day. The seven were probably not part of an organized band.

The next evening Grant sent a second dispatch suggesting that if Sheridan could spare a cavalry division he should send it into Loudoun County "to destroy and carry off the crops, animals, negroes and all men under fifty years of age capable of bearing arms. In this way you will get many of Mosby's men. All male citizens under fifty can fairly be held as prisoners of war, and not as citizen prisoners."[48]

With a reinforced Confederate army in his rear, Sheridan chose to ignore this suggestion. Confident that Mosby was not a threat, he continued with the northward movement.

Lowell and the 3rd Brigade left Cedar Creek at 9 A.M. on August 17.[49] Following orders from Torbert's cavalry headquarters, Lowell sent details from each regiment to go out on the flanks and burn every bit of forage they could find.[50] Sergeant Corbett described the morning with perfect aplomb: "Left Cedar Creek 9 AM and moved toward Winchester. Burned all hay along the Valley and drove away the stock. Cooked dinner 2 miles from Winchester."[51]

Colonel Lowell was not happy with the orders: "I had the right rear, with orders from Grant to drive in every horse, mule, ox or cow, and burn all grain and forage— a miserable duty which continued till Winchester."[52]

Heavy skirmishing began at about 1 P.M. during the retreat to Winchester. Lowell's orderly described the activity:

There was a piece of wood mounted on two wheels of a wagon to represent a cannon. The Colonel ordered it to be taken along. We raised a little hill and there we made a stand. The Rebs were getting range on our cavalry, so the Colonel ordered this piece of wood to be brought out and go through the motions of loading. The Rebel artillery took range on that wood, and while they were firing at that, the Colonel shifted his cavalry under cover of the hill, out of range of the artillery. We went down a hill and through the woods, and in a field we found our ammunition trains that had not been moved. The Rebs were on top of the hill behind us, and the Colonel had to turn and charge and drive them back from the ammunition trains; then he dismounted the men behind stone walls, and held them in check until they moved the ammunition.[53]

The 2nd Massachusetts arrived at Winchester during the afternoon and joined the army's rear guard, which included Wilson's cavalry division, lately arrived through Snicker's Gap, and a New Jersey infantry brigade from the VI Corps. Sam Corbett, now a veteran of skirmishing, reported: "Within one mile of Winchester we met the Rebel skirmish line. The battle opened immediately. The fighting is getting hotter and more of it (and) some one will get hurt if they are not careful" [54]

The fighting continued until dark. The Confederates charged three times but were repulsed each time. Lowell was discouraged by the retreat from Cedar Creek and the continuous fighting. He wrote his bride that night: "Torbert made a stand with Wilson's Division and my Brigade of cavalry and a small Brigade of infantry. He stood until nightfall, just long enough to lose nearly the whole of the infantry Brigade and some of Wilson's Cavalry—my men were only engaged in the very beginning and were withdrawn as soon as Torbert discovered he had infantry in front of him."[55]

That evening, the brigade fell back to the Opequon crossing on the Berryville Pike, and by 9 P.M. the Union infantry was back on the Clifton–Berryville line. Merritt's cavalry division, falling back along the Front Royal Pike, was ordered back to the neighborhood of White Post.

There is one account stating that during this period Dolly Richards's Company B from Mosby's command killed or captured a squad from "Lowell's Reserve Brigade."[56] However, it could not have come from the Reserve Brigade since Lowell did not take command of it until September 8.[57] The troopers still may have come from the 2nd Massachusetts, however, as the regiment did lose eight men from Companies K and G and a Californian from Company L during the retreat (see Appendix). One of the prisoners, Pvt. William Harmon of Company K, deserted while in captivity and joined the Confederate Foreign Legion. The rest of the captured men survived their imprisonment and were paroled in early 1865.

The opening of Sheridan's Valley campaign had not been auspicious. Nothing much had been accomplished other than the destruction of a few farms near Strasburg and Middletown. The army was back where it started. In spite of Mosby's later claims, the withdrawal was planned before the Berryville raid and was predicated on the information available to both Grant and Sheridan. All of the intelligence indicated that Early outnumbered the Army of the Shenandoah. The Valley had been the site of Union defeats for three years; another defeat there in 1864, an election year, was politically intolerable. A little caution now would give Sheridan time to sharpen his troops and perhaps catch Early off guard. Wisely, he decided to take the time and wait.

9 | Opequon Creek and Fisher's Hill

About August 19 or 20, accounts vary, Mosby crossed the Shenandoah at Castleman's Ferry with about 250 men with the intention of once again attacking Sheridan's supply line. As they approached Berryville, a scout reported that a brigade of cavalry was posted nearby. Mosby decided his party was too large to remain concealed for very long, so he split the force into three groups. One group, under the command of Capt. William Chapman, moved to a house owned by the Mountjoy family. Chapman sent a party accompanied by one of the Mountjoys as guide to reconnoiter the Federal encampment. On their return they approached a picket from the 5th Michigan Cavalry. Chapman later claimed that he sent a man to approach the Union picket from the rear while he engaged the man in conversation and thus take him prisoner. The flanker took too long and Chapman finally demanded the picket's surrender. According to Chapman, he and the picket fired at the same time and his shot killed the bluecoat.

The dead soldier was twenty-one-year-old Cpl. Alpheus Day of Riley, Michigan. Chapman claimed no one witnessed the exchange of gunfire, however at least one other federal picket claimed Day had talked with a group of men dressed as civilians. After they asked a number of questions about the brigade's position, the man said the civilians shot Day and rode off. A picket from the 7th Michigan reported that he saw a party of men dressed in blue uniforms in a nearby wood and that they had fired on him, taking off two fingers from his right hand. Two other pickets from the 5th Michigan were captured and two men from the 7th Michigan who had gone beyond their lines to purchase food disappeared without a trace.[1]

After hearing the accounts of the pickets, General Custer, the brigade commander, was convinced that local citizens had attacked his men. He was outraged and, characteristically failing to think through the possible consequences of his actions, ordered that five of the more prominent homes in the area be burned—this in spite of Sheridan's standing orders that private homes were not to be damaged.

The next day, Capt. George Davis and fifty men from Companies C, L, and M of the 5th Michigan set out to punish the local citizens. Custer ordered Davis and the three lieutenants accompanying the party to inform the citizens why their homes were being destroyed. The first house fired was the Sower's residence near Corporal Day's picket post. Next was the M'Cormack house. Rebel chief Chapman, camped nearby, spotted flames and smoke coming from the vicinity of M'Cormack's home. Fearing the worst, he mounted his horse and rode to the home, which he found in smoldering ruins. The M'Cormacks were in the yard when Chapman rode up. They told him that the burning was in retaliation for the attacks on the picket posts and the murder of Corporal Day. Chapman sent word back to bring up the guerrilla band and they immediately set off in pursuit of the Union raiders. They reached the blazing Sower house, where they found a woman and her children weeping in the yard. The woman explained that they had been able to extinguish the first fire but that the Yankees had returned and started a second fire and restrained her from putting it out. After the war, Chapman's men claimed the sight of the bereft mother and children aroused them to rage and justified their subsequent actions.[2]

In the meantime, Captain Davis had ordered Lt. James Allen to take about forty men and wait at Shepard's Mill Road while he went ahead about a half mile to Colonel Morgan's house, the final home selected for burning. Allen saw a column of about eighty riders approaching and, seeing blue uniforms on the lead riders, assumed they were Union troopers—until they suddenly charged. Allen's men were caught completely by surprise and the guerrillas were among them before they could form into line. The neighboring fields were crisscrossed with stone walls and fences, thwarting the outnumbered Federals' attempt to flee. Those that were not shot down tried to surrender.

One Michigan trooper, Pvt. Sam Davis, handed over his pistol to a Southerner dressed in civilian clothes. After taking the weapon, the man cursed him and shot Davis in the face. Another Michigander, John Lutz, fell wounded alongside him. As they lay on the ground a second group of Confederates rode up. One of the rebels was going to shoot Davis but his companion, seeing Davis's bloody head wound, told him not to waste his powder. After they left, Davis crawled away and hid in the nearby underbrush. A second group of rebels rode up and asked Lutz where his companion had gone. Lutz may have answered, "Gone away." The Confederate questioning him replied, "You won't get away," and shot him dead.[3]

Lieutenant Allen and a handful of his men who escaped the carnage returned to the scene with reinforcements, eager to engage the rebels. The guerrillas were gone but the nearby fields were littered with twelve Union dead. Most of the men had been shot in the back of the head; two had their throats slit. Lieutenant Allen found Private Davis cowering in the brush. Two other wounded men were picked up but both died later. Only Davis survived.[4] The story of the massacre quickly spread throughout Sheridan's army and many determined that the killings must be avenged.

On August 20, the Confederates probed the picket lines in front of the 2nd Massachusetts. Fighting broke out again and "Shot and Shell flew pretty thick for a while."[5] The rebels brought up more guns and at about 5 P.M. charged the 2nd Massachusetts's skirmish line.[6] The firing lasted about an hour. With darkness approaching, the fighting at last died down and the brigade fell back to a camp about a mile from Berryville. Losses were light: only one man was wounded.

Everything was quiet until about ten the next morning, when "The enemy advanced and the firing commenced. Co. A was dismounted and placed on the skirmish line. We held our position till 2 PM at which time we were compelled to fall back amid the howling of shells and hissing of bullets. At the redoubt near Berry-ville they charged us through the woods and were repulsed. It was terrific and we did our duty well. Grant [Grout] and Ward were wounded. Co. A left the skirmish line at 9:20 P.M. Joined the column on the pike to Charlestown."[7]

John O'Leary, a Massachusetts recruit in Company E, was killed and eight men were wounded during the fight (see Appendix).

By 5 A.M. Monday, August 22, the brigade, still serving as part of the army's rear guard, reached Charlestown.[8] The rebels continued to follow closely but a strong skirmish line protected the rear of the retreating column. As the head of the col-umn neared the Union lines, entrenched artillery opened up on the advancing Confederates. The brigade filed through the infantry line and moved to the left. The rebels launched an attack at 6 P.M., but it was repulsed and about twenty Con-federates were taken prisoner. Captain John Philips, commanding Company C, was badly wounded during the fighting. He was later discharged for disability after a long stay in the hospital.

Lowell sent the 2nd Massachusetts out in force the next day to scout the Con-federates just north of Charlestown. Reflecting on the withdrawal, Colonel Lowell wrote: "We have had the rear guard nearly every mile of the way down—have had no real heavy fighting, but a great deal of firing; have got off very well, losing in the whole brigade not over seventy-five."[9]

Firing along the picket line started at sunrise on the twenty-fourth and con-tinued until sunset. The 2nd Massachusetts made a mounted attack on the Con-federate lines and brought back several prisoners. The regiment lost just one man wounded.

In three consecutive days Lowell, who was always in the thick of the fighting, lost three of his horses. Two were shot and one suffered a broken leg. One of the wounded mounts belonged to Major Forbes, who had been captured in July. "Yes-terday," wrote Lowell, "I tried Billy [Forbes's horse] and a bullet went through his neck, it will not hurt him at all, however,—will add to his value in Mr. Forbes's eyes at least a thousand dollars."[10]

General Early decided that same day to make a move toward the Potomac in an attempt to draw Sheridan out of his fortifications and bring on a battle on ground of his choosing. The plan called for Breckinridge to move toward Shepardstown followed by Gordon, Ramseur, and Rodes. Fitz Lee's cavalry division was sent to-ward Williamsport, threatening another raid across the Potomac. Kershaw was or-dered to make a demonstration on the right to conceal the movement. The next morning Kershaw's division opened fire all along the front of General Crook's line. Sheridan correctly sensed that the heavy fire on the left was intended to distract attention from movement on his right flank and ordered Torbert to send Merritt's and Wilson's cavalry divisions toward Kearneytown in an effort to determine if the Confederates were trying to slip by his right flank. The Union cavalry quickly found the head of the Confederate column. Thinking he was facing only cavalry, Torbert ordered an attack. When the cavalry broke through the Confederate screen they discovered they were facing the head of Breckinridge's division. Supported by three other Confederate divisions, Breckinridge counterattacked and drove Merritt and Wilson back in confusion. Early, with the element of surprise gone, ordered his forces to retreat back up the Valley and concentrate at Smithfield and Bunker Hill.

Now it was Sheridan's turn. Reasoning that Early had weakened his right to support Breckinridge, he ordered Crook, supported by Lowell's brigade, to attack Kershaw's division. Lowell ordered a mounted charge against Kershaw's line. For some unknown reason the Union infantry on the cavalry's right failed to charge and Lowell's assault was flanked and repulsed. Thirteen rebel prisoners were taken but Captain Eigenbrodt of Company E was killed and one man was wounded.[11] Eigenbrodt's body was left near the Confederate lines.

The next morning the enlisted men on both sides, who were not privy to the grand strategies of the campaign, eagerly attempted to find out who was winning during a lull in the fighting. While the officers stayed in camp, the privates, who had been trying to kill each other the day before, took charge. "This morning an armistice was agreed upon between the Rebel pickets and our boys. It lasted four hours. The boys traded papers, coffee and tobacco with the Rebels."[12]

Sheridan ordered another attack in the afternoon. Lowell's brigade was not part of the cavalry Sheridan had brought with him from the Army of the Potomac, so he decided to ride over to observe the brigade as it attacked the Confederate line:

> General Sheridan and staff came over just as the Colonel had four companies ready to charge the Rebel lines. The Colonel went up a hollow,—he could go within two hundred yards of them. Before they could see him, he went out of the hollow, and formed in line and charged. The Rebels had rails piled up to form breastworks. The Rebels fired a volley into the men. They stopped and the Colonel rode out ahead and waved his saber and cheered them. Then the men started, and he led them, and he was the first man to jump the rail-pile in to the Rebs; then they broke and ran, and the Colonel captured sixty-seven privates and seven commissioned officers. General Sheridan's orderly told me that when the Colonel jumped the rail pile, the General said "Lowell is a brave man."[13]

Two rebels were clubbed to death with muskets in the hand-to-hand fighting when the brigade tore down the rail barricade. In the ensuing scramble the charging cavalry captured a lieutenant colonel, three captains, three lieutenants, and sixty-nine enlisted men from the 15th South Carolina Infantry.[14] Two Californians, 1st Lt. Charles Meader, commanding Company A, and Pvt. James Ackerman, also of Company A, were killed. Two other enlisted men were wounded.[15]

On August 27 Lowell and the 2nd Massachusetts got as far as Charlestown before they encountered rebel pickets. Skirmishing continued for most of the day and the regiment took three prisoners. In the latter part of the afternoon they had a sharp skirmish with Lomax's cavalry. Two Massachusetts recruits, Cpl. Thomas Martin and Pvt. John Marden of Company K, were killed. One Californian was wounded and a Massachusetts recruit was captured. The regiment was also able to retrieve the bodies of Lieutenant Meader and Private Ackerman. They were buried that evening with military honors. Captain Eigenbrodt's grave was located and marked for removal by an embalmer.[16]

Based on the information gained from this patrol, Sheridan ordered the infantry to move to Charlestown the following morning. Merritt moved to Leetown with the 1st, 2nd, and Reserve Brigades of his division and attacked the rebel cavalry there, driving them through Smithfield. Lowell's 3rd brigade moved to the north fork of Bullskin Run near Charlestown and camped for the night on the army's left flank. During the march Pvt. John O'Connell of Company F was severely wounded. O'Connell, whose real name was Michael Walsh, had deserted from the 2nd California Volunteer Infantry on April 23, 1863, to join the California Battalion.[17]

Lowell's brigade continued its advance on the morning of the twenty-ninth. The 2nd Massachusetts left the Smithfield Pike at 6 A.M. "and joined the Brigade on the Berryville Pike. Heavy cannonading in the direction of Smithfield. Our forces are reported to have fallen back near Charlestown. One PM we left the pike and moved up on the Winchester road as far as Haynes Station [Summit Point]. All quiet with us with the exception of a little picket shooting just at dusk on a picket north of the Station."[18]

Although there was very little skirmishing, when the brigade made camp the men discovered that the location was almost surrounded by rebel pickets. Sam Corbett wrote that they "utilized a little strategy by bringing out the fife and drums of the band and playing to make the Rebels think we had a force of infantry with us." They slept somewhat uneasily that night but the next morning they found that "Our strategy last evening was completely successful as we captured several prisoners during the night and the first thing they asked when we got them into camp was 'Where is your infantry.' Our own pickets, when they heard the drums thought we had been reinforced."[19]

The ruse did not work for long, however. Cole's battalion of Marylanders manning the picket post was driven in by a sudden assault. The 2nd Massachusetts counterattacked and drove the rebels back three miles, killing one captain, a lieutenant, and several privates and took five prisoners. After the skirmish the brigade moved to the Smithfield Pike and set up camp for the night.

The brigade spent the thirty-first picketing the army's left flank. Picket posts were set up at Summit Point on the brigade's left, and Smithfield and Leetown on the right.[20]

On Friday, September 2, the VI and XIX Corps broke camp and started moving toward Berryville. Lowell's men drew rations and then broke camp and started moving south. Over the next week the 2nd Massachusetts was in constant contact with the retreating rebels. On the fourth a heavy rainstorm started in the morning, slowing the fighting and thoroughly soaking the men. Lowell wrote: "We are on the right flank of the Army again—indeed are the only cavalry there—and are constantly on the go. By the way, Billy got another bullet yesterday; it struck the ring of his halter and shivered it,—has bruised and cut him a little, but we cannot decide where the bullet is."[21]

The wagons caught up with them on the fifth and the men were able to set up their tents and dry out but no rations were issued. "Everybody and everything wet, cross and hungry," grumbled Sam Corbett.[22] The infantry skirmishing continued on the right in the direction of Berryville and cannon fire could clearly be heard at the brigade's position.

Rations were finally issued in the evening, and as the smell of hot coffee and frying bacon wafted through the sodden camp, the morale of the troops improved.[23] The next day, just after sunrise, Lowell led the brigade down to Sack's Ford. Concealed by a belt of trees, the sergeants aligned the men. Colonel Lowell moved out in front, the buglers sounded charge, and the brigade galloped across the little stream. With pistols banging and sabers flashing the sudden surge drove the surprised Confederate skirmishers back against the main body. The Confederates counterattacked and for a few moments there was a swirling melee of horsemen as the two sides met. The outnumbered regiment took casualties and was forced to fall back to the cover of the trees.

John Storer of Company D was killed and John Smith, also of Company D, was badly wounded. Smith died of his wounds at the hospital at Annapolis, Maryland, on October 1. Three Californians were wounded. One Californian, George Small of Company F, was captured. He later died at Andersonville.

On September 8 Lowell moved the brigade about a mile to a field "noted for mud and weeds."[24] The rain continued, and with the tents back at the last camp, whatever dry clothes the men had quickly became soaked. The 1st Cavalry Division reorganized its brigades that same day. Lowell's 3rd Brigade was broken up. The 25th New York was sent to the 1st Brigade, Custer's old command, and the 1st Maryland Home Guards were sent back to Harper's Ferry. The 6th Pennsylvania's enlistment period was over and it was sent to Pleasant Valley to muster out. The 2nd Massachusetts joined three regular army regiments, the 1st, 2nd, and 5th Cavalry, in the Reserve Brigade. Lowell assumed command of the reconstituted brigade and Lieutenant Colonel Crowninshield continued to command the 2nd Massachusetts.[25]

Colonel Lowell was pleased:

> The change looks like making the Second Massachusetts a permanent member of the Army of the Potomac, or that portion of it which is here. I am now where, if there is anything to be done for Mr. Linkum in the way of fighting. I may have a chance to do it.[26] I have stepped into a rather trying position now,—the regular Brigade is hard to run; there are many prides and prejudices,—and then, too, much more is expected from an officer commanding it, than from one commanding a little patched-up affair like my last command. However, I shan't worry at all, but shall try to do what I can. I don't think I now care at all about being Brigadier-General. I am *perfectly* satisfied to be a Colonel if I can always have a brigade to command—That's modest isn't it?[27]

Several weeks before the cavalry was reorganized, Sheridan called for volunteers for a battalion of scouts that would carry out special missions for his headquarters. Major H. K. Young of the 1st Rhode Island Infantry commanded the new battalion.

The volunteers wore Confederate uniforms and thus faced summary execution if captured.[28]

In mid-August, two of the new scouts discovered an elderly black man who moved freely through the lines of the two armies selling fresh vegetables. Major Young proposed that the old man be used to procure information from inside Winchester. General Crook, who was familiar with some of the Union sympathizers in the town, proposed to Sheridan that the old man contact a schoolteacher named Rebecca White. Miss White was a Quaker and Crook was sure she could be trusted. The old man agreed and informed the generals he knew Miss White very well.

Sheridan corresponded with Miss White on a regular basis for about three weeks. The old man carried the messages, written on tissue paper and wrapped in tinfoil, in his mouth when he passed through the lines.[29] On September 8 Sheridan learned from Miss Wright that Kershaw's division had left Early and was moving to Front Royal en route to Richmond. Sheridan decided to wait two more days before moving forward to attack. The wait would insure that Kershaw was far enough away to be beyond recall.

On September 9 the men in the Reserve Brigade camp were issued three days' rations. It had rained most of the night but the sky was clear in the morning. The 2nd Massachusetts was sent out toward Winchester to burn a mill on Opequon Creek that had somehow escaped destruction during the army's withdrawal. A fire was set and the regiment moved back toward camp. But the mill was very wet from the recent rains, and when the rear guard discovered the fire had gone out the regiment returned to finish the job. As the troopers approached the mill they encountered a rebel force that had come up. Rather than risk a fight, the raiders fell back and returned to camp.[30]

The next day the sky was overcast and rain threatened to delay Sheridan's proposed attack. Lowell's brigade saddled up at about 11 A.M. and then waited for orders for several hours in a battle line facing the rebel skirmishers. During the wait Valorus Dearborn of Company A was shot in the head and killed by a Confederate sharpshooter. Another man was wounded by the accidental discharge of a pistol. At last orders came sending the brigade to camp with the hapless Dearborn's body draped over his saddle.

At headquarters that evening "we had the band up and they were quite sentimental in their choice of music, and I grew as homesick as possible." Colonel Lowell enjoyed the serenade so much that he ordered the band to play every evening. The order also spoke to the band's skill level: Lowell further required that the bandsmen practice three times a day. That night there was a torrential downpour and Lowell wrote that he and the brigade's doctor "were quite washed out, our tent seemed to be a through drain for all the surrounding countryside."[31]

On September 13 the Reserve Brigade joined the 1st Brigade in a demonstration at Locke's Ford on the Opequon, capturing one lieutenant and ten privates from Breckinridge's corps.[32] The action was almost a disaster. The skirmish line in front of the brigade ran into the rebel lines and was captured en masse. The 2nd Massachusetts was then ordered to charge, recapturing all of the brigade's men and taking the first line of rifle pits. After some cannonading the Union troopers fell back. The brigade lost a total of twenty-two men killed or wounded. In the 2nd Massachusetts, Alexander Logan of Company D was killed and seven troopers were wounded. One wounded man, Winfield Wilbur of Company I, died that evening. John Shiffer of Company F and William Colgan of Company C died a few days later in the hospital at Frederick (see Appendix).[33]

The rainy weather continued through the fifteenth. During the lull in the Valley fighting the Northern press began pushing for Sheridan to launch an offensive. Some editors were concerned that the Shenandoah Valley had stymied yet another Union general. Even Grant was concerned that Sheridan was being overcautious: "My purpose was to have him attack Early, or drive him out of the valley and destroy that source of supplies for Lee's army. I knew it was impossible for me to get orders through Washington to Sheridan to make a move, because they would be stopped there and such orders as Halleck's caution (and that of the Secretary of War) would suggest would be given instead, and would, no doubt, be contradictory to mine."[34]

Grant instead went directly to Charlestown, once again bypassing the War Department, even though the trip took him through the capital. Before departing he sent a courier to Sheridan informing him of the meeting. Grant had prepared a plan of campaign for Sheridan before starting on the trip. When the two finally met, Grant asked Sheridan if he had a map showing his positions and those of the enemy. "He at once drew one out of his side pocket, showing all roads, and streams, and the camps of the two armies. He said that if he had permission he would move so and so (pointing out how) against the Confederates, and that he would 'whip them'."[35]

Sheridan's confidence reassured Grant; the plan he had prepared never left his pocket. Sheridan told Grant he would be ready to move at daylight on Monday, September 19. Grant immediately returned to City Point. By the eighteenth the men in the ranks knew that Grant had been at Charlestown. A general inspection of all the cavalry in the army was held and a rumor spread that General Grant was expected to review the troops. Then came orders that rations and forage were to be issued and the men prepared to move at a moment's notice, a sure sign that a movement was imminent.

The 2nd Massachusetts mounted up at 7 P.M. expecting to move out, but then the order came down to fall out. The horses were unsaddled and the men went to their campfires. That night, the main body of the army, screened by the cavalry, moved south to the Berryville-Winchester Pike. The battle would start at dawn.

The next day started early for the 2nd Massachusetts. Reveille was at 1 A.M. The men quickly built up the cooking fires and started coffee and bacon cooking. The tents had been packed in the wagons the night before. The horses were saddled and by 1:30 the companies were assembling and roll was taken. At two the column moved toward the Opequon. They encountered no resistance until they reached the creek. The rebel pickets on the east bank retreated across the creek and General Merritt sent Custer's brigade to Locke's Ford. Lowell's brigade was sent to try a crossing at Seivers's Ford. The 2nd Massachusetts and 2nd U.S. Cavalry were put in the front rank. The 1st and 5th U.S. Cavalry formed a second line in reserve. At Lowell's order the two regiments charged across the creek. The rebel pickets fired a volley and then ran to the rear, leaving forty stragglers behind who were quickly rounded up. On the other side of the stream, the 2nd U.S. Cavalry made a mounted charge on a battery in the face of particularly heavy fire from a band of Confederates concealed in a railroad cut. The attack was repulsed by the batteries' infantry support. Farther down, Custer's brigade charged across the creek at Locke's Ford and was driven back. Custer then extended his position to connect his left flank with Lowell's right and the firing intensified.[36]

The main infantry attack was along the Berryville-Winchester Pike. The XIX Corps was on the north side and the VI Corps along the south side of the pike. Crook's VIII Corps was in reserve behind XIX Corps. Wilson's cavalry, which had led the advance, moved to the left of VI Corps when the infantry came up. Ramseur's division opposed the advance, assisted by most of Early's artillery. The VI Corps's wagons and guns delayed XIX Corps[37] and it was hours before the lines were formed. The delay gave Early time to bring up Gordon's and Rodes's divisions, select the ground they would defend, and prepare for the Union attack. Sheridan was furious but decided to go forward. At first the Union troops drove the Confederates back. The XIX Corps broke the left of Early's line, throwing it into confusion. Rodes counterattacked, striking the juncture between the two Union corps. The counterattack was just barely stopped by troops from VI Corps. Rodes, who was one of Early's best generals, was killed during the attack.

A lull in the fighting occurred as Sheridan brought up Crook to attack Early's left. Early took advantage of the break in the fighting to reorganize his line. On the left, Breckinridge's troops were demoralized by the constant attacks by Merritt's cavalry as they fell back through the open ground east of Stephenson's Depot. When they arrived back at the main body they were disorganized and worn out. Early placed them on his left flank in a line perpendicular to his main front in a position he thought would be quiet. The Confederate cavalry fell back to a position west of the Valley Turnpike. Casualties had so depleted Breckinridge's force that he was unable to connect with the Confederate cavalry.[38]

Merritt's cavalry, following the retreating Confederate cavalry, hit the new position before they and Breckinridge's left had time to reorganize.[39] By noon the Reserve Brigade had become scattered. Lieutenant Colonel Crowninshield joined the 2nd Brigade with two squadrons from the 2nd Massachusetts in an assault on the rebels' infantry at 2 P.M. According to Crowninshield:

> all the cavalry had come together on the Martinsburg & Winchester Pike; the whole line of the enemy's cavalry was just in front of us—the country was very open and a splendid place for a cavalry fight. Averell was on the left of the road with Custer just behind him. Merritt was on the left of the road—I had two squadrons of my Regt. deployed as skirmishers. A part of Merritt and I was supported then with two more. Soon the Rebel Cavalry charged and drove back our skirmishers on the right & left of the road; I had posted my reserve just on the edge of a wood and I managed to

check the rebels on the left of the road. In the mean while our cavalry was formed in line ready to charge. Soon the bugler blew; on they came, 6 or 7 thousand men with sabers drawn and shouting like demons. It was a splendid sight. I never shall forget it. We rode completely over the rebel cavalry, the (two indecipherable words) the rebel cavalry have not stopped running yet. We charged the infantry and routed them taking over 900 prisoners 9 battleflags & 2 guns, three caissons. If night had not closed in so soon we should have destroyed Early's army. Everyone says that this was the most splendid cavalry fight of the war. I had two officers mortally wounded and lost some very good men.[40]

Colonel Lowell and the 5th U.S. Cavalry charged a battery of guns from Breckinridge's corps, capturing two with their caissons and wagons. Once again Lowell's horse Billy was hit, shot in three places during the assault. The wounded animal had to be destroyed.[41]

Sheridan ordered Crook to attack Early's left. Crook's troops swung in a wheeling movement against the remnant of Breckinridge's infantry. Pressed on the right by Crook's infantry, and with his unprotected left flank being assaulted by Merritt's cavalry, Breckinridge's line collapsed. As the Confederate troops facing the VI and XIX Corps became aware of firing in their left rear, they too began to fall back. Soon a chaotic retreat was underway all along the front.[42]

A Union officer who had been captured earlier saw the final attack of Merritt's division and wrote:

> The confusion, disorder and actual rout produced by the successive charges of Merritt's division would appear incredible did not the writer actually witness them. To the right a battery with guns disabled and caissons shattered was trying to make to the rear, the men and horse impeded by broken regiments of cavalry and infantry; to the left the dead and wounded, in confused masses around the field hospitals—many of the wounded in great excitement seeking shelter in Winchester; directly in front an ambulance, the driver nervously clutching the reins while six men in great alarm were carrying to it the body of General Rhodes.[43]

As the Confederates retreated through Winchester the local ladies came out in the streets and pleaded with the fleeing rebels to stand and fight. A few stalwart brigades slowed the Union pursuit just long enough for Early to extricate the forces on the Berryville Pike and start them south.

Jubal Early knew that he had been soundly defeated. He accepted none of the blame for his defeat nor did he offer the slightest praise for the fighting abilities of the Union troops. In his typical choleric manner, he criticized Sheridan's lack of ability. After the war he wrote that Sheridan should "have been cashiered for this battle" and should "have destroyed my whole force and captured everything I had." He asserted that his "escape from utter annihilation is due to the incapacity of my opponents."[44]

The 2nd Massachusetts was not effective as a unit in its first major battle. In the morning's advance part of the regiment was dismounted during the crossing of

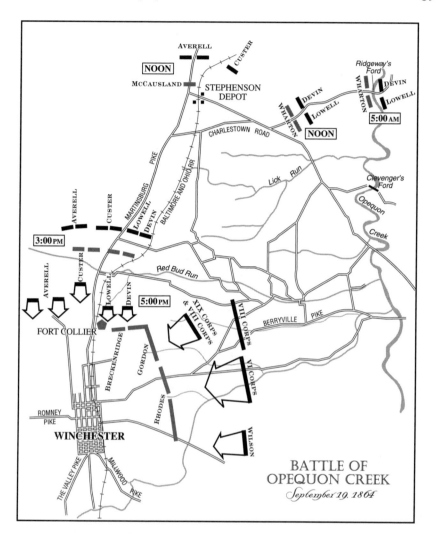

BATTLE OF
OPEQUON CREEK
September 19, 1864

Opequon Creek. The rest of the regiment was in support. Somehow the units became separated as the brigade moved toward Winchester. Perhaps the companies that had fought on foot at the creek crossing were slow in retrieving their horses. In any event, almost half the regiment ended up with Averell's division on the other side of the Martinsburg-Winchester Pike and did almost nothing. That night, a weary but jubilant regiment finally regrouped and camped about two miles from Winchester.

When a final count was made it was found that casualties were slight: ten wounded and four captured. One of the wounded, George Emerson of Company I, died a few days later from his wounds (see Appendix). Among the wounded was 1st Lt.

Josiah Baldwin of Company L. At first it was thought he would die, so he was left at a nearby farmhouse. That action may have saved his life, for he avoided the infections and poor care at the army hospitals. Baldwin was very popular and during his convalescence men from the regiment often visited him. He was discharged for disability on May 5, 1865.[45]

The Confederate army took up positions on Fisher's Hill, where the impenetrable Massanutten massif and a U-shaped curve in the north fork of the Shenandoah River made an assault on Early's east flank impossible. Little North Mountain anchored the western flank. The hill had been entrenched earlier and was considered to be a very strong position.

Wilson's and Merritt's divisions, less Devin's brigade at Cedar Creek, moved toward Front Royal with Torbert in command. His orders were to move down the Luray Valley to New Market while Sheridan and the army's main body attacked Early at Fisher's Hill. Wilson's division, operating about six miles in front, met Wickham's cavalry division at Front Royal. Wilson attacked and drove the Confederates back up the valley. The advance was halted by rebels occupying a strong position at Gooney Run, about six miles south of Luray. Merritt set out with Lowell's and Custer's brigades at 2 A.M. and marched across the north fork of the Shenandoah at Buckton Ford, then moved east through Front Royal. They camped about a mile and a half beyond the village.[46] Rations had run out the day before and there was some grumbling around the campfires.[47]

During the night, cannonading could be heard from the right, toward Strasburg. Custer's brigade crossed the south fork of the Shenandoah before sunrise and moved down the east bank toward McCoy's Ford in the rear of the rebel position at Gooney Ford. Lowell's brigade broke camp at 5 A.M. and moved up the valley toward Luray.

The Confederates, anticipating Custer's movement, had withdrawn to the south bank of Milford Creek the night before. The Luray Valley becomes a narrow gorge at this point. The left flank of the Confederate line was anchored on the Shenandoah, which runs so close under the mountains that it was impossible to turn. The right flank rested against a high mountain. The position was entrenched with "loop hole breast works" that ran clear across the narrow valley.

Torbert decided the position was too strong to be turned and that a frontal attack would result in very heavy casualties. "Not knowing that the army had made an attack at Fisher's Hill, and thinking that the sacrifice would be too great to attack without that knowledge, I concluded to withdraw to a point opposite McCoy's Ferry."[48]

Torbert's statement about the attack at Fisher's Hill is misleading. According to Sgt. Sam Corbett, cannonading could clearly be heard from the vicinity of Fisher's Hill on the other side of Massanutten Mountain all day.[49] Torbert ordered the two divisions to return to Front Royal and assigned the Reserve Brigade the task of escorting the wagon train of ambulances.

One of the most controversial incidents of the Civil War occurred during the march up the Luray Valley to Front Royal. The accounts vary and the *Official Records* are silent, other than the mention of a skirmish with Mosby. The incident might never have occurred if Mosby had been in charge, but he had been wounded a few days earlier in a skirmish in Fairfax County and Capt. Sam Chapman was temporarily placed in charge of Mosby's band. He decided to make a hit-and-run raid on a picket post at Chester Gap, not far from Front Royal. Leading 120 guerrillas, more than enough to overwhelm any picket post, he moved through the gap without meeting any resistance and discovered that the pickets had been withdrawn earlier. The guerrillas camped the night of the twenty-second on the Chester Gap road about halfway between the gap and Front Royal. During the evening Chapman learned from residents of Front Royal about the Union troop movements that day and that heavy firing had been heard in the direction of Milford, up the Luray Valley.

On the morning of the twenty-third Chapman and several scouts rode to a home on the Gooney Manor Grade from which he could see the Federal camp at Milford. In a short time a report came that an ambulance train led by a small cavalry escort had left the camp and was heading north toward Front Royal. The full length of the train was hidden by low hills. Chapman sent word to the guerrilla camp to quickly move toward Fort Royal and set up an ambush. A party commanded by Capt. Walter Frankland was ordered to make a circuit over Graveyard Hill and move to a position in front of the column at a point where the road passed between a wooded hill and a small ravine just out of town. Chapman took the rest of the guerrillas to a position where he could attack the rear of the column near the turnpike tollhouse.[50] As Frankland moved into position, Chapman headed south, screened by intervening hills on the parallel road. He was confident the attack would be a success; ambulance trains were rarely heavily guarded and he was in an ideal position to capture or destroy the whole lot. Chapman rode to the crest of a nearby hill to take one last look at his quarry. At first glance it was apparent his reconnaissance had been faulty. The train was much longer than he had supposed and then, at the rear of the column, he counted three distinct stands of colors.[51] He turned and raced back to Frankland yelling, "Call off your men, you are attacking a brigade." Frankland told him it was too late, besides he was driving the enemy back.[52]

Frankland had struck the advance guard of Lowell's Reserve Brigade. In a matter of minutes the rest of the brigade was charging down the fields alongside the pike. They came on "like a swarm of bees," according to one eyewitness. The guerrillas panicked and scattered in every direction. A group of cavalrymen from the 2nd U.S. Cavalry led by Lt. Charles McMasters climbed the bank alongside the road and raced toward the lane leading to the road used by Chapman in his approach.

Almost all the rebels were racing toward the same road or the wooded hillsides on either side. McMasters, out in front of his charging troopers, lost control of his horse, probably because the reins were cut by a bullet. He fought for control and when the animal finally slowed, he dismounted. Out in front by himself and without support, he tried to surrender. The panic-stricken rebels, closely pursued by the

Federals, ignored his pleas and riddled his body with bullets as they thundered past. When the Union troopers reached the fatally wounded lieutenant, he told them he had been trying to surrender when the guerrillas gunned him down.[53]

Major John Scott excused the murder with the brutal observation that "The fate of this officer was not singular, for it is a fact in the history of this locality that no Yankee has ever visited Hominy Hollow and returned to tell the tale."[54]

Mosby later denied that McMasters was ever taken prisoner and added that "even admitting that McMasters offered to surrender," his men might not have realized it in the confusion or perhaps had refused to grant him quarter. A resident of Front Royal wrote in her diary on September 25: "Our men had captured a Colonel [she was incorrect about McMasters's rank] and were overtaken by the enemy. Our men shot the Colonel, giving him several shots after his begging and pleading with them not to kill him."[55]

Lowell reported that thirteen rebels led by Capt. R. P. Montjoy were killed but he did not include any count of prisoners.[56] However, Lowell's report was less than candid; the brigade took six prisoners.[57] All of the prisoners were part of Montjoy's company, which is probably why Lowell attributed the attack to that unit. Five of the captives—Philip Jones, Lucien Love, Thomas Carter, Thomas Anderson, and William Overby—were veteran guerrillas. Jones had been captured once before and paroled. The last prisoner was seventeen-year-old Lafayette Rhodes of Front Royal, a local youth who, on a lark, borrowed a horse from a neighbor and joined in the guerrilla attack hoping to capture a horse and some plunder from the Yankees.[58]

General Merritt, accompanied by Custer and his brigade, arrived at Front Royal after the fight was over and while the dead and wounded were being gathered. General Torbert rode in at about the same time. All three heard how McMasters was shot. The record is not clear, but one of the three, or perhaps all of them, ordered the six prisoners executed.[59]

The Union troopers and the Californians needed little encouragement. All of the frustrations of the past months came to the forefront. The attacks on isolated picket posts; the twenty-nine dead Michigan troopers at Colonel Morgan's house, ten of them with bullets in the back of their heads; Pvt. Oscar Burnap of Company E, crippled for life; Owen Fox, shot while trying to surrender as he lay trapped under his fallen horse; the ambush of Captain Reed's squadron, the bodies of their friends—stripped of their clothing, boots, and dignity—all of this came back to the tired officers and enlisted men of Lowell's command. Five men and one foolish boy paid the price for months of rebel depradations. The prisoners were not executed, they were savaged. They were killed by a mob that could not and would not be stopped. Justice was irrelevant; this was what the war in this part of Virginia had become.

With Custer's personal band playing a dirge, the prisoners, ropes around their necks, were led through the town. Jones and Love were taken behind the Methodist Church and shot by a squad of cavalrymen. Thomas Anderson was hanged from a tree on Perry Criser's farm. Poor Lafayette Rhodes was dragged up the main street of his hometown lashed to the saddles of two Union troopers. His mother pleaded for his life but one his captors, a gruff Michigan trooper, threatened to behead her with his saber. They dragged the boy to a hill owned by the Richardson family. There they untied his bindings and he fell to the ground. One of the Michigan troopers mercifully shot him dead as he lay in the dirt among the horses' hooves.

A large crowd of men, largely from Lieutenant McMasters's regiment, had Overby and Carter. General Torbert ordered Capt. Theodore Bean, Merritt's provost marshal, to question them. Bean asked the prisoners to reveal the location of Mosby's headquarters, but both men refused. [60] Two horses were brought over and the prisoners were set in the saddles. The ropes around the men's necks were then thrown over the limb of an adjacent walnut tree. Bean again questioned the men, who stubbornly refused to answer. Carter asked for a bible, read a little, then prayed. Overby was defiant to the last. He told the Union troopers that "Mosby'll hang ten of you for every one of us." Two whips cracked, the horses bolted, and the two guerrillas were dead. [61]

There is some question about whether the 2nd Massachusetts participated in the murders. Lowell said the regiment was not involved, and Colonel Crowninshield wrote: "We fell back to Front Royal. We there had a fight with Mosby and killed and hung 14 of his men. I am glad to say that my Regt. had nothing to do with this." [62]

At least one Californian was involved. Sam Corbett wrote that he "Fell back five miles last night. This morning when near Front Royal on a flank movement Mosby guerrillas charged in to our advance guard. We pitched in to them driving them to the mountains killing seventeen and taking four prisoners, two of them we shot and the other two we hung in retaliation for shooting two of our men that they had captured. I had the pleasure of capturing one of them myself. We passed through the town then came back." [63]

All of this was a minor issue to most of those involved, excepting the men who were executed. Only a few of the participants felt any qualms of conscience. Five guerrillas and seventeen-year-old Lafayette Rhodes were murdered. Their deaths had virtually no effect on the outcome of the war. The seeds of inhumanity had been planted by Custer's foolish order to burn houses. Chapman's barbaric massacre at Colonel Morgan's house started the chain of murders. At Front Royal the brutality escalated. There would be another senseless atrocity in November before wiser heads regained control.

10 | "A Crow Will Have to Carry His Own Provisions"

As the cavalry at Milford Creek retreated down the Luray Valley, Sheridan was attacking Early at Fisher's Hill. He won a staggering victory and once again Early's army was routed with heavy losses. Massing VI and XIX Corps on his left, Sheridan made Early believe the attack would fall on the Confederate right. In the meantime Crook, using the intervening terrain and thick woods on Little North Mountain to conceal his movements, suddenly fell on Early's unguarded left flank.[1] Crook rolled the rebel line up like "a row of tenpins."[2]

In a telegram to Grant, Sheridan wrote:

> While Crook was driving the enemy in the greatest confusion and sweeping down behind their breastworks, the Sixth and Nineteenth Army Corps attacked the rebel works in front, and the whole rebel army appeared to be broken up. They fled in the utmost confusion. Sixteen pieces of artillery were captured; also a great many caissons, artillery horses &c. I am tonight pushing on down the Valley. I cannot say how many prisoners I have captured, nor do I know either my own or the enemy's casualties; only darkness has saved the whole of Early's army from total destruction. . . . The First and Third Cavalry Divisions went down Luray Valley today, and if they push on vigorously to the main valley, the results of this day's engagement will be still more signal.[3]

The next morning he added, "If General Torbert has pushed down the Luray Valley according to my directions, he will achieve great results. I do not think there ever was an army so badly routed. The Valley soldiers are hiding away and going to their homes."[4]

The news that Torbert had retreated back to Front Royal arrived later in the morning. Sheridan was enraged. In his memoirs he noted that

> The only drawback was with the cavalry, and to this day [published in 1888] I have been unable to account satisfactory for Torbert's failure. No doubt, Wickham's position was a strong one, but Torbert ought to have made a fight. Had he been defeated in this, his withdrawal then to await the result at Fisher's Hill would have been justified, but it does not appear that he made any serious effort at all to dislodge the Confederate cavalry: his impotent attempt not only chagrined me very much, but occasioned much unfavorable comment throughout the army.[5]

Sheridan immediately ordered Torbert to turn around and attack the Confederates at Milford Creek. The order arrived at about 4 P.M., after the killing of the prisoners in Front Royal. The troops immediately countermarched and were back at the positions they had left that morning. It was too late; the Confederates had fled up the Valley. The 2nd Massachusetts camped in the rebel entrenchments on Milford Creek that night.[6]

At daylight on September 24, Merritt's division led the advance. Wickham's brigade of Virginia cavalry was discovered about three miles north of Luray. Custer's brigade charged, supported by two squadrons from the 2nd Massachusetts. Seventy prisoners were taken. Private Philip Baybutt of Company A, a Massachusetts recruit, captured the battle flags of the 6th Virginia Cavalry. A few weeks later he was awarded the Medal of Honor for the deed. After dispersing the Confederates, Merritt's troopers passed through Luray onto the New Market Pike and camped west of the Shenandoah at the foot of the pass leading over Massanutten Mountain.

Lowell wrote his wife that night:

> We have been in Luray Valley and entirely away from communications. I send you a little purple Gerardia, picked for you by General Wilson (whom you don't know, but who must have heard Mr. Dana speak of you): he had just handed it to me, when my unfortunate Adjutant-General was shot right behind us (not fatal, though we feared so for some time), so it has not very pleasant associations. We did capture a battle flag yesterday, so I'm tolerably satisfied. If you could only look in here for a minute,—it's in the loveliest mountain scenery you can imagine.[7]

Lowell's adjutant general was 2nd Lt. H. F. Woodman, who enlisted in San Francisco as a corporal in Company A on December 10, 1862. He rose through the ranks and was commissioned a second lieutenant in May 1864. Woodman suffered a compound fracture of a leg. At first the wound was thought to be serious, but not mortal. He was carried by ambulance with the army for a couple of days, but developed a fever and was left at Mount Jackson when Sheridan's army retreated up the Valley. He died there as a prisoner on October 9, 1864.[8]

John Moeglen of Company M, a forty-three-year-old farmer from Lancaster, Massachusetts, was badly wounded. His son Philip, also of Company M, had been captured two days earlier at Front Royal. Philip was released on October 8, eleven days after his father died from his wounds in a Winchester hospital.

General Averell also drew Sheridan's wrath. On the morning of the twenty-third Averell had been ordered to pursue the retreating rebels. Instead he went into camp. He finally started out about noon but maintained a lethargic pace. Sheridan relieved him of his command and ordered Col. William H. Powell to take command of the division.

Sheridan subsequently blamed Averell for giving Early time to collect his scattered forces and occupy a highly defensible position east of the north fork of the Shenandoah on commanding terrain about two miles south of Mount Jackson.[9]

The ground was completely open and offered Powell and Devin no opportunity to conceal flanking movements. With VI and XIX Corps following, the Confederate army fell back, marching through New Market and Keezletown before stopping at Brown's Gap on the same ground occupied by Stonewall Jackson's army in 1862. Sheridan halted the Union infantry at New Market and sent Devin's brigade forward as bait in an attempt to get Early to stop long enough for Torbert to come up in the rear, but the rebels declined the opportunity.

Kershaw's division, which had been ordered to retrace its march after the fight at Opequon Creek, joined Early's forces at Brown's Gap. Wickham, who had held up Torbert in the Luray Valley, and Lomax, who had acted as rear guard in the retreat from Fisher's Hill, joined the main body of the Confederate army the next day. General Gordon wryly described the elation in the Confederate camp when Kershaw's troops marched in:

> Cheer after cheer came from their husky throats and rolled along the mountain cliffs. . . . "Hurrah for the Palmetto Boys!" "Glad to see you South Ca'liny!" "Whar did you come from?" "Did you bring any more guns for Phil Sheridan?" We had delivered a number of guns to that officer without taking any receipts for them; but the Confederate authorities at Richmond were straining every nerve to supply us with more. Among the pieces of artillery sent us by the War Department was a long black rifle-cannon on which some wag had printed in white letters words to this effect: "Respectfully consigned to General Sheridan through General Early."[10]

At sunrise on September 25, Torbert's troops marched over the pass from the Luray Valley to New Market, where they stopped at about noon to feed and water their horses. The men received four days' rations, the first they had had in eight days. In the afternoon they continued on to Harrisonburg, where they joined the main body of Sheridan's army. They camped about ten miles south of New Market that night, "arriving many hours later than expected."[11]

Reveille sounded at 4 A.M. on the twenty-sixth. General Merritt was ordered to move to Port Republic with his 1st Brigade to cover the army's left flank. Devin and the 2nd Brigade were at Keezletown on the Port Republic–Harrisonburg Road. He would join Merritt in the advance to Port Republic. Wilson's 3rd Division, General Torbert, and Lowell's Reserve Brigade were ordered to move to Staunton and then Waynesboro. On the way they were to pick up Colonel Powell's 2nd Division, which was on the Valley Turnpike about eight miles ahead. General Custer would ride with Torbert. He had been assigned to relieve Colonel Powell and take command of the 2nd Division. Torbert's orders were to destroy the railroad bridge at Waynesboro and drive off cattle and burn forage, "breadstuffs," and flourmills on the way back.[12]

The troops moved out at 5 A.M. Powell's division, moving down the Valley Turnpike and following the enemy in his front, turned east toward Piedmont. Torbert moved directly to Staunton. The Union cavalrymen spent the twenty-sixth and most of the twenty-seventh destroying the considerable military supplies stored in the town.

"The latter place [Staunton] is very pretty, one of the finest places I have seen in the Confederacy," wrote Sam Corbett. "The Rebels are supposed to be making tracks for Linchburg, they left a great many of their wounded at Harrisonburg and Staunton. . . . [W]e have been at work nearly all day destroying commissary and quartermasters stores of the Rebels and the Rail road. The Johnies must have left here in a hurry as they left at deal of stuff for us to destroy. They had a large Boot and Shoe factory here which we burned. 150 dollars in Confederate Script is the price of a common pair of cowhide boots."[13]

Colonel Lowell was looking forward to the time when the brigade would go into winter quarters and Josephine could join him:

> I didn't tell you what a magnificent spring wagon I have now,—four stylish white horses and driver to manoeuvre them, it beats Tyler's red turnout, I think: it's for you to ride out in next winter. In this army (and in the Army of the Potomac) some such affair is a recognized part of a brigade commander's equipment, general orders always mention a spring-wagon for each headquarters, &c., so you see we are likely to be very magnificent this winter, as commanding the Regular Brigade I am expected to indulge in even more luxe than my neighbors, we shall quite disappoint the world, shan't we, with our republican simplicity! I haven't told you either that, the day before yesterday at Luray, I organized a small black boy, bright enough and well brought up; his name is James, but as we have already two of that name about here, I call him Luray, which is quite aristocratic. You can teach him to read and write this winter, if you have time. The Doctor thinks you would find more satisfaction in him than in your pupils of Vienna.
>
> I wish you could see the splendid country we are in, we are about one mile beyond Staunton, facing towards the Blue Ridge—we have found out pretty well where the Rebs are, and I have a notion that we shall be getting back pretty soon toward the infantry.[14]

General Torbert reported that his command had destroyed or captured "300 muskets, 75 sabers, 50 cartridge boxes, 70 sets horse equipment, 60 rounds fixed ammunition, 200 sets harness, 350 saddle trees, 200 tents, 65 head of beef cattle, 57 prisoners, 25 wagons, 5 tons salt, 100 barrels flour, 500 bales hay, 1,000 bushels wheat, 125 barrels hard bread, 50 boxes tobacco, 50 horses, medical supplies &C."[15] By 3 P.M. they were moving toward Waynesboro. General Custer, escorted by a full regiment, was sent to Piedmont to find the 2nd Division. Lowell's brigade, again serving as rear guard, marched until 11 P.M. When the column halted, Lowell set up a picket line at Rockfish Gap and ordered it to push out toward New Hope, a few miles out of Waynesboro. The rest of his troops camped near the town. Wilson's troopers moved out at dawn to the iron bridge across the south fork of the Shenandoah intending to dismantle it, but the structure proved to be more than they could handle and remained standing in spite of their best efforts. Other Federals burned the railroad depot and government buildings in the town.[16]

The strain of the campaign was beginning to wear on Lowell. On the twenty-eighth he wrote a strange and unusually somber letter to his wife: "I used to look forward to things somehow—now I don't look forward, but all the old pleasure of looking forward seems to be stirred in with things as they come along. I can't explain what I mean, but the difference is immense."[17]

At about 5 P.M. a force of Confederate infantry and a battery of artillery suddenly appeared on the left flank of Lowell's picket line and opened fire. The brigade slowly fell back toward Waynesboro, covering the rest of the Union troops, who by this time were retreating towards Harrisonburg. "Musket balls and shells flying around quite lively," Sergeant Corbett recorded in his diary. "The Rebels are flanking us and whipping us at the same time, the fighting is getting quite hot."[18]

The 2nd Massachusetts bore the brunt of the fighting. Brigader General John Pegram's veteran infantry division and all of Wickham's cavalry attacked. The brigade was badly outnumbered and lost heavily. Some of the men who had dismounted and were unable to keep up with the retreating brigade became prisoners.[19] Californians Robert Burns and Cpl. Edward Kingsley of Company L, Sgt. Benjamin Williams of Company E, and Massachusetts Pvt. William Hurley were killed. Five men were wounded. One, James P. Hunter from Company L, died of his wounds on Christmas Eve in Philadelphia. Six men were captured. One of them later died in prison (see Appendix for a detailed list of casualties).

Colonel Crowninshield had a horse shot out from under him and Lowell's horse was wounded. An unnamed sergeant from the 2nd Massachusetts claimed he saved Lowell's life "by running in and getting badly sabred himself."[20]

The Reserve Brigade was driven through the center of the little town. There it received some help from Torbert's headquarters guard and a squadron of Rhode Island cavalry that was acting as the provost guard. Captain George Bliss of the 1st Rhode Island Cavalry described the action:

> Looking toward the enemy I saw Colonel Charles Russell Lowell, who had been in command of the picket line, riding toward us with his horse in a walk—the last man to fall back before the advance of the enemy. The Confederate bullets were whistling about him, and frequent puffs of dust in the road showed where they struck right and left of the brave soldier. Putting spurs to my horse, I rode forward to meet him and the following conversation ensued:
>
> "Colonel Lowell, I had but a few of the Provost Guards, and did what I could with them to help you."
>
> "Well Captain, we must check their advance with a sabre charge. Isn't that the best we can do?"
>
> "I think so Colonel."
>
> By this time we had come up to the Third New Jersey Cavalry, known in the army as the "Butterflies" on account of their gay uniforms, and Colonel Lowell said to the officer in command: "Major, let your first squadron sling their carbines, draw their sabres and charge." The order was given "forward," but not a man moved; they were completely disheartened by having seen the other troops driven back. The Captain in charge of the squadron said,
>
> "Corporal Jones are you afraid," and the Corporal made no reply.

The men wavered and Colonel Lowell said, "Give a cheer boys, and go at them," and at once, suiting the action to the words spurred his horse at the gallop towards the enemy, followed by myself, both of us waving our sabres. The squadron at once cheered and followed.[21]

Lowell fell back to organize added support as Bliss led the charging Federals. Out in front, Bliss found himself alone among the Confederates, who were retreating in the face of the squadron's charge, and was captured when his horse was shot down. The valiant officer spent the rest of the war in Richmond's Libby Prison.

The Reserve Brigade formed both the advance and rear guards for the division during the retreat. The men marched all night, passing through Staunton at midnight, and finally went into camp at 4 A.M. at Spring Hill.[22] After a short break the brigade marched to a small patch of woods about a mile from Mount Crawford on the left of the three infantry corps. Both horses and men were about played out from the constant marching and fighting and needed rest. Sixty-five new recruits for the 2nd Massachusetts came into camp at noon to make up the losses the regiment had suffered in the past two weeks. A picket line was set up from Cross Keys to Rockland Mills to cover the army's flank.[23]

While Torbert was raiding up the Valley, Merritt occupied Port Republic. By coincidence, Merritt arrived there the same day Kershaw was marching through Swift Run Gap on his way to rejoin Early with four infantry brigades. The Southerners attacked immediately and Merritt's outnumbered cavalrymen were pushed back toward Cross Keys. Sheridan ordered up infantry support to join Merritt at Cross Keys, hoping the maneuver would provoke an attack. Instead, Kershaw retreated and joined Early at Rockfish Gap. Merritt then reoccupied Port Republic.

During the day, word came that General Wilson was being reassigned to Maj. Gen. William T. Sherman's Military Division of the Mississippi as chief of cavalry. Custer, who had not yet taken command of the 2nd Division, was sent to take over the 3rd Division, and Col. William Powell retained command of the 2nd Division.[24]

Sheridan stretched his supply line with each mile he advanced up the Valley. The number of wagons was limited. Since the trains had to carry forage for their own mules, the tons of supplies that could be carried to the army were inversely proportional to the number of miles between the army and its supply base. Brigadier General Jonathan D. Stevenson, the commander at Harper's Ferry responsible for organizing the wagon trains and escorts that supplied the army, pleaded for additional teams: "There ought to be at once at least 300 wagons sent to this post and Martinsburg to carry forward necessary supplies to be held as post teams independent from army supply. This would enable us to meet promptly unexpected demands and is a reserve absolutely requisite for an army the size of General Sheridan's operating so far from its base."[25]

In late September Grant asked Halleck for his views on opening up the Manassas Gap Railroad to Strasburg as an alternate to the long wagon trains. Halleck at first reported that it would take a week. Then, later that same afternoon, he sent a more detailed response: "I now learn the Manassas Gap Railroad can be put in running order to Piedmont, sixteen mile from Front Royal, in three days. From there to Front Royal, all of the iron of the track has been carried away, and it will require about a week to replace it. From Front Royal to Strasburg all the bridges, which are very long have been destroyed and the rails removed. . . . We can picket it from Alexandria to Thoroughfare Gap but General Sheridan must defend it beyond."[26]

At Secretary of War Stanton's request, General Stevenson offered an alternative. He proposed to repair the railroad to Winchester and make that point Sheridan's base for operations in the lower Valley. He also suggested that if Sheridan intended to move south toward Lynchburg there be no supply base in the Valley and that the army be supplied by way of Luray Gap and the Orange and Alexandria Railroad.[27]

The Manassas Gap Railroad's easterly terminus was at Manassas Junction. If either Halleck's plan (a base at Strasburg) or Stevenson's second route (supply via the Orange and Alexandria) was selected, the railroad as far as Manassas Junction would have to be repaired. Without selecting a plan, Grant ordered the repair work on the Orange and Alexandria started. From there it would be up to Sheridan to decide which route would be the best.

Sheridan, who opposed moving into the upper Valley wrote Grant that

> My judgment is that it would be best to terminate this campaign by the destruction of crops, &c., in this valley, and the transfer of the troops to the army operating against Richmond. If the Orange and Alexandria is opened it will take an army corps to protect it. If the Front Royal road is opened, it will take as many troops to protect it, as there is no enemy in the Valley to operate against. Early is, without doubt, fortifying at Charlottesville, holding Rockfish Gap. It is no easy matter to pass these mountain gaps and attack Charlottesville, hauling supplies through difficult passes, fourteen miles in length, and with a line of communication from 135 to 145 miles in length, without the organization of supply trains, ordnance trains, and all the appointments of an army making a permanent advance. At present we are organized for a raid up the Valley, with no trains except the corps trains. . . . With my presents means, I cannot accumulate supplies enough to carry me through to the Orange and Alexandria Railroad.[28]

The long wagon trains from Martinsburg and Harper's Ferry were a unique opportunity for organized guerrilla bands to change the course of events. In spite of roving bands of stragglers and Mosby's guerrillas, the flow of rations and supplies to Sheridan's army during the crucial period of the campaign never stopped. Between September 19 and October 19, seven major trains were sent to the front, all without mishap. The size of these trains varied, the largest was about a thousand wagons and the smallest around 250. They carried rations, forage, ammunition, tents, and medical supplies. On the return leg they carried a steady stream of prisoners, wounded, and refugees. The escorting troops never exceeded two thousand men. Most of the escorts were made of up of remounted cavalry, returning convalescents, men back from furlough, or second-line regiments from the defenses around Washington. Only two brigades, Col. Leonard D. H. Currie's 3rd Brigade from Brig. Gen. William Dwight's division of XIX Corps and Brig. Gen. Oliver Edwards's brigade from VI Corps's 1st Division, were detailed from the frontline forces.[29] That was hardly a major diversion of frontline strength.

About the fourth or fifth of October, when the difficulties of pursuing Early to Charlottesville and Gordonsville became apparent, Sheridan decided to return down the Valley. The move would shorten his supply lines and permit him to complete the destruction of the Valley as a supply source for the Confederacy.

Sheridan now held a line across the Valley from Port Republic to Mount Crawford to the Back Road near Briery Branch Gap in the Cumberland Mountains. Custer's division was on the right covering the Back Road, and Torbert covered the Valley Turnpike with Powell's division and Lowell's brigade. The remainder of Merritt's division picketed the army's left flank.

The first three days of October were rainy and cold. The 2nd Massachusetts was camped in a small wood near Mount Crawford. The nearby woods and fields concealed groups of rebel stragglers and the troopers took a number of prisoners during the day. On October 2 the regiment skirmished with the advancing rebels for most of the day. At the end of the day they moved to a new camp to the rear of the picket line. During the afternoon of the third the brigade conducted a reconnaissance down the pike as far as Bridgeport, chasing away a band of rebels guarding a bridge and taking several prisoners.[30]

At dusk that evening one of those tragic events so common in this war occurred. It was tragic because a young man who had shown much promise lost his life, and because it caused a bitterness and anger that lasted for decades after the war. Twenty-one-year-old Lt. John Meigs, who was Sheridan's topographic engineer officer, a member of the West Point class of 1863, and the son of Maj. Gen. Montgomery Meigs, was murdered within the Union lines. Lieutenant Meigs and two assistants had spent the day plotting the country around the Union positions. They started back toward camp as the sun dipped below the mountains. Riding along the Swift Run Gap road, they came upon three men dressed in Union uniforms about a mile and a half from Sheridan's headquarters. Lieutenant Meigs and his companions saw the blue uniforms and, considering the proximity to Union headquarters, assumed the three strangers were friends. They rode on a bit and then suddenly were ordered to surrender by the three men. Without a pause the trio opened fire. Meigs was killed without the opportunity to surrender or resist. One of his assistants escaped and one was captured.[31]

Confederate accounts claimed that the three assailants were scouts.[32] According to General Early, Meigs refused to surrender and fired first, wounding one of the Confederates.[33] The Union soldier who escaped to Sheridan's headquarters denied the rebel's claim. The useless murder incensed Sheridan. He ordered Custer to burn everything within a five-mile radius. The next morning, as Custer began carrying out his orders, the Confederates paroled the topographer they had captured. Sheridan in turn called a halt to the burning. Only a few houses had been destroyed, but it was enough to express vengeance.[34] After the war General Meigs, bitter that his only son had been murdered by guerrillas, offered a $1,000 reward for their capture. Although the killers were known throughout the Shenandoah, the reward was never claimed. General Meigs, one of the major architects of the Union victory, died in January 1892, bitter to the end.

On October 6 Sheridan started the army moving toward Strasburg. Custer's division moved to the Back Road and Merritt covered the Valley Turnpike. Powell was at Front Royal. As the army marched north, the cavalry was ordered to destroy all supplies, mills, and barns and drive off all livestock.[35] "Near Harrisonburg an order was issued this AM for all Citizens to pack up and leave this valley, either go North or South," Sam Corbett recorded in his diary. "Men are now riding through the country issuing this order. This evening we commence burning all the barns and store houses in the Vicinity. . . . Last night the heavens were lit up for miles with the glow of burning buildings, houses[36] and barns alike destroyed. The intention is to clean out this valley completely."[37]

Back in August, when Grant appointed Sheridan to command the Army of the Shenandoah, he told him to destroy the agronomy of the Valley "so a crow will have to carry his own provisions." For the next week, as the cavalry withdrew down the Valley, flames and destruction marked their path and a gray haze covered the landscape.[38]

The gray haze ominously concealed a resurgent, reinforced rebel host that was still dangerous.

II | The Woodstock Races

After the battle at Fisher's Hill, Lee sent Cutshaw's light artillery battalion, Kershaw's infantry division, and Rosser's Laurel Brigade to the Valley. Rosser had been Custer's roommate at West Point and, earlier in the year, had badly beaten him in a cavalry fight at Trevilian Station.[1]

When Fitz Lee, commanding one of Early's cavalry divisions, was wounded at Opequon Creek, Rosser took command of the division and Col. Richard Dulaney took over the Laurel Brigade. The division now included the Laurel Brigade, Wickham's brigade, now commanded by Munford, and Col. W. H. F. Payne's small brigade. Lomax continued to command Early's other cavalry division. Unlike Sheridan's cavalry, there was no overall cavalry commander.

As the Union army moved down the Valley in late September and early October, burning and destroying its production capacity, Rosser's division nipped at the heels of the Union army, picking up stragglers and attacking the cavalry rear guard at every opportunity. The Confederate cavalry was often dangerously ahead of its infantry support, a fact that did not escape Sheridan's notice.

On October 7, under the cover of a thick fog and smoky haze, Rosser came up against Custer's division on the Back Road at Mill Creek. He split his force and struck Custer on the flank while his main body attacked in front, down the Back Road. Custer's men were pushed steadily back.[2] On the Valley Turnpike near Woodstock, another portion of Rosser's troops attacked the cavalry wagon train, but was repulsed by the 2nd Massachusetts and the Reserve Brigade guarding the train, in a bloodless skirmish.[3]

The next day, the wagons, followed by the remainder of Merritt's division, crossed a small stream called Tom's Brook. Torbert sent down orders to halt and form a battle line. Shortly afterward the 1st Brigade was ordered to move back toward Woodstock on reconnaissance. A regular cavalry regiment from the Reserve Brigade and one from the 2nd Brigade were ordered out on the flanks to protect the movement. Soon after the 1st Brigade started, Custer sent word that he was heavily engaged on the Back Road, about four miles from Tom's Brook. Torbert ordered Merritt to send two brigades to strike the Confederate flank. Merritt sent the Reserve Brigade and the 2nd Brigade, which marched cross-country and started skirmishing with the enemy. The Confederates turned to face the new threat and the fighting became heavy. The two Union brigades, now facing Rosser's complete division, were forced back across Tom's Brook. Custer, now on the enemy's right flank, was expected to attack but, for some unknown reason, the attack never came.

Meanwhile, Colonel Lowell had another horse shot out from under him. That evening he wrote: "We had another skirmish yesterday with their cavalry. Lieutenant Tucker wounded and Sergeant Wakefield;—the roan horse killed, and today I shall have to ride the gray unless I can find Sergeant Wakefield's. Enos has been looking for him for two hours."[4]

Wakefield's horse, its saddle creased by a rebel bullet, was found later that day and Lowell rode him throughout the next day's fighting. Although the infantry had beaten the Confederates at every turn since the battle at Opequon Creek, the total smashup of Early's army had eluded Sheridan. At Winchester and Fisher's Hill the cavalry pursuit had been lackadaisical, and Torbert's failure to stop the retreating rebels at New Market was disappointing. Sheridan was dissatisfied with his cavalry and its leader. Frustrated by the Confederate cavalry's steady pursuit during the army's withdrawal, he decided to put some fire into his mounted arm. On the evening of October 8 Sheridan ordered General Torbert to "whip the Rebel Cavalry or get whipped himself." Sheridan added that he was going to the top of nearby Round Top Mountain the next day to watch the fight.

The order was reminiscent of Sheridan's confrontation with Meade in April 1864. During the movement toward Spotsylvania, Meade had issued orders directly to several of Sheridan's cavalry divisions. Sheridan was furious and confronted Meade. In a bitter, face-to-face shouting match, Sheridan offered his resignation and then said that if Meade would let him use cavalry the way it should be used, he would go and "whip Jeb Stuart out of his boots." Meade went to Grant and told him everything Sheridan had said, fully expecting that Sheridan would be brought up on charges of insubordination.

When Meade told Grant that Sheridan had said he would whip Stuart, Grant looked up and replied, "Did he say so? Then let him go out and do it."[5]

Sheridan delivered on his promise, soundly beating the Confederate cavalry in four days of almost continual fighting during the second week of May. The Union troopers also destroyed about ten miles of the Virginia Central Railroad, two hundred thousand pounds of bacon, and nearly all the Army of Northern Virginia's medical supplies. On May 11, at a small village called Yellow Tavern, Stuart's cavalry and the bluecoats came together in a confused, swirling fight. Sheridan's men routed the rebels and chased them back to the lines surrounding Richmond. Casualties were severe on both sides. Stuart, the leader of Lee's cavalry and the darling of the Confederacy, was among the dead. It was the first major defeat of Confederate cavalry in the war. Yellow Tavern was the standard by which Torbert would be measured.

Torbert started to move his troops into position for an attack the next morning. Merritt's division was camped at the foot of Round Top Mountain just north of Tom's Brook, where the fighting had ended that afternoon. Custer had fallen back about two miles and was now about six miles away to the north and west, in the rear of Merritt's division.

Rosser's three brigades were on the Back Road at Tom's Brook behind several stone walls and hastily erected barricades. The men in these brigades were all veterans from Stuart's Cavalry Corps and most were reasonably well equipped with sabers and carbines. Lomax was on Merritt's front along the Valley Turnpike with Jackson's and Johnson's brigades. His other two brigades were on detached duty. Jackson's and Johnson's were a wild and undisciplined group, more interested in plunder than real fighting. They were armed with infantry rifles, shotguns, and whatever they had gathered during two years of roving the Valley.

Custer was ordered to move up the Back Road and attack Rosser at daybreak. Merritt's movements were to conform to Custer's and provide support on his left flank. Colonel James H. Kidd's brigade, less one regiment to support Lowell, was sent to reinforce Custer's left and support his attack. As the fighting spread from the right flank, Merritt was to attack Lomax's division in his front.[6]

It was very cold on the morning of October 9; there had been snow flurries during the night.[7] The troops were up long before sunrise, brewing coffee and cooking bacon and hardtack. The Reserve Brigade, led by the 2nd Massachusetts, had the assignment of leading the frontal assault up the Valley Turnpike. Lowell's brigade was reduced to three regiments, the 2nd Massachusetts and the 1st and 2nd U.S. Cavalry Regiments. The 1st New York Dragoons, from Kidd's brigade, was on the left in reserve, and the 5th U.S. Cavalry had been assigned to headquarters as Merritt's reserve.

They had only to wait for Custer, and for once he was on time. At 7 o'clock, just as the sun rose over the Blue Ridge, the distinctive crack of Spencer carbines was heard over on the right flank. The sound grew in intensity and then the horse artillery started banging away, answered by a boom from a battery of Confederate guns. Merritt ordered Devin's 1st Brigade to move to the center between the two roads to maintain a continuous division front and provide reinforcements to either wing as needed. The men of the 2nd Massachusetts mounted their horses, and, under the prodding of the company sergeants, shook out into a line of battle across the Valley Turnpike. The 1st and 2nd U.S. Cavalry Regiments formed a second line behind the Californians and Massachusetts men.[8] In front, the ground dipped down to a line of maples clad in their red and yellow fall foliage, marking the course of Tom's Brook.

The two lines splashed across the brook at a walk, opposed by a smattering of fire from the Confederate pickets. About a quarter of mile past the brook, at a small creek called Jordan's Run, they came upon two Confederate brigades that had dismounted and established a defensive line behind cover. Suddenly, six rebel guns opened up on the right flank and the Confederate cavalrymen opened fire, driving Lowell's troopers back. The brigade retreated about a half mile in some confusion. The officers rallied the shaken troopers and reformed the lines. Lowell sent a courier to Merritt asking for help. The division commander responded by sending the 1st New York Dragoons and 5th U.S. Cavalry to his aid. Lowell put the 1st New York on the pike, supported by the 5th U.S. Cavalry. The 2nd Massachusetts was split and placed on the flanks and the smaller 2nd U.S. Cavalry was left behind to support a section of artillery. As Lowell was reorganizing in preparation for resuming the attack, Devin's brigade flanked the Confederate artillery battery, which fell back. The second attack, no longer plagued by galling artillery fire from the flank, slowly drove the Confederates back down the pike.

At first the retreat was stubbornly contested as Lomax skillfully used the broken ground and small woods to shield his men. However, the countryside opened up at Woodstock, and the Union soldiers, fighting on horseback, could see their enemy in front. This was cavalry country. Lowell gave the order to charge and buglers sounded the call. The Union troopers drew sabers and moved forward, first at a trot and then at a gallop. The Confederate line broke and the battle degenerated into a running fight. Lowell's men, their sabers flashing, chased the rebels, who "ran like sheep,"[9] for ten miles. Several times the rebel artillery tried to make a stand. Near Woodstock, two guns halted and fired on the advancing troopers. Lowell ordered a charge and his men captured the guns. Everyone who offered resistance was cut down. At Edenburgh, two more guns with several caissons and wagons shared a similar fate. The Reserve Brigade was finally halted at Stony Creek, more for the sake of the horses than any resistance on the part of the enemy. Two regiments from the 2nd Brigade continued pursuit and did not halt until the demoralized Confederate cavalry reached their infantry support at New Market.[10]

Rosser's division held together somewhat better against Custer's attack. The fighting was heavier but Custer, supported by Devin's brigade and two of Kidd's regiments from Merritt's division, drove the Confederates steadily to the rear.

The two Union cavalry divisions captured eleven guns. The 2nd Massachusetts took five of the eleven. Merritt's division captured forty-two wagons, three ambulances, four caissons, five forges, twenty-nine mules, thirty-nine horses, and took fifty-two prisoners. In addition, Lowell's troopers took a Confederate battle flag.

Later that night the battle got another name not recorded in the official reports: the men called it the "Woodstock Races" as they sat around their camp fires discussing the day's events.[11] Next to Sheridan's fight with Stuart in May, it was the worst defeat Confederate cavalry suffered during the war. From that day on, Sheridan's cavalry would dominate their rebel counterparts.

Casualties in the 2nd Massachusetts were light. Lawrence Lawson was killed and James Collins was mortally wounded. He died at the hospital in Winchester two weeks later. Both troopers were from Company C. Six men were wounded, including 2nd Lt. Samuel Tucker of Company L and 1st Sgt. Elhana W. Wakefield of Company F.

In a dispatch to General Lee that night, Early wrote:

> I have not heard from General Rosser, but he is, I understand, falling back in good order, having rallied his command, which is on what is called the Back Road, which is west of the pike; but Lomax's command, which was on the pike, came back to this place in confusion. This is distressing to me, and God knows I have done all in my power to avert the disasters which have befallen this command; but the fact is that the enemy's cavalry is so much superior to ours, both in numbers and equipment, and

the country is so favorable to the operations of cavalry, that it is impossible for ours to compete with his. Lomax's cavalry are armed entirely with rifles and have no sabers, and the consequence is that they cannot fight on horseback, and in this open country they cannot fight on foot against large bodies of cavalry; besides, the command is and has been demoralized all the time. It would be better if they could all be put in the infantry; but if that were tried I am afraid they would all run off.[12]

Early correctly identified the reason for the rout. The Confederate cavalry was an armed rabble compared to the superbly equipped and disciplined Federal troopers. Without pistols, sabers, and repeating carbines, the Confederates were not equipped to fight mounted cavalry. The Confederate system was also partially responsible. Confederate cavalrymen supplied their own horses. The local countryside had been stripped of horses by both armies. A Confederate cavalryman whose horse was shot out from under him could quickly find himself in the infantry.[13] Confederate troopers were stubborn fighters on foot because their horses were protected. Rebels engaged in a mounted fight had good reason to run if their horses were endangered.

One wonders what happened to all the horses, arms, and equipment supposedly captured by Mosby the year before. Captured equipment and animals were supposed to be purchased by the government at fair prices established by the Confederate quartermaster corps. The horses and material Mosby claimed to have captured in 1863 should have been enough to supply several cavalry divisions. Either Mosby's accounts were exaggerated or the captured mounts were sold in more lucrative markets.

That night the Reserve Brigade moved back and camped at Woodstock. The next morning, October 10, they started at daybreak and moved to within three miles of Strasburg, where they camped on the left of the 2nd Brigade. The supply wagons came up and issued four days' rations that night. They passed through Strasburg the next morning at seven, and then went into camp at 4 P.M. on the banks of the Shenandoah, about four miles from town. Lowell's troopers spent the remaining daylight hours washing clothes and cleaning up for the first time in a long spell.[14]

With the defeat of the Confederate cavalry, Sheridan concluded that the campaign was over. He ordered VI Corps to move to Front Royal. He intended to send VI Corps, followed by a division of cavalry, to Petersburg via Alexandria by way of the Manassas Gap Railroad in the next few days. By the twelfth, however, after several attacks on the railhead and one on a supply train, the work had been slowed.[15] Sheridan ordered the VI Corps to move toward Ashby's Gap. From there the troops would march to Alexandria, where transports would take them to City Point.[16]

A reconnaissance party from Merritt's division was sent down the Valley Pike, and Custer's division sent scouts up the Back Road. Both patrols went about twelve miles without finding any Confederates. Lowell's brigade was ordered to Cedar Creek and arrived there on the twelfth. A heavy rain fell as the troops set up camp.

The Reserve Brigade was camped on the army's left on flat ground alongside Cedar Creek on the J. Cooley farm. Powell's 2nd Cavalry Division was posted several miles farther left, toward Front Royal. Pickets were sent out along the river.[17] In spite of the rain, Colonel Lowell ordered the brigade out for dismounted drill. The enlisted men were delighted when General Merritt sent word to stop the drilling because he wanted the men to rest.[18]

At midnight the 2nd Massachusetts was sent to Rectortown to escort a courier party. Couriers were increasingly the targets of the numerous stragglers from Early's army and communications had occasionally been disrupted from time to time by these roving bands. Earlier Sheridan had written Grant: "Lieutenant Colonel Tolles my chief quartermaster and Asst. Surg. Emil Ohlenschlager, medical inspector on my staff, were both mortally wounded by guerrillas to-day, on their way to join me from Winchester; they were ambuscaded. Three men killed and five wounded out of an escort of twenty-four. The refugees from Early's army, cavalry and infantry, are organizing guerrilla parties, and are becoming very formidable and are annoying me very much."[19]

On the afternoon of October 12 General Grant sent a wire to Halleck regarding the future disposition of Sheridan's army. The dispatch was the first in a chain of events that set the stage for the destruction of the Confederate army in the Shenandoah: "After sending the Sixth Corps and one division of cavalry here, I think Sheridan should keep up as advanced position as possible toward the Virginia Central road, and be prepared with supplies to advance on that road at Gordonsville and Charlottesville at any time the enemy weakens himself sufficiently to admit of it. The cutting of that road and the canal would be of vast importance to us."[20]

Halleck sent a slightly reworded version of this dispatch to Sheridan. However, the rewording changed the whole emphasis of Grant's intent: "General Grant wishes a position taken far enough south to serve as a base for future operations on Gordonsville and Charlottesville. It must be strongly fortified and provisioned. Some point in the vicinity of Manassas Gap would seem best suited for all purposes. Colonel Alexander, of the Engineers will be sent to consult with you as soon as you connect with General Auger."[21]

Setting up a fortified base was not in Sheridan's nature. The authorities in Washington knew he was opposed to Halleck's ideas and would not endorse the plan. A later dispatch from Secretary of War Stanton suggested a meeting to settle the issue: "If you can come here, a consultation on several points is extremely desirable. I propose to visit General Grant and would like to see you first."[22]

The second in the chain of events delayed Sheridan's trip to Washington. On October 13, Early, now reinforced with Kershaw's division, pushed a force out from his entrenchments at Fisher's Hill and attacked an infantry force commanded by Colonel Thoburn at Hupp's Hill, just beyond Strasburg. Thoburn was forced back to the north bank of Cedar Creek. Sheridan concluded that this attack indicated Early intended to resume the offensive. He decided to issue orders recalling VI Corps.[23]

The next day Lowell's regular cavalry regiments moved to a new camp on the

Belle Grove Plantation about two miles south of Middleburg, to the right and rear of army headquarters.[24] The 2nd Massachusetts returned from Rectortown in the afternoon and joined the regulars there.[25] The cavalry picket line on the left of the infantry was withdrawn and Crook's corps took over the position.

Sheridan intended to attack Early at Hupp's Hill as soon as Wright returned with VI Corps. After Wright arrived, scouts determined that Early had returned to Fisher's Hill. Sheridan, positive the enemy at Fisher's Hill "could not accomplish much," decided to go to Washington and "come to some definite understanding about my future operations."[26] He ordered Torbert to accompany him with Merritt's division. On the evening of the October 15, Sheridan, leading the column, rode to Front Royal on his way to Rectortown to meet with General Auger. From there he would take the train to Washington. He planned to return to the army on the nineteeth by way of the Baltimore and Ohio Railroad to Martinsburg and then by horse to Winchester. Torbert, in the meantime, would continue through Chester Gap and destroy the Virginia Central bridge over the Rivanna River at Charlottesville.[27] General Wright would temporarily command the army during Sheridan's absence.

The 2nd Massachusetts and the Union cavalry arrived at Front Royal at 1:30 A.M. and went into camp. Sheridan stopped at a house on the north bank of the river. While there, the third and final event in the chain leading to the destruction of Early's army occurred. Sheridan was handed a dispatch from Wright stating: "I enclose [for] you [a] dispatch which explains itself. If the enemy should be strongly reinforced in cavalry, he might, by turning our right, give us a great deal of trouble. I shall hold on here until the enemy's movements are developed, and I shall only fear an attack on my right, which I shall make every preparation for guarding against and resisting."[28]

The dispatch Wright enclosed was addressed to General Early and said, "Be ready to move as soon as my forces join you and we will crush Sheridan."[29]

Ominously, it was signed "Longstreet, Lieutenant General." The message had been read as it was being flagged by the Confederate signal station on the top of Three Top Mountain, a steep escarpment at the end of Massanutten Mountain, overlooking the Union camp at Cedar Creek. Federal signal officers who had the Confederate cipher were able to decode it.[30] Sheridan suspected the dispatch was a ruse, but to be on the safe side he ordered Torbert to take the cavalry back to Cedar Creek. Reveille sounded at 3:30 A.M. and by six the cavalry was on the road back to Middletown. "The cavalry is all ordered back to you; make your position strong," Sheridan instructed Wright. "If Longstreet's dispatch is true, he is under the impression that we have largely detached. I will go over to Auger, and may get additional news. Close in Colonel Powell, who will be at this point. If the enemy should make an advance I know you will defeat him. Look well to your ground and be well prepared. Get up everything that can be spared. I will bring up all I can, and will be up on Tuesday, (October 18) if not sooner."[31]

Torbert led Merritt's and Custer's divisions back to the Cedar Creek area in the afternoon, Powell's division remained at Front Royal, and Sheridan went on to

Washington. At Cedar Creek, Merritt's division returned to the camp near Belle Grove. Future moves would await the return of General Sheridan.

Cedar Creek meanders down the Valley in an easterly direction. Just north of the Valley Pike crossing, it turns sharply to the southeast. About a mile after passing under a stone bridge at the Valley Pike it turns back to the east and joins the Shenandoah another mile and a half downstream. The Shenandoah runs along the south side of Strasburg, then tight against the base of Three Top Mountain before joining Cedar Creek. After the juncture, the Shenandoah continues in an easterly direction toward Front Royal. Middletown is about two and a half miles north of the stone bridge on the Valley Pike. The western side of the pike is flat and open, sloping up from Cedar Creek to a crest just beyond the town. There are no natural obstacles to a flanking attack in this portion of the field. Northeast of the Valley Pike, Cedar Creek is fordable in October, but the banks are steep and not passable for wagons or guns except at established fords. Two fords cross the creek. Hottle's Mill Ford is nearest to the pike. It crosses the creek on the southeast leg, about a mile upstream from the stone bridge. A small creek, Meadow Brook, running from north to south in a shallow ravine, flows into Cedar Creek near Hottle's Mill Ford. Cupp's Ford, the second crossing on the north side of Cedar Creek, is about four miles northwest of Middletown. East of the pike the ground slopes much more sharply down to the Shenandoah. Two creeks cross the slope and run east to the river below. The ravines along these creeks are deeper and steeper.

The ground drops abruptly to the creek below south of the Cedar Creek bridge. There are three fords in front of the high ground. The first, Bowman's Mill Ford, is about a mile and a half south of the bridge at the point where Cedar Creek turns east. Two fords with graded approaches cross the Shenandoah. The first, McInturff's Ford, is another mile downstream; the second, Bowman's Ford, is about a half mile downstream from McInturff's Ford. A small country road connected the two Shenandoah fords directly in front and below Thoburn's entrenchments. Both fords are shallow and have good gravel bases. In 1864, McInturff's and Bowman's Fords were only accessible by narrow footpaths on the south side.[32]

On the night of October 16, General Rosser, still smarting from the defeat at Tom's Brook, set out to attempt to capture General Custer. After obtaining Early's permission, Rosser took five hundred picked men from Brig. Gen. Bryan Grimes's North Carolina infantry brigade. The infantrymen were mounted behind cavalrymen and the force moved out along the south side of Cedar Creek. They headed toward Old Forge, where Custer's headquarters was supposedly located. The column turned right and stopped at a prearranged location where a scout was to meet them and guide them to the camp. The scout mistook the Confederates for Union troops and remained concealed. In exasperation, Rosser decided to proceed anyway and moved slowly forward. He split his force into two parts, then charged, only to find a small picket post at the site of the former Union headquarters. The two Confederate columns became confused and a brisk little firefight broke out between them. At last, after several rebels were wounded, someone got the firing

stopped and they withdrew with only a few Union pickets to show for their efforts.[33]

The Union army was spread over the ground between the stone bridge and
Middletown. Crook's VIII Corps was camped on the high ground overlooking the
junction of Cedar Creek and the Shenandoah. Emory's XIX Corps was echeloned
behind Crook on the west side of the Valley Pike about three-quarters of a mile to
the right rear, in front of the Belle Grove Plantation house. The VI Corps was
about a mile to the right rear of Emory's position. Wright believed an attack on the
left was impossible, but he was greatly concerned with his right flank. Rosser's
aborted raid reinforced his convictions. He decided to move Merritt's division to
the right to reinforce Custer. Merritt sent pickets out along Cedar Creek connecting with Custer's picket line.

In the new camp Lowell wrote to his wife:

> I get the Chaplain's "Army and Navy Journal" for the present. . . . It's notices
> about this Shenandoah campaign have not been very good: it has been wrong in
> some most important facts and some of its' criticisms. It has been entirely wrong to in
> praising ———— so constantly; ———— from the beginning has been the laughing
> stock here, his absurd newspaper reporter may have caused this, but worse than that,
> his false dispatches to the general and his constant habit of having "infantry" in front
> of him, and of falling back "pressed" have on two occasions come very near causing
> great disasters.[34]

Although Mrs. Lowell edited the missing name from the letter long after the
war, it is obvious that Lowell was writing about Custer. He probably was referring
to the fights at the Luray Valley and Tom's Brook.

On October 16 and 17 several members of the Confederate command reconnoitered Sheridan's position. Early's chief topographical engineer, Jed Hotchkiss, General Gordon, Brig. Gen. Clement Evans, and Gordon's chief of staff, Maj. Robert
Hunter, climbed to the signal station atop Three Top Mountain. Evans, who had
been wounded during the Maryland raid in July, had only been back with his troops
a few days.

The Union camps were laid out at the Confederate officers' feet like a gigantic
map. While Hotchkiss sketched out the federal positions, Gordon, Evans, and
Hunter planned their strategy. Early favored an attack on the Union right. From
their vantage point Gordon and Evans became convinced that if a route could be
found, an attack on the Union left would give them the victory the Confederates
so badly needed. The exhausted party did not get back to camp until long after dark
and Gordon decided to wait until morning to present his plan of attack to General
Early.

The next day Hotchkiss found a concealed route on which Gordon's division
could advance. Little more than a footpath, it ran along the base of Massanutten
Mountain behind Strasburg and led to Bowman's and McInturff's Fords. At a con-
ference with General Early, Gordon's plan was adopted. Gordon's troops, supported
by Pegram's and Ramseur's divisions, would cross the Shenandoah at Bowman's

Ford, move to the right of Thoburn and the VIII Corps, and then attack in a westerly direction. Payne's small cavalry brigade would move with Gordon and make a dash at the Belle Grove Plantation house in an attempt to capture General Sheridan. Kershaw would cross at McInturff's Ford and Brig. Gen. Gabriel C. Wharton would follow the Valley Pike. Both would then move north and attack VIII Corps. Rosser was ordered to take the cavalry and make a feint against Custer's troops at Cupp's Ford. Lomax's cavalry would move up the Front Royal–Winchester Pike to cut off the Federals' line of retreat.[35]

The stage was set for one of the war's most decisive battles. Early and Halleck had ensured that Sheridan's army would be concentrated. Halleck's revision of Grant's dispatch had angered Sheridan enough to get him to stop all movement until the future of his army was determined. Early's attack on Hupp's Hill, the bogus message from Longstreet, and Rosser's aborted raid had then convinced Sheridan to revert to his earlier cautionary stance. The generals were finished with their meddling; now the common soldiers would decide the issue.

Sergeant Gilbert Merritt, Company M, California Battalion, convalescing at Camp Meigs. Merritt suffered a broken leg while breaking a horse. The leg was not properly set and resulted in his medical discharge and a lifelong disability. (Courtesy of the U.S. Army Military History Institute, Carlisle Barracks, Pennsylvania)

An unidentified member of the California Hundred. One of the few selected from among the many who applied for enlistment, he holds his saber and proudly displays his Colt revolver and California Hundred kepi. (Courtesy of the U.S. Army Military History Institute, Carlisle Barracks, Pennsylvania)

Second Lieutenant John C. Norcross, Company E. Norcross's horse was killed in a charge at Ashby's Gap on July 12, 1863, and he was taken prisoner. He was imprisoned at Libby Prison in Richmond until his escape in March 1865. (Courtesy of the U.S. Army Military History Institute, Carlisle Barracks, Pennsylvania)

Colonel Charles Lowell as a captain in the 3rd U.S. Cavalry. (Courtesy of the U.S. Army Military History Institute, Carlisle Barracks, Pennsylvania)

Colonel Caspar Crowninshield. Crowninshield commanded the regiment when Lowell took command of the brigade. After the war he was active in the Military Order of the Loyal Legion of the United States (MOLLUS). He died in 1890. (Courtesy of the U.S. Army Military History Institute, Carlisle Barracks, Pennsylvania)

Captain J. Sewell Reed, Boston-born businessman, Alameda County Supervisor, California Militia Officer, and first captain of the California Hundred. (Courtesy of the U.S. Army Military History Institute, Carlisle Barracks, Pennsylvania)

Sergeant John M. Locke, Company M. At thirty-one, Locke was one of the older men in the regiment. Wounded in the battle at Anker's blacksmith shop, he returned to duty after a short hospital stay. He was promoted to sergeant in 1864 and was in all of the fights in the Shenandoah Valley. After the war Locke returned to California and raised a family in the foothill town of San Andreas. (Courtesy of the U.S. Army Military History Institute, Carlisle Barracks, Pennsylvania)

Charles Atmore, a sailor from Boston and one of the Massachusetts recruits who filled Company A's thinning ranks in March 1864. He was captured at Mount Zion Church in July and died in Andersonville Prison on September 26, 1864. (Courtesy of the U.S. Army Military History Institute, Carlisle Barracks, Pennsylvania)

Corporal William DeForrest, Company M. Deforrest was shot in the head July 12, 1863, at Ashby's Gap and taken back to camp in an ambulance wagon, where Colonel Lowell reported he was mortally wounded. Deforrest survived and was discharged on September 4, 1864, "because of wounds." (Courtesy of the U.S. Army Military History Institute, Carlisle Barracks, Pennsylvania)

Lieutenant Henry Crocker holding the sword presented to him by members of the Oakland Home Guards militia company. An Oakland barkeeper, Crocker was awarded a Medal of Honor in 1896 for his gallantry at the Battle of Cedar Creek. (Courtesy of the U.S. Army Military History Institute, Carlisle Barracks, Pennsylvania)

Corporal James Eby, Company M. A telegraph operator, twenty-nine-year-old Eby was promoted to commissary sergeant. This photo has only recently been identified as that of Corporal Eby. (Courtesy of the Tibbals Collection)

Lieutenant George Plummer, Company A. One of the first recruits in the California Hundred, he was mustered on December 10, 1862. Plummer was wounded at Rockville, Maryland, but returned to the regiment. He was promoted to corporal, then sergeant, and was commissioned a second lieutenant on March 23, 1865. (Courtesy of the Tibbals Collection)

Abraham Loane, Company A. Loane was captured at Mt. Zion Church on July 6, 1864. He spent the balance of the war in Confederate prisons and was finally released on April 28, 1865. (Courtesy of the U.S. Army Military History Institute, Carlisle Barracks, Pennsylvania)

Left: Corporal James McKay, Company H. McKay was captured at Rockville, Maryland, on July 13, 1864. He was sent to Andersonville, survived, and was paroled at Annapolis, Maryland, on February 22, 1865. (Courtesy of the U.S. Army Military History Institute, Carlisle Barracks, Pennsylvania)

Below: 2nd Massachusetts Camp at Vienna, Virginia. The camp is stockaded with vertical timbers set in the ground. The officers' wall tents face the streets between the rows of Sibley tents and stables. (Courtesy of the Tibbals Collection)

Captain Archibald McKendry, Company G. Promoted to major, McKendry was second in command of the regiment in the latter part of 1864 and the spring of 1865. The enlisted men nicknamed him "the old badger." (Courtesy of the U.S. Army Military History Institute, Carlisle Barracks, Pennsylvania)

The 2nd Massachusetts band. In the center with the book of music and an alto cornet is Bandmaster Sgt. Samuel Corbett. The second man to his right is Bugler Peter White. The fourth man to Corbett's right may be Bugler Everd Irving. Colonel Crowninshield is standing on the steps of the building in the background. (Courtesy of the Tibbals Collection)

Captain George Manning, Company M. The eldest of two brothers in the regiment, Captain Manning was captured at the fight at Anker's blacksmith shop on February 22, 1864. (Courtesy of the U.S. Army Military History Institute, Carlisle Barracks, Pennsylvania)

The 2nd Massachusetts Cavalry's battle flag. In the center is the Great Seal of the State of California. The names of the regiment's battles are around the side. This flag was presented to the California veterans in commemoration of their service during the war. (Courtesy of the U.S. Army Military History Institute, Carlisle Barracks, Pennsylvania)

Corporal John L. Finley, Company L. Finley enlisted in San Francisco on February 16, 1863. He was promoted to sergeant and then commissioned a second lieutenant on January 10, 1865. Before the war he was a miner working the gold fields in the Mother Lode. (Courtesy of the Tibbals Collection)

Corporal Edward B. Campbell. Among those arrested at Gloucester Point, Campbell served throughout the war as a private. He was not promoted to corporal until after his discharge. (Courtesy of the Tibbals Collection)

Bugler Everd Irving, Company F. Irving was an eighteen-year-old clerk before the war. He served as Company F's bugler throughout the war and played in the regimental band. (Courtesy of the Tibbals Collection)

John Mosby, fabled guerrilla leader of Northern Virginia. (Courtesy of the National Archives)

Sheridan and his generals. *From left:* Wesley Merritt, David McM. Gregg, Sheridan, Henry Davies, James Wilson, and Alfred Torbert. (Courtesy of the National Archives)

12 | Sabers at Cedar Creek

Just after dark on October 18 a small patrol from the 2nd Massachusetts returned from a scout toward Strasburg. The troopers rode down the sloping bank on the south side of Cedar Creek near Cupp's Ford and started to cross. Suddenly, there was a shouted warning and a spattering of carbine fire from the opposite bank. The troopers scattered, splashing back across the creek into the trees lining the edge of the little stream. A few drew their weapons and returned the fire. Someone shouted to stop firing. There was a string of oaths and then the shooting stopped. The patrol crossed the little creek and moved past several very abashed Union pickets.

The Reserve Brigade was camped near Middle Marsh Brook about a half mile to the rear of Devin's 2nd Brigade and about a mile west of VI Corps's camps. The Michigan Brigade, now commanded by Colonel Kidd, was camped behind the Reserve Brigade. Pickets from the Michigan Brigade were strung out along Cedar Creek covering the fords. Custer's division was a mile away, along the creek and northwest of Kidd's camp. The picket firing had broken the quiet of the evening but nobody was alarmed; firing along the creek was common. The sergeant in charge of the patrol complained about the nervous Union troopers who had fired on his returning men and reported that all was quiet on the other side and there did not appear to be any Confederates near Strasburg, other than a few pickets. A courier went to General Merritt's headquarters with the sergeant's report. As a precaution against similar incidents, messengers were sent to Colonels Devin and Kidd and General Custer reminding them that the Reserve Brigade would be sending out another reconnaissance patrol at daybreak.[1] There was no expectation of anything but a normal day on the morrow.

After the war, Colonel Kidd recalled that "somehow I had a vague feeling of uneasiness that would not be shaken off. I believe now and have believed for many years, that there was in my mind a distinct presentiment of the coming storm. I could not sleep and at eleven o'clock, was still walking outside the tents. It was a perfect night, bright and clear. The moon was full, the air crisp and transparent. A more serene and peaceful scene could not be imagined."[2]

Colonel Lowell may have had some of the same feelings when he wrote a few days earlier: "I don't want to be shot till I've had a chance to come home. I have no idea that I shall be hit, but I want so much not to now, it sometimes frightens me."[3]

Reveille sounded at 3:30 A.M. for the 2nd Massachusetts and the rest of the

Reserve Brigade.[4] The men rolled out of their tents and built up their campfires. A thick fog had settled over the low ground along the Shenandoah and Cedar Creek, blanketing most of the landscape and damping the men's voices as they prepared for the day's work. As usual, breakfast was fried bacon, a piece of hardtack, and government-issue coffee. About 4 A.M. there was a scattering of picket firing along Kidd's front at Minebank Ford, three and a half miles from the turnpike bridge across Cedar Creek, and the picket line began falling back in front of a heavy force of Confederate cavalry. Kidd sent word to Merritt, who ordered him to reinforce the pickets with his whole brigade.

About 4:30 the Reserve Brigade mounted, formed into a column, and moved toward the creek, about a half mile away. The jingle of the harnesses and the muf-fled steps of the horses were the only sounds to be heard above the scattered picket firing upstream. Then the sound of "Boots and Saddles" coming from the direction of Custer's camp proclaimed that the 3rd Division was also under attack. Colonel Lowell, at the head of the column, hesitated, listening to the firing on his right. After a few moments he sent several scouts wading across the creek while the main body waited on the east bank. In a short time there was a scattering of fire from the woods on the other side of the creek and the scouts returned and reported encoun-tering Confederate cavalry nearby on the south bank. Lowell ordered the brigade to cross and dismount. The troopers formed a strong skirmish line and began firing into the fog-shrouded figures to their front.[5]

Without warning, a heavy volley of rifle fire blasted the morning air on the army's far left. It was about 5:15 A.M. A few minutes later some ragged firing was heard, then another, even louder, volley.[6] The veterans knew that sound. It was the massed fire of a large infantry formation in line of battle. Lowell immediately sent a courier scurrying back to the camp guard with orders to break camp and prepare to move. In a short time the tents were packed and the brigade's wagons were moving to the rear. Soon after that the camp guards joined the rest of the brigade along Cedar Creek. The sounds of the firing from the left grew heavier, with artillery batteries from across the creek adding to the roar. The fog obscured the view and diffused the sound so that it was difficult to determine whether the firing was mov-ing or stationary. At about 7:30, Lowell received a dispatch directing him to sup-port Kidd. He immediately ordered the brigade to fall back.[7] As they recrossed the creek, Lowell rode ahead to a small hill, where Kidd had his headquarters. The fog completely hid the ford. Lowell told Kidd his orders were to support the Michigan-ders if needed. Kidd replied that no support was needed because his brigade had driven the Confederate cavalry back across the creek.[8]

The Confederates in front were Rosser's two brigades, about nine hundred strong. After brushing Kidd's picket away, the rebel cavalrymen moved across the creek and set up their horse artillery on the opposite bank, awaiting developments. Another brigade crossed near Custer's division. Rosser's orders were to create a diversion on the Union right and hold the enemy cavalry until the attack on the Union left succeeded. Badly outnumbered and still smarting from his defeat at

Tom's Brook, Rosser was overly cautious and, when Kidd counterattacked with his whole brigade, fell back to the south side of the creek. He was content to harass the Federals with his artillery and, if the chance presented itself, pursue a defeated Union army.

As the firing along the creek died down, it was clear to both colonels from the sounds of the gunfire on the left that the main Confederate effort was in front of the infantry encampments. However, because of the fog, they could only follow the battle by the noise. Above it all was the unmistakable, animal-like, terrifying "YIP-YIP-YAHOO!" of the rebel yell as thousands of Confederate infantrymen swept across the plateau.

The veteran cavalrymen in the Union regiments knew that a major attack was underway. The two colonels listened to the sounds, trying to derive some sense of what was happening from the crashing noises. After a while, Colonel Kidd remarked that it seemed to him the army was retreating.

"I think so," Lowell replied. There was a pause as they considered what they should do. Then Lowell said, "I shall return."

Kidd, who had been in command of the Michigan Brigade for only seventeen days, had experienced an abrupt introduction to brigade command. When Custer got word of his promotion, Kidd recalled that Custer, after "hastily summoning me, went away, taking his staff and colors with him. I was obliged while yet on the march to form a staff of officers as inexperienced as myself. It was an unsought and an unwelcome responsibility."[9]

Now, without orders and realizing that a major battle was underway, he was hesitant and unsure. The last orders he had received were to send his whole brigade to the support of his pickets. The firing along the creek had died down, now there was only the crashing of the guns to the east. Looking for support he finally asked Lowell, "Colonel, what would you do if you were in my place?"

Lowell, as always, wanted to move toward the firing. Sheridan had made it clear that no one would go wrong if he moved to the sound of the guns. Rosser's cavalry was an unknown threat but for now seemingly content to stay on the other side of the creek. The choice for Lowell was clear: "I think you ought to go too," Lowell replied. Then he turned in his saddle and, as the senior officer present, said, "Yes I will take the responsibility to give you the order." With that both brigades started moving toward the Valley Pike—and destiny.[10]

Lowell led the two brigades northeast toward the ridge north of Middletown following farm lanes and country roads.[11] The fog, thinned by the rising sun, no longer obscured the view below. The column came out onto open ground overlooking the sloping plateau where the army's encampments had been located.

After the war Kidd wrote:

> The full scope of the calamity which had befallen our arms burst suddenly in view. The whole battlefield was in sight. The valley and intervening, the fields and woods were alive with infantry, moving singly and in squads. Some entire regiments were

hurrying to the rear, while the Confederate artillery was raining shot and shell and spherical case among them to accelerate their speed. Some of the enemy's batteries were the very ones just captured from us. It did not look like a frightened or panic stricken army, but like a disorganized mass that had simply lost the power of cohesion.[12]

Lowell led the two brigades across the front of XIX Corps, which was forming on the reverse slope of the ridge. The column was about three-quarters of a mile long. They marched across the high ground, battle flags and swallow-tailed guidons snapping in the wind, in full view of the triumphant Confederates below. A Confederate battery fired at the column. One round struck part of Kidd's brigade, neatly slicing out one set of four men and their mounts in a burst of scarlet. The column hesitated, then closed ranks and moved on, leaving the dead and dying by the side of the road.[13] It was nine in the morning.[14]

The cavalry continued on through the broken masses of infantry to a point on the main road northeast of Middletown as Confederate artillery fire rained down. Not a single cavalryman left the ranks unless he was wounded. They moved with the quiet precision of troops on parade.[15]

The sight of the cavalry troopers crossing calmly to their front had an electrifying effect on the shaken Union infantry. Brigadier General William Dwight, a division commander in XIX Corps, watched the passing troopers and recorded later that "They moved past me, that splendid cavalry; if they reached the Pike I felt secure. Lowell got by me before I could speak, but I looked after him for a long distance. Exquisitely mounted, the picture of a soldier, erect, confident, defiant, he moved at the head of the finest body of cavalry that to-day scorns the earth it treads."[16]

It was clear to the cavalrymen marching along the ridge that the army had been badly beaten. The Confederate attack had been a complete surprise. Under the cover of the early morning fog, Gordon's divisions crossed as planned and formed in a field northeast of Thoburn's fortifications. By coincidence, the Reserve Brigade had camped in the same field two days earlier, before moving to Front Royal. Hidden from sight in the low ground, Gordon's and Kershaw's brigades attacked and smashed the VIII Corps. Many Union troops were bayoneted in their tents; others fled half clothed. The XIX Corps, next in line, had just a few minutes to form. Some men ran, but most retreated, fighting desperately every step but outflanked and overwhelmed. Some brigades remained intact while others reformed when they reached the low hills to the rear of their camps.

The only infantry still actively engaged when the cavalry moved to the turnpike was the VI Corps. When the fighting broke out that morning, General Ricketts, the acting VI Corps commander, was seriously wounded while leading his divisions forward. Major General George Getty,[17] commanding the 2nd Division, assumed command of the corps. The 3rd Division, on the right, inundated with fugitives from VIII Corps and pressed back by the retreating XIX Corps, fell back as a unit, providing cover for the demoralized troops from the two corps. The 1st and 2nd

Divisions moved forward but the 1st Division was forced to fall back when the 3rd Division's withdrawal exposed its right flank to a galling fire from the advancing rebels. Only Getty's 2nd Division stood firm and provided a solid front to the advancing Confederates. At about 8 A.M. Getty ordered his men to fall back to a hill west of town, where the town cemetery is located, and formed a line along Hite Chapel Road north of the cemetery.[18] Getty's defense of this position was so fierce that Early, thinking he was fighting the entire VI Corps, concentrated all his artillery on the 2nd Division. Getty held for about an hour, and then pulled back to the Old Forge Road. Early's exhausted troops did not follow. After a few minutes' rest, Getty pulled the line back another half mile to the ridge where the rest of the army was reforming.

Gordon, Ramseur, Kershaw, and Pegram followed the retreating Union soldiers to Hite Chapel Road. There they stopped to reorganize and consolidate. To cover their flank, Early brought Wharton's division up on Pegram's right, extending the Confederate line east of the turnpike.

During the lull in the fighting General Wright ordered General Torbert to mass all the cavalry on VI Corps's left. Torbert opposed the move and, acting on his own responsibility, decided to keep three regiments from Custer's division on the army's right flank. Lowell and Kidd were already on the way, so Torbert ordered Custer to leave one brigade to watch Rosser and move to the army's left flank with the rest of his division. Earlier, Devin's 2nd Brigade and the 5th U.S. Cavalry, Merritt's escort, had moved to the Valley Pike to set up a line to halt the fleeing infantry.

Devin later recalled that "With some difficulty I checked the rout at this point (between the turnpike and the cavalry camp), it being necessary in several instances to fire on the crowds retiring, and to use the saber frequently."[19] Devin then moved his command to the Valley Pike north of Middletown, where he found Col. Alpheus Moore's brigade of Powell's division. Moore had just come in from his picket post at Bucktown Ford and set up a mounted skirmish line across the pike. Devin immediately formed his brigade on Moore's right, extending his line across the northern limits of Middletown.

A few minutes after Devin was in position, a strong Confederate skirmish line emerged from a line of trees south of town. The Confederates, from Pegram's division, moved up the pike toward Moore's skirmishers, overlapping his left flank. The fire from Moore's mounted troopers' carbines was not accurate enough to halt the determined Confederates, and the Union troopers began to fall back. Devin, his flank in danger of being turned, rode over to Moore and suggested they dismount and move up behind a series of stone walls perpendicular to the road at the north end of the village.[20] Colonel Moore refused, saying his men had great objections to fighting on foot.[21]

As Devin was remonstrating with Moore, Lowell's Reserve Brigade and Kidd's 3rd Brigade, still in column of fours, moved behind VI Corps on Old Forge Road, reaching the Valley Turnpike north of Middletown at about 9:30 A.M. As the column approached, Devin rode over to Lowell. He explained the position and pointed to the stone walls. Lowell immediately ordered the van, commanded by 2nd Lt.

William Hussey of Company C,[22] to dismount and seize the position.[23] With Lowell in front, the rest of the brigade charged the advancing Confederates, drove them back to the line of trees, then turned and galloped back out of range of the Confederate musket fire. Lowell's horse was shot out from under him at the beginning of the assault, the thirteenth he had lost during the thirteen weeks of the campaign.[24] He quickly got another from an aide and met the returning troopers. Captain Rufus Smith, the commander of Company A, and 1st Lt. Henry Kuhls of Company L were wounded during the attack. Smith died later that evening.

The firing at Lowell's men behind the stone walls was murderous. Confederate sharpshooters fired out of second floor windows and from the roofs of nearby houses. Lieutenant Hussey, shot in the shoulder, continued to direct his men's fire. A battery of Confederate artillery rode up, unlimbered, and began pounding the position. Lieutenant Colonel Crowninshield sent another company to help.

Another rebel line appeared in front of the trees. The Confederates fired a volley, then reloaded and started forward. Two regular army artillery batteries temporarily assigned to Devin, commanded by Lt. Franck Taylor, were ordered out in front on the pike to stop the rebel advance. Most of VIII and XIX Corps' artillery had been captured and VI Corps's artillery had retreated, so for a time Taylor's batteries were the only Union artillery on the left of the Union line. Taylor's gunners opened fire and once again the rebels retreated to the shelter of the trees.

The fighting became very fierce all along the line.[25] Part of Devin's brigade moved up to reinforce the men at the stone wall. Custer's brigades arrived and were placed to the rear of Lowell's brigade. Kidd was on Lowell's left, in reserve. With two divisions of cavalry in their front threatening to attack, the Confederates fell back to another line of stone walls at the edge of the town.

On the Confederate side, General Gordon had made preparations for one final attack on Getty when General Early arrived at the front. Early was convinced the battle was won when he saw Getty withdraw from the cemetery. Gordon recorded their conversation in his memoirs:

> "Well Gordon, this is glory enough for to-day. This is the 19th. Precisely one month ago to-day we were going in the opposite direction."
>
> His allusion was to our flight from Winchester on the 19th of September. I replied, "It is very well so far, general; but we have one more blow to strike, and then there will not be left an organized company of infantry in Sheridan's army."
>
> I pointed to the Sixth Corps and explained the movements I had ordered, which I felt sure would compass the capture of that corps—certainly its destruction. When I had finished, he said
>
> "No use in that; they will all go directly." "That is the Sixth Corps, General. It will not go unless we drive it from the field." "Yes it will go too, directly."[26]

Gordon later claimed that Lomax's cavalry was on that flank and had already advanced to a point within a few miles of Winchester. In his memoirs Gordon brushes off the presence of about five thousand fresh Union cavalrymen on the Confederate right and the dogged defense at Middletown's stone walls: "It is

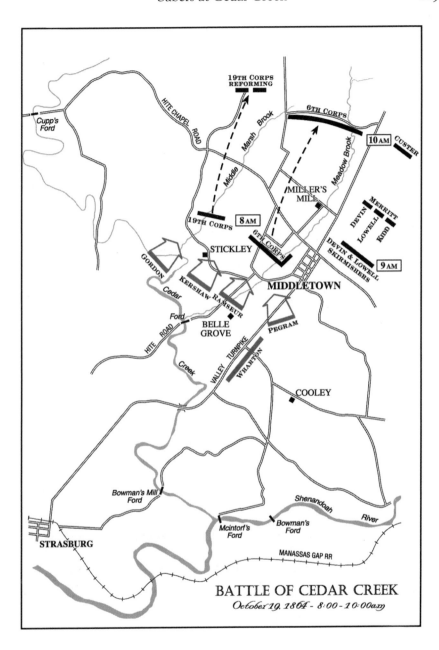

BATTLE OF CEDAR CREEK
October 19, 1864 - 8:00 - 10:00am

claimed by the Confederate commander that we were threatened with cavalry on our right, whereas General L. L. Lomax of the Confederate cavalry, who combined the highest qualities of great courage and wise caution, was on that flank and had already advanced to a point within a few miles of Winchester."[27]

Lomax had been sent to Front Royal to attack Chapman's cavalry division and then swing behind the Union army and cut the Valley Turnpike. After Tom's Brook, it was a task well beyond the abilities of the beleaguered Lomax and his weary troopers. Lomax was, in effect, out of the picture. The only Confederate cavalry on this part of the field was Lomax's old brigade, now commanded by Brig. Gen. William Payne. Gordon fails to explain how Lomax at Winchester could help Early's right flank at Middletown. Gordon's memoirs were first published in 1903, eight years after Early's death so, he had "the last word." The rancor between the two men never eased after the war; the "fatal delay" is still part of the "what-ifs" of the Civil War. To be fair, Gordon may have underestimated and Early overestimated the threat from the Union cavalry. Both positions expressed the mind-set of the two leaders. Still, Early was the army commander, and his view of the tactical situation would guide the army's actions. An ungainly horseman with little understanding of how to command cavalry, he had the infantryman's inborn fear of a massed cavalry charge. Those fears had been realized tenfold at Opequon Creek, and in mentioning September 19 to Gordon he undoubtedly recalled how Merritt's and Custer's men slashed into his left flank. In his report, written two days after the battle he explained his estimate of the situation:

> the enemy's cavalry was threatening our right flank and rear, and the country being perfectly open, and having on that flank only Lomax's old brigade, numbering about 300 men. It became necessary to make dispositions to prevent a cavalry charge, and a portion of the troops were moved to the right for that purpose and word was sent to Gordon, who had got on the left with his division, and Kershaw, who was there also, to swing around and advance with their divisions, but they stated in reply that a heavy force of cavalry had got in their front, and that their ranks were so depleted by the number of men who had stopped in the enemy's camp to plunder that they could not advance them. Rosser also sent word that when he attacked the cavalry he encountered a part of the Sixth Corps supporting it; that a very heavy force of cavalry had massed in his front, and it was too strong for him, and that he would have to fall back.[28]

General Early thus far had dominated the morning's battle, forcing the Federals to react to his moves. At 10:30 A.M. that changed with General Sheridan's arrival on the field.

Sheridan reached Winchester by horse about 3:30 P.M. the day before, after a train ride to Martinsburg. He sent a courier to the front to bring back a report of current affairs, then took General Halleck's engineering officer, Col. Barton S. Alexander, out to look over the area around Winchester. They returned to Sheridan's headquarters after dark. A courier arrived from Cedar Creek and reported all was quiet. He informed Sheridan about the proposed reconnaissance in the morning. Sheridan retired about 10 P.M., expecting to make a leisurely ride to his headquarters the next morning.

At about 6 A.M. the officer on picket duty woke him up and reported that artillery firing could be heard from the direction of Cedar Creek. Sheridan asked if it was continuous and was told it was not. He tried to go back to sleep but grew so restless he finally got up and dressed. The picket officer returned and reported the firing was still going on. Once again Sheridan asked if it sounded like a battle and once again the officer replied it was not. Sheridan, still concerned, ordered that breakfast be served quickly and the horses saddled. He and his party moved out between 8:30 and 9 A.M. and

> As we were proceeding up the street which leads directly through Winchester, from the Logan residence where [General] Edwards was quartered, to the Valley Pike, I noticed that there were many women at the windows and doors of the houses, who kept shaking their skirts at us and who were otherwise markedly insolent in their demeanor, but supposing this conduct to be instigated by their well known and perhaps natural prejudices, I ascribed to it no unusual significance. On reaching the edge of town I halted a moment, and heard there quite distinctly the sound of artillery firing in an unceasing roar.[29]

Sheridan soon realized the women in Winchester had received intelligence from the battlefield by a "grape vine telegraph." He moved forward, listening and trying to interpret the sounds from the front. At Mill Creek his escort fell behind the pace he was setting. At a crest beyond the creek he came upon "the appalling spectacle of a panic stricken army." The road was crowded with slightly wounded men, throngs of demoralized unhurt men, and supply wagons—all pressing to the rear. The fugitives tried to assure Sheridan the army was broken up and in full retreat. He sent word to Edwards to form a picket along the south side of Winchester and round up the fleeing men.[30] Accompanied by two aides and fifty of the best mounted men from his escort, Sheridan stepped up the pace from a trot to a gallop. Later, his ride to Cedar Creek would be immortalized in a poem that would be memorized by every schoolboy in the North.[31]

As Sheridan drew closer to the army, the sound of the guns could be clearly heard, and he saw "now and then a wounded officer or enlisted man on horseback or plodding along on foot, with groups of straggling soldiers here and there among the wagon-trains or in the fields, or sometimes sitting or lying down to rest by the side of the road, while others were making coffee in their tin cups by tiny campfires."

There was no stopping to plead with the stragglers, however. "The general would wave his hat to the men and point to the front, never lessening his speed as he pressed forward. It was enough; one glance at the eager face and familiar black horse[32] and they knew him, and starting to their feet they swung their caps around their heads and broke into cheers as he passed beyond them; and then gathering up their belongings and shouldering their arms, they started after him for the front, shouting to their comrades further out in the fields, 'Sheridan! Sheridan!'"[33]

He rode past the debris of the army—the hastily improvised hospitals with the groaning wounded, broken wagons, ambulances, stragglers, and walking scarecrows —to where Getty's division had formed in line of battle on the right of the pike with "its standards flying and evidently well in hand." The first officer he met was

General Torbert, who said, "My God! I am glad you've come!" Sheridan then turned and rode past Getty's men, passing in front of the barricades the troops had piled up. He rode to the right, to where General Crook's troops were in position. "Men," he told them, "by God, we'll whip them yet. We'll sleep in our old camps tonight." To a man VI Corps rose and cheered. Sheridan then rode east behind Getty's division and "a line of regimental flags rose up out of the ground, as it seemed, to welcome me. They were mostly the colors of Crook's troops, who had been stampeded and scattered in the surprise of the morning."[34]

Sheridan's staff joined him behind Getty's division. He met with Generals Wright—bloodied by a wound in the face—Emory, and Crook. A little later he went to a small knoll west of the pike where he could get a good view of the field and set up his headquarters.

When word reached the cavalry that Sheridan was now on the field, "a cheer went up from each brigade in this division; every officer in the command felt there was victory at hand."[35]

Sergeant Corbett reported a similar response in the 2nd Massachusetts "when General Sheridan came on the ground as soon as it was known that he was with us everything was so more cheerful aspect, the boys began to cheer as he rode down the line and new courage seemed to be inspired all through the army."[36]

Major James W. Forsyth of Sheridan's staff was sent to meet with Colonel Lowell. They rode down the Reserve Brigade's line of battle. To the south, at the line of trees, they could see Pegram's division of rebel infantry forming up as if to attack. Forsyth asked, "Can you hold on here for forty minutes?"

"Yes," Lowell replied.

Forsyth then asked if he could hold for sixty minutes.

"It depends," Lowell answered, "you see what they are doing. I will if I can."[37]

While Forsyth and Lowell were reviewing the Reserve Brigade's position, Gordon and Ramseur persuaded Early to renew the advance. As Sheridan watched from his knoll behind Merritt's cavalry, the Confederates began forming a strong skirmish line all along their front. A few Union pickets in front of Gordon's and Kershaw's divisions rose, fired, and ran for the safety of the Union infantry line. Along Pegram's front, the troopers of the 2nd Massachusetts opened fire from their position at the stone wall. Pegram's men returned the fire but the rapid firing Spencers wielded by the cavalrymen were too much for them. The rebels fell back to the cover of the tree line. Wharton, on Pegram's right, conformed and fell back, covering Pegram's flank. When Ramseur saw Pegram's line rebuffed by the strong point at the stone wall, he ordered his rightmost brigade to wheel so that it faced east and covered the gap left by Pegram's retreat. Gordon's and Kershaw's divisions and Ramseur's remaining two brigades continued to advance, threatening the still partly disorganized Union infantry on the ridge. The advance slowed when it became apparent that any further forward movement would stretch Ramseur's brigade on the right to the breaking point and expose the flank of the battle line to a Union cavalry attack. The advancing Confederates finally halted, after moving about four hundred yards, at a small country road running parallel to Hite Chapel Road. On the right, Ramseur's line now faced north as well as east, with the angle anchored at Miller's Mill.

Pegram was ordered to renew his attack and drive the Union cavalry from the position at the stone walls. Colonel Benjamin Crowninshield, cousin to Lt. Col. Caspar Crowninshield and a member of Sheridan's staff, described the cavalry action over the next couple of hours:

> In this battle, as at the battle of Winchester, Torbert's cavalry had to fight infantry in the open fields. That is to say, our cavalry was not protected by woods, and presented a fair mark all day for the Rebel musketry and artillery. Stone walls and houses protected the rebels themselves, so that no proper opportunity for charging occurred. Feeling that the holding of the pike depended on them, the cavalry pushed in against the rebel infantry under circumstances which made success almost impossible. They charged right up to the stone walls and close to the rebel guns. . . . These charges were repeated several times, only to be repulsed.[38]

During the last attack Lowell was struck in the chest by a bullet that probably ricocheted off the stone wall where his men were crouched. His aides escorted him to the rear. The bullet made him feel faint and he lost his voice. The aides laid him on the ground and covered him with an overcoat, waiting for his strength to come back. Lowell was determined that he was going to lead the mounted charge everybody knew was coming. He coughed up some blood and said, "It is only my poor lungs."[39]

He had the satisfaction of knowing he was better than his word; the Reserve Brigade held its position for five hours. It was a crucial defense because it created a weak link in the Confederate line. The continuing threat of a massed cavalry charge on the right persuaded Early to suspend the advance. Control of the battle swung now to Sheridan. With the Confederate advance stalled by the Californians and Massachusetts men at the stone walls, he decided to wait until "my thin ranks were further strengthened by the men who were continually coming up from the rear, and particularly till Crook's troops could be assembled on the extreme right."[40]

During a lull, Sheridan, concerned that the message of the sixteenth regarding Longstreet may have been real, ordered Merritt to attack the skirmish line in front and take some prisoners for questioning. Merritt ordered Lieutenant Colonel Crowninshield to make the attack.

Henry Crocker, in command of the picket reserve, was with Crowninshield when the courier arrived. Crocker had taken command of Company E after Captain Eigenbrodt was killed at Halltown on August 25 and was promoted to captain on September 3. Before the war Crocker had been a barkeeper in Oakland, California. In 1861, after news of the battle of Bull Run reached the West Coast, he attended the organizational meeting of a local militia company called the Oakland Home Guards and was elected orderly sergeant. The company, which wore uniforms consisting of red shirts, black pants, and black glazed hats, drilled at Camp Downey, the former site of the Racetrack.[41] The Home Guards saw active service once. One night a small naval cannon, on display in the town square, disappeared.

The Home Guards mustered the next morning and immediately arrested Jack Cochrane, a Confederate sympathizer and head of the local Copperheads. The militiamen promptly escorted Cochrane to the estuary at the lower end of Broadway and threw him in the water. The militia waited at the water's edge for Cochrane to either drown or tell them where the cannon could be located. Cochrane's Confederate sympathies quickly vanished and he disclosed the gun's location. It was promptly restored to the town square, where it remained for the rest of the war.[42]

Crocker was one of the first to sign up for the California Hundred but, perhaps because of his occupation or the fact that he was a city dweller rather than an experienced rural horseman, he was not selected. He later joined Eigenbrodt's company and was commissioned as a second lieutenant. Now, with a chance to prove himself, he asked Crowninshield for permission to make the attack.

Years later, Crocker recalled the conversation:

> The colonel gave his consent, but cautioned not to advance too far, and if possible, bring back some prisoners. I hurried back to my company and told the boys, very much to their satisfaction, of the work before us. We waited until we knew that the advancing force could give us but one volley before we could reach them, then I gave the command: Forward! Trot! Gallop! Charge! And away we went with sabers flashing in the sunlight. The expected volley was received, saddles were emptied and horses went down, but on we went. In less time than it takes to tell we were among them, their line was broken and we demanded their surrender.[43]

Lieutenant Crocker was hit below the left knee during the charge but he kept riding. On the way back, Lieutenant Crocker stopped to pick up Lt. Isaac McIntosh of Company A, whose horse had been killed. In January 1896 Henry Crocker was awarded the Medal of Honor for his actions that day thanks to the efforts of his congressman and Colonel Crowninshield.

The troopers returned with fourteen prisoners who revealed that only Kershaw's division was present. While the captives were being questioned, a report came announcing that General Longstreet was marching toward Winchester on the Front Royal Pike. Sheridan once again delayed until word came from Powell at Front Royal with assurances that the report was not true.

In front of the cavalry, Pegram's and Wharton's Confederates were concealed behind a pile of logs and rails in a line of trees that stretched clear across the battle line. Payne's small brigade was on the extreme right. Closer to the pike was a series of low stone walls shielding the Confederate infantry and several batteries of guns. Three ravines cut the ground between the timber and the higher ground occupied by the Union cavalry. The ravines were just deep enough to offer some cover to an attacker approaching the Confederate position. A strong rebel skirmish line was located on the slope leading up to the timber from the last ravine.[44]

"During the entire day," General Merritt reported, "the enemy kept up an artillery fire on our position which was truly terrific; it has seldom been equaled for accuracy of aim and excellence of ammunition.[45] The batteries attached to this division did nobly, but were overpowered at times by weight of metal and superior ammunition. So excellent was the practice of the enemy that it was utterly impossible to cover a cavalry command from the artillery fire; a number of horses and men were destroyed by this arm during the day."[46]

Finally satisfied that Early had not received large reinforcements, Sheridan ordered the attack to proceed. The 1st Cavalry Division moved into line of battle in an open field on the left side of the pike. Devin was on the right on the edge of town, Lowell was in the center, and Kidd lined up on the left. A little later Moore's brigade, still mounted, moved in on Kidd's left. However, before the attack commenced, Moore was ordered to join his division at Newton.[47] Earlier Custer, ordered to "take charge of affairs on the right,"[48] moved his division behind VI Corps on the army's right flank. He established contact with Col. William Wells, commander of the brigade watching Rosser's division along Cedar Creek.

A 4:15 P.M. the order was given for an all-out counterattack. The reorganized XIX Corps and all three divisions of VI Corps stepped out against the main body of Early's infantry. Merritt ordered Lowell to lead the assault on the left. Aides helped Lowell onto a new horse, his fourteenth in the campaign. When the skirmishers at the stone wall fell back to get to their horses, the VI Corps infantry on the flank hesitated, then started to retreat. When the troopers returned, newly mounted, the infantry moved forward once again.[49]

The cavalry brigades formed a line two ranks deep and five hundred yards long stretching from the Valley Pike toward the river. Regimental commanders moved out in front of the line. Orders rang out and were repeated by the company commanders. With a hiss of steel sliding against steel, three thousand cavalrymen drew sabers and waited for the order to advance. The Confederate infantry hunkered down along the barricade in the trees. Ricketts's infantry division advanced slowly on the cavalry's right flank, driving the rebel skirmish line through Middletown, building by building.

A bugle call sounded from the center and was echoed on both sides of the line. The three thousand cavalrymen started moving forward at a trot. In the center, the 2nd Massachusetts, with Colonel Lowell in front, moved forward to the first ravine. As the regiment came on up the high side, the Confederate line fired a volley. The artillery on both sides opened up and the field was covered with smoke.

Colonel Lowell, despite being in excruciating pain from his earlier wound, was out in front with his saber upraised, pointing toward the enemy. He could only whisper his orders to his aides, who then shouted them out over the pandemonium of battle.

There was a snakelike undulation as groups of men moved to their places in the line. At first they moved forward at a walk, taking about a hundred yards to straighten their alignment. The national colors were out in front, a flurry of red white and blue; red and white guidons marked positions of the companies.

Colonel Lowell was shot as the line surged forward. He reeled in the saddle and then fell heavily to the ground. In the smoke-filled air things were in a fog. Al-

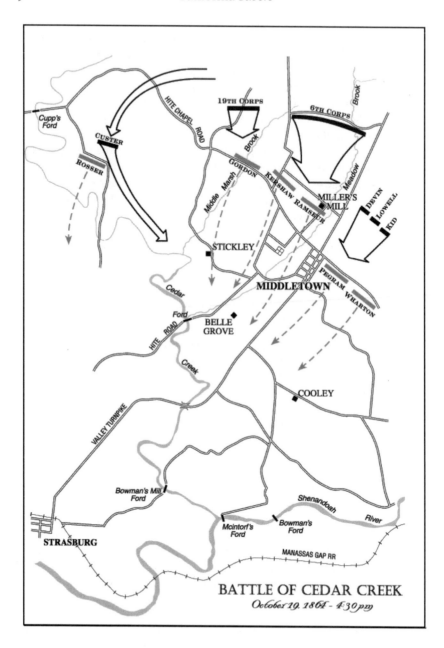

BATTLE OF CEDAR CREEK
October 19, 1864 - 4:30 pm

though there are differing accounts of what happened, most observers thought the shot came from a sharpshooter in the second floor of the Brinker house on the outskirts of Middletown. Lowell's aides quickly moved him to the rear.[50]

The brigade bugler sounded a couple of notes and the pace eased into a gentle trot, then quickened. The waiting Confederates could hear the drumming of the horses' hooves as the line pounded up the slope from the ravine.

"It was a glorious sight to see that magnificent line sweeping onward in the charge," wrote Colonel Kidd. "Far, far away to the right it was visible. There were no reserves, no plans for retreat, only one grand, absorbing thought—to drive them back and retake the camps."[51]

As the line came nearer, a few nervous rebels fired, but most of the defenders at the barricades waited for the order from their officers. A few more notes from the bugles and the trot turned into a ground-eating gallop. On they came, sabers flashing in the setting sun. For the rebels who had been at Winchester, it was a nightmare revisited. All along the rebel line commanders shouted the order to fire and rifles and cannon crackled with flame. Exposed to a crossfire as it fought through gardens and enclosures, Devin's brigade wavered and then slowly fell back. While the smoke obscured the scene the cavalry line, staggered by the volley, fell back to the first ravine. Only a few downed horses and wounded bluecoats lay on the ground in front, marking the limits of the first assault.

Sheridan rode forward and joined Lieutenant Colonel Crowninshield, who had taken command of the Reserve Brigade after Lowell was hit.[52] "I checked him from pressing the enemy's right," Sheridan wrote later, "in the hope that the swinging attack from my right would throw most of the Confederates to the east of the Valley Pike, and hence off their line of retreat through Strasburg to Fisher's Hill. The eagerness of the men soon frustrated this anticipation however, the left insisting on keeping pace with the center and right, and all pushing ahead till we regained our old camps at Cedar Creek."[53]

Protected from the Confederate fire by the depression, the sergeants, bawling orders, realigned the men. The colors moved back to the front and buglers sounded the charge. Once again the thin blue lines galloped onto the flat plateau. The charging cavalry got ahead of the infantry line on the right and again started taking flanking fire from Confederates concealed in the buildings along the outskirts of Middletown. The troopers rode through the second ravine but the musketry from the right was taking effect. In spite of the galling fire, the blue line rode right up to the skirmish line posted on the slope of the last ravine.

This time the troopers fell back to the second ravine. After a brief time they again moved forward into the smoke that lay between them and the Confederate barricade. This time the firing from the rebels was ragged. After almost breaking through, the charging cavalry fell back and sought cover in the third ravine. It seemed that the Confederates might hold out indefinitely if the flanking fire from the houses in Middletown could not be stopped.

The Confederate collapse started on the right, where the Union troops faced Gordon's division. Rosser had remained at Cupp's Ford, leaving a gap between his cavalry and Gordon's left flank. Custer, ordered to protect XIX Corps's right flank, decided to follow his own course. Claiming that Rosser was advancing, he moved to attack the Confederate cavalry and drive it back across Cedar Creek.

Brigadier General Clement Evans's Georgia brigade of Gordon's division was on the extreme left of the Confederate line. After the morning sweep through the Union camps, Evans's brigade had turned north and advanced toward the hill behind Middletown. The fighting in the center and the appearance of the massed cavalry on the right had drawn Early's attention away from his left. Gordon, whose line was stretched paper thin, appealed for reinforcements. Unfortunately, none were available. As XIX Corps's unguarded right flank approached, Gordon's division attacked, causing considerable confusion.[54] The Union infantry wavered under the volleys of rifle fire from Evans's Georgians and it seemed that the Union attack might be forced back. Brigadier General James McMillan commanded the 2nd Brigade on XIX Corps's right. The brigade included the 8th Vermont, one of the best infantry regiments in the army. Under heavy fire, the Vermonters wheeled to the right, perpendicular to the main battle line, and delivered a shattering blast at the Georgians. Meanwhile, McMillan ordered a second regiment to turn and fall in beside the Vermonters. As soon as they were in position McMillan ordered a charge and soon the Georgians were cut off and fleeing. McMillan then wheeled his regiments to the left, back into line, and the advance continued. As they moved forward Sheridan rode up and told McMillan to move to the left but hold up the attack until Custer was in position.

While they were talking, Custer arrived, "riding at full speed himself to throw his arms around my neck," Sheridan wrote. "By the time he had disengaged himself from this embrace, the troops broken by McMillan had gained some little distance to their rear, but Custer's troopers sweeping across the Middletown meadows and down toward Cedar Creek, took many of them prisoners before they could reach the stream—so I forgave his delay."[55]

Once again Custer's luck held. Sheridan was probably not aware of why Custer was not where he was supposed to be on XIX Corps's right flank. If the army's attack had stalled because of Custer's failure to protect XIX Corps's flank, as it might have except for General McMillan, it is doubtful that Sheridan would have been so forgiving.

With Custer's cavalry to their rear and XIX Corps now overlapping their flank, the rest of Gordon's division collapsed.[56] Kershaw's and Ramseur's divisions, in the center with their left now exposed and their right threatened by the charging cavalry, fell back. Ramseur was wounded as he tried to rally his troops. He was loaded into an ambulance and was headed for the rear when he was captured by Union troops. Later he was brought back to Sheridan's headquarters, where he was visited by a number of former West Point classmates before he died.

As the Confederate center fell back, the rebels in front of Merritt's charging troopers wavered. Devin rallied his men and, with Colonel Kidd and Lieutenant Colonel Crowninshield in front, the cavalry troopers turned. Dust swirled and bugles blared as they raced up the slope right into the muzzles of the Confederate guns. In a letter to his mother two days after the battle, Crowninshield wrote:

> You probably have seen by the papers all about our great victory of the 19th. I will
> not go into particulars. It was the most desperate fight I ever saw. Up to 3 o'clock we

were beaten & had lost 21 pieces of artillery. Sheridan was not on the field in the morning but when he did get up he found our men badly beaten—he got them rallied & pitched in & won a splendid victory taking 45 pieces of artillery & 2500 prisoners. Our cavalry had desperate fighting to do & behaved splendidly. . . . We charged over an open field on the enemies infantry posted behind a stone wall and with 4 or 5 pieces of artillery. We charged almost up to the wall but could not carry it. The fire was *perfectly fearful*; grape and canister & musket balls came into us in (a) perfect shower. We were driven back with considerable loss. How any of us escaped I don't see but thank God who spared me.[57]

Payne's Confederate cavalry brigade was fighting dismounted in front of Kidd's brigade. As Kidd's troopers reached the barricade, Payne's troopers were outmatched and overwhelmed. It was the sad end for the famed "Black Horse Cavalry." Wharton's and Pegram's infantry held as long as possible. With their flanks collapsing and faced with the gleaming sabers of Lowell's and Devin's brigades, they finally scattered and ran. Some, stricken or just too tired to run, dropped their weapons and raised their hands in surrender. A few who were slow to drop their weapons were sabered into submission. It was over in a few minutes. The Union brigades followed at a gallop, racing for the crossings at Cedar Creek.[58]

Custer had left Col. Alexander C. McW. Pennington with three regiments at Cupp's Ford to deal with Rosser and protect the rear of his division as it moved around the Confederate left. Pennington had instructions to leave one regiment to watch Rosser. When the collapse started, he sent the 1st Vermont and 5th New York to join Custer, who led the two regiments across Cedar Creek at a ford about a half-mile above the bridge. Hupp's Hill concealed the movement from the Confederates fleeing across Cedar Creek Bridge. A line of rebel infantry posted on the hill poured heavy fire into the two regiments. Custer quickly formed them into a battle line and they charged up the ridge. The Confederates fled toward Strasburg and the charge became a pursuit.

Strasburg is bounded on the south by a wide loop of the north branch of the Shenandoah. On the north side of the loop, near the edge of town, a small, steep-sided creek joins the river. The Valley Pike turns west through Strasburg and then southwest before it crosses the creek. A narrow stone bridge with wood flooring spanned the creek. Sometime in the late afternoon, the rear wheel of a wagon fleeing the battlefield broke through the bridge's planking. The wagon tipped over, blocking the roadway for everything but foot traffic. A half dozen men easily could have thrown the wagon into the creek, but nobody in the fleeing mob stopped long enough to consider such a step. With the bridge blocked, almost all of Early's guns and wagons were trapped on the north side of the creek.

Custer ordered the 1st Vermont and 5th New York to continue the pursuit while he stayed near the pike awaiting the arrival of the rest of his command.[59] Devin's brigade, racing up the Valley Pike, crossed the bridge at Cedar Creek. Kidd's brigade made a right wheel and began gathering prisoners.[60] The Reserve Brigade crossed Cedar Creek at the lower fords and reached Strasburg before it was directed to stop and recross the creek, leaving the pursuit to Devin. Custer, waiting at the pike, met Devin's advance regiment and advised it to follow his two regiments. General Devin arrived and set up headquarters on Hupp's Hill. As batches of prisoners started arriving, Devin's staff and escort secured them before sending them back to Sheridan's headquarters.

For some reason, none of Custer's other regiments reached him. The 1st Vermont and the 5th New York went as far as Fisher's Hill before they returned. Meanwhile, Custer showed up at Belle Grove, where he clutched Sheridan in his arms and proclaimed, "we've cleaned them out of their guns and got ours back."[61] It was a shameful performance that embarrassed even the publicity-hungry Phil Sheridan. None of the fighting cavalrymen were surprised, though; it was what they had come to expect from the curly-locked boy general.

While the pursuit was still ongoing, the wounded were being gathered up and moved to houses that were being converted into makeshift hospitals in Middletown. Lowell's aides carried him to a small, white house across the road from the old stagecoach inn.[62] They laid him on a table in the front room, where Dr. Oscar C. DeWolf, the 2nd Massachusetts surgeon and Lowell's tentmate, took a brief look at him. DeWolf, seeing that the wound was fatal, moved on to administer to the other wounded. The bullet had hit Lowell below his right arm and probably penetrated his lungs and nicked his liver. The bullet, or a fragment of it, had severed his spinal cord and he was paralyzed from the shoulders down. Lowell knew he was dying.[63] He spent much of his last hours comforting one of his officers who lay dying on a nearby couch. He also issued complete orders concerning the minutiae of the brigade and wrote a few private messages of affection. Word came in that Col. Henry S. Gansevoort, Lowell's successor in Fairfax County, had captured Mosby's complete artillery train consisting of a twelve-pounder howitzer, a three-inch rifle, and two small mountain howitzers with limbers, caissons, ammunition, and sets of harness. Lowell expressed pleasure over the victory. Just before dawn he wrote a farewell note to Josephine with Dr. DeWolf's help.[64] As the sun rose on October 20 Lowell became silent. He quietly died about midmorning. Charles Russell Lowell was twenty-nine years old, one year short of the age his prewar doctors had told him he could expect to lead a normal life.[65]

Two days after the fight, Lieutenant Colonel Crowninshield wrote in a letter to his mother:

> When the Colonel was shot I took command of the Brigade & am in command of it at present I suppose that some Colonel or General will soon relieve me. Colonel Lowell died like a hero & he certainly was one of the bravest of the brave, he is universally regretted & is a great loss to this *army & to the country*. Before he died he told Dr. DeWolf what he wish to have done with his things; he said "give my pistol to Caspar I was very fond of him." I wish some of the young men at home could have seen him leading his brigade in that terrible charge & then have seen him on his death bed & have heard him say, "My only regret is that I can not do something more for our cause." No hero of old was more fearless than he. It makes me very sad to think his poor wife, she is to be confined in a month.[66]

Lowell's body was sent to his mother's house at Cambridge. He was buried October 28 at Mount Auburn Cemetery. Edward Emerson described his funeral:

> I remember, one rainy day when the sudden gusts blew the yellow leaves in showers from the College elms, hearing the beautiful notes of Pleyel's Hymn, which was the tune to which soldiers were borne to burial, played by the band as the procession came, bearing Charles Lowell's body from his mother's house to the College Chapel; and seeing the coffin, wrapped in the flag, carried to the altar by soldiers; and how strange in contrast with the new blue overcoats and fresh white and red bunting were the campaign soiled cap and gauntlets, the worn hilt and battered scabbard of the sword that lay on the coffin.[67]

Lowell was buried beside his brother in the family plot. Lowell's promotion to brigadier general had been approved and the orders were on the way to him when he fell. A letter from a contemporary said, "I do not think there was any officer in all the army so much beloved as Lowell." Custer recorded: "We all shed tears when we knew that we had lost him. It is the greatest loss the Cavalry Corps has suffered." General Sheridan concluded, "I do not think there was a quality which I would have added to Lowell."[68]

Lowell was not universally loved by the enlisted men of the 2nd Massachusetts even though they, more than once as individuals, had taken risks or been wounded protecting him. They endangered their lives because they knew his worth to the regiment. Officers and men strove to match his courage and zeal for the cause. He was a strict disciplinarian, a patrician, and an elitist—none of which were admirable traits to the independent-minded Californians. Nevertheless, they followed him through the smoke, fire, and sheer terror of battle—wherever he led them —never faltering. They were never beaten when Lowell rode at their head, and he always got them out of tough spots safely. He had turned them into soldiers, which was not an easy task. Every man in the regiment and the brigade would sorely miss him.[69]

In all, Merritt's division lost 149 men killed, wounded, or missing. The Reserve Brigade alone lost thirty-seven officers and men killed, wounded, or missing.[70] (See Appendix for a complete listing of 2nd Massachusetts casualties.) Many of the losses occurred during the fighting for the stone walls. The defense at the walls did not win the battle but it is fair to say that the battle would have been lost if Pegram and Wharton had been able to conform with Ramseur's advance and reached VI Corps's left flank. The determined defense by the 2nd Massachusetts and Devin's brigade was crucial to the subsequent victory.

Custer's division lost a total of only thirty-four killed, wounded, or missing—less than a third of Merritt's losses and less than the casualties in the Reserve Brigade. In spite of this disparity, Custer tried to claim the laurels so ably earned by Merritt's troopers. In his report written after the battle, Custer claimed his two regiments captured most of the prisoners and all of the guns taken during the pursuit: "All guns taken from the enemy were left standing on the pike with perhaps a guard to every second or third gun, it being dark and the regimental commanders wisely forbearing to weaken their commands by leaving strong guards. It was owing to this fact that the troops of General Devin's command, arriving on the ground and seeing so many pieces of artillery without guards, volunteered their assistance, which was gratefully accepted on the part of my men."[71]

Rumors of Custer's claims circulated through the army's camps in the weeks after the battle. The rumors were confirmed when Custer's congratulatory order appeared in the newspapers. General Merritt was incensed: "I did not think it possible, from what I knew of the pursuit of the enemy on the south side of Cedar Creek, that such an unfounded assertions . . . could receive the support or endorsement of General Custer. . . . I think it my duty to my officers and men to declare the statement . . . as without foundation in truth."

The controversy over the guns lasted a long time. Custer's two regiments may have well ridden by the guns during the pursuit but capturing them meant securing the material. Guns with only one guard for every three or four were not secure from recapture by a counterattack. Merritt had receipts for twenty-two guns secured by his division. Custer tried to steal them to add to his own reputation. The 3rd Division was never heavily involved in the fighting during the Battle of Cedar Creek. In the morning, before Sheridan's arrival, the 3rd Division was in reserve behind Merritt's division, and it did not reach the battle line in the afternoon until after the Confederate left had collapsed. Just two 3rd Division regiments were involved in the pursuit of the retreating rebels. It was an act of "over-weaning greed" on Custer's part to claim these captures and one that did not make him popular with his fellow officers.

Between August 1 and October 31, Sheridan's cavalry lost a total of 2,634 men. The heaviest losses were in Merritt's division, which lost 186 men killed, 778 wounded, and 504 missing for a total of 1,558 or about 60 percent of the Cavalry Corps's losses. The 1st Division was credited with capturing as many guns as the 3rd Division despite Custer's claims. In the sixty days of active campaigning, the 1st Division destroyed over 410,000 bushels of wheat and took over thirty-two hundred head of cattle, sheep, and swine—far more than the other two divisions combined. The destruction was as complete as that visited on Georgia by General Sherman and would make the surrender of Lee's army inevitable. The Valley of the Shenandoah was no longer the breadbasket of the Confederacy.

The Battle of Cedar Creek was one of the most complete defeats of any army, Union or Confederate, during the war. The victory gave Sheridan complete dominance of the Shenandoah. In addition to the forty-five guns that were captured, Early lost practically all of his wheeled transportation. Twelve hundred men were captured and could not be replaced. Early lost many of his finest combat commanders, including General Ramseur and Brig. Gen. Cullen A. Battle, a promising brigade commander who was severely wounded, and a host of regimental and company officers whose loss would be sorely felt in the weeks and months to come.[72]

The victory occurred about two weeks before the 1864 presidential election. A former commander of the Army of the Potomac, George B. McClellan, was the Democrat's candidate. Whether he would have continued the war is problematical. The Northern populace was ambivalent. The numbers of dead and wounded suffered during Grant's 1864 campaign were overwhelming. There was war weariness throughout the North and Lincoln's reelection was in doubt. Then, on September 2, Sherman captured Atlanta. His triumph was followed by the stunning victory at Cedar Creek. These two battles showed that the war was being won, that the sacrifices of the last three and a half years were not in vain. The victories at Atlanta and Cedar Creek, coming so close before the election, changed the public will and Abraham Lincoln was reelected. The war would continue until the South was conquered.

13 | Burning "Mosby's Confederacy"

On October 20 Merritt took the 1st Division up the Valley Pike to Fisher's Hill. A small force of rebel cavalry blocked the road but was quickly dispersed and the division moved on to the small village of Woodstock. Rebel prisoners and a few friendly citizens reported that the Confederates were still some distance in advance, so Merritt sent the Reserve Brigade forward to locate the enemy. The brigade went beyond Edenburgh without meeting any rebels but it did capture a number of abandoned supply wagons, ambulances, and caissons. After destroying the captured equipment, the brigade returned and joined the division at Fisher's Hill, where they camped for the night.[1]

The division returned to Cedar Creek the next day and the Reserve Brigade camped on the left of the infantry in a field near the juncture of Cedar Creek and the Shenandoah. The skies opened up during the night and a torrent of rain fell on the encampment. The brigade's tents had not come up, so the men were out in the open. They were camped below the brow of a hill with no protection from the weather, making for a long and miserable night. After thoroughly soaking everyone, the rain eased off in the morning but the temperature turned cold before sunrise.[2]

After the morning muster many of the men went out souvenir hunting. The battlefield was still littered with discarded muskets and knapsacks dropped by the fleeing rebels. One of the favorite finds was letters. Throughout the war, the officers and men of both sides searched the knapsacks of the enemy dead for letters or diaries. Daguerreotypes of an orphaned child or a now-bereft wife were prized finds and often sent home. The practice at first may seem macabre, but in this war between brothers it was as if there was a need to know the men they had killed.

While the army rested, life in the brigade returned to the normal routine of picket duty and patrols. Chaplain Humphreys returned to the regiment on the twenty-fourth. He had been imprisoned for over three months before being exchanged.[3] The men welcomed the popular chaplain's return.

Washington rewarded the West Pointers who had fought at Cedar Creek. Sheridan was promoted to major general in the Regular Army and Merritt was made a brevet major general. Newly promoted Bvt. Brig. Gen. Alfred Gibbs, who had commanded a regiment in Devin's brigade, replaced Lieutenant Colonel Crowninshield as commander of the Reserve Brigade. Crowninshield was promoted to colonel on October 21 and returned to the command of the 2nd Massachusetts Cavalry.

Alfred Gibbs, the regiment's new brigade commander, was born on April 22, 1823, to a prominent New York family. He went to school at White Plains and Dartmouth before receiving an appointment to West Point. He graduated forty-second in the class of 1846 and served in Mexico, where he was wounded in action. He was given a brevet first lieutenancy for gallantry. From 1856 to 1861 he was stationed in New Mexico and was captured during the Confederate invasion of New Mexico in 1861. He was paroled but not exchanged until September 1862, when he took command of the 130th New York Infantry. Gibbs was with General Erasmus Keyes's division during the 1863 attack on the South Anna bridges. In August 1863 his regiment was reorganized as the 1st New York Dragoons (later the 19th New York Cavalry). The regiment guarded the Orange and Alexandria Railroad through most of 1863. During the spring campaign of 1864 Gibbs's regiment was heavily engaged. He was a short, stocky man with a tendency to be overweight. He was an excellent rider and no one could question his personal bravery, but Gibbs never became popular with the men of the 2nd Massachusetts.

The main body of Sheridan's army moved down the Valley on November 9 and camped where the Valley Pike crosses Opequon Creek just outside Kernstown, a few miles south of Winchester. Sheridan, along with the engineer officers brought from Washington, decided to fortify Kernstown so that a smaller force could hold the lower Valley when the VI and XIX Corps were sent back to Grant at City Point. To readily supply the troops that would hold the Kernstown position, reconstruction of the Winchester Potomac Railroad from Harper's Ferry to Stephenson's Depot was set in motion.

The army's rear area was infested with Confederate stragglers, deserters, and freebooters looking for the opportunity to ambush a sutler's wagon or an unwary Union soldier. The 2nd Massachusetts lost three men to some of these unorganized rebels during the two weeks they camped at Cedar Creek. In addition, three men from the 1st U.S. Cavalry were captured and sent to Richmond. However, they were recaptured by a detachment from the 1st New York Cavalry, which paid a stiff price for its good deed: four foragers from the regiment were captured by guerrillas and hanged. A sign reading "This is the fate of all foragers" was pinned to each of the corpses.[4]

The bushwhackers posed a real threat to the unarmed railroad work parties. From the beginning, ninety-day militia units had been sent from Harper's Ferry to guard the work on the railhead. But conditions had changed. On November 1, General Stevenson at Harper's Ferry reported that the terms of enlistment for four regiments assigned to Brig. Gen. William H. Seward Jr. at Martinsburg were expiring and the men were returning home. Stevenson sent Seward Cole's Maryland cavalry, thus reducing the garrison at Harper's Ferry to a single cavalry regiment. "By using every man that can be spared it is not possible to protect the party working on Winchester road [railroad] beyond Charlestown," he noted. "I think there should be with (the) construction party all the time a good regiment of infantry and at least 500 cavalry. They have to use a large number of wagons, and small parties cutting ties are dispersed along the road. They can only be protected by cavalry."

Sheridan agreed. The next day he wired Stevenson: "I will send at once a brigade of cavalry to Summit Point, and to cover the working party out on the road from Halltown. Please inform the engineer in charge."[5]

The Reserve Brigade was selected to guard the construction project. The troopers broke camp on November 3 during a light rain and headed north. The 2nd Massachusetts's bandmaster, Sergeant Corbett, ordered the playing of "patriotic Union music" as they rode through Middletown and Kernstown to annoy the rebel inhabitants. At sunset the regiment camped near Winchester. The rain continued through the night but cleared in the morning. The next day's march took the regiment through Winchester, Bunker Hill, Smithfield, and Charlestown. In each, the band played loudly and lustily. The regiment camped near Halltown on November 5 and the next morning moved closer to Charlestown and set up camp "near corn feed in a fine oak grove."[6]

On November 7, George H. Sowle, an eighteen-year-old trooper from Company G, 5th Michigan Cavalry, reached the Union lines around Winchester. Sowle, an escaped prisoner, related a terrible story of savagery by Mosby's guerrillas. According to Sowle, Mosby had ordered the execution of seven men, selected by drawing lots from a group of twenty-three Union prisoners, in retaliation for the killing of the guerrilla prisoners at Front Royal the month before.

Mosby had spent much of October recovering from the wound he received at the hands of the New Yorkers. At the end of the month he wrote General Lee: "During my absence from my command the enemy captured six of my men, near Front Royal; these were immediately hung by order and in the presence of General Custer. They hung another lately in Rappahannock. It is my purpose to hang an equal number of Custer's men whenever I capture them."

There was no mention of the slaughter of the trapped Michigan men at the Morgan house, or that the six executed at Front Royal were part of a group that had shot a Union officer in the act of surrendering. Lee, with only partial information, and concerned with the protection of those under his command, replied: "I do not know how we can prevent the cruel conduct of the enemy toward our citizens. I have directed Colonel Mosby, through his adjutant, to hang an equal number of Custer's men in retaliation for those executed by him."[7]

Early in November, Mosby gathered his battalion at Rectortown after General Lee issued his directive to hang prisoners from Custer's division. Mosby was not so selective, however: Twenty-seven Union prisoners from various commands were chosen for the lethal lottery. Mosby, perhaps lacking the stomach for brutal murder, put Capt. A. E. Richards in charge and left the scene. After his departure the prisoners were drawn up in a single line. Twenty-seven slips of paper were placed in a hat and each man was ordered to draw one. Seven slips had numbers on them. The men with blanks would be sent to Richmond; those who drew the numbered slips would be executed.

Among the unlucky ones was a young drummer boy. The prisoners appealed and asked that the boy be spared. After some consideration, Captain Richards agreed. The numbered slip was placed back in the hat along with the twenty blanks and a luckless artillery officer drew it. A detail was formed to guard the doomed men and the party set out through Ashby's Gap toward Winchester, where the executions would take place. During the march they met Capt. R. P. Montjoy, who was escorting another batch of prisoners. Montjoy was a Mason, and when the Union artillery officer gave him a secret Masonic signal of distress, Montjoy substituted two of his prisoners for the artillery officer and another Mason.

The little column stopped at sunset at Rosemont near Berryville. During the night, one of the condemned men escaped. Richards decided to carry out the executions before any more managed to flee. Three of the men were hanged without ceremony from nearby trees. The remaining three, including Sowle, were dragged into the nearby scrub. Two were shot but Sowle, in an act of final desperation, struck the guerrilla holding him and eluded capture by hiding in the nearby brush. When the killings were over and the murderers gone, he stole out of hiding and headed for the nearest Union encampment.

Mosby, unaware that only five prisoners had been killed, sent Sheridan a letter recounting the execution of the guerrillas at Front Royal. "Hereafter," Mosby concluded, "any prisoners falling into my hands will be treated with the kindness due to their condition, unless some new act of barbarity shall compel me reluctantly to adopt a line of policy repugnant to humanity."[8]

The executions were an act of common brutality. The circumstances leading up to the killings at Front Royal were never explained to Lee. After the war Mosby conveniently forgot them. It was an act of pure revenge that neither lengthened nor shortened the war. Sadly, it only added a chapter to the ever-expanding litany of brutality that characterized the guerrilla warfare in Virginia and elsewhere. Later, in the spring, the memory of the five dead would be a palliative for the consciences of normally humane men as they exacted their revenge on "Mosby's Confederacy."

The national election was held in the North on November 8. Unlike soldiers from many states, the Massachusetts men in the regiment could not cast absentee ballots. Earlier in the year, the California State Supreme Court had declared that a law permitting California volunteers to vote was unconstitutional.[9] Still the election was important to the men, and they took an informal vote that evening. When the votes were counted there were 349 for Lincoln and 111 for McClellan. Among the Californians, there were only five votes for McClellan. The soldiers in the Union armies throughout the country echoed the count in the regiment. The men who would have to do the fighting voted overwhelmingly for Lincoln.[10]

On November 10 the Reserve Brigade, keeping pace with the railroad working party, moved its camp to the grounds of an estate owned by George Stephen Washington, a descendant of the first president.[11]

By the eleventh the railroad to Summit Point Station was nearly complete. Detachments from the Reserve Brigade went out every day to escort the working parties cutting ties. Another brigade, an infantry unit, protected the road from Summit Point back to Charlestown to ensure that track and materials got through to the railhead safely. Troops from Harper's Ferry covered the road between that point and Charlestown.

Twenty-five guerrillas commanded by Capt. John W. Mobberly[12] attacked two wagons and eleven men from the 2nd U.S. Cavalry. The guerrillas, dressed in Union uniforms, caught the escort off guard. They took the mules and both of the wagons. One sergeant was killed and five men were captured. The guerrillas tore up approximately a half-mile of the new railroad track before a patrol from the 1st New York Cavalry caught up with them and killed seven of the guerrillas and recaptured the wagons.[13] Another group from the 12th Pennsylvania Cavalry recaptured two mules. Colonel Crowninshield reported that, according to scouts, Mosby had about seven hundred men in the area, including men from White's, Imboden's, and Mobberly's commands.[14]

Also on the eleventh, Early made a demonstration toward the army's position at Kernstown. Merritt and Custer attacked the flanks of the advancing rebel column and the Confederates retreated. When everything was pieced together and the prisoners questioned, it was found that Early had moved his whole force from New Market to north of Cedar Creek. But with Union cavalry on both his flanks, he quickly retreated to New Market.[15]

Two days later the Reserve Brigade moved to a camp near Summit Point and camped on the same ground it had occupied in early September.[16] The brigade remained there for four days before moving to a patch of woods where it had fought during the Battle of Opequon Creek. The weather continued to be cold with frequent rains. The rest of the army started constructing winter quarters at Newton while the men of the Reserve Brigade continued to live in their Sibley tents while protecting the railhead.

With the railroad nearing completion, Sheridan issued a strong warning to the local inhabitants. In the event the railroad was attacked, the male citizens of Shepardstown, Charlestown, Smithfield, Berryville, and "the adjacent country would be sent to Fort McHenry, there to be confined during the war." In addition, the army would "burn all grain, destroy all subsistence, and drive off all stock belonging to such individuals, turning the stock so seized to the Treasury agent for the benefit of the Government of the United States."[17]

The troops guarding the railroad working party had a small brush with a band of guerrillas on the nineteenth. They killed four and drove the rest off.[18] Colonel Crowninshield reported that the railroad construction had been completed a half-mile beyond the crossing at Opequon Creek. With the work going well, the dismounted men in the brigade went to the remount camp to pick up new horses.[19] That afternoon the regimental band serenaded Lt. Josiah Baldwin, who was recovering at a nearby farmhouse from a wound received at Winchester on September 19.[20] Baldwin was very popular with the men. One letter writer wrote: "No officer in this regiment is so universally esteemed as is Lieutenant Baldwin. His known bravery, his zeal for our cause combined with his uniform kindness and affable manner are a ready passport to the hearts of all with whom he comes into contact."[21]

The dismounted troopers returned from the remount camp on November 23 with a hundred new horses. During the night the rain changed to hail and snow and by morning the water in canteens had frozen. An order was given to not cut down any more trees in the area because this was to be the site of the brigade's winter camp. However, the order to prepare for the oncoming winter did not come with it and the question on everybody's mind was, "When do we go into winter quarters?"[22]

Six 2nd Massachusetts band members went foraging on the twenty-sixth. Sergeant Corbett, one of the foragers, described the venture: "got a few pounds of sausage given to us by our Quaker friends. One young lady that I was talking with thought I was quite a curiosity being from California. She was alright on the Union and wished I would settle in this part of the country when the war is over."[23]

The Reserve Brigade had a dress parade, mounted and dismounted, each day for a week in preparation for a sweep that would destroy Loudoun Valley, Mosby's sanctuary. Sheridan was still angry about the bushwhacking murders of two of his staff officers earlier in the year.[24] On November 26, in a note that expressed his frame of mind, General Sheridan wrote General Halleck:

> I will soon commence work on Mosby. Heretofore I have made no attempt to break him up, as I would have employed ten men to his one, and for the reason that I have made a scapegoat of him for the destruction of private rights. Now there is going to be an intense hatred of him in that portion of this Valley, which is nearly a desert. I will soon commence on Loudoun County, and let them know there is a God in Israel. Mosby has annoyed me considerably, but the people are beginning to see that he does not injure me a great deal, but causes loss to them all that have spent their lives in accumulating. Those people who live in the vicinity of Harper's Ferry are the most villainous in this Valley, and have not yet been hurt much. If the railroad is interfered with I will make them poor. Those who live at home, in peace and plenty, want the duello part of this war to go on; but when they have to bear their burden by loss of property and comforts they will cry for peace.[25]

General Merritt was ordered to march into Loudoun Valley and destroy all means of support for the guerrillas. The movement started at daylight on November 28. The Reserve Brigade, still at Summit Point, was ordered to march to Snicker's Gap the next day and join the rest of the division. Merritt's orders were clear:

> This section has been the hot bed of lawless bands, who have, from time to time, depredated upon small parties on the line of the army communications, on safe guards left at houses, and on all small parties of our troops. Their real object is plunder and highway robbery, . . . you will consume and destroy all forage and subsistence, burn all barns and mills and their contents, and drive off all stock in the region the boundaries of which are described. This order must be literally executed, bearing in mind, however, that no dwellings are to be burned and that no personal violence be offered to the citizens.[26]

Sheridan told General Stevenson at Harper's Ferry: "Should any complaints come in from the citizens of Loudoun County tell them that they have furnished too many meals to guerrillas to expect much sympathy."[27]

Stevenson wired back that a force of 150 to two hundred guerrillas had attacked one of his patrols about six miles from Point of Rocks. The thirty-four-man patrol was badly beaten. Survivors reported that the guerrillas turned back and marched toward Hamilton. Stevenson proposed that if Snicker's Gap could be closed he would send his cavalry to close the lower gaps. In that way, Merritt, who was moving north, could trap the guerrillas. Mosby's only escape would be east through Leesburg. Sheridan agreed and Stevenson moved his troops immediately.[28]

General Auger in Washington offered to send his cavalry to help. Sheridan instructed Auger to send his troops to Leesburg and report to General Merritt, who would arrive there in the evening. The plan fell apart when Auger's troopers, commanded by Col. Nelson B. Sweitzer of the 16th New York Cavalry, did not leave until 1:30 P.M. on the thirtieth. By then it was too late to trap Mosby. However, Sheridan was sure that Stevenson's information was incorrect, so Sweitzer escaped any censure for his tardiness.[29]

Merritt, whose division now included the Reserve Brigade along with Stagg's and Devin's brigades, camped at Ashby's Gap on the night of the twenty-eighth. Over the next four days the three brigades moved through the Loudoun Valley, much like a line of upland bird hunters moving across a field. Anything—barns, mills, corncribs, chicken coops, haystacks, smokehouses, and root cellars—that might provide sustenance to the guerrillas and their horses was destroyed. Livestock—including horses, cattle, and sheep—was confiscated and driven to army depots. Union sympathizers and rebels were treated alike.[30] Devin noted that "The work has been very thoroughly done."[31] High plumes of black smoke marked the paths of the three brigades as they worked their way through the valley. The local populace, Union and Confederate alike, was left destitute in the face of the oncoming winter.

The 2nd Massachusetts had a brief brush with a party of guerrillas, but it was the only flicker of resistance. Throughout the four days of destruction the guerrilla leader never offered any organized resistance in defense of "Mosby's Confederacy." One report said Mosby and about three hundred of his men were encamped near Waterford, seven miles east of Lovettsville, on the night of the thirtieth. That evening he watched the fires burning on the horizon.[32]

One officer in the 2nd Massachusetts commented: "It was a terrible retribution on the country that for three years had supported and lodged the guerrilla bands and sent them out to plunder and murder. Women and children shrieked: men begged for mercy. This was the most unpleasant task we were compelled to undertake."[33]

Sergeant Sam Corbett was not so sensitive: "The raid was a complete success, the boys cleaned out Loudoun Valley to a tee, foraging was the order of the day and the order was lived up to."[34]

Colonel Crowninshield reported that the 2nd Massachusetts alone had burned 230 barns, ten thousand bushels of hay, twenty-five thousand bushels of grain, eight flourmills, and one distillery. The regiment seized eighty-seven horses, 474 head of cattle, and a hundred sheep in just one day. He estimated the value of the destruction and captured animals to be $411,620.[35] On December 1 the 1st and 6th U.S. Cavalry Regiments drove the herds across the Shenandoah and went into camp near the river. The 2nd U.S. Cavalry and the 2nd Massachusetts returned to camp the next day.

One of the many stories about Mosby concerns the return of VI Corps to City Point. According to some, Sheridan delayed VI Corps's movement and kept the 2nd Division because Merritt's cavalry had failed to capture the guerrilla leader during the Loudoun Valley sweep. The transfer of VI Corps had always been intended to occur when the Valley was secured. When Sheridan fortuitously halted the movement just days before Early's assault at Cedar Creek, VI Corps saved the army from a disastrous defeat. Early's resiliency after the defeat at Fisher's Hill had surprised everyone. When the Union army moved back to Kernstown the lesson was not forgotten. Sheridan, with the responsibility of shielding the capital from another invasion, was particularly wary of moving too quickly.

Sheridan ordered General Torbert to take the 2nd and 3rd Cavalry Divisions on a reconnaissance to determine if Early had indeed been recalled. The first reports indicated that only Kershaw's division had gone to Richmond. Torbert sent a report to Sheridan on November 21 verifying that only Kershaw's division, with about five thousand men, had returned. Torbert took fifteen prisoners back for questioning. According to the captives, the balance of Early's army was at New Market. On the twenty-third Torbert returned and reported that Kershaw had started leaving the Valley on the eighteenth.[36] Sheridan asked that a group of scouts be sent to watch the railroad at Gordonsville.

On November 24 Sheridan wrote that Early still had four divisions of infantry and seven brigades of cavalry in the upper Valley. He estimated that the infantry divisions had five thousand men apiece and that the cavalry force numbered about seventy-five hundred.[37] "Unless there is some great necessity for sending off the Sixth Corps immediately," he suggested, "I deem it best to wait until the season is a little further advanced."[38]

Sheridan notified Halleck and Grant that he would start VI Corps back to City Point on the thirtieth. Arrangements were made with the Baltimore and Ohio Railroad to have cars ready to move the troops from November 30 through December 2. At 6 P.M. on the twenty-eighth Sheridan received a report that Gordon's division was leaving Early's army for Richmond. In Washington, General Halleck, cautious as ever, expressed concern about sending VI Corps back to Grant.

Sheridan was busy on the twenty-ninth moving troops in an attempt to catch Rosser returning from a raid on New Creek in West Virginia. He took time to reassure Halleck that he did not feel any concern about sending VI Corps off if Grant needed it for an immediate offensive.

The VI Corps began its move on the thirtieth as scheduled. The 1st Division left Stephenson's Depot at 11 A.M. on December 1 and the 3rd Division left at 12:30 P.M. on the third. At noon on the fourth, Sheridan wrote Halleck that he would like to keep Getty's 2nd Division "for a few days." He added that the departure of all of VI Corps would leave him with only ten thousand infantry. Grant agreed at 1:30, deferring to Sheridan's judgment. About an hour later, Sheridan expanded on his reasons for keeping Getty: "If this division remains here for a few days it gives me security, and the movement of the other two divisions forces the enemy to move one way or another."³⁹

In all the dispatches between Sheridan, Grant, and Washington there is no mention of the failure to capture Mosby. During the entire period Sheridan was concerned with the size of Early's infantry force. The retention of Getty's division was a precautionary measure in case Early decided to advance. When Lee first became aware of the movement on December 5, he immediately ordered Early to send Gordon's division to Richmond and to get another division ready for departure.⁴⁰ Sheridan ordered Getty to move as soon as the Confederate movements became known. The division left on December 9.

The first weeks of December were quiet and uneventful for the Reserve Brigade and the 2nd Massachusetts. On December 3, the brigade marched through Winchester and camped about three miles south of town. The Brigade contributed men to the picket line in front of the army on a regular basis. The 6th U.S. Cavalry and the 1st Rhode Island Cavalry, commanded by Maj. John Rogers, joined the brigade. The 2nd U.S. Cavalry was reassigned to army headquarters as the escort guard.

The weather turned bitterly cold and wet on the eighth and remained that way for a week. A hundred men went out on a scout to Fisher's Hill on the eighth but could find no rebels. The scouting party returned the next day during a storm that piled up eight inches of snow. No orders had come down to go into winter quarters, but the men started stockading their tents anyway.

Colonel Crowninshield went home on leave on the thirteenth. General Gibbs, perhaps with a better ear for music than Crowninshield (or perhaps poorer), dismissed the 2nd Massachusetts Band as the brigade band and sent it back to the regiment. There the bandsmen were again placed under the command of Maj. Archibald McKendry. McKendry was not too popular with the enlisted men, who nicknamed him "the badger."⁴¹

The cold weather continued, hampering efforts by scouts to verify the movements and locations of Early's troops. Most signs indicated that the bulk of his infantry had been sent to Richmond.

Throughout the month of November Grant had urged Sheridan to conduct a cavalry raid on Gordonsville and the Virginia Central Railroad. Before the destruction of the Valley in September, the Virginia Central had carried foodstuffs from the Shenandoah's rich agricultural harvest to Lee's besieged army. Grant had ordered the destruction in the Valley but probably was not aware of the success of his policy. Sheridan believed that breaking the Virginia Central Railroad line would not be of any value because he was "satisfied that no supplies go over the road toward Richmond from any point north of the road or from the Shenandoah Valley. On the contrary the rebel forces here in the Valley have drawn supplies from the direction of Richmond."⁴²

Sheridan was correct. As early as November 9 General Early wrote Secretary of War Seddon: "The supplies are so limited in the Valley that unless they are kept here my troops cannot be subsisted. I have, therefore, directed that all supplies be stopped unless by your special permission. I hope none will be granted, as it is a case of necessity."[43]

Grant, ever aggressive, wrote Sheridan: "If the enemy are known to have retired to Staunton, you will be either able to make a dash on the communications north of the James, or spare part of your force. Let me know your views as to the best course to make a dash on the central Railroad and canal or detach your command."[44]

Sheridan recommended that more of the infantry force in his command be withdrawn. He told Grant that it was impossible to do anything to the Virginia Central until the weather changed. He proposed to send Crook's VIII Corps because "They are too near their homes and should go among strangers."[45] Grant agreed, but asked Sheridan to send separate regiments or divisions rather than a corps because then they could be added to the corps at City Point without adding another headquarters.[46]

On December 16 General Sheridan ordered a hundred-gun salute celebrating the defeat of Lt. Gen. John Bell Hood's Army of Tennessee at Franklin, Tennessee, on November 30. A second hundred-gun salute was fired the following day when word came of the complete destruction of Hood's army by Maj. Gen. George H. Thomas on December 15. It was clear to all that the war in the west was winding down. Sheridan's orders starting Crook's VIII Corps toward Washington and City Point went out with Grant's approval on December 18.[47] Captain William McKinley, an aide on Crook's staff and future president, prepared the movement orders.[48]

That same day, Sheridan ordered General Torbert to lead a raid through the Blue Ridge to capture a herd of cattle being gathered by the rebels at Bloomfield and Union. Additionally, Torbert was told to attack the Virginia Central Railroad at Gordonsville if possible.

The members of the 2nd Massachusetts band, stung by their demotion from brigade band to regimental band, decided they did not want to go on the forthcoming raid. After reveille on the nineteenth, Sgt. Sam Corbett went to Major McKendry, "the old badger," and requested that the band be excused. McKendry refused Corbett's request. Corbett and the bandsmen mounted the worst horses they could find and reported that the animals were not fit for the trip. The band lined up on the right of the regiment and McKendry came out to inspect the troops. When he looked at the band's horses he was forced to excuse them. "He was awful mad and hated to do it but we didn't care how mad he was so that we got clear of going."[49]

As a diversion, Torbert decided to send Custer up the Shenandoah to draw off Early's cavalry and drive it back on the infantry. After that was accomplished, he was to be "guided by your own better judgment." Meanwhile Torbert would lead Merritt's and Powell's divisions across the Blue Ridge through Chester Gap. Four days' rations and eighty rounds of carbine ammunition were issued to each man the night before. Custer's orders did not limit the number of wagons he could take along; the orders to Merritt's division limited the train to six ambulances and eight wagons.

Custer moved up the Valley and camped at Lacey's Springs, a crossroads about nine miles beyond Woodstock. He sent a courier back to Sheridan boasting that he was planning to spend Christmas in Lynchburg. Four regiments were sent out to picket the flanks and front. Pennington's brigade camped on the left of the pike and Brig. Gen. George H. Chapman's brigade camped on the right. Reveille was ordered at 4 A.M., with the command to move out at about 6:30.

In the morning, reveille sounded and the regiments on picket fell back to the main body. It was raining and the rain turned to ice as it fell. The roads were icy and it was bitterly cold. Chapman's brigade mounted and moved onto the pike in a column of fours in the dark long before sunrise. As the brigade came up, the troopers were startled by a Confederate line of battle sweeping toward the campsite they had just left. The Confederate line charged past the pickets and headed for the division's now vacant campsite. Pennington, in the rear of Chapman's column, quickly mounted his troops and moved forward. The Confederates, assailed on several sides, withdrew, leaving ten dead. Custer lost two men killed, twenty-two wounded, and twenty captured. Afterwards, Custer claimed to have killed and wounded a hundred Confederates.[50]

The sudden attack unnerved Custer, who quickly forgot the idea of Christmas in Lynchburg. He had been thoroughly surprised and badly beaten. His troops had exhausted their rations and forage the night before. Prisoners reported he was facing three Confederate brigades and that a division of infantry was coming up. Later he claimed that Rosser was supported by Kershaw's infantry and, in some very convoluted reasoning, decided he "was convinced that if it was decided to return, the sooner my return was accomplished the better it would be for my command."[51]

The miserable weather probably influenced his decision, although he did not mention it as a factor. Sheridan, always protective of the "boy General," noted that 230 men in Custer's command had frostbite. Custer remained sensitive about this affair. He blamed the failure on Torbert, who only issued him three days' rations, and two Confederate scouts who discovered the column early on the nineteenth. It is hard to understand how Custer thought he could penetrate all the way to Staunton without being noticed by Confederate scouts. General Torbert and the two scouts were useful scapegoats for his bruised ego. After his return, Torbert's chief of staff sent a note asking how it happened that the enemy overran his camp. Custer replied in a tone bordering on insubordination: "I have gone into the details of that affair more than I otherwise should, particularly as my previous dispatches contained all the information which I deemed of value or interest."[52]

The assault was planned and executed by Custer's West Point roommate, Tom Rosser, who took with him all the mounted men he had in his division and Payne's small brigade. Near Custer's camp, Rosser and Payne rode out to reconnoiter. The campfires stretched for miles, so they decided on a surprise attack. The sudden, early morning rush when the Union troopers were still groggy with sleep was a complete surprise. After a short fight, Rosser ordered his men to retreat. The attack accomplished its purpose. On the twenty-third, with Custer back at Kernstown, Early was able to send part of Wharton's division and all of Rosser's cavalry to thwart General Torbert's attack at Liberty Mills.[53]

Concurrently with Custer's movement, Torbert moved out with the 1st and 2nd Divisions. The force consisted of about five thousand cavalrymen. The horse artillery was left behind. The two divisions, with the 2nd Massachusetts (minus the band) leading, marched to Front Royal and then to Chester Gap, where they camped for the night. It had rained all day. After sunset, the rain turned to sleet. Chaplain Humphreys described the night: "A bleaker camp could not be imagined. The winter as a whole was exceptionally severe for Virginia, snow falling frequently, and the mercury sinking sometimes to zero. It was excruciating at this climax of this inclement season to be perched at the top of a pass in the Blue Ridge and to face the icy blasts as they sucked and swirled through the narrow gorge."

The cold made sleep a nearly impossible thing. The men built large campfires and slept with their feet toward the flames. Humphreys continued: "I was so weary with the long day that I slept from nine to twelve o'clock, when the extreme cold awakened me. I got up and paced back and forth for an hour trying to get warm; but I could not, the wind was so piercing. So I huddled up again under the blankets as near as possible to the fire; but do my best the wind would creep in, and blew away all sleep."[54]

The skies were cloudy on the morning of the twentieth as they moved through the gap and then turned south and passed through Washington and Sperryville, a total of about twenty-nine miles. The 1st Division camped on the Hazel River. The 2nd Division was nearby on the Hughes River. They managed to build a few fires to cook coffee and rations before the weather turned.

It was snowing when reveille sounded the next morning. The men tried to light fires but the wood was just too wet. As the column moved out, the snow changed to a cold, driving sleet and then to an icy rain. The horses suffered as much as the men. Many were so stiff from the previous day's march and so cold from being in the open during the night that they had to be walked to warm up. After the column started moving, a ten-minute halt was called at two-hour intervals to rest the horses. About 4 P.M. they halted at the summit of one of the hills surrounding Criglersville. After a short rest, they descended into the valley below. The temperature dropped and the ground was frozen. The column marched toward Madison Courthouse, near Montpelier, the estate of former president James Madison. General Torbert noted that this was one of the worst roads he had ever traveled.

At about 8 P.M. Merritt's division reached the courthouse. The advance guard briefly skirmished with Jackson's cavalry as the rest of the division was formed into a battle line. The advance guard drove the rebels from the village with a slight loss. The main body was then ordered to fall back into the woods to set up camp.[55]

The 2nd Massachusetts camped in a small pine forest, where the thick branches shielded the men from the wind. The men trimmed off the larger boughs and laid them on the snow for beds. They also stuck boughs in the ground in a circle around a blazing campfire to form a windbreak, and thus were able to obtain a modicum of warmth for the first time in three days.

The march resumed the next day, December 22, with the 2nd Division leading the way through Madison Courthouse and on toward Liberty Mills and Gordonsville. The horses slipped on the frozen ground "like hogs on ice." Jackson's and

McCausland's brigades from Lomax's cavalry division tried to hamper the advancing column but they were easily driven back by the advance guard, which pushed the rebels across the bridge over the Rapidan at Liberty Mills. As the Union troopers moved forward under heavy fire from Confederates entrenched on the opposite bank, they discovered that the planking on the bridge had been torn up. The troopers dismounted and began laying down covering fire while an assault party approached the bridge. Suddenly, a huge explosion destroyed the span in their faces.

General Torbert, knowing failure would bring Sheridan's wrath on his head again, decided to flank the rebel position. Merritt's 1st and 2nd Brigades and Col. Henry Capehart's brigade from Powell's division were ordered to move to the fords above and below the bridge and march down the south side of the river. The movement took most of the waning afternoon. The remaining brigades, including the Reserve Brigade, kept up a desultory fire, attempting to distract the Confederates on the opposite bank.

Breaking through the ice on the frozen Rapidan, the troopers forded the river below the rebel trenches. Merritt's two brigades came in sight about dusk and charged the Confederate position while Powell's troopers and the Reserve Brigade furnished covering fire for the flank attack. Merritt's charge drove the Confederates back toward Orange Courthouse, where they were struck by Capehart's brigade coming in from the east. The fighting ended as darkness fell. It was becoming difficult to tell friend from foe, and when Union troopers began firing on each other, commanders issued the order for the men to cease firing and hold their positions for the night.[56]

The Confederates fell back through the gap in Southwest Mountain and moved into a commanding position on Haxall's Mountain overlooking Gordonsville and the juncture of the Orange and Alexandria and Virginia Central Railroads. They left behind two artillery pieces that were captured during the skirmishing.

Torbert launched an attack on the Confederate position with about half his force the next day, but the rebels, who were strongly posted behind rail and earthen breastworks, repulsed the Union troopers. He then sent a column off to the north to find a way to flank the rebel position. After the flanking column moved off, the sounds of a train arriving at Gordonsville could be heard. About an hour later, Wharton's and Rosser's divisions, fresh from their ambush of Custer, started to file into the breastworks, relieving the beleaguered defenders. With the appearance of the reinforcements, Torbert decided it was useless to make another attempt to hit the railroad. He ordered a withdrawal back across the Rapidan.

Eight Union troopers were killed and about forty wounded in the fighting. One Californian, James Harding of Company F, was slightly wounded.[57] Because the retreating column had no ambulances, the wounded who could not stay in the saddle were left behind. Torbert also paroled about thirty prisoners because they would be a handicap during the withdrawal. The captured guns were brought along.[58]

The 2nd Massachusetts returned to the same pine forest where it had been the night of the twenty-second. The atmosphere around the camp was not as cheery as before, however. The men and their clothing were soaked, and the day's work had exhausted them. Most spent a sleepless night huddled around a campfire. Reveille sounded at 5 A.M. and the troops cooked the last of the coffee. They had started out with four days' rations, expecting to forage for the remainder of the time. The rations had run out and foragers were sent ahead of the column.

The horses' hoofs could not break the frozen crust of ice on the roads, and the constant rain and sleet made building fires almost impossible. Horses weak from hunger gave out and had to be left behind, forcing their riders to continue on foot.[59] The sky finally cleared, but it became bitterly cold. That night the regiment camped on a hillside so steep "we had to crawl on our hands and knees to keep from falling."[60]

The next day, Christmas Eve, the 2nd Massachusetts was at the rear of the retreating column. Chaplain Humphreys described the day's march:

> There were many places where an obstruction or break in the road made it impossible for more than two horses to pass abreast; and, as we generally marched by fours, the column at such places would be drawn out to twice its normal length . . . at such a place, the advance [guard] waits for the rear to catch up, as a caterpillar when it meets an obstruction huddles up, fixes its tail, then lengthens out over the obstacle, fixes its head and, drawing in its lengthened body, huddles up again, then creeps on as before with equal length.[61]

The regiment camped about five miles from Culpepper Courthouse and spent a cheerless Christmas Eve.

On Christmas Day the column forded two branches of the Rappahannock, but not until the troopers had cut a passage through the ice. During the march they frequently had to dismount to lead the horses down steep hills. The horses' shoes were now so smooth that it was difficult for the animals to maintain their footing, even on level ground. The troopers' boots were soaked and close to freezing. In order to keep the leather flexible, the men regularly dismounted and walked for a time. Foraging parties went out hoping to find something for Christmas dinner, but to no avail. One foraging party from the Reserve Brigade came upon a stockpile of rebel arms. They destroyed 150,000 Sharps carbine cartridges, a million percussion caps, two hundred muskets, and ninety blankets and took four prisoners.[62]

A few stragglers on broken-down horses or on foot and out of sight of their officers preyed on the local citizens. Young William Nalle of Culpepper, hearing about the retreating column, rode to his grandmother's house on Christmas Eve. He was chased away by several troopers who were ransacking the place. The next day, he and several friends carrying loaded pistols decided to join the bushwackers harassing the column. They searched for a small group of Union soldiers, hoping for an easy fight. Instead they found only one mortally wounded trooper lying in the road. They left him and rode away. On New Year's Day Nalle met a Union sergeant named Barker who claimed to have wandered away from his regiment.[63] Nalle and Barker had a long talk. Later Nalle found a wounded trooper and three dead Federals near his grandmother's ransacked house. The wounded man was taken to a nearby home. After dark, a group of Mosby's men came and killed him.[64]

On December 26, the column moved through Jefferson and the 2nd Massachusetts made camp about three miles from Sulphur Springs, a popular spa before the war. The once-luxurious hotel there was a ruin and utterly deserted. During the evening some of the men slipped away to try the water from the famous spring. Three men from Company H, probably out foraging or visiting the old springs, were taken prisoner.

The next day, when they reached Warrenton, the column split. The 2nd Division went through Salem to Paris, and the 1st Division marched through New Baltimore to Middleburg. Merritt's division, which included the 2nd Massachusetts, finally reached Winchester and its old camp on the twenty-eighth.

The raid had taken ten days, and it rained or snowed on six of those days. It was probably the most grueling march the cavalry made during the war.[65] The 2nd Massachusetts and the rest of the Reserve Brigade were played out and needed rest. So did General Torbert, who took leave shortly after returning to Winchester—perhaps to escape Sheridan's wrath. Remarkably, Custer was never criticized for his precipitous retreat and the failure to create a believable diversion in the Valley.

14 | Virginia Mud

The year 1865 started out with a heavy snowstorm, suspending all military activities in Northern Virginia.[1] Ironically, at the height of the storm, the 2nd Massachusetts was finally ordered to go into winter quarters. Sam Corbett, who had been ready for at least a month, wrote, "Rather late in the season for that I should think."[2]

The men raised the Sibley tents to provide more headroom. Sidewalls were constructed with logs cut from the local woods or with lumber pilfered from local barns and sheds. Some tents were even floored with sawn lumber. Makeshift stables were built from barn siding, fence rails, and anything else the troops could gather. Within a week the men were snugly settled in their winter huts and ready for the worst the skies could bring. Sheridan, commenting with some pride on the ability of his veteran soldiers to improvise, reported that all the men and horses were under cover "without expense to the government."[3]

The 2nd Massachusetts and the Reserve Brigade, along with most of Sheridan's cavalry, were at Camp Russell, near Kernstown, about three miles south of Winchester on the Valley Pike. Three brigades were detached: Devin's brigade was at Lovettsville covering the lower Loudoun Valley, and two brigades were back at Summit Point. Except for Devin's brigade all the cavalrymen and their horses could be supplied by the newly constructed railroad from Harper's Ferry.

During the cold nights a few rebel deserters came in seeking food and warm quarters. They confirmed that most of Early's army had been sent to Richmond. According to their reports, the only Confederate troops still near the Valley were Wharton's infantry at Staunton, Rosser's cavalry at Lexington, and Lomax's cavalry on the Rapidan. Lomax and Pegram, who had come up from Richmond and then returned, had opposed the cavalry attack at Gordonsville.[4] With these reports in hand, plus information from the regular cavalry patrols, Sheridan decided to order the XIX Corps's 2nd Division to leave for Baltimore on January 6.[5]

On January 12, Colonel Crowninshield, temporarily in command of the brigade while Gibbs was on leave, sent Major McKendry and a party of two hundred men from the 2nd Massachusetts to scout the upper Valley. They went through Strasburg and as far as Fisher's Hill before returning that evening. Other than a few scouts, they did not find any Confederate force in the immediate area. McKendry reported that local citizens told him all but a few rebel cavalry squadrons had been dismounted and the horses sent to the rear where forage was available.[6]

A reinforcement of 176 new recruits and remounted men assigned to the 2nd Massachusetts arrived on January 20. They would be a welcome addition for the spring campaign.

In preparation for the forthcoming campaign, Grant sent Sheridan a wire asking whether Sheridan thought he could spare a cavalry division to join Sherman's army as it moved northward through the Carolinas.[7] Sheridan delayed replying for one day until a grand review of the Cavalry Corps was completed. The reviewing party included Pauline Cushman, the famous Union spy who was visiting Sheridan's headquarters. Cushman, "The Spy of the Cumberland," is described as "a woman well endowed with female traits." She was a mediocre actress, but her female "endowments" made her very popular. She was not a very capable spy and eventually was caught and condemned to death. She escaped hanging when the Confederates holding her were reluctant to carry out the sentence and retreated in the face of an advancing Union column, leaving her behind. She came back north to Washington, where James Garfield, a future president and Republican Party luminary, got Lincoln to give her an honorary appointment as a major of cavalry in recognition of her services. The commission was approved before her visit to Sheridan's army, and it was in her new capacity that she was invited to attend the review.

These were Cushman's golden days. After the war she moved to San Francisco and went on the lecture circuit. She remarried, was widowed, and, as her popularity fell, slipped into alcoholism, morphine abuse, and promiscuity. She died December 2, 1893, of an opium overdose while living in abject poverty at a boarding house on Market Street in San Francisco. The coroner picked up her body and she would have been buried in a potter's field grave except that someone from the San Francisco chapter of the Grand Army of the Republic learned of her death. The men of the post paid to have her remains sent to a local mortuary, embalmed, and buried with full military honors in the military section of the city cemetery. A bugler from the Presidio sounded taps over her grave. There is no doubt that some of the men present at the review on that cold day in 1865 were at her funeral.[8]

After the review Sheridan wrote Grant: "I have now 10,000 cavalry in pretty good condition, and in another month it will be in excellent condition. I would like to comply with your wishes, and if the division is much needed it would perhaps be best to take a little risk."[9] There was twelve inches of snow on the ground at Winchester, so all major movements were postponed. Patrols and pickets invariably returned with men suffering from frostbite. The supply of horses continued to be a major problem. General Meigs reported that he had supplied 8,265 remounts to Sheridan's cavalry between December 1, 1864, and February 20, 1865—fully three quarters of the 11,214 horses reported as "present for duty" at the time.[10]

In a decision that changed the lives of many in the 2nd Massachusetts, the federal government announced on January 21 that it would resume the practice of exchanging prisoners, which had been suspended at the start of the 1864 campaign. The moratorium began when the Confederates refused to treat black soldiers in the same manner that they treated whites. Captured blacks, even those who were freedmen, were liable to be returned to slave masters. This policy was politically unacceptable to an administration now fighting a war under the aegis of emancipation. The government refused to exchange any more troops until the Confederacy changed its position. The stance, while morally correct, nonetheless played havoc on Union soldiers in captivity during the summer and fall of 1864. Confined in overcrowded hellholes like the Andersonville and Libby prisons, they died by the thousands from malnutrition, inept prison management, and the collapse of the Confederate supply system.

Some believe the policy may have been only a smoke screen because only a few blacks were in frontline combat positions and apt to be captured. They contend that a more likely rationale is that many Northern leaders believed the exchange system benefited the South more than the North. Captured rebels, who had been housed in barracks and fed regularly, were immediately available for duty in the Confederate army upon their exchange, whereas Union prisoners were in dreadful physical condition and, without exception, had to be hospitalized or allowed a long period of convalescence before returning to active service. Recognizing that the war was nearing its conclusion and faced with increasing pressure from the Northern populace to relieve the suffering of captured Union troops, the government decided to end its moratorium on prisoner exchanges. The movement of men from both sides started in late January. However, it was too late for nearly a quarter of the 264 2nd Massachusetts men captured during the war; sixty of them died in Confederate prisons.[11]

In February the parole camp at Annapolis, Maryland, was soon flooded with human wreckage from Georgia, the Carolinas, and Virginia. On March 27 the Commissary General of Prisoners, Brig. Gen. William Hoffman, notified Grant that 16,700 Union prisoners had arrived at Annapolis since February 1. At the same time, because of the better transportation system in the North, 24,200 Confederates had been sent south.[12] Among the February Union returnees were fifty-eight survivors from the 2nd Massachusetts, including forty men on February 2 alone. Most of them had been imprisoned since their capture at Rockville in July 1864. Only a handful were physically able to rejoin the regiment during the closing months of the war.

Meanwhile, Grant contemplated sending Sheridan south to join Sherman in North Carolina for the spring campaign. He wrote Sheridan that he would reach a decision about future moves when Sheridan arrived in Lynchburg. Sheridan intended to start his move south on February 25 but the bad roads delayed Devin's return from Loudoun County and the delivery of the canvas pontoon bridge train essential for crossing the Virginia rivers in February and March.[13]

Major General Winfield Scott Hancock, convalescing from a wound received at Gettysburg, was temporarily assigned to take Sheridan's place as commander of the Department of West Virginia and the Middle Military Division. A total of about four thousand men were left to guard the Baltimore and Ohio Railroad and occupy the lower Shenandoah Valley. Another twelve thousand to fourteen thousand troops garrisoned West Virginia.[14]

Chapman's division, formerly Averell's command, was broken up. Colonel Henry Capehart's 2nd Brigade was transferred to Custer's division, leaving only Col. William B. Tibbits's 1st Brigade at Winchester. Tibbits's brigade was the same unit that had refused to fight on foot on Devin's left at Cedar Creek. A court of inquiry later exonerated Tibbits, but the incident made the brigade expendable in Sheridan's mind.

On the morning of February 26, after a regimental inspection, the 2nd Massachusetts, drew four days' rations—hardtack, bacon, coffee, and sugar—and was ordered to be ready to move out the next morning.[15] The horses carried thirty pounds of forage and each man carried seventy-five rounds of ammunition.[16]

On a wet and rainy morning, the cavalry brigades turned out of their snug winter camps one by one and formed up on the Valley Pike. The column, consisting of ten thousand cavalrymen, a train of eighty-three wagons, and two batteries of artillery, took several hours to clear Kernstown. The train was minimal, with just twelve ambulances, two medical wagons, sixteen ammunition wagons, a pontoon train of eight canvas boats, and forty-five supply wagons. The supply wagons carried fifteen day's rations of coffee and sugar only. Once their four-day issue of bacon and hardtack was consumed, the men would have to live off the countryside or go hungry.[17]

General Torbert, who had asked for and received a leave extension in January, returned the same day but was not included in the expedition. Torbert's handling of the advance into the Luray Valley during the battle of Fisher's Hill and the Gordonsville fiasco had convinced Sheridan that he was not capable of leading a major expedition.[18] General Merritt was named Chief of Cavalry in his place, and General Devin took over Merritt's 1st Division. Colonel Peter Stagg was given command of Devin's 1st Brigade.

The column moved through Middletown and passed the Cedar Creek battlefield. The surrounding mountains were covered with snow that was fast disappearing under the continual rain. All the creeks and rivers along the line of march were running full and deep. The spring floods had carried the old bridge over Cedar Creek away, so the creek had to be forded. The soggy column reached Woodstock by sundown.

Major Albert Morrow of the 6th Pennsylvania went forward to Edenburgh with five hundred men from the Reserve Brigade's 6th Pennsylvania and 6th U.S. Cavalry regiments to hold the bridge across Stony Creek overnight. There was some skirmishing with rebel pickets during the afternoon's march and one Confederate was killed and three were captured.[19]

The column mounted up at five the next morning. Custer's division was in front, followed by the wagons, and Devin's division was in the rear. A courier went ahead to Major Morrow with orders for him to seize the bridge across the north fork of the Shenandoah at Mount Jackson. When Morrow sent word that the bridge had been destroyed some time earlier, Merritt ordered the pontoon train pushed forward. Capehart's brigade forded the river and established a skirmish line on the other side. The river was running fast and one man and several horses drowned during the crossing.[20] The 2nd Massachusetts waited at New Market for the pontoon train to come up. The regiment and the pontoons finally arrived at Lacey's Springs at 3:30 A.M. just as reveille was sounding for the rest of the column.[21]

Merritt sent Capehart's brigade out at reveille to occupy Harrisonburg. The main body, now led by Devin's division, followed and by 10 A.M. was passing through Harrisonburg. In the meantime, Capehart's brigade was ordered to move rapidly to Mount Crawford to secure the bridge across the North River. As they arrived at the bridge, some of Rosser's cavalry attempted to set fire to the span. Capehart's troopers forded the river above and below the bridge, flanking the Confederate rifle pits. The Confederates were dispersed or killed and thirty rebels—including a colonel, a major and a captain—were taken prisoner.[22] With the crossing site secure, the pontoons were laid across the river. The main body moved on to Mount Sydney and then across the Middle River bridge before setting up camp for the night four miles from Staunton.

The Confederates evacuated Staunton during the afternoon. Early and his staff got off at 3:45 but the last train did not leave until 4:30. Jed Hotchkiss, Early's topographical engineer, had a special problem: "My servant, William got drunk in Staunton and got out of the way, and I left Staunton without him and I did not know of his whereabouts until I got to Waynesborough, so I rode back in the night, very dark and mud very deep, to John Hamilton's, and got my servant and horse and came back about 2 A.M. of the 2nd, and slept a while at a refugee camp as I could not find my own."[23]

Unbeknownst to him, Hotchkiss just missed being captured by Union cavalry. That evening Colonel Stagg took his brigade through Staunton to destroy the railroad bridge at Christian's Creek. Stagg brushed aside the small detachment of rebels left to guard the bridge and his men set fire to it and returned to Staunton. However, the bridge was only slightly damaged because a heavy rain quenched the blaze.

The weather had been dismal, with a bone-chilling, cold rain ever since the column had left Winchester. The Valley Pike was macadamized, but it had seen hard usage throughout the war and was falling into disrepair. Out in front, before the column went by, the road was still passable but it quickly became a muddy quagmire with the passage of ten thousand horses in the unrelenting rain. The strain on the horses was beginning to exact a toll. The first to go were the horses pulling the pontoons. At best the horses that were originally provided were in sad shape. After a few days of pulling the heavy wagons through the constant rain and mud, they began to fail. Teams were made up with horses from the supply train and any captured horses that could be found. Merritt tried to ease the strain on men and animals by alternating the order of march, but each day found more men on foot. Californian Sam Corbett recorded: "The mud is very deep. It is impossible to take a piece of artillery out of the road. We have lost 2,500 horses through fatigue since leaving Winchester."[24]

Reveille sounded at 3 A.M. on March 2. The Reserve Brigade was in the rear behind the wagons. Custer's division, leading the column, was ordered to "proceed to Waynesborough, ascertain something definite in regard to the position, movements, and strength of the enemy, and if possible destroy the railroad bridge over the South River at that point."[25]

Word about the attack at Christian's Creek reached Early at Rockfish Gap in the early morning. He ordered General Wharton to march to Waynesboro at daybreak with about a thousand infantrymen, a battery of six guns, and the remnants of Rosser's cavalry. When they arrived, Early formed the little force in a line across a low ridge just to the west of town.[26] Accounts vary, but there may have been as many as fifteen hundred or as few as twelve hundred determined Confederates ready to dispute the Federal advance.

The South River runs behind the ridge on the east side of the town. The river runs roughly north-south as it passes the town but on the south side it takes a sharp turn to the west. In 1865 two bridges crossed the river, one was on the Waynesborough to Rockfish Gap road to the south. The other was the steel bridge on the Virginia Central Railroad on the north side of the village.[27] The railroad bridge was planked for foot and wheeled traffic.[28]

Both Confederate flanks were unprotected by any natural barriers. The left flank ended in a clump of trees about five hundred yards from the westerly loop of the river. The right flank ended at a group of cabins near the railroad. Conditions were miserable; a freezing sleet was falling and no one thought to dig entrenchments in the soggy ground. A few rebels cleared the surrounding area of fencing and carried the rails to the battle line to form a barricade for protection. The pickets from Christian's Creek reported that the Union troops were returning to Staunton after burning the bridge, so it appeared the threat was over. Early issued an order to let the men fall back into the adjacent wood where they could build fires and warm themselves. Just before the order could be passed on, a courier brought the alarming news from the picket line at Fisherville, a few miles up the road, that Union troops were coming down the road in strength.

Custer's van brushed aside the pickets at Fisherville at a trot, driving them back on Waynesboro. When the head of his column reached Waynesboro at about 2 P.M., he sent Colonel Wells forward with the 2nd Brigade to probe Early's line. There was a brief firefight and Custer hesitated, even though he outnumbered Early by about four to one. The boy general convinced himself that a frontal assault on the Confederate position would be costly and ordered a careful reconnaissance of Early's position. "The enemy had a heavy force of infantry behind his works, while ten pieces of artillery were in position and completely covered his front," Custer reported after the fight. "One point seemed favorable for attack. The enemy's left flank, instead of resting on South River, was thrown well forward leaving a short gap between his left and the river."[29]

Custer ordered Colonel Pennington, with three of his First Brigade regiments armed with Spencers, to dismount and move to the right under cover of the woods while Wells's brigade skirmished with the rebels in front. Capehart's brigade was ordered to be ready to make a mounted charge. A battery of horse artillery came up behind Wells. Early, seeing the movement to his left, sent orders to Wharton to guard his flank but, before the courier could find him, the attack started. The little Union battery banged away at the Confederate line as Wells and Capehart moved to attack in the front. On signal, Pennington's mud-spattered troopers charged through the woods and up the ridge toward Wharton's exposed flank. It was over in minutes. Early's once invincible infantry, now reduced to demoralized ragamuffins, fired one volley and ran pell-mell for the river.

When the little army collapsed, Early and his staff leaped on their horses and raced for the bridges. They narrowly escaped being captured by Capehart's charging troopers. Early's poor scarecrows were not so lucky; the rampaging cavalrymen captured most of them. From a concealed spot on the wooded hills behind Waynesboro, a dejected Jubal Early watched as his men were rounded up and started on their way to Northern prisons.

Custer claimed the capture of more than eighteen hundred Confederates, fourteen artillery pieces, two hundred wagons and ambulances, and General Early's headquarters wagon.[30]

Although it was only a minor battle, it marked the end of effective, organized resistance in the Shenandoah Valley.

There was an abundance of battle flags carried by the remnants of the many depleted Confederate units in Early's little force. Custer's Division reaped the harvest. Sixteen Confederate flags were taken, including General Early's headquarters national standard. In addition to the sixteen Confederate flags, the attackers recovered General Crook's headquarters flag, which had been taken earlier in the year at Boonsboro.[31]

In comparison to other Civil War battles, the "Battle" of Waynesboro was barely a skirmish. Early's choice of the position for his troops was faulty to the point of incompetence. A defense from the other side of the South River at the bridges would have offered a better position. Considering the disparity in the size of the contending forces, Early should have fallen back to Rockfish Gap. Early's lapse gave Custer his first unaided victory of the war.

Always irascible, General Early blamed his troops for the failure: "The only solution of this affair which I can give is that my men did not fight as I had expected them to do. Had they done so, I am satisfied that the enemy could have been repulsed; and I was and am still of opinion that the attack on Waynesboro was a mere demonstration, to cover a movement south towards Lynchburg."[32]

In the days that followed a rumor spread that Early was drunk on the day of the battle. Although in the past he had a reputation for being a temperate person, there is reason to suspect there may have been some validity in the claim considering his performance that day. General Lee never again entrusted him with a troop command, and Early returned to his home in Rocky Mount, North Carolina, apparently sick with pneumonia. His war was over.

While Custer was battling Early's small force, Devin's 1st Division and the 2nd Massachusetts spent March 2 marching through Staunton to Christian's Creek. A group from the 20th Pennsylvania went to Swoope's Station and destroyed the depot and four barns filled with commissary and quartermaster supplies. As the column marched through Staunton, the 6th New York Cavalry was detailed to destroy all Confederate supplies found in the town. They destroyed a blacksmith shop, a large tannery, and a number of wagons and stagecoaches. It was a difficult march for the rest of the division, which trailed the wagons. The ground was so soggy it was impossible to take a gun or wagon off the road. The division camped east of the railroad crossing at Christian's Creek after covering just twelve miles.

Nearly ten thousand troopers rode out of Winchester on February 26. Five days later, fifteen hundred of them were without horses. The weather, the fighting, and the road conditions had taken their inevitable toll. That evening the dismounted men in both divisions were mustered and organized into a column commanded by Col. John Thompson of the 1st New Hampshire Cavalry. The column was to escort the Confederates captured thus far in the campaign north to Winchester.[33]

The column began moving north early in the morning on March 3. None of the prisoners had any rations, and the escort had only coffee and sugar. When the column reached Staunton, Colonel Thompson ordered the citizens there to provide food as the column marched through the town. Several women offered a few baskets, hardly enough to feed the nearly three thousand men. Thompson, not to be denied, ordered all available flour and bacon to be taken from the local insane asylum to feed the prisoners and guards.

Rosser, operating in the area with about a hundred of his own men and Capt. John McNeill's ranger company, decided to try to free the prisoners. He sent dispatches to the citizens and guerrillas ahead of the column directing them to rendezvous at Mount Jackson and hold the fords at the North River. Rosser hung on the flanks of the column as it moved north. At night he slipped some of his men into the column in an effort to prepare the prisoners for a mass escape attempt when he made his attack.[34]

The head of Thompson's column reached the river on the sixth and found a force of about two hundred rebel irregulars holding the fords. Thompson tried to build a bridge by felling trees but was not successful. The river was falling rapidly, so he waited until morning to send a column to a ford upriver to drive the rebels away. The water was breast high with a rapid current, so the dismounted troopers and prisoners crossed in groups of fifty, holding each other by the arms. Rosser attacked the rear of the column with about three hundred men as the last of the men were crossing the river. Much to Rosser's chagrin, none of the prisoners tried to escape. After losing ten men killed and twenty-five captured, Rosser retreated and returned to Woodstock.

The column reached Cedar Creek on March 7 and camped in the earthworks there. Word came that Mosby's men would join Rosser during the night to make another attempt, but Mosby failed to appear and the threat disappeared. The column reached Winchester the next day. After a march of more than a hundred miles through enemy country infested with guerrillas and pursued by regular cavalry, instead of losing prisoners the column arrived with a total of 1,395 Confederates, an increase of thirty-four rebels taken from would-be rescuers.[35] It was a remarkable journey. The lack of citizen concern for the hungry prisoners and the failure of any of the prisoners to aid their rescuers is evidence of the overwhelming war weariness among the population, the guerrillas, and the soldiers in that part of Virginia.

After the departure of the dismounted men, the 2nd Massachusetts and the rest of the Reserve Brigade broke camp at 5 A.M. on March 3 and marched to Waynesboro, arriving in midmorning. The roads were almost impassable after the passage of Custer's column. Devin's 1st and 2nd Brigades were ordered to follow Custer's division through Rockfish Gap toward Charlottesville.

The 2nd Massachusetts remained at Waynesboro and destroyed all Confederate property in the area.[36] The men were appalled at the scene. Custer had failed to bury the Confederates killed in the previous day's fight, so a detail was ordered to gather the dead. Another detail, made up of miners from California's gold country, was sent to destroy the steel railroad bridge over the South River. They built a caisson made of railroad ties and timbers under the center of the span and filled it with about a hundred barrels of captured cannon powder. Having no fuse, they laid a trail of powder over boards and then touched it off. The resulting explosion "raised up the whole center of the bridge and then dropped it into the river."[37] In addition, the troopers destroyed a limber and caisson, a hundred wagons, and threw a large quantity of ammunition and muskets into the river. In the afternoon they marched up the mountain through the smoke of blazing Confederate supply wagons and continued on through Rockfish Gap. A little after midnight, the brigade finally halted and went into camp two miles beyond the little town of Brooksville. The 1st and 2nd Brigades were camped at Ivy Station on the Virginia Central line about seven miles from Charlottesville.[38]

On March 4 there was a steady downpour throughout the day. The head of the column had a break while waiting for the wagon train to close up. When the train arrived at 1 P.M., the 1st and 2nd Brigades moved on to Charlottesville and camped for the night. The 2nd Massachusetts, again at the rear of the wagons with the Reserve Brigade, marched until about midnight.

Custer's division occupied Charlottesville, the site of Thomas Jefferson's home and university, earlier in the day. A deputation of citizens led by the mayor met the young general at the outskirts of town. The delegation formally surrendered the town by handing over the keys to all the public buildings and the University of Virginia. The ceremony only slightly delayed Custer, whose men continued on and captured a small body of Confederate cavalry and three guns just beyond the town.[39] After chasing the remaining rebels off, the cavalrymen destroyed the railroad bridge across the Rivanna River and two railroad bridges over the north and south forks of the Hardware River.[40] The town and university were spared.

The march between Staunton and Charlottesville was arduous for Devin's division. Merritt reported that "The state of the roads from Staunton to Charlottesville defies description. Heavy rains that fell during the march rendered the stiff, yellow clay of that section of the country soft and almost impassable. Great injury resulted to the horses of the command from marching over these roads. The disease called the hoof-rot was generated by the mud in this march."[41]

Bandmaster Sam Corbett seconded Merritt's report: "Ploughed through the mud until half past twelve last night, then went into camp. We are now through the Gap, I believe it is called Rock Fish Gap. We made but eight miles yesterday. Broke camp this morning at 7 o'clock. We are guarding the wagon trains as it is our turn to be in the Rear to day. We had to abandon one of our Bass Drums as it was impossible to carry it all day the rain has been pouring down upon us everybody wet through."[42]

The march resumed at daylight on the fifth. The 2nd Massachusetts had managed to get five hours sleep. At Charlottesville the troopers were issued the last of the coffee and sugar rations and the empty supply wagons, now surplus, were burned. The brigade, exhausted from the past three days' exertions, stopped and set up camp at 3 P.M. Pickets were sent out and the horses were fed the last of the forage. The men built fires and the aroma of army coffee spread through the camp. Except for the few who had picked up something in Waynesboro, or the even fewer who had saved some hardtack and bacon from Winchester, there was nothing to eat. The only cheering prospect was that they were at last out of the Valley and neither army had ravaged the country ahead. They camped at Joy Hill, which was "anything but Joy for us."[43]

In the morning the 1st Brigade and three regiments from the 2nd Brigade were detailed to destroy the Virginia Central Railroad south of Charlottesville. They used a technique perfected earlier in the war. First, a long line of men armed with crowbars would assemble on both sides of a length of track and pry the rails from the ties. After lifting several hundred feet of track, the ties were gathered, piled up, and set ablaze. The rails were then placed across the roaring fire. When the iron became white-hot, teams of men with large tongs would bend them into U shapes, sometimes called "Sherman hairpins," or twist them around the nearest trees. In one day the 1st and 2nd Brigades destroyed about three miles of the Virginia Central Railroad line and two fifty-foot-long bridges.

The remaining regiments from the 2nd Brigade destroyed two thousand pounds of tobacco (less what ended up in their haversacks), fifteen wagonloads of grain, and a tannery with a thousand hides. The Reserve Brigade, not to be outdone, burned Ivy Station and several warehouses containing tobacco and commissary stores. War had finally come to the upper Shenandoah, and the sky was covered with the black smoke that had become so familiar to the citizens of the lower Valley.[44]

General Sheridan marched toward Lynchburg with Custer's division on March 6. A squadron from the 2nd Massachusetts commanded by Capt. Henry Kuhls accompanied Sheridan. During the march the troopers destroyed a number of railroad bridges and culverts along the Virginia Central Railroad.

General Merritt led the 1st Division to Scottsville on the James River, arriving at about 3 P.M. On the way they destroyed three canal barges.[45] One contained ninety-six hundred artillery shells; the other two were loaded with commissary stores. All three were destroyed along with all the nearby locks and canal bridges. At 5 P.M. the 1st and 2nd Brigades marched to Howardsville, twelve miles up the canal. The 6th Pennsylvania moved out to destroy a masonry aqueduct at the Hardware River and a detachment of the 2nd Massachusetts was sent to raze another aqueduct west of town at Tooler's Creek. Both aqueducts were made of masonry and, in spite of their best efforts, could only be damaged with the tools the men had available. The Reserve Brigade stayed at Scottsville to complete the destruction of government properties and then went into camp at midnight.

Sheridan had planned to cross the James River and destroy the Southside Railroad as far as Appomattox Station. Because of the constant rain over the past week, the James was running full and was too wide to cross with the eight pontoons accompanying the expedition. The nearest bridge was at Hardwicksville, about twelve miles upstream from Howardsville. A second bridge led to Duguidsville, about fifteen miles upriver on the south bank.[46] Both were covered wooden bridges.

At 2 A.M., the 1st New York Dragoons from Devin's 2nd Brigade moved rapidly up the canal towpath to attempt to seize the bridge at Hardwicksville. As the troopers approached the bridge, rebel pickets set it afire. Each end of the bridge had been filled with straw and creosote, and the fire was just too hot to extinguish. The rest of the 1st and 2nd Brigades spent the day destroying canal locks and aqueducts from Warminster to New Market, and set up camp at New Market that evening.[47] That night's campground was only twenty miles north of a small Virginia village called Appomattox Courthouse.

The 2nd Massachusetts remained at Scottsville with the Reserve Brigade burning a large cloth mill, a five-story flourmill, a candle factory, a machine shop, and a tobacco warehouse. Some of the local women helped themselves to whatever they could carry before the fires were started.[48] Some houses near the flourmill were slightly damaged by the intense heat but there was no loss of life. In the afternoon the brigade marched along the towpath toward New Market, a distance of thirty-two miles. During the march they burned and destroyed whatever the 1st and 2nd Brigades had missed. At Warren they destroyed a large mill, and at Howardsville a large wagon and plow factory, several railroad bridges, and warehouses containing tobacco and food were put to the torch.[49] At Tredick Hall Station they burned one of the largest tobacco factories in Virginia.[50] A few rebels trailed the advancing Union column along the opposite side of the river. The brigade went into camp a mile from New Market at about 11 P.M.[51]

After dark the 6th and 17th Pennsylvania Cavalry regiments were ordered to move quickly down the towpath and seize the bridge across the James at Duguidsville.[52] Again the effort was thwarted. Before the two regiments were within a mile, the rebels set the bridge on fire.

Sheridan continued down the Virginia Central Railroad toward Lynchburg with Custer's division, destroying bridges and tracks for about twenty miles. By March 7 they had reached Buffalo Run near Amherst Courthouse. Duguidsville was only fifteen miles away, due east across the Buffalo Ridge. Throughout the march, scouts

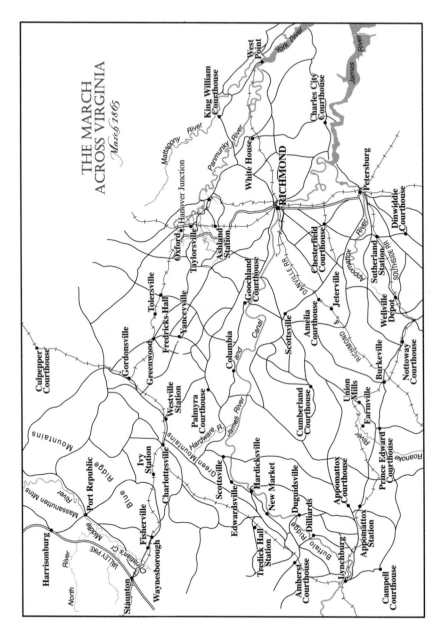

THE MARCH ACROSS VIRGINIA
March 1865

kept both columns aware of each other's position. Scouts sent word from Lynchburg that the enemy was concentrating there to oppose Sheridan's advance. The rebel force was formidable, consisting of Pickett's division from Longstreet's corps and Fitz Lee's cavalry.[53] All of this served as a rationale for Sheridan to give up the idea of capturing Lynchburg and moving south to join Sherman. When word came that the bridges across the James had been destroyed, Sheridan decided to join the armies of the lieutenant general in front of Petersburg instead of going back to Winchester.

The truth is that Sheridan never intended to join Sherman. It was always his intent to go to Petersburg. After the war he wrote: "I was master of the whole country north of the James as far down as Goochland; hence the destruction of these arteries of supply could be easily compassed, and feeling the war was nearing its end, I desired my cavalry to be in at the death."[54]

A heavy rain began falling the next morning. Sheridan ordered Custer to march to New Market to join Devin's division and start moving east. Devin's 2nd Brigade was ordered to make a forced march and occupy the town of Columbia. The 2nd Massachusetts and the 1st Brigade destroyed a dam and breached the canal wall at New Market. From there they moved down the towpath to Duguidsville and await-ed orders. The move was made to ensure that the way was clear for Custer to move to New Market.[55]

When the brigades arrived, Devin massed them on the hill overlooking the canal as a show of force to the watching Confederates on the other side of the river. At 4 P.M. orders came down to return to New Market. The 1st Brigade and a battery of artillery moved onto the towpath. As the brigade stretched out along the path, a party of rebels on the other side of the river opened fire. Devin ordered the 5th U.S. Cavalry from the Reserve Brigade to dismount and provide cover for the retiring troops. The artillery battery opened up on the town. The cannon fire quickly damp-ened the spirits of the bushwhackers, who quickly dispersed.

The 2nd Massachusetts returned to New Market with the Reserve Brigade by way of the ridge road, avoiding the skirmish along the canal and covering the column's left flank. The march that night was one of the most difficult the brigade ever made. "It rained all day yesterday and all last night," Sam Corbett wrote. "It was intensely dark and the mud was so deep that we would have to dismount and feel our horses through it."[56]

When the troopers arrived at New Market, the headquarters detachment man-aged to find a barn where they could spend a dry night. Unfortunately, "We found it occupied by about 500 Negroes, men, women and children all thrown in Promis-cuously. We made them take one side of the building while we camped at the other."[57]

The 2nd Massachusetts and the Californians had never encountered blacks in such large numbers. In the Shenandoah and Loudoun County there were only a few slaves, mostly house servants and an occasional field hand. East of the moun-tains, below Charlottesville, there were a number of extensive tobacco plantations requiring large numbers of slaves. As the Union troops moved through the area, the blacks left the plantations and followed them in search of freedom.

Reveille sounded at four the next morning. The rain continued and the mud was knee deep. The Reserve Brigade, along with Custer's Division and accompa-nied by General Merritt, took the Back Road to Columbia. It was a somewhat longer route but it offered protection for the column's left flank. The brigade marched all night, passing through Howardsville and finally reaching Scottsville at noon on March 10.[58] After resting about an hour, the march resumed and the command arrived a few miles east of Columbia, where it went into camp at about 10 P.M.[59]

The 2nd Brigade reached Columbia at daybreak on the morning of March 9 after a fifty-six-mile forced march in knee-deep mud and continual rain. Detachments went out on the Richmond and Palmyra roads and brought back the information that Fitz Lee's cavalry was south of the James, marching toward Columbia.[60]

The 1st Brigade accompanied the wagon train to Columbia on the canal towpath, arriving on the eleventh. Because of the condition of the roads, the march had been exceedingly difficult. The Negroes following the column pitched in and helped move the column along.[61]

At about three in the afternoon the 2nd Massachusetts and the Reserve Brigade rode through Columbia across the canal and camped in some woods about two miles from town. That evening they drew seven days' worth of coffee and sugar. It continued to rain most of the day and night but the trees provided some welcome cover.[62]

During the day Sheridan sent two pairs of scouts to General Grant at City Point. All four men carried the same message: "Sheridan is moving to the White House (on the York River); send supplies, forage, extra horses and ammunition." Each pair was allowed to select its own route. The first duo to make it through Confederate lines, J. A. Campbell and A. H. Rowland, reached Grant's headquarters on the evening of the twelfth while General Grant and his staff were eating dinner. The wives of the commanding general and chief of staff were visiting and at the dinner table when a waiter announced the arrival of two very strange men asking to see the general. A staff officer went outside and brought them into the dining room when he found out that their instructions were to hand the dispatch personally to General Grant. The message was written on a piece of tissue paper and enclosed in a ball of tinfoil that one of the scouts carried in his mouth. Grant unrolled the wrapper and read the message aloud to his staff and the two ladies. When he finished, Grant questioned them. The ladies, intensely interested in the exchange, also directed questions at the two very tired men. After a while Grant excused himself and took the men away for more questioning by his staff.

The story of their journey is one of the truly heroic adventures of the war.[63] After leaving Sheridan at Columbia, they were overtaken twice by Confederate patrols but claimed they were members of Imboden's cavalry brigade. Another patrol chased them all the way to the Chickahominy River, where they stripped to their underwear and swam their horses across. On the other side they came to a row of pilings. The horses could not get through the barrier, so the scouts abandoned them. They came across a canoe and used it to get ashore, all while under fire from the Confederates on the opposite bank. They then walked to Harrison's Landing, eleven miles away, where they met a party of Union soldiers. After identifying themselves they were given some spare clothing and taken by boat to City Point and Grant's headquarters. The second pair of scouts arrived two days later after six attempts to get through Confederate lines. Both parties were given a meal of the best food the headquarters cooks could provide, new horses and clothing, and sent to the White House to await Sheridan's arrival. The next day Grant issued orders arranging for supplies to be transferred to the White House in readiness for the Cavalry Corps.[64]

On March 12 the Reserve Brigade marched through Yanceyville with Devin's division to the South Anna River. The 1st Brigade forded the river and moved east to cover the 2nd and Reserve Brigades with the wagon train as they crossed the Yanceyville Road bridge. The three brigades then camped on the north bank of the river.[65]

Early the next morning they continued their march north to Tolersville on the Virginia Central Railroad, where the whole division was put to work pulling up rails, burning the ties, and heating, bending, and twisting the rails. About three miles of track between Tolersville and Frederick's Hall were destroyed and rendered useless. The 5th U.S. Cavalry also burned a large tannery at Tolersville. At about 6 P.M. work halted and the men mounted up. The division moved on to Frederick's Hall and went into camp at about ten.

Custer's division marched directly to Frederick's Hall. Dispatches captured at the telegraph office indicated that General Early, who was headed home to North Carolina, was nearby with about a hundred men. Custer captured some of these men and a couple of members of Early's staff. Early and a single orderly escaped and made their way to Richmond.[66]

To assist in the chase of Sheridan's column, Pickett's division and Fitz Lee's cavalry were ordered to leave Lynchburg and report to General Longstreet in Richmond. They arrived on March 13. The next day, Longstreet moved the force toward Hanover Courthouse. Longstreet asked for a pontoon bridge and halted the column to await its arrival. The bridge never arrived, perhaps because none were available in the dwindling Confederacy.

As Pickett and Fitz Lee were arriving in Richmond, Custer's division was crossing the South Anna at Ground Squirrel Bridge and marching toward Ashland Station, where he was expected to block any Confederate forces moving from Richmond.

Devin was ordered to move to the railroad bridges across the South Anna. He led the division along the Virginia Central Railroad then, after crossing the tracks at Anderson's Turnout, headed southeast to Taylorsville. The troopers arrived there at about 4 P.M. About a mile to the south was the long bridge over the South Anna on the Richmond, Fredericksburg, and Potomac Railroad. To the left, about three miles downriver, was the newly rebuilt Virginia Central bridge—the site of the California Hundred's first fight back in June 1863. The Reserve Brigade was assigned the task of destroying the bridges. The 6th Pennsylvania and 6th U.S. Cavalry regiments were ordered take the long bridge on the Fredericksburg line just beyond Taylorsville. The two regiments did not meet any resistance and started to work destroying the bridges. Another detachment went to destroy the bridge over the Little River. The 2nd Massachusetts, supported by the 5th U.S. Cavalry, marched out to destroy the Virginia Central bridge. The 5th U.S., traveling by a different road, reached the bridge before the 2nd Massachusetts. The advance guard, led by Colonel Crowninshield with men from both regiments, charged across the bridge at the rear of the Confederate works, driving the defenders off and capturing three guns. The Confederates rallied about eight hundred yards away and started to counterattack but the cavalrymen, using the Confederate's own guns, drove them off.[67] The captured guns were then spiked and thrown in the river.[68]

By midnight all three bridges were demolished. These were major spans. The RF&P bridge over the South Anna was a thousand feet long, the Little River bridge was seven hundred feet long, and the Virginia Central bridge measured six hundred feet. The destruction of these bridges effectively isolated Richmond from northern Virginia and the Shenandoah. That it was accomplished without any resistance indicated the Confederacy was at last nearing its end.

The brigade camped near the Little River that night. On the fifteenth it crossed the river and halted. Regiments from the 1st Brigade were sent to destroy another RF&P bridge over the North Anna and a trestlework across a swamp near Hanover Junction. The 6th U.S. Cavalry was sent out as skirmishers. Orders arrived early in the day from the Cavalry Corps headquarters directing that a detachment be sent across the South Anna to Hanover Courthouse. The river was too deep for fording and all the bridges had been destroyed, so scouts went to locate a crossing. They found a wagon bridge two miles to the west. Lieutenant Colonel George R. Maxwell took his 1st Michigan Cavalry and a squadron from the 2nd Massachusetts to secure it. At Hanover Courthouse they encountered the advance guard of Longstreet's corps.[69] Heavy skirmishing continued most of the day. Strong scouting parties were sent out toward Ashland to open communications with Custer.

Custer arrived at Ashland early in the morning. There he learned that Pickett was moving toward Ashland with a strong force to intercept Sheridan. Custer ordered his division to move north to join the 1st Division, leaving Pennington's brigade behind as rear guard and dispatching couriers to Sheridan at the South Anna. When Sheridan received Custer's report he decided to cross the North Anna and move down the north bank of the Pamunkey River to the White House. Pennington set fire to the wagon bridge as the last of Custer's troops moved out.

Custer's hurried retreat left the 1st Michigan and the 2nd Massachusetts squadron alone and unsupported on the rebel side of the South Anna. At 5 P.M. Devin received orders to move north and cross the North Anna at Oxford. He sent orders to Maxwell to return to the South Anna, cross at the wagon bridge, and rejoin the division. When Maxwell arrived at the bridge it was on fire even though Devin had ordered that it be spared until the detachment returned. After some anxious minutes and a search in the fast-fading light, a place where a crossing might be made was eventually found. The water was high and flowing very swiftly. As the regiments crossed, the river took its toll. Seven men needlessly drowned that night, swept away by the raging current because Pennington had too hastily burned the wagon bridge. Once on the other side, the angry and sodden column moved to the North Anna River, crossed over, and camped that night with the rest of the division at Oxford.[70]

Custer's division led the march the next day followed by the wagons and then Devin's division. The column moved through Chesterfield to Mangohock Church, arriving about 10 P.M. The weather was warm and pleasant for a change, and the roads were finally mud free. The march was comparatively easy because of the slow-moving wagons. The column was now on the north bank of the Pamunkey, which is formed by the conjunction of the North and South Anna Rivers and the Little River. On March 17 the column marched through Aylett's Station to King William Courthouse and went into camp at two in the afternoon. The next day they moved slowly to the White House, arriving at 2 P.M. Two gunboats patrolling the river and a brigade of infantry on the bank greeted them. The stores and forage requested by Sheridan were already there. After drawing five days' rations and forage, the command crossed the Pamunkey at 6 A.M. and was assigned campsites on the south side.[71] The Reserve Brigade camped at Hill's plantation, just one mile from where Company A made camp in July 1863.[72]

Rosser's cavalry joined Longstreet's corps on the south side of the Pamunkey. On the sixteenth, Longstreet had ordered Rosser to ford the Pamunkey and follow Sheridan. Pickett's infantry and artillery were delayed while a bridge was built using the timbers from an old barn near the river.[73] Part of Longstreet's command crossed over on the morning of the seventeenth, too far behind to catch the Union cavalry. On the eighteenth, Longstreet decided the chances of confronting Sheridan were gone, so he ordered his troops to return to Richmond.[74]

It had been an exhausting time for the Union cavalry. The loss of horses was staggering. General Merritt reported that he had 1,323 dismounted men and 2,161 unserviceable horses, which meant 3,484 animals were needed to completely remount the command.[75] As for the 2nd Massachusetts, in January there were fifteen officers and about five hundred mounted men present for duty. By the end of March more than a third were on foot.

"The raid has been a trying and severe one on both men and horses, but as hard as the latter were worked, they have suffered far more from disease than from fatigue, and I can say with confidence that were it not for the ravages of grease heel, and rotten foot, and black tongue, that the losses of horses would have been comparatively slight in this command. The conduct of men and officers had been admirable whenever there was work to do. Such excesses as may have been committed while foraging are chargeable to the lawless men, whom of late there has been scant opportunity to ferret out and punish"[76]

The material damage to the economy of Virginia was staggering. Thirty-one factories, mills, and forges had been destroyed, along with twenty-six government warehouses. Twenty-three railroad bridges and culverts were burned. The Virginia Central and RF&P Railroads were rendered inoperable for considerable time. One engine, four cars, seven depots, and eleven water tanks were destroyed, and almost fifty miles of track had been pulled up and twisted beyond repair. Six major bridges over two hundred feet long were destroyed on the Little River and the North and South Anna Rivers. The destruction on the James River canal included thirty boats, thirty-nine canal and road bridges, thirty locks, and two aqueducts. During the raid, 158,000 pounds of wheat, 118,000 pounds of flour, seven tons of cotton, a hundred thousand pounds of tobacco, 836 sacks of salt, a thousand pounds of bacon, and 150,000 feet of bridge lumber went up in smoke.

The raid also resulted in the capture of 1,603 prisoners, 2,164 horses and mules, seventeen artillery pieces, 281 wagons, 1,976 muskets and carbines, and countless boots, uniforms, harness sets, and tents. The command marched over 350 miles, with some units covering up to five hundred miles. Devin's division lost four men killed, eight wounded, and forty-six missing. Three of the dead and two of the wounded were from the Reserve Brigade; none were Californians. Custer lost five men killed, five wounded, and sixteen missing.[77]

The Richmond papers bravely noted that "It is no longer a state secret, we believe, that General Sheridan and his raiders came within fifteen or twenty miles of the city last week, produced one of those periodical bell ringing which only serve to alarm timid women and children, and after resting his force escaped to the Yankee lines below Richmond."[78] The papers neglected to mention the destruction to the state's economy and its ability to sustain the Army of Northern Virginia. The havoc visited on the central part of the state would slow Virginia's recovery for many years after the war was over.

There would be no more supplies from the bountiful Shenandoah Valley for General Lee's beleaguered army. Two major railroads and the James River canal were destroyed. The Army of Northern Virginia and the refugee-swollen populations of Richmond and Petersburg would have to look south for rations. Unfortunately for them, William Tecumseh Sherman and sixty thousand hungry men were inexorably on the march in North Carolina.

15 | Dinwiddie Courthouse

The cavalry stopped at the White House for one week. The men and horses were exhausted. Hard marching through the mud and rain had taken its toll. Merritt, with more than his usual vigor, acted immediately. He ordered Devin and Custer to have each regiment inspected. All the Negroes were gathered up and turned over to the Provost Marshal on the north side of the railroad bridge. Later they were sent to Fortress Monroe. Twenty-five forges arrived on the twentieth for reshoeing the horses. The 17th Pennsylvania, currently at Winchester, was ordered to join the command, and all line and regimental officers at the Pleasant Valley remount camp had to report to the White House. The men got a welcome morale boost when mail arrived on March 23. It was the first they had had since leaving Winchester.

Only about a thousand remounts were available. The remaining dismounted men and disabled horses went by steamer to Washington, then on to the remount camp at Pleasant Valley.[1] To Bandmaster Sam Corbett's chagrin, dismounted band members were exempt because General Sheridan thought bands were important for the troops' morale. The band was provided with new mounts, including some mules.[2]

West of the White House lay the long line of trenches in front of Richmond and Petersburg. The Union's Army of the James and Army of the Potomac had been struggling with Lee's embattled veterans here since early in the fall. The opposing trenches zigzagged between strong redoubts, sometimes only a few hundred yards apart. The terrain is flat, with patches of marshy ground, and has only a few low-lying hills. For the most part the land was covered with woods, with only an occasional clearing where some hardy farmer attempted to grow a crop. The woods provided ample timber for the construction of the redoubts and bombproofs that dotted the entrenchments.

The siege lines started at the Chickahominy River to the north and ran to Hatcher's Run to the south. Two rivers dominated the arena. To the north the James River, after passing Richmond, meanders generally in a southerly direction and then, after several wide curls, turns east and flows to the ocean. At Petersburg, about thirty miles south of Richmond, the Appomattox River runs east to west with Petersburg on the south bank. About two miles west beyond town the river takes a sharp turn to the north and continues for about six miles before it turns east and joins the James near City Point, where Grant established his headquarters and the main supply base for the Union armies. A military railroad ran behind the line from the Appomattox to the Weldon Railroad and then to City Point. The total line of fortifications was thirty-seven miles long.[3]

At the start of the war, six railroads supplied Richmond and Petersburg. One by one they had been cut or denied to the Confederates. The West Point Railroad was closed early in the war. In the fall of 1864 the Union armies cut the Weldon and Norfolk and Petersburg Railroads, which had been supplying Petersburg. The destruction of the Virginia Central and RF&P bridges at the North and South Anna Rivers left Lee with just one line, the Southside Railroad, to supply his besieged army. The Southside ran east to west from Petersburg to Lynchburg in the upper Shenandoah. The Richmond and Danville Railroad joined the Southside at Danville west of Petersburg and provided access to North Carolina. Cutting the Southside west of Petersburg and east of Danville would strand Lee's army.

Early in the morning on March 25 the Confederates launched an attack on Fort Stedman, a strong point on the right of the IX Corps line near the Appomattox River. The attack was planned and led by General Gordon, who had planned the assault at Cedar Creek. Gordon's troops captured the fort and about a mile of the front line. For a couple of anxious hours there was concern that the rebels might achieve a breakthrough and head straight for the supply dump at City Point. In time, Maj. Gen. John G. Parke, the IX Corps commander, rallied his troops and recaptured Fort Stedman, inflicting heavy losses on the rebels, including the capture of two thousand prisoners.

The attack was an attempt by Lee, who was aware of the impending buildup on his right flank, to delay the inevitable. At the end of the campaigning season in the fall of 1864, Grant had stopped at Hatcher's Run only because the winter weather would render the roads to the Southside Railroad impassable. With the onset of spring and the arrival of Sheridan's hard-hitting cavalry in the Richmond-Petersburg lines, it was only a matter of time before the Southside Railroad would be cut. The attack on Fort Stedman was an attempt to disrupt Parke's IX Corps so that it would not interfere with the Confederate withdrawal from the Petersburg fortifications. A secondary goal was to cause enough consternation to force Grant to temporarily abandon his effort to turn Lee's flank. One of Grant's traits was to never let his actions be determined by those of his enemy. Unflappable and stolid, General Grant recognized the attack for what it was and sped up the planning for the final thrust that would end the war.

On March 26, after a week of rest and refitting, Merritt's two divisions resumed the march, crossing the Chickahominy River at Jones's Bridge. They camped at Westover Church near Harrison's Landing. The next day, the pontoon bridge across the James at Deep Bottom was dropped down to Four-Mile Creek.[4] The bridge was ready for use at 6:30 A.M., but Sheridan's column did not start crossing until 1 P.M. By 6:30 that evening the end of column had crossed over the river.[5] On the twenty-seventh they camped alongside the military railroad at Hancock's Station, where they were joined by the 2nd Cavalry Division, commanded by Bvt. Maj. Gen. Henry E. Davies.

Grant decided that the Cavalry Corps would continue to operate independently under Sheridan's command. While his cavalry was moving to Hancock's Station, Sheridan rode to City Point to meet with Grant. Grant's plan called for Sheridan to move to the left of the army and then drive west and southward, cutting the Southside and Danville Railroads. If his return was cut off or if he was unable to get to the railroad, Sheridan was to continue south along the Roanoke River, get in the rear of Gen. Joseph E. Johnston's army in North Carolina, and help Sherman complete its destruction.[6]

In the orders to Generals Meade, Sheridan, and Edward O. C. Ord was a paragraph pertaining especially to the cavalry: "The cavalry under General Sheridan, will move at the same time (29th inst.) by the Weldon road and the Jerusalem plank road turning west from the latter before crossing the Nottoway, and west with the whole column before reaching Stony Creek. General Sheridan will then move independently under other instructions which will be given him."[7]

According to Grant, Sheridan "seemed somewhat disappointed at the idea, possibly, of having to cut loose again from the Army of the Potomac, and place himself between the two main armies of the enemy." Grant, knowing "that unless my plan proved an entire success it would be interpreted as a disastrous defeat. I said to him, General, this portion of your instructions I have put in merely as a blind; and gave the reason for doing so. . . . I told him that as a matter of fact, I intended to close the war right here, with this movement, and that he should go no farther."[8]

That afternoon Grant asked Sheridan to accompany him on a trip up the James River on the steamer *Mary Martin*. After they boarded, Grant told Sheridan that President Lincoln was also aboard the *Mary Martin*. The ship steamed upriver to the pontoon bridge where Sheridan's cavalry column was crossing and the three leaders spent an hour or so watching the veteran troopers pass over the river heading south.

Sheridan returned to Hancock's Station on March 29 to prepare the orders for the movement. That afternoon he got a telegram from Grant saying, "General Sherman will be here this evening to spend a few hours, I should like to have you come down." Fearing Sherman would persuade Grant to change the orders and send the cavalry south to join his army in North Carolina, Sheridan got on the military railroad and, after a bumpy ride, arrived at City Point at about 7 P.M. The three generals once again discussed whether Sheridan should join Sherman. Finally Grant, seeing that Sheridan was opposed to the idea, reiterated his orders of the day before. After the meeting broke up, Sherman came to Sheridan while he was in bed and renewed the discussion, but when he saw Sheridan was firmly against the idea, Sherman dropped the subject and left.[9]

The next morning Sheridan returned to Hancock's Station and Grant, Sherman, Rear Adm. David D. Porter, and the president went up the James River. Some time during the day, General Crook arrived and assumed command of the 2nd Cavalry Division, relieving General Davies. Crook, who had been captured by guerrillas in late February, was exchanged on March 18 and was now available for duty. At first Grant had wanted Maj. Gen. Frank Wheaton of Wright's VI Corps to take the division, but Meade reported that Wheaton suffered from piles and thus would not be of much service to the cavalry. Grant had some misgivings about Crook, based on conversations with him after he left Richmond, but went ahead because of Crook's seniority.

That night Sheridan received another written order from Grant. The new order included information regarding the movements of V and II Corps, which would be supporting the flanking movement, as well as the option of joining Sherman in North Carolina. The latter caused Sheridan some concern,[10] but he chose to trust that "matters would so come about as not to require compliance with those portions relative to the railroads and to joining Sherman."[11]

During the evening each trooper was issued five days' rations, thirty pounds of forage, and forty rounds of ammunition to be carried on the horses. There were 9,000 men under Sheridan's command, including 5,700 in the 1st and 3rd Divisions, and 3,300 in Crook's 2nd Division. Major General Ranald S. Mackenzie's cavalry division from the Army of the James, numbering about a thousand men, would join Sheridan later.[12] The Reserve Brigade was still commanded by General Gibbs and consisted of the 1st, 5th, and 6th U.S. Cavalry regiments and the 2nd Massachusetts. Gibbs's entire command had only 437 men and twenty officers, making it about the size of an average infantry regiment.[13]

Major General Gouverneur Warren's V Corps, with 685 officers and 15,576 men present for duty,[14] started out at three the next morning, following the old stage road to Rowanty Creek. The head of the column arrived at the crossing at 4:45 A.M. The engineers quickly installed a pontoon bridge while the infantry scrambled across on the wreckage of a former bridge. At 8 A.M., the advance guard reached the junction of the stage road and Vaughan Road, the corps' first objective.

Major General Andrew A. Humphreys's II Corps, with 1,064 officers and 20,107 men,[15] moved out at 6 A.M., crossed Hatcher's Run, and formed into line of battle, with each division holding about a third of its strength in reserve. The right of the line was at Vaughan Road and within supporting distance of Crook's troops, who had taken over the position occupied by II Corps the day before. The left was near Gravelly Run, about a half mile from the Quaker Road.

Humphreys sent a mounted scouting party up Gravelly Run to the Quaker Road while the line of battle was being formed. The scouts drove the Confederate cavalry pickets beyond an old sawmill to the enemy's infantry picket line. Skirmishers were sent out ahead of the battle line to develop the rebel position. They quickly determined that the Confederate entrenchments extended from Hatcher's Run to the vicinity of the Quaker Road. Any further advance was delayed by Meade's orders.[16]

The cavalry started out at 5 A.M. With Devin's 1st Cavalry Division leading the way, the column marched down the Jerusalem Plank Road through Gary's Church and Ream's Station to Malone's Crossing on Rowanty Creek. Since Warren's V Corps infantry had been assigned to the only graded road in the area, the cavalry had to move on country lanes. The 1st Division moved into line at the rear of Crook's column at about 8 A.M. Custer's 3rd Division, assigned the task of accompanying the wagon train, brought up the rear. Warren's column was still passing over the V Corps bridge, so Sheridan's engineers constructed another pontoon bridge farther downstream. The advance guard met a small rebel cavalry picket on the other side and drove it to the left toward Stony Creek. A few prisoners were taken and Sheridan's scouts learned from them that the bulk of the Confederate cavalry was to the south at Stony Creek Station on the Weldon Railroad.[17]

Sheridan ignored the cavalry force on his flank and pressed on to the day's objective, Dinwiddie Courthouse. The advancing troopers drove off a small rebel picket at the courthouse and sent their own pickets out on the four roads radiating out from the village before setting up camp. These roads, leading toward all four points of the compass, made Dinwiddie Courthouse an important but not very imposing crossroads. The village "was far from attractive in feature, being made up of a half dozen unsightly houses," Sheridan wrote. It had "a ramshackle tavern propped up on two sides with pine poles, and the weather-beaten building that gave the official name to the crossroads. We had no tents—there were none in the command—so I took possession of the tavern for shelter for myself and staff."[18]

The 2nd Massachusetts, marching at the rear of Devin's division, moved into camp a few miles east of the crossroads at 11 P.M.

No attempt was made during the night to establish contact with Warren's corps on the Boydton Plank and Quaker Roads. When the wagons came up the next day, Sheridan intended to move toward Five Forks and the Southside Railroad.

The progress of the wagon train and Custer's division was much slower. The weather was clear on the twenty-ninth but the roads, which ran across swampy, low-lying ground, had to be corduroyed the whole distance to keep the wagons from sinking to their axles.[19] The train got only as far as the pontoon bridge at Malone's Crossing by the end of the day.

Some time after nightfall, the sky clouded over and a heavy rain began falling. The roads, which during the day had been difficult, promised to become quagmires by morning. It was just like the storms that the cavalrymen had experienced a month earlier. However, there was one big difference. During the march from Waynesboro to the White House, Custer's division had been out in front grabbing the headlines. Now it was Custer's turn to be bogged down with no one to help. As the rain poured down, the 1st Division troopers huddled around their campfires, boiled coffee, and ate hardtack. There must have been at least a few smug grins when they thought about the wagon train, Custer, and his newspaper reporters stuck in the mud fifteen miles to the rear.

At Sheridan's tavern headquarters, the night brought good news:

> The wagon containing my mess e quipment was back somewhere on the road, hopelessly stuck in the mud, and hence we had nothing to eat except some coffee which two young women living at the tavern kindly made for us; a small quantity of the berry being furnished from the haversacks of my escort (the Sixth Pennsylvania

Cavalry of the Reserve Brigade). By the time we got the coffee, rain was falling in sheets, and the evening bade fair to be a most dismal one; but songs and choruses set up by some of my staff—the two young women playing accompaniments on a battered piano relieved the situation and enlivened us a little. However the dreary night brought me one great comfort; for General Grant, who that day had moved out to Gravelly Run, sent me instructions to abandon all idea of the contemplated raid, and directed me to act in concert with the infantry under his immediate command, to turn, if possible, the right flank of Lee's army.[20]

Sheridan slept "most soundly" that night on a Virginia feather bed assigned to him by his staff, confident the cavalry could now become the noose that would catch the Army of Northern Virginia.[21]

A couple of miles north of Warren's position on the night of the twenty-ninth was Burgess's Mill, which marked the end of the strong Confederate fortifications protecting Petersburg. Dinwiddie Courthouse, Burgess's Mill, and Five Forks are at three corners of a triangle. From Dinwiddie Courthouse, the apex of the triangle, Boydton Plank Road runs northeast to Burgess's Mill. Another road, running northwest, goes from Dinwiddie Courthouse to Five Forks. White Oak Road, the base of the triangle, runs east to west from Burgess's Mill to Five Forks. The Southside Railroad is just a little over a mile to the northwest of Five Forks.[22] West of Burgess's Mill, Hatcher's Run turns west.

While the Union troops were moving on the twenty-ninth, General Lee ordered Lt. Gen. Richard H. Anderson's corps and Pickett's division from Longstreet's corps to move into line west of Burgess's Mill, covering the approaches to the Southside Railroad. The force had about fifteen thousand infantry and eighteen hundred cavalry. When the Confederates reached their new positions they began digging entrenchments along White Oak Road south of Hatcher's Run for a distance of about three miles. At the end of the new line, the trenches turned north along a road leading to Sutherland Station on the Southside Railroad.[23] Pickett's division, with four brigades, was on the right. Major General Bushrod R. Johnson's division from Anderson's corps held the left. Fitzhugh Lee's cavalry division was sent on to Five Forks. Brigadier General William P. Roberts's small brigade of North Carolina cavalry from Rooney Lee's division picketed the woods between Fitz Lee and the new entrenchments. Facing these Confederates were about forty thousand Union soldiers in the II and V Corps.[24]

During the night Meade instructed Warren to extend his line to the left as far as possible. At daybreak on the thirtieth the rain continued to fall and Warren became hesitant and overly cautious. At 5:50 A.M. he sent Meade a dispatch questioning the order because "My left, on the plank road, cannot be extended with propriety till I can get some idea of General Sheridan's movement."[25]

Meade remained firm and, at 8:30 A.M., again directed Warren to extend his left using Maj. Gen. Samuel W. Crawford's and Maj. Gen. Romeyn B. Ayres's divisions. He told Warren that Sheridan had been ordered to attack or turn the Confederate right but "you must act independently of Sheridan and, protecting your flanks, extend to the left as far as possible. If the enemy turns your left, you must attack him."[26]

Ayres moved to the left without encountering any opposition and halted. He reported seeing infantry moving to the west along the White Oak Road. Because of Warren's inaction and Ayres's failure to cut White Oak Road in the morning, three brigades from Pickett's division and two from Bushrod Johnson's were able to reinforce the Confederate cavalry at Five Forks.[27] Except for a weak demonstration by the Confederates at about 4:30, the fighting on Warren's front was over in the early afternoon.

When Warren's maneuvering was completed, II Corps and Brig. Gen. Charles Griffin's division from V Corps were in front of the Confederate entrenchments at Burgess's Mill. Crawford was in reserve near Boydton Plank Road, and Ayres was in the woods to the left of Boydton Plank Road with one brigade pushed out about three-fourths of a mile from White Oak Road.

The continuing rain and the swampy nature of the ground made movement difficult for the cavalry, but Sheridan was not to be deterred. Gregg's brigade from Crook's division went down Boydton Plank Road to the crossing at Stony Creek. The 2nd Massachusetts led the 1st Division and Davies's brigade from Crook's division on a reconnaissance toward Five Forks early in the morning. Custer remained stuck in the mud at Malone's Crossing.

As the cavalry left, Sheridan received an order from Grant confirming the instructions regarding the change of objectives. He directed Sheridan to keep enough troops to hold his present position and send the rest back to the military railroad, where the horses could be supplied with hay and grain.[28]

According to the account in Sheridan's memoirs, after receiving this dispatch he decided to ride over to Grant's headquarters to get a clear idea of Grant's intent. When he arrived Sheridan found Grant's staff congregated around a large bonfire, standing on boards to keep from sinking in the knee-deep mud. According to Sheridan's account, Grant was with his chief of staff, Bvt. Maj. Gen. John A. Rawlins, discussing the question of suspending operations until the weather improved. Rawlins was for continuing but Grant thought the army should wait for better weather. Seeing that there was a difference of opinion, Sheridan quietly withdrew. Grant joined him a little later and said that because of the rain and mud it seemed necessary to suspend operations. Sheridan, perhaps drawing on his experience during the march across Virginia earlier in the month, begged him to continue. He raised the specter of the ridicule heaped on Burnside after his "mud march" in January 1863, and told Grant the cavalry was ready to move despite the difficulties.[29]

Grant's memory of that interview was diametrically different from Sheridan's recollections. According to Grant, it was General Rawlins who favored returning to City Point and the lines around Petersburg. Grant admits only that Sheridan's confidence influenced him insofar as he was more determined than ever to continue the operation.[30]

Grant's memoirs were published in 1885 shortly after his death; Sheridan's were published in 1888. Furthermore, there were no other witnesses to their meeting. Considering Grant's character and past performance it seems that Sheridan, knowing he could not be refuted, was apparently embellishing his own image.

While they were discussing whether or not to continue the operation, Sheridan asked Grant if he could have Wright's VI Corps for the flanking movement. Grant replied that the weather and road conditions precluded moving any infantry and that he would have to take Five Forks with his cavalry.[31] Sheridan's preference for Wright was to be expected after they had worked so well together during the Shenandoah campaign. Moreover, he may have felt some antipathy toward Warren, who would be on his right, after learning of Warren's lack of aggressiveness during the previous two days.

On the way back to Dinwiddie Courthouse, Sheridan went by Warren's headquarters. Finding Warren asleep, he went to the tent of Col. William T. Gentry, one of Warren's staff members and an old friend. While he was talking with Gentry, Warren came in and discussed the activities of the past two days. Sheridan wrote that Warren spoke "rather despondently of the outlook, being influenced no doubt by the weather." By the time Sheridan reached his headquarters, he knew Warren would be a problem.[32]

When Sheridan reached the Dabney Road, he sent a member of his staff toward Five Forks with orders for Merritt to develop the enemy's position and try to determine his strength. Merritt promptly ordered the Reserve Brigade to move on the enemy positions. The 5th and 6th U.S. Cavalry regiments moved out along the road heading directly to Five Forks with the 6th Pennsylvania on the right facing toward White Oak Road and the 2nd Massachusetts to the right of the Pennsylvanians facing north along Boydton Plank Road. The 1st Brigade was massed at the J. Boisseau House with one regiment across Gravelly Run toward White Oak Road and behind the Reserve Brigade's right flank. The 2nd Brigade was concentrated at the intersection of Brook Road and the Five Forks road with one regiment out on Boydton Plank Road.

As the Reserve Brigade's regiments pushed forward, heavy skirmishing took place all along the front in spite of the weather, indicating that the enemy held White Oak Road and Five Forks in force. In front were Fitzhugh Lee's dismounted regiments with about thirteen hundred men. Pickett's infantry was preparing to defend the crossroads behind the cavalry screen. At about 3 P.M., 150 men of the 5th and 6th U.S. Cavalry regiments pushed the rebels to within three-fourths of a mile of Five Forks. In front was Chamberlain's Swamp, a low-lying boggy area in front of the Five Forks fortifications. Suddenly a large enemy force came charging out from a line of trees on the far side of the swamp and surrounded Morris and his troopers. He was forced to cut his way out, losing three officers and twenty men in the process. The 2nd Massachusetts charged, driving the rebels back in confusion to White Oak Road. The line of skirmishers, led by Captain Kuhls of Company L, was forced back by deadly fire from a strong line of entrenchments. Colonel Crowninshield, thinking the trenches might be lightly held, formed a battle line and ordered a charge. Once again the rebel fire drove the Union troopers back. Chaplain Humphreys described the ensuing scene: "Here, Captain Kuhls, an enthusiastic hot-blooded German, who seemed crazed by the excitement of the onset, refused to quail before the belching blaze of death, and I could see him as, without a follower, he galloped his horse defiantly up to and over the breastworks, utterly oblivious of the fact that alone he was charging upon Pickett's Division of ten thousand veteran infantry. I think his daring must have struck such amazement into the enemy that they refrained from shooting him at such close range."[33]

Kuhls was captured unharmed. He had enlisted in Company L at San Francisco on January 24, 1863, and was made a sergeant. He was commissioned a second lieutenant February 5, 1864, and six weeks later was promoted to first lieutenant. He made captain on August 31. He was exchanged ten days after his capture. Kuhls died in 1883 in Idaho.

The 1st Brigade, the 1st U.S. Cavalry, and two regiments from the 2nd Brigade were sent to relieve the Reserve Brigade. The reinforcements tried to retake the position reached by Morris but they were forced back by a strong line of Pickett's infantry. The 2nd Massachusetts and 6th Pennsylvania, unable to drive back the enemy in front of them, held their positions under increasing pressure. At sunset the three brigades retreated to the Boisseau's house and encamped.[34] That evening, Sheridan reported that the Confederate cavalry had been reinforced by Pickett's division. Grant replied that if Sheridan thought he could turn the enemy's right flank the next morning with the assistance of a corps, Grant would detach the V Corps and "place the whole under your command for the operation." Grant added that Ord, Wright, and Parke had been instructed to be ready to assault at daylight but that they would not make the attack until Grant gave the order.[35]

Sheridan declined the offer and again asked for VI Corps, saying that with Wright's men and his cavalry he could turn Lee's flank.[36] The next morning Grant answered that the VI Corps could not be moved and offered II Corps instead. Sheridan did not reply as events along his front required all of his attention.

During the evening of the thirtieth, Rooney Lee's cavalry division, fifteen hundred strong, and Tom Rosser's division with twelve hundred veterans of the Shenandoah Valley campaign arrived at Five Forks and joined Fitz Lee's division. The three divisions were formed into a corps with Fitz Lee in command.[37]

The rain finally stopped on the morning of the thirty-first and the 1st Brigade from Devin's division was sent out on the right toward White Oak Road. The Reserve Brigade, with the 2nd Massachusetts, was massed at the intersection of Brook Road and the road to Five Forks. The 2nd Brigade, supported by Davies's brigade on the left, was dismounted and put in motion toward Five Forks.[38] As the brigades marched toward the swampy ground in front of Five Forks, they encountered considerable opposition. Eventually the rebels were pushed back and Five Forks was taken and occupied. At about 2 P.M., Pickett sent a force across a ford farther upstream and attacked the Union left. A strong party of rebel cavalry assailed Davies's front and his troopers broke and retired in confusion. While the fighting was going on at Five Forks, Crook sent Bvt. Brig. Gen. Charles H. Smith's 3rd Brigade northwest from Dinwiddie Courthouse to Fitzgerald's Crossing at Chamberlain's Creek to cover the 2nd Brigade's left. Gregg was sent to Smith's right and rear in support. Smith's brigade held the ford through several heavy attacks during the midafternoon.

Colonel Charles Fitzhugh was ordered to fall back from Five Forks with his 2nd Brigade and move by the left flank to meet the advancing infantry. The 6th New York was ordered to remain in position and hold the road to Five Forks. Fitzhugh slowed the enemy's advance on the left but soon after a heavy line of infantry appeared in the right rear, moving down Crump's Road from White Oak Road toward the 6th New York. These Confederates were the same troops that had repulsed Warren's attack earlier in the day. The 1st Brigade sent a regiment to support the beleaguered 6th New York. The two regiments slowed the Confederate advance but at about the same time the Confederates on Fitzhugh's front attacked his left flank, driving the Union line across the road to Dinwiddie Courthouse and threatening to surround the brigade. Devin, who was with the 1st Brigade, ordered Fitzhugh to retreat and connect with the 1st Brigade. Fitzhugh conducted a fighting withdrawal, twice halting his troops to charge the enemy.

The 2nd Brigade joined Col. Peter Stagg's 1st Brigade along Brook Road. Devin called for the held horses and was preparing to charge down Brook Road when General Davies, who was senior to him, rode up. Taking command, he ordered Devin to move his two brigades to the east and out of the fight. Before the order could be executed, however, Pickett ordered a left wheel so that his battle line faced north, trapping both of Devin's brigades between his division on the south and west and the rebel battle line advancing down Crump's Road.

When the Confederates pushed Fitzhugh back across the Five Forks road, Sheridan moved Gregg's brigade over to support the 2nd Massachusetts and the Regular Army regiments at the intersection of Brook Road and the Five Forks road. As the Confederate battle line moved through the left wheel, its right and rear were exposed to the two brigades. Gibbs and Gregg's troopers quickly dismounted and fired into the rear of the rebel line. The surprised Confederates stopped, made a quick about-face, and returned the fire. The change in front gave Devin a brief respite and he was able to safely withdraw the beleaguered 1st and 2nd Brigades. They moved east through the woods toward Boydton Plank Road and made their way back to the courthouse without opposition.

Pickett turned his full attention to Gibbs's Reserve Brigade and Gregg's men. Heavily outnumbered, the two cavalry brigades fought dismounted, contesting every yard of ground. Their determined defense gave Sheridan time to organize a line to defend the courthouse. Capehart's brigade and General Custer arrived and were directed to a low ridge to the left of the Five Forks road. As Custer finished placing Capehart's brigade, Smith's brigade, sorely pressed by Fitz Lee's cavalry, fell back from Chamberlain's Creek. The Confederates, unaware of the arrival of Capehart's brigade, made a sudden dash at Smith's troopers as they fell back across an open field. Capehart's troopers opened up with a withering blast of carbine fire on the charging rebels' left flank, throwing them into confusion. They turned and ran for

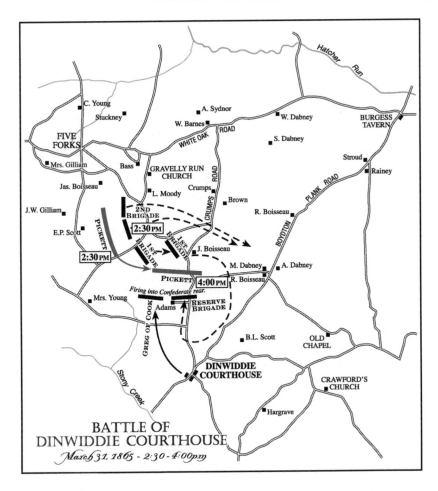

the protecting woods on the far side of the field, giving Smith time to halt and set up a battle line on Capehart's flank. Gibbs's and Gregg's exhausted troopers moved to the right rear of Capehart's brigade to replenish their ammunition, leaving a gap for Pennington's brigade, which was expected momentarily. The horse artillery, which had been stuck in the mud, arrived on the scene and was quickly posted along the line. A few minutes before sunset the rebels formed a solid battle line in preparation for an attack. As the line was forming, Pennington arrived and quickly filled the gap in the Union line.

Sheridan was now ready. His line, about a half-mile west of Dinwiddie Courthouse, was anchored on the left at the thick woods near the junction of Chamberlain's and Stony Creeks. From there the line ran in a northeasterly direction to a clump of trees near Boydton Plank Road. The artillery was in position and ready to open up. The men quickly erected a breastwork of fence rails and brush for some minimal protection. Generals Sheridan, Merritt, and Custer rode along the line with members of Sheridan's staff to encourage the men. The reception Sheridan received from the Union troopers was enthusiastic and showed their resolve to hold the position. The parade of mounted officers drew a different kind of reception from the Confederates. Rebel sharpshooters opened up, wounding a few men, including Theodore Wilson, Custer's *New York Herald* correspondent, much to the glee of the men of the 2nd Massachusetts.

The desultory firing and shouting stopped and an expectant hush fell over the field. The troopers watched as the solid lines of infantry, veterans of the attack on Cemetery Ridge, emerged from the line of trees in the front, bayonets gleaming in the fading sun. They were just discernible in the dim light at the tree line, then grew larger and larger as they came on, red battle flags in front. The horse artillery set up a racket, banging away at the approaching line, sharp orange flashes in a ball of white smoke. Sheridan had ordered all the brigade bands to the front and they were playing loudly. According to one of Grant's staff officers who was there that afternoon,

> Sheridan always made effective use of his bands. They were usually mounted on gray horses, and instead of being relegated to the usual duty of carrying off the wounded and assisting the surgeons, they were brought out to the front and made to play the liveliest airs in their repertory, which produced excellent results in buoying up the spirits of the men. After having several of their instruments pierced by bullets, however, and the drums crushed by shells, as often happened, it must be admitted that the music, viewed purely in the light of an artistic performance, was open to adverse criticism.[39]

In the center, Custer's two brigades waited, the troopers' pockets full of brass Spencer cartridges. The Californians and the 2nd Massachusetts counted out the few rounds they had remaining. When the Confederates neared the line, the cavalrymen opened fire. The troopers worked the levers on their carbines rapidly, sending volley after volley crashing into the rebel ranks. The tattered gray and butternut line reeled, turned defiantly, and then sullenly fell back to the line of trees. It was over; Sheridan and his weary troopers still held Dinwiddie Courthouse. Five brigades of cavalry behind hastily constructed fence-rail breastworks had held off five brigades of infantry and a division of cavalry. Mercifully, darkness ended the fighting.

Pickett employed all of his infantry and Fitz Lee's cavalry in this action—nearly eleven thousand men. During the final attack in front of Dinwiddie Courthouse, Sheridan had only about forty-seven hundred men in the defensive line.[40] Regardless of the odds, the Spencer repeating carbines were more than a match for the rifled muskets carried by Pickett's veteran infantry.[41]

Sheridan lost about 450 men killed and wounded in the Battle of Dinwiddie Courthouse, as the day's fight became known.[42] The Reserve Brigade lost five officers and fifteen men killed or captured. Only one of the casualties was a Californian: Cpl. William H. Moore from Company E, who was severely wounded.

BATTLE OF
DINWIDDIE COURTHOUSE
March 31, 1865 - 5:00pm to Sunset

Dinwiddie Courthouse was not a decisive battle. The Confederate infantry still blocked the road to Five Forks. Beyond Five Forks was the Southside Railroad. If the railroad could be cut, Lee would have to leave the trenches and fight the numerically superior Union army on open ground. As the weary troopers huddled around the campfires that night everyone knew that the morning would bring a renewal of the fighting.

16 | The Five Forks Shad Bake

The Union infantry units along White Oak Road, despite their superior manpower, had done little to ease the pressure on Sheridan's badly outnumbered cavalry at Dinwiddie Courthouse. After some indecisive skirmishing across Gravelly Run, General Warren, ever cautious, called a halt while he conducted a reconnaissance of the Confederate position. Later, at about 5:15 P.M. on March 31, Warren was ordered to send a brigade down White Oak Road to cooperate with Sheridan. Bartlett's brigade from Griffin's division got as far as the J. Boisseau house at the intersection of Crump's Road and the Five Forks road and encamped without making contact with Sheridan's beleaguered cavalry.

Grant sent Sheridan the following dispatch at 10:45 P.M.: "The Fifth Corps has been ordered to your support. Two divisions will go by J. Boisseau's and one down the Boydton road. In addition to this I have sent Mackenzie's cavalry, which will reach you by the Vaughan road. All these forces except the cavalry should reach you by 12 tonight. You will assume command of the whole force sent to operate with you and use it to the best of your ability to destroy the force which your command had fought so gallantly today."[1]

Sheridan wrote Warren at 3 A.M.: "I am holding in front of Dinwiddie Courthouse on the road leading to Five Forks, for three-quarters of a mile, with General Custer's division. The enemy are in his immediate front, lying so as to cover the road just this side of A. Adams' house, which leads out across Chamberlain's bed or run. I understand you have a division at J. Boisseau's; if so, you are in the rear of the enemy's line and almost on his flanks. I will hold on here. Possibly they may attack at daylight; if so attack instantly and in full force. Attack at daylight anyhow, and I will make an effort to get the road this side of Adams's house, and if I do you can capture the whole of them."[2]

At about ten that night, Generals Pickett and Fitz Lee were sleeping side by side just behind the Confederate line in front of Dinwiddie Courthouse when pickets sent word that Union troops were moving toward the Boisseau house.[3] The two generals decided to fall back to Five Forks.[4] The wagon train started as soon as the teams could be hitched up. Brigadier General Matthew W. Ransom's brigade, on the left of Pickett's infantry, started at about 1 A.M. The rest of the infantry pulled out of the line from left to right and followed Ransom throughout the early morning hours. Fitz Lee's cavalry withdrew a little after sunrise.[5]

Ayres's division from Warren's V Corps moved down Boydton Plank Road early in the morning of April 1. One of Sheridan's staff officers met the head of the column and guided them west along Brook Road directly into the left flank and rear of the position the Confederates had held the night before.

The 1st and 3rd Cavalry Divisions were ordered to follow the retreating Confederate cavalry. As the troopers moved out, Mackenzie and his division reported to Sheridan at Dinwiddie Courthouse. Sheridan ordered him to rest and await orders.[6] Crook's division remained to guard the wagon trains and cover the crossing at Stony Creek. When the cavalry reached the intersection with Brook Road, Custer's 3rd Division dismounted and, with Chamberlain's Creek on the left, headed cross-country for the Widow Gilliam's house on Scott's Road. Devin's 1st Division continued up the Five Forks road.

Warren ordered Griffin's division to move in the direction of Dinwiddie Courthouse on White Oak Road at 5 A.M. and report to General Sheridan.[7] The troops marched about a mile to the intersection with Crump's Road, then down Crump's Road to the Five Forks road. There they met Devin's cavalry moving toward Five Forks. Griffin halted and sent word to Warren about his location. Sheridan arrived on the scene and ordered Griffin to move his division to the vicinity of the Boisseau house and await further instructions.

General Crawford's 3rd Division was in camp near White Oak Road when Warren told him the entire corps was going to move toward Dinwiddie Courthouse.[8] The division formed into line of battle and fell back in a southwesterly direction until it reached the country road used earlier by Bvt. Maj. Gen. Joseph J. Bartlett's brigade from Griffin's division. There they formed into a column of fours and continued to Crump's Road, arriving at the intersection of Crump's Road and Five Forks Road late in the morning after Devin had passed.[9]

When Colonel Stagg, leading the advance guard of Devin's division, reached Chamberlain's Swamp, a line of Confederate infantry appeared, ready to contest any further passage. The 2nd Brigade dismounted and Devin ordered Colonel Fitzhugh to cross the swamp farther up to find a position from which he could provide covering fire for an attack by the 1st Brigade.

When the two brigades were in position, Devin ordered Stagg to charge. Fitzhugh's men opened fire as Stagg's troopers splashed across the muddy ground. The attack drove the Confederates clear through the wood to a strong line of entrenchments filled with rebel infantry. The attack was so sudden that some of Stagg's men crossing the open ground rode in front of the entrenchments and came within twenty yards of the startled Confederates. Some of the 2nd Brigade's dismounted men raced forward behind Stagg's mounted troopers and caught and dragged away fleeing rebels just as they reached the parapets. After a heavy exchange of fire, the cavalrymen fell back to the cover of the woods about fifty yards to the rear.

Companies I and K of the 2nd Massachusetts had been assigned to serve temporarily as General Gibbs's escort, and Capt. Henry Alvord, commanding Company K, was made Gibbs's acting aide de camp. According to Alvord, the 2nd Massachusetts was on the Reserve Brigade's right flank at the far end of the cavalry line. The brigade was operating independently of the division commanders, taking orders directly from General Merritt and Sheridan.[10]

Alvord wrote that the

brigade had been in advance the day before . . . as far as Five Forks. . . . It had been pretty badly used up towards night on March 31st, and we had been sent back to the rear to reorganize somewhat, . . . we were in the rear as we moved forwards from Dinwiddie Courthouse. We passed General Sheridan's headquarters a mile or so out from Dinwiddie, and then the left the main road to Five Forks road; crossing through the woods and then dismounted soon after we left the Five Forks Road; left our horses and moved forward. It was then about the middle of the day. Devin's division was direct in our front as we came up, and the line was pressing the enemy back at the time, between twelve and one o'clock—about twelve o'clock, because by one o'clock we were in line on the right of Devin's division. Colonel Stagg, I think, of the Michigan brigade was in command at that time; was still mounted and on our right. We left our horses in the woods and moved forward through heavy timber fronting the White Oak Road, formed in sight of the enemy's works—their outer line of works—before one o'clock.

We were practically in front of the left of the enemy's works. . . . We were really on the right of the dismounted line of cavalry facing the left of the enemy's works.[11]

Custer's division followed Scott's Road to Five Forks and arrived in front of the Confederate entrenchments at 11 A.M. He precipitously organized a mounted charge on the Confederate line that was quickly repulsed. Both sides then settled down and continued to exchange skirmish fire. Fitzhugh was on Devin's left, tied in with Pennington's brigade of Custer's division. The Reserve Brigade was on Fitzhugh's right, opposite the end of the Confederate line. Devin ordered Stagg's brigade to mount up and move to the right and rear of the Reserve Brigade. The 1st U.S. Cavalry remained mounted directly behind the Reserve Brigade, ready to charge if the enemy line was broken. The rest of the brigade dismounted and the horses were led to the rear. A heavy skirmish fire was maintained to keep the Confederates in the entrenchments until the infantry moved up.[12]

The Confederate entrenchments were about a mile and three-quarters long. At this stage of the war, experienced troops automatically built fortifications any time it appeared they were going to be in a fight. If they stayed in place for even a few days, the works became virtually impenetrable. Pickett's men had constructed some of the works near Five Forks the day before. The rest of the line was thrown up after the troops returned from Dinwiddie Courthouse. Generally it consisted of barricades of logs and rails with an earth covering. Other obstructions, including tree slashings, were set in front of the position. At the eastern end, in front of the 2nd Massachusetts, the entrenchments turned and ran north for about two hundred yards, protecting the rebels' left flank. The entrenchments had one weakness: the Confederates had not had sufficient time to clear much of the ground in front. In some places, the tree line sheltering the Union troopers was only forty yards from the Confederate line.

Rooney and Fitz Lee's cavalry divisions were posted on the right. One regiment from Fitz Lee's division, now commanded by General Munford, was placed on the left, connecting with the pickets from Roberts's North Carolina cavalry in the woods along White Oak Road. Tom Rosser's troopers, pleading fatigue after their long march on the thirtieth, were placed in reserve on the north side of Hatcher's Run, so they could feed and rest their horses. The rebel supply wagons were parked near Rosser's division.

At about 2 P.M. Sheridan sent orders for the infantry to come up. Despite repeated orders from Sheridan to hurry up, it took the three divisions about two hours to march the two miles to the open ground around Gravelly Run Church. [13] Brevet Major General Joshua L. Chamberlain, commanding Griffin's lead brigade, described the march:

> We turned off on a narrow road said to lead pretty nearly to the left of the enemy's defenses at Five Forks on the White Oak Road. Crawford led, followed by Griffin and Ayres,—the natural order for prompt and free movement. The road had been much cut up by repeated scurries of both the contending parties, and was even yet obstructed by cavalry led horses[14] and other obstacles, which it would seem strange had not been got off the track during all this halt. We who were trying to follow closely were brought to frequent standstill.[15]

The corps was formed into a two-division front with Ayres on the left and Crawford on the right. Griffin's division would follow Crawford and be ready to send help to either of the two other divisions. As the troops were moving into position, Sheridan and Warren gathered the division and brigade commanders around to discuss the maneuver. Sheridan drew his saber and sketched his plan of attack in the soft ground at his feet. The plan was simple: V Corps would cross White Oak Road and make a counterclockwise left wheel, swinging around to attack the entrenchments on the rebels' left flank as the cavalry attacked in front. Ayres would strike the corner of the Confederate line while Crawford, supported by Griffin, would move to the Confederate rear. Custer's and Devin's divisions would maintain a heavy skirmish fire while the infantry came up and moved into position and then charge as the infantry attack developed. Custer's mounted brigade would pursue the fleeing Confederates. Before the attack commenced, Mackenzie would move east on White Oak Road to drive off any reinforcements, then turn around and attack on the right of V Corps as it hit the Confederate flank. The 2nd Massachusetts Cavalry, on the right flank of the cavalry line, was the pivot point for Warren's left wheel.

By 4 P.M. everything was ready and the order to march was passed down the line. The V corps moved forward on the Gravelly Run Church Road, its front supposedly parallel to White Oak Road. Shortly after the divisions started moving, a sketch of the movement, hand drawn by General Warren, was circulated among the commanding officers.

Chamberlain later said the sketch "showed our front of movement to be quite

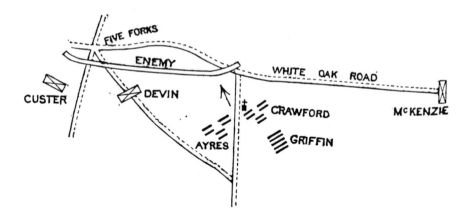

oblique to the White Oak Road—as much as half a right angle with Crawford's Division directed upon the angle, and Ayres, of course, thrown far to the left, so as to strike the enemy's works halfway to Five Forks. Griffin's Division was shown following Crawford; but the whole direction was such that all of us would strike the enemy's main line before any of us could touch the White Oak Road."[16]

The sketch, instead of helping, wound up causing confusion and doubt among some of the division and brigade commanders as their troops plunged forward through the tangled brush and trees along their route. The sketch was seriously flawed in two respects. First, the Confederate entrenchments did not extend as far as the intersection of Gravelly Run Church Road and White Oak Road. Secondly, the corps was facing north, not northwest as indicated.

When the battle line crossed White Oak Road the attack plan fell apart. Crawford's division crossed before Ayres's because of the road's southeasterly direction. Then, after crossing the road, Crawford ordered a half-left wheel[17] to the heading indicated by Warren's sketch. Griffin's division followed Crawford through the turn. Because of the erroneous map, Crawford's and Griffin's divisions were now marching northwest—right out of the fight along White Oak Road.

Ayres, at the pivot of the turning movement, ignored the oblique front. His division continued on as it had started, with the 2nd and 3rd Brigades in front in an east-west alignment with the 2nd Brigade on the left. The 1st Brigade followed in reserve. The division crossed White Oak Road and moved into the heavy brush and woods, pushing back the rebel cavalry pickets. After advancing a short distance, the left regiments received a heavy volley of rifle fire from the flank. Ayres ordered the 2nd Brigade to change its front to the left and attack. Then he ordered the 1st Brigade to move into the front line to the left of the 2nd Brigade as the 3rd Brigade had lost contact with him and was continuing slowly north. One more brigade also entered the fray: Joshua Chamberlain, commanding Griffin's left flank brigade, moved toward the sound of the guns and came in on Ayres's right. Together they attacked the Confederate flank.

Devin's division, which included the Reserve Brigade, attacked at about the same time Ayres's attack began on the right. According to Devin:

> The whole division was dismounted and ordered to advance and again charge the enemy's works. Captain Lord, First US Cavalry was ordered to keep his regiment mounted and in readiness to charge should the enemy's line be broken. The whole line advanced under a terrible fire from the enemy's works; but the regiment on the right of the Third Division giving way, the Third Division was halted and reformed. On the second charge the troops on our left again fell back; but notwithstanding this defection, the division pressed forward, the enemy's works were carried after an obstinate struggle, the right was connected with the left of the Fifth Corps, the front of the division changed to the left, and the enemy pursued for two miles. As the works were carried Captain Lord was ordered to charge with his regiment, and gallantly responded, clearing the breastworks at a bound and charging far in advance of the division.[18]

Captain Alvord reported that Ayres's division carried the first Confederate position to its front. Alvord said the Reserve Brigade broke from cover when Ayres's division moved into an open field behind the Confederate position and attacked on Ayres's left, causing "quite a confusion at that time"[19]

Under attack from the cavalry and Ayres's infantry, the Confederate line along White Oak Road disintegrated. Hundreds of rebels ran for cover in the adjoining woods, even more dropped their arms and surrendered. Captain Henry Chambers of the 49th North Carolina described the action from the Confederate perspective:

> Much to our surprise and consternation, in a short time one or two regiments of our men came running back to within an hundred yards of our immediate rear saying the enemy had completely flanked both them and us and were moving in a heavy column on a line parallel to ours and in rear of us, thus almost completely surrounding us. These regiments soon rallied and drove the enemy in their front back a considerable distance, but could not affect the main flanking column. Col. Rutledge, commanding brigade, received no orders from the Commander of Division, and either would not or could not determine upon any course of action. Col. McAfee, commanding the regiment, was equally undecided, not knowing what to do, or fearing to assume the responsibility of moving. The men, seeing they were flanked, awaited orders. It was suggested that we form a line of battle perpendicularly to ours so as to protect our flank and rear, but no order to that effect was given. Again these regiments (the 25th N. C. and 23rd S. C., I believe) which had before driven, were forced back. The men could stand it no longer. Without doing something we would be captured or annihilated where we were. Men and Officers immediately moved obliquely to the rear and were rallied, or partially (for many did not stop) where it had been proposed to form the line of battle, The enemy immediately occupied our works by coming up from a pine in our rear. The 24th and 25th Regiments, doubtless not comprehending, or not being able to follow this movement, were thus cut off and completely surrounded. The enemy were in considerable force between us for I counted three national colours.[20]

General Munford's cavalry and fugitives from the Confederate regiments east of Five Forks patched together a new line on Ford's Road assisted by Col. William J. Pegram's battery of three guns. Two cavalry brigades, Pennington's from Custer's division and Fitzhugh's from Devin's, made a dismounted charge over the entrenchments and captured the guns, mortally wounding Pegram. Rooney Lee fell back with his cavalry division and Brig. Gen. Montgomery D. Corse's infantry brigade and set up another line in the open ground at the Widow Gilliam's plantation west of Five Forks.

Often, random happenings change the course of history. One of those occurred during the Battle of Five Forks. To fully explain it, we must go back a couple of days. On March 30, while on his way to join Fitz Lee at Five Forks, Tom Rosser and his division crossed the Nottoway River. It was just coincidence that the shad were making their spring run up the Nottoway. He stopped on the riverbank as his men moved past. Since his orders did not say "report immediately," and after the deprivation of the previous winter, Rosser could not resist the temptation to stop and fish. Rosser, a Negro servant, and a few members of his staff borrowed a net from a nearby farmer and waded into the stream. His division, led by his able regimental commanders, continued down the road toward Five Forks. Rosser and his staff were amply rewarded with a fine catch of large shad that they stored in the headquarters wagon. When they arrived at Five Forks that night, he and his staff enjoyed a choice dinner of baked fish. A large number of the big fish were still left, however, so Rosser decided to invite Pickett and Fitz Lee for lunch when things were a little more settled.

On the morning of April 1, after the retreat to the fortifications at Five Forks, Rosser sent invitations to Pickett and Lee. The invitations were promptly accepted and preparations were started. Before Fitz Lee left, General Munford rode up with a dispatch that said the enemy had penetrated the picket line between Five Forks and the main entrenchments at White Oak Road. Lee, eager to get to Rosser's luncheon, ordered him to investigate and report back. Pickett and Lee then left and hurried on to Tom Rosser's camp, two miles in the rear. No one on the Confederate side expected an attack that day, and both generals neglected to tell their seconds in command that they were vacating the field or where they could be located.

Rosser, every bit the Southern gentleman, proved to be an excellent host. His Negro servants offered wines and liquors to the guests as they arrived. They were gratefully accepted, although there is no evidence that anyone overindulged. The shad was cooked in the traditional way, split and placed flat on small branches over a hot bed of coals by Rosser's manservant. The luncheon went well and was greatly enjoyed by the three generals. It was a brief return to life as it had been before the war, and each of them relished the moment. In retrospect, knowing what each of them had undergone over the past four years, it is hard to be critical.

The generals lingered around the table for several hours. About three o'clock, two pickets from Rosser's division galloped up with the startling news that the

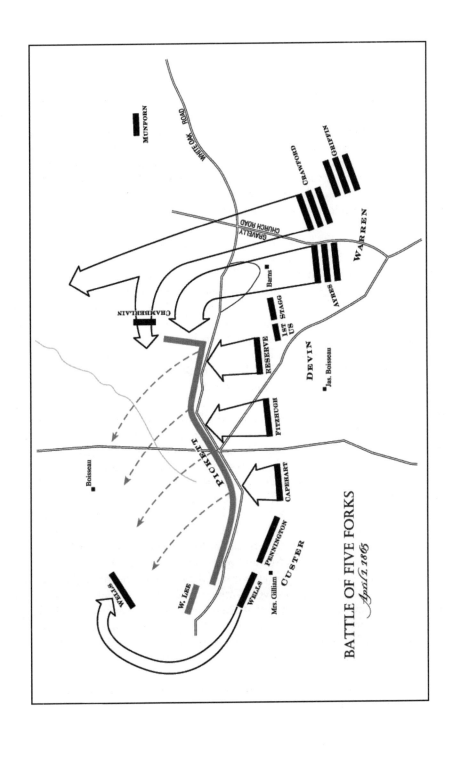

BATTLE OF FIVE FORKS
April 1, 1865

Yankees were approaching the division's camp and, even more alarming, a large enemy force was moving down White Oak Road. The officers heard the pickets' report and then listened for the sound of gunfire from Five Forks. Hearing none, they decided the threat was minimal and continued to enjoy each other's congenial company.[21]

Sometime around four, Pickett asked Rosser for someone to deliver a dispatch to Five Forks. Rosser gave him two couriers. The first man would ride ahead and, if he was taken, the second could detour and still deliver the message. Shortly after the couriers rode off there was a rattle of musket fire and the three generals watched as the first courier to cross Hatcher's Run was captured. The second courier galloped back with the unwelcome news that the woods on the other side of the run were filled with Yankees.

Pickett mounted his horse and rode across Hatcher's Run to try to reach his command but found that the Union infantry barred his way. He returned to Rosser's camp and asked for a company of cavalry to serve as an escort. Accompanied by some of Rosser's men, Pickett headed toward Five Forks. Across the run he met Tom Munford, who Lee had left in command of the cavalry screen in front of Crawford's advancing troops. He appealed to Munford to hold the enemy until he could get through. A platoon of sharpshooters laid down covering fire and Pickett escaped amid a shower of minié balls, crouching on his horse like a Plains Indian. Fitz Lee tried to follow but was forced to fall back.[22]

The troops between Rosser's camp and the Confederate trenches were from Crawford's division and two of Griffin's brigades. Earlier, General Warren, realizing that Crawford was marching right out of the fight, went after the errant division. During his search for Crawford, Warren came across Crawford's 1st Brigade, commanded by Col. John A. Kellogg. He faced it south to act as a guide for a new alignment, then went in search of the rest of the division to bring it into line. One of Sheridan's staff officers came upon Kellogg's halted brigade and ordered him to move up and join the fight on White Oak Road. Kellogg questioned his authority and some harsh words were exchanged, but Kellogg finally decided it would be wiser not to incur Sheridan's wrath and ordered his men to advance. Crawford's 3rd Brigade also turned toward the south and followed Kellogg into the fighting.[23]

Warren finally located Crawford and got him turned. Griffin's division followed. The two divisions moved down on the rear of the Confederate entrenchments, but by then most of the fighting was over. Warren sent his chief of staff, Col. Broderick T. Locke, to Sheridan to report that Warren was in the enemy's rear and had captured a large number of prisoners. In spite of the victory Sheridan was furious. The V Corps attack had been slow and badly bungled. The three divisions had been sent in piecemeal and, except for Ayres and Chamberlain, were not at the brunt of the fighting.

When Locke made his report Sheridan retorted, "By God sir, tell General Warren he wasn't in that fight."

Locke was shocked. "Must I tell General Warren that, sir," he asked.

"Tell him that sir," was the reply.

"I would not like to take a verbal message like that to General Warren. May I take it down in writing?" Locke asked.

"Take it down sir; tell him, by God, he was not at the front!" Locke wrote out the message and then rode off. Sheridan met Griffin shortly afterward and placed him in command of V Corps.[24]

Pickett, after following a roundabout route, finally arrived at the Widow Gilliam's plantation, where he was met by a swarm of bullets from Union infantry. He formed some of the fugitives in the woods behind Corse's brigade on the Confederate right. Crawford's errant division, led by Kellogg, came in on the rebels' left. Warren personally led an attack by one of Crawford's brigades. After reaching the Confederate line and driving the defenders back, he returned to his headquarters and was handed a dispatch from Sheridan directing him to report to Grant for further orders.[25]

Under attack by dismounted cavalry[26] and threatened on the left by Kellogg's brigade and to the front by Ayres and Chamberlain moving parallel to White Oak Road, the defenders were completely demoralized. Corse's and Rooney Lee's troops, still maintaining their organization, were able to make their way across Hatcher's Run to join Tom Rosser. Pickett's division ceased to exist.[27] Charged with the responsibility of holding Five Forks "at all costs," Maj. Gen. George Pickett had failed completely. The strength of the Union 1st and 3rd Cavalry Divisions could not have exceeded 5,250 men. Furthermore, after deducting horse holders from the dismounted units, the dismounted mounted brigades were left with only about forty-five hundred effectives to cover the entire Confederate line.[28]

Custer's weak attack early in the day may have led Pickett to believe that was all the Federals could muster that day and that it would be safe to accept Rosser's invitation. Thus it was that a batch of fresh-caught Virginia shad and two cavalry divisions—particularly the three dismounted cavalry brigades that maintained a continual fire for four hours—kept Pickett's veteran infantry, about sixty-four hundred strong, in place until the slow-moving Union infantry came up to spring the trap.

Most of the Confederates who escaped fled west. They reached Hatcher's Run because there was no organized pursuit. Contrary to orders, Custer had decided earlier to mount two of his brigades, leaving only Pennington to join the assault with Devin's division. Before the infantry attack started, he led the two mounted brigades around the extreme right of the Confederate line. When the dismounted brigades attacked, Custer turned and faced the two brigades to the south and formed a battle line about a mile behind the Confederate entrenchments. Custer never explained his actions; apparently he intended to block an escape to the northwest. Instead of pursuing the demoralized Confederates, the two brigades merely forced the Confederates to retreat to the west. By the time Devin's dismounted brigades brought up their horses, the fleeing Confederates were gone.

A few days after the fight, General Devin proudly wrote about his troopers that day, "In some regiments every squadron commander was killed or wounded. With regard to the conduct of officers and men it is sufficient to state that under the hottest fire not a straggler could be seen along the whole line—every man was in his place and at his work."²⁹

About four thousand Confederates were taken prisoner. Hundreds more rebels lay dead in the trenches and the woods and fields behind the line. The Reserve Brigade lost eleven men killed, wounded, or captured.³⁰ Among the dead in the 2nd Massachusetts were two Californians: Cpl. George Thayer and 1st Lt. Lewis Munger, both of Company F. Munger had been wounded at Summit Point in September 1864. He returned to the company and was promoted to first lieutenant after Cedar Creek. He was in command of Company F when he was killed while leading the charge on the Confederate works. Newly promoted first lieutenant Samuel Tucker of Company M, who returned to the regiment after being wounded at Tom's Brook, was wounded again. Four other enlisted men, including two Californians, were wounded. Three men were captured. One of them, James Smith of Company B, disappeared and was never returned after the surrender.³¹

The Cavalry Corps camped on the battlefield that night. The wounded from both sides were gathered up and put into ambulances for the long, painful ride back to the field hospitals.

By early evening on the first, after the rout of Pickett's troops, Grant was aware that the entrenchments in front of Petersburg had been stripped to reinforce the line at Hatcher's Run. He issued orders for an all-out assault. The cannonade started about midnight and the Federal armies attacked at 4:40 A.M. on April 2. The Confederate defensive line quickly began to dissolve. The defenders were able to hold in a few places, but for the most part, the overwhelming numbers of Union soldiers forced the ragged rebels out of their fortifications. Hundreds of men, weary because of the lack of rations and barefoot and benumbed by the onslaught of thousands of fresh Yankees, surrendered.

Lee had anticipated this day for the past month. The only hope for the Confederacy seemed to be for the Army of Northern Virginia to join Johnston's army in North Carolina, strike Sherman, then turn and smash Grant. Under the circumstances it was a forlorn hope. When the lines collapsed, Lee set his plans in motion. The army would cross to the north side of the Appomattox River and make a rapid march to the west. After a short march up the Appomattox, they would recross to the south side near Amelia Courthouse, then march to Danville for the meeting with Johnston. There was one flaw in the planning: Pickett had failed to report the extent of the disaster at Five Forks. Lee was not aware until after the retreat started that Sheridan would be in on the race for the Danville Railroad.

At 10 A.M. Lee sent a telegram to Secretary of War John C. Breckinridge advising him of the plan and recommending that the Richmond area be abandoned that night.³²

On Sunday morning, April 2, a messenger brought a note from Breckinridge to St. Paul's Church and handed it to President Jefferson Davis, who was attending the services. He read the paper and turned pale. Without a word he stood and quietly left. The service continued, but everyone in the church knew something momentous had occurred. That afternoon the contents of Lee's wire became apparent as the evacuation of Petersburg and Richmond began.

Pickett was later released from the army as a supernumerary and the remnants of his command were merged with Anderson's corps. When Lee learned about the shad bake, perhaps from his own son, Fitz Lee, who freely admitted his part in the debacle, Pickett was arrested and remained with the army during the retreat. One day he passed Lee on the road. Lee, with uncharacteristic contempt in his voice, was heard to remark, "Is that man still with this army?"[33]

The Union cavalry's bugles sounded before sunrise on April 2 and the men rolled out of their bedrolls in the half-light before dawn. The smoldering fires were re-kindled, coffee was boiled, and before daylight they were back in the war. The 2nd Massachusetts, in the van of Devin's division, led the way north along Ford's Road. The column reached the Southside Railroad midway between Sutherland Station and Ford's Depot about 10 A.M. Rooney Lee's cavalry division was guarding the track. A line of skirmishers dismounted and their horses were sent to the rear as they spread out to probe the Confederate position. Devin ordered Capt. Marcus F. Miller's battery to the front. The horse artillery clattered up and the caissons were swung to the rear. The guns ran forward and fired three or four rounds at the Confederates. It was enough. The rebels turned and moved back into the screen of woods to the north.

With the Confederates out of the way, the hard work began. The rest of the men dismounted and the number fours took the horses. The crowbars came out and the sergeants spread the men out along the tracks. In a short time, a half mile of railroad was torn up, the ties burned, and the track bent into unusable scrap.[34]

After noon the division mounted up and marched out on Cox's Road, this time with Fitzhugh's brigade in the van. Once again they came upon Rooney Lee's division formed in a skirmish line. Devin ordered Fitzhugh to dismount and advance on Lee's weary rebels. Fitzhugh drove the Confederates back about five miles to Scott's Crossroads, where the troopers came upon a heavy line of infantry at about 5 P.M. The 1st Brigade dismounted and deployed to support Fitzhugh, and Miller's battery was brought up and placed in position on the road. The 2nd Massachusetts, still mounted, came up on the right near Exeter Mills to support the battery. For a while the firing was heavy and several rebel attacks were driven back. During the fighting a rebel battery got the range of the 2nd Massachusetts band, killing two horses and slightly wounding one man. The Confederates finally fell back to a line of log barricades across the road. At about eleven the 2nd Massachusetts and the rest of the Reserve Brigade moved to the front and bivouacked on the skirmish line. The remainder of the command retired about half a mile to the rear.[35]

The V Corps, now commanded by General Griffin, followed the Cavalry Corps and camped at the intersection of Namozine Road and Cox's Road.[36] Crawford's division was sent forward to support the Cavalry Corps the next morning and the II

Corps marched on Sutherland Station. During the day, an attack by Maj. Gen. Nelson A. Miles's division of the II Corps drove the Confederates from the entrenchments at Sutherland Station, turning the left of the Petersburg line.

The next day was uneventful for Devin's division. The march started at 7 A.M. and ended at 7 P.M. Custer's division, leading the advance down Namozine Road, ran into the rebels at Namozine Creek. Part of the rebel force took the road to Bevill's Bridge on the Appomattox; the rest continued toward Amelia Courthouse. Custer split his force, driving both groups of Confederates. The rebels made a stand at Sweat House Creek, forcing Custer to halt.[37] He brought up his reserves but the enemy retreated before they could attack. Devin's division came up after the fighting was over and the two divisions camped on Namozine Road at Sweat House Creek that night.[38] The V and II Corps and Crook's cavalry division bivouacked a few miles to the rear.

The retreat of Lee's army was in full swing by April 3. Anderson's corps, with the remnants of Pickett's command and Fitz Lee's cavalry, was south of the Appomattox, skirmishing with Custer all day. Confederate trains and large bodies of infantry could clearly be seen north of the river heading for Bevill's and Goode's Bridges. Longstreet's corps was in the van and Gordon's corps served as the rear guard. Farther north, Ewell led a force of about three thousand men out of Richmond and began moving west to link up with Longstreet.[39] The march was directed toward Amelia Courthouse on the Danville Railroad. Originally they intended to cross to the south side of the Appomattox at Bevill's Bridge, but the rains had flooded the approaches. The column was forced to turn north for about five miles and cross at Goode's Bridge. By early morning on the fourth, Longstreet and his men were across the Appomattox and on the road to Amelia Courthouse, about ten miles away. They would arrive in early afternoon.[40]

In spite of a number of warnings from Lee in the weeks preceding the withdrawal from Petersburg, President Davis and the Confederate government had not taken any steps to prepare for a possible retreat. A sense of disbelief seemed to grip the Confederate authorities in the waning days of March. Vital government records and the Treasury Department's gold bullion were still in Richmond when Lee sent his fateful message. Inexplicably, no preparations had been made to stockpile food and ammunition along the line of retreat. When Lee left Petersburg, one of his last requests to Secretary of War Breckinridge was that all available rations be sent to Amelia Courthouse. The dispatch to the War Department was received in the evening and no action was taken as chaos gripped the Confederate capital. In the end, the warehouses holding the rations meant for Lee's half-starved army were opened up to the populace before the first Union troops entered the city.

The first train out of Richmond on April 2 carried the last of the gold bullion left in the Confederacy. The second train carried only Davis, his cabinet, and a few records, and left hundreds of would-be refugees stranded. Only one more train went out that day, and it carried artillery ammunition to Amelia Courthouse. One can only wonder what Lee's reaction was when the train supposedly carrying rations for his starving veterans was found to be carrying artillery ammunition.[41]

On April 4, as the Army of Northern Virginia gathered at Amelia Courthouse, Lee's immediate problem was finding food. Unaware that Union cavalry was approaching, he prepared a wire to the authorities at Danville and Lynchburg to ship two hundred thousand rations to Jetersville. When it was discovered that the telegraph was broken somewhere north of Burkesville, several couriers were dispatched with copies. As a temporary measure, he ordered every available wagon out to forage for foodstuffs. Word came during the evening from General Ewell that he expected to reach Goode's Bridge at 9 P.M. Lee ordered him to move his wagons to Painesville, a route that would take him a little north and west of Amelia Courthouse. Lee intended that the main body, now at the courthouse, would move through Jetersville to Burkesville, the next day.[42]

Devin's division rose before sunrise on April 4. While the troopers cooked breakfast word came round that Richmond had fallen. The column moved out at 6 A.M. The Confederates in front had already departed. Mackenzie's command joined Devin and Custer in the march and cleared the obstructions at the best ford on Deep Creek. After it was cleared, however, they found that the ford was too deep and muddy—impassable for wagons and unsafe for mounted men. Devin, Custer, and all the wagons marched south and crossed at the shallower headwaters. Custer and Devin took the Deep Creek Road to Drummond's Mill on Beaver Pond Creek. Mackenzie marched north to Bevill's Bridge Road, then west toward Amelia Courthouse. Throughout the march the road was littered with the signs of the breakup of the Confederate army.[43]

Sergeant Corbett noted that "The boys are all in good spirits, and the Rebels are doing the tallest kind of Skeddadling. The road is full of abandoned caissons, forges and guns. We buried some of the latter and marked the spot with head Boards."[44]

One regiment from Fitzhugh's brigade was sent to reconnoiter toward Bevill's Bridge on the Appomattox. The rest of the command reached Beaver Pond Creek at about sunset. As darkness settled in, the Union advance guard suddenly came up against a Confederate line in newly dug earthworks across the road. Unbeknownst to the Union cavalry, the works were manned by two brigades of rebel infantry commanded by General Anderson and supported by Fitz Lee's cavalry. Thinking the troops approaching their lines were from Maj. Gen. Henry Heth's division, expected to arrive on the same road, the Confederates allowed the Union cavalry to get very close. The lieutenant colonel of the 4th Virginia Cavalry, sent out to find out who the approaching troops were, walked into the line of Union skirmishers. When he was captured, the questions the Union soldiers asked were clearly heard by the rebels in the entrenchments. The rebel lieutenant colonel's capture alerted the Confederates, who fired a few confused shots. No damage was done, and the Union troopers fell back.

The advance guard joined the main body and the 1st Brigade established a picket line. Several pickets were sent forward to probe the rebel position. The 2nd Massachusetts and the 2nd Brigade fell back across the creek and went into camp. Skirmishing lasted until dark.[45]

On the upper road, Mackenzie got within two miles of Amelia Courthouse before being checked by entrenched infantry. He reported that the enemy was in full force both there and out in front in the race to Burkesville. Mackenzie was ordered to remain where he was, stay alert, and not push the enemy. Sheridan decided to order the rest of his forces to make a forced march and cut the Danville Railroad.

At 10 P.M. most of the 2nd Massachusetts troopers were rolled up in their blankets asleep when the order came down to sound reveille and then "Boots and Saddles." In less than a half-hour, Merritt's cavalry was underway. Devin's division, including the 2nd Massachusetts, followed Ayres's Church Road to Dennisville. Custer may have used the road just to the west. A heavy rain started falling and continued all day.[46] The cavalrymen reached Namozine Road a little before daybreak. At Dennisville both divisions turned west on Namozine Road and headed to Fergusonville and Jetersville.[47] Sheridan, accompanied by his escort, the 1st U.S. Cavalry on temporary assignment from the Reserve Brigade, arrived before the main body. He had the escort deploy and cover the roads leading to Dennisville. In a short time they captured a man on a mule headed in the direction of Burkesville. He was arrested and searched. A copy of Lee's request that rations be forwarded to Amelia Courthouse was found in his boot. Sheridan's men were short of rations, too, so he decided to try to capture the supplies for their use. Major H. K. Young, commanding the scouts, sent out four of his best men. They each carried a copy of the dispatch. Two headed toward Lynchburg and two toward Danville. At the nearest telegraph station they were to send the dispatch just as it had been written.[48] After this subterfuge Sheridan sent word to General Ord to speed his march to Burkesville. Another courier was sent to the V Corps with orders for Griffin to move as rapidly as possible to Jetersville.

Crook's 2nd Cavalry Division was the first to arrive. The division had stayed at Dinwiddie Courthouse guarding the Cavalry Corps trains after the fight at Five Forks. On April 3 the division marched through Sutherland Station with the trains, headed west on Namozine Road, and camped at Deep Creek behind the V Corps. On the morning of the fourth Sheridan ordered Crook to strike the Danville Railroad above Burke's Station, then turn north toward Jetersville. When the division arrived at Jetersville early in the morning on April 5, Sheridan immediately ordered Crook to send Davies's brigade toward Painesville at daybreak to determine if the Confederates were trying to escape. Davies came upon a portion of Ewell's train containing 180 wagons escorted by a large cavalry force. He attacked, destroying the wagons and capturing five guns, four hundred animals, and 320 prisoners. Fitz Lee responded by sending Rosser's division out from Amelia Courthouse, almost cutting Davies's brigade off from Jetersville. Crook sent Gregg and Smith out in support and, after some hard fighting, Davies got through and rejoined the main body.

The V Corps left Deep Creek at 5 A.M. and marched west on Namozine Road in support of Crook's advance. The corps' main body reached Jetersville ahead of Merritt's cavalry and quickly set up a line of battle across the Danville Railroad. Custer's division arrived later in the morning and was placed on the right flank.

For Merritt's troopers, the afternoon of the fifth was the first opportunity since Dinwiddie Courthouse to rest for a few hours. Crook's division brought along the Cavalry Corps's wagon train and Merritt's weary men were issued five days' worth of coffee and sugar, the first they had had since leaving Five Forks.

Humphreys started II Corps moving at about 1 A.M. on April 5. About a mile and a half from Deep Creek, the road at Dennisville was filled with Merritt's cavalry column coming in on the roads from Amelia Courthouse. Humphreys stopped and waited until about eight and then started off again. During the forced halt he distributed rations, the first his men had had in two days. The head of the corps column arrived in midafternoon and the 1st and 2nd Divisions moved into the line on V Corps's left. The 3rd Division was massed on V Corps's right. When the 3rd Division moved up, Merritt's cavalry moved to the rear and set up camp. A few hours later the van of General Wright's VI Corps reported to Sheridan's headquarters and the trap was complete. The VI Corps, veterans of the Shenandoah campaign, went into camp about two miles to the east of V Corps.[49] During the night a line of rifle pits was constructed in front of the army.[50]

At about 1 P.M., Lee, unaware that Sheridan was astride the Danville Railroad, started his army marching toward Burkesville. In the lead was Longstreet's corps, screened by Rooney Lee's cavalry. They were followed by the remnants of Lt. Gen. A. P. Hill's corps, a line of wagons, and Anderson's corps with some of the survivors of Five Forks. Ewell, recently arrived with a small force from Richmond, followed Anderson. Another wagon train followed Ewell. Gordon's corps, which had been at Cedar Creek and included some of Lee's most dependable infantry, brought up the rear.

Reports reached Lee that his son Rooney was skirmishing with cavalry at Jetersville. Lee rode ahead of his column, determined to send forward an infantry force to drive off the enemy cavalry and clear the way to the rations that should now be moving toward him. As he got closer, he realized that the return fire was from infantry, not cavalry. Rooney Lee rode up and reported that the road to Burkesville, Danville, food for the weakened army, and juncture with Johnston was blocked. General Lee, realizing that the one-day delay at Amelia Courthouse had given Sheridan time to catch up, decided to make one more try. He ordered the army to turn west through the maze of country lanes and try to reach Farmville on the Southside Railroad. If rations could get through to them from Lynchburg, there was still a chance they could join up with Johnston and continue the war.

The march would be across Sheridan's front; to be successful it would have to be quick. The weary and hungry Confederates would have to march all night to reach Farmville and the railroad. Orders were issued and the van of Longstreet's corps made a short countermarch, then turned west toward Amelia Springs, a small resort town on the road to Farmville. The rest of the rapidly disintegrating, once-proud Army of Northern Virginia would follow. It was a last desperate gamble.[51]

Road Block at Appomattox

Lee's change in direction was soon reported to Sheridan. He sent a courier to Grant with word that the Confederates were retreating to the west and asking him to come to Jetersville. Another courier went to General Ord at Burkesville with orders directing him to move to Farmville to intercept the Confederate column. Crook was ordered to attack the enemy's trains and burn the bridges across the Appomattox before the Confederate main body arrived. Merritt's cavalry was ordered up in support, and he and Crook devised a plan of attack that involved leapfrogging divisions. The lead division would hold fast if it found the enemy force guarding the trains was too strong; a second division would then pass to the left, moving up the column. If it found that the next point along the road was too heavily defended, a third division would come up on the left. The divisions would continue moving up the length of the supply train in this manner until a weak point was found.[1]

Early in the morning on April 6, Crook led the column in the initial advance toward the trains, followed by Custer's and then Devin's division, which included the 2nd Massachusetts. After a short ride on a road running parallel to the enemy column, the three divisions turned and moved cross-country, probing for a weak point. The ground was broken and intersected with ravines and ditches, making the approach march very difficult. Crook's division reached the road at the center of Anderson's column. Confederate infantry and artillery quickly swung into line as the cavalry approached. Custer and Devin immediately pulled back and started moving to the left looking for an opening. Colonel Stagg remained behind with the 1st Brigade from Devin's division and a section of artillery. Custer, in front and on Devin's left, discovered a gap between the rear of Longstreet's column and the van of Anderson's corps and set up a roadblock. Anderson halted his troops and formed a battle line. The rebels hurriedly gathered fence rails and brush and made a protective breastwork, then waited for orders.

Ewell said Anderson greeted him as he approached and reported that the road ahead was blocked by at least two cavalry divisions. Anderson recommended that they either unite their forces and attempt to break through, or that they move to the right through the woods and take another road to Farmville. Ewell recommended the latter alternative and left the dispositions up to Anderson because he knew the area. However, the Union VI Corps appeared behind Ewell's column as they were talking and Anderson said he would make the attack in front if Ewell would hold off the enemy force to the rear.[2]

Ewell formed a line across the road on the high ground overlooking Sayler's Creek. The veteran VI Corps troops waded across the swollen creek and attacked but were thrown back by Ewell's rebels. Ewell ordered an immediate counterattack, but it sputtered out at the creek's edge.

At about the same time, Anderson fell on Custer's division just as Devin started moving around Custer's rear. Custer sent an urgent request stating that he was being attacked and driven back by the enemy and needed help securing prisoners. Devin moved in at a gallop on Custer's right and after several heavy volleys of carbine fire, stopped the rebel advance. Devin's division then resumed its leftward movement. It had barely arrived at its new position when orders came to return and assist Custer's troopers, who were again being pushed back by Anderson. Devin moved back to Custer's right and the two divisions counterattacked. Anderson's corps was routed and dispersed and the fugitives fled through the woods to the west.

Anderson lost twenty-six hundred men killed and captured—his corps ceased to exist as a unit. The cavalry had only 172 casualties. None were from the 2nd Massachusetts.

Meanwhile, back at Sayler's Creek, Wright ordered another attack on Ewell's position. This time the Union infantry overran the Confederate line as a heavy line of skirmishers swung around the rebel left and closed off Ewell's only escape route. Stagg's cavalry brigade, left in place when Devin's division moved out that morning, attacked Ewell's right flank as Wright's infantrymen stormed across the creek. The cavalrymen took over three hundred prisoners. Trapped by VI Corps to his front and left and by the Union cavalry to the right and rear, Ewell tried to escape down the road, followed by the remnants of Anderson's corps. Eventually he and his staff and three thousand tired and hungry Confederates surrendered to a cavalry officer from Custer's command.[3]

To the north of Wright's fight, Humphreys's II Corps attacked Gordon's corps just as his wagons were crossing over the confluence of Big and Little Sayler's Creeks. Gordon and his seven thousand men made a stand on the nearby high ground. Humphreys, with 16,500 men, sent a flanking column around Gordon's left and the Confederates were forced to retreat toward Rice's Depot.[4]

Custer's division secured the prisoners and camped on the field that night. Devin's division, with the Reserve Brigade, moved cross-country and reached the road near Rice's Depot just after dark. Pushing on, they struck the enemy's rear guard, forcing the Confederates back across the upper crossing of Sayler's Creek. Major General William Mahone's infantry division covered the crossing from the other side, supported by rebel artillery. When the Union troopers drove in the pickets, the Confederates responded with heavy musket fire and canister at short range. The cavalrymen fell back, taking some casualties and losing a number of horses. They went into camp half a mile to the rear.[5]

After the debacle at Sayler's Creek, Lee ordered the surviving Confederates to retreat to High Bridge. Mahone was ordered to hold the High Bridge crossing until

Gordon's corps crossed before joining them there. Longstreet, at Rice's Depot, was ordered to move along the south side of the Appomattox and cross at Farmville. When all the guns, wagons, and troops were across, Confederate engineers were to burn the bridges.

Three trains were ordered to bring rations from Lynchburg and meet the army at Farmville. With the bridges destroyed and rations on the way, it seemed possible that the weary Confederates would have a chance to get a day's rest.[6]

Tom Rosser's cavalry division led Gordon's and Longstreet's corps toward the bridges on the morning of April 7. About two miles from High Bridge they encountered a Union detachment from Crook's division, including about 160 cavalrymen led by Col. Francis Washburn of the 4th Massachusetts. Formerly a captain in the 2nd Massachusetts, Washburn and his troopers fought with a fierceness that belied their small numbers. Washburn was killed and the rest of his men were either killed or captured. The fight convinced Lee that a large Union force must be within supporting distance on the south side.

Lee made preparations for Longstreet's arrival. His column would leave Rice Station during the night and arrive at Farmville in the morning. Lee would issue rations to his men and then cross to the north bank of the Appomattox.

When it became apparent that Lee was heading toward the north side of the Appomattox, General Ord, at Burke's Station with the Army of the James, was directed to move toward High Bridge along the Southside Railroad. General Merritt was ordered to take his two divisions south on the most direct route to Appomattox Station. General Sheridan rode with Merritt's cavalry. Sam Corbett recalled that reveille sounded at 4 A.M. on the seventh and that the fighting along their route of march commenced at eight. "It seems the Rebels did not get enough of it yesterday but want to try us on again," he recorded in his diary. The ensuing battle lasted three hours and Corbett says the 2nd Massachusetts captured a large number of prisoners. The regiment followed the retreating rebels closely and finally made camp at ten that night about five miles from Prince Edward Courthouse.[7]

Meanwhile, the remainder of Lee's ragged band reached Farmville during the morning. The rations sent by train from Lynchburg had arrived and were distributed to Longstreet's men as they marched across the bridges to the north side of the Appomattox. The remnants of Anderson's and Gordon's corps crossed the river at High Bridge and Lee rode out to meet the column. Everything seemed to be in place for his beleaguered army to get a much-needed day's rest when the rear guard sent word that the span at High Bridge had not been destroyed. The plan to use the river as a barrier had failed because Mahone, under pressure, had simply forgotten to order the bridge set on fire.[8]

Lee immediately sent a courier to the engineers with orders to burn the bridge but it was too late. The soldiers in Humphreys's van drove the engineers off just as they started setting the fires and put out the flames. The II Corps's lead units then crossed over the river and by 9 A.M. the chase was on.[9]

When Mackenzie's cavalry division reached Prince Edward Courthouse on the seventh, Sheridan ordered him to march across Buffalo Creek and move toward

Prospect Station west of Farmville to determine if Lee's army had gotten ahead of the cavalry. Merritt's divisions followed Mackenzie and camped alongside Buffalo Creek that night. When Crook reported that the Confederates had crossed over to the north side of the Appomattox, Sheridan ordered him to join the cavalry column the next day at Prospect Station.[10]

General Grant reached Farmville in the afternoon. Concerned that Humphreys's II Corps had become isolated on the north side of the Appomattox, he ordered VI Corps to cross the river. As the troops moved through the village in the early evening, bonfires were lit alongside the road. Grant sat on the verandah of a little country hotel and the march became a sort of parade and review. The men cheered as they marched by the commanding general. After the end of the column passed, Grant went inside and wrote a formal letter to General Lee suggesting he surrender. "The results of the last week must convince you of the hopelessness of further resistance on the part of the Army of Northern Virginia in this struggle," wrote Grant. "I feel it is so, and regard it as my duty to shift from myself the responsibility of any further effusion of blood, by asking of you the surrender of that portion of the Confederate States army known as the Army of Northern Virginia." The letter went out that night under a flag of truce.[11]

Lee's reply reached Grant on the morning of April 8. "Though not entertaining the opinion you express on the hopelessness of further resistance on the part of the Army of Northern Virginia," Lee wrote, "I reciprocate your desire to avoid useless effusion of blood, and therefore, before considering your proposition, ask the terms you will offer on condition of its surrender."[12]

Grant, probably echoing the conditions outlined by President Lincoln during their last meeting, wrote: "In reply, I would say, that peace being my great desire, there is but one condition I would insist upon—namely, that men and officers shall be disqualified for taking up arms again against the Government of the United States until properly exchanged."[13]

Earlier that morning, when Grant and Lee were exchanging notes, one of Sheridan's scouts reported that four trains carrying rations for Lee's army were nearing Appomattox Station. Merritt and Crook were ordered to quickly take the cavalry to Prospect Station, then to Walker's Church, and on to Appomattox Station. During the march Devin sent a staff officer with a regiment from the 1st Brigade to Cut Bank Ford to determine if the enemy was trying to recross the river. The officer reported that the Confederates were continuing to march along the north side of the Appomattox.[14]

With Custer's division in the lead, they reached Appomattox Station without meeting any opposition and quickly secured the four supply trains from Lynchburg. Railroad men from the cavalry manned the locomotives and ran the trains back up the track toward Farmville, where they would be out of the rebels' reach. Word came that the enemy was moving a large wagon train toward the railroad from the direction of Appomattox Courthouse. Custer immediately ordered his whole division to attack.[15]

The rebel wagon train was heavily guarded and all of Custer's attacks were repulsed. Devin's division arrived at about 3 P.M.,[16] dismounted, and moved into the line on Custer's right. When the troopers were in position, the 1st and 2nd Brigades, with the 2nd Massachusetts and the Reserve Brigade in support, advanced on the wagon train. They captured the train and drove the Confederates back through Appomattox Courthouse until they encountered a strong line of Confederate infantry that counterattacked and drove the Federals back. The fighting continued until after dark. When the fighting finally died down, the 2nd Massachusetts came up and established a picket line about a half-mile south of the village.[17]

That night Sam Corbett wrote: "The Rebels seem to be demoralized and do not fight with their usual vigor and well they may be for we have kept them going for the last two weeks."[18]

Sheridan's cavalry captured twenty-five artillery pieces, a hospital train, and four trains loaded with supplies. During the night, Sheridan sent couriers to Grant, Generals Ord and John Gibbon of the Army of the James, and General Griffin commanding V Corps, telling them that if they came up quickly, Lee would be trapped. Sensing victory, the Union infantry accomplished some extraordinary feats of marching on the eighth. The V Corps camped about two miles west of the courthouse at 2 A.M. after an eighteen-hour march covering twenty-nine miles. Ord's troops left Farmville at 5 A.M. on the morning of the eighth and marched west on the Lynchburg road. The march was halted at midnight and the troops were allowed to catch three hours' sleep. After starting again at 3 A.M. on the ninth, the column was nearing Appomattox Station by sunrise. Meanwhile, General Humphreys's II Corps, which left Farmville early that same morning, was about three miles east of Appomattox Courthouse to the rear of Lee's army.

Grant's message outlining the terms of surrender reached General Lee at the end of the day. Lee responded by first disavowing the need to surrender, then proposed a meeting at 10 A.M. on the Richmond road to discuss the restoration of peace. The letter was carried to Humphreys's lines under a flag of truce. Unbeknownst to Lee, Grant had crossed over to Sheridan's line of march on the south side of Appomattox Courthouse and did not receive the letter.[19]

The Reserve Brigade manned the picket line just outside the small village of Appomattox Courthouse. Just before daybreak on the ninth the rest of Devin's 1st Division moved up to support it. The surviving Californians and the rest of the 2nd Massachusetts were in the front line. As the sun rose, they could see a heavy line of Confederate infantry, the remnants of Gordon's corps, moving out of the village.

Devin's cavalrymen were ordered to fall back slowly and give the large Union infantry column time to shake out and form into a battle line. The heavy skirmish fire from their repeating carbines slowed the advancing Confederates as the cavalrymen fell back, trading ground for time. Custer brought his division up and extended the skirmish line on the left. When the cavalrymen reached the waiting Union infantry, the troopers fell back through the line and moved to the right flank.[20]

The Confederates became jubilant as they watched the cavalry troopers fall back, certain that the road west was finally open. However, as the firing died down they were greeted by the sight of a solid blue line of V Corps infantry slowly emerging from the clearing smoke to their front. Ord's three divisions were deployed in the woods to V Corps's right, and the Union cavalry was reforming on the left. With fire coming from three sides, the dismayed Confederates began to fall back.

"I have fought my troops to a frazzle," General Gordon wrote in a dispatch to Lee, "and I fear I can do nothing unless I am heavily supported by Longstreet."[21]

Sergeant Sam Corbett, recalling the events of that morning, wrote: "We had nothing to oppose Lee but cavalry and nobly did they do their work. We fought them dismounted. They tried hard to break our lines and poured in the shot and shell with their musketry until the air seemed full of it. At half past eight the V Corps came up, the fighting lasted but one hour longer when at 9:30 AM Lee sent in a Flag of Truce."[22]

Unfortunately for Gordon, Longstreet was being pressed by Humphreys's II Corps and was in no position to help. Lee finally accepted the inevitability of defeat. Assuming Grant had received his note regarding a meeting at 10 A.M. on the Richmond road, he passed the time sitting with Longstreet and his staff. Shortly before ten, Lee—accompanied by Col. Charles Marshall, Lt. Col. Walter Taylor, and Sergeant Tucker, his orderly—rode to the rear of Longstreet's line on the Richmond Stage Road. Sergeant Tucker rode out between the lines with a flag of truce. Colonel Marshall rode forward to join Tucker when a line of Union skirmishers began to approach and was given a note from Grant by a member of Humphreys's staff.[23]

The note advised Lee that Grant had no authority to discuss peace terms and rejected Lee's request for a 10 A.M. meeting. Grant concluded with an appeal to Lee to bring an end to the bloodshed and destruction by surrendering.[24]

When Lee read Grant's note he at last understood there would be no negotiations. The conditions for surrender were as originally stated. Lee turned to Marshall and asked him to write down his reply. The note Marshall prepared simply acknowledged receipt of Grant's message and asked for a meeting "in accordance with the offer contained in your letter of yesterday for that purpose."[25]

Marshall gave the note to Humphreys's staff officer and asked that fighting be suspended until it reached Grant. Lee then sent a messenger to Gordon, facing the Union troops at Appomattox Station, to seek a truce.[26]

When Gordon received Lee's message he directed Col. Green Peyton, a member of his staff, to find a white flag and communicate with General Ord, whom he assumed commanded the infantry in his front. Instead of Ord, however, Peyton encountered General Custer and guided him back to Gordon. Custer reported "with faultless grace and courtesy, saluted me with his saber and said, 'I am General Custer, and bear a message to you from General Sheridan. The General desires me to present to you his compliments, and to demand the immediate and unconditional surrender of all the troops under your command.'"

All of this was bravado on Custer's part. When Custer met Peyton he sent a message to Sheridan notifying him that a flag of truce had come through. Sheridan was aware of Grant's negotiations. Without waiting for instructions from Sheridan, Custer followed Peyton back to Gordon, and issued his inane demand. It was a flagrant attempt at headline grabbing and Gordon, recognizing the absurdity of the situation, told Custer he would not surrender his command to him. Custer then boldly announced, "He directs me to say to you, general, if there is any hesitation about your surrender, that he has you surrounded and can annihilate your command in an hour."

Gordon then told the blustering Custer about the truce arranged between Grant and Lee and said that if General Sheridan decided to continue, the bloodshed would be his responsibility. That done, Gordon sent Custer off with another staff officer to try out his bravado on General Longstreet.[27]

The boy general took the same tack with Lee's senior corps commander, announcing, "In the name of General Sheridan I demand the unconditional surrender of this army."

Longstreet reminded Custer that "I was not the commander of the army," and that Custer was within his lines without authority and addressing a superior officer—an act of "disrespect to General Grant as well as myself." Custer, somewhat chastened, replied that it would be a pity to shed more blood. Longstreet then suggested that the truce be respected, and said, "As you are now more reasonable, I will say that General Lee has gone to meet General Grant, and it is for them to determine the future of the armies."[28] With that, he sent the chastised cavalryman back to the Union lines.

About the time Custer left Gordon, Sheridan and a large escort appeared in front of the Confederate lines under a flag of truce. Gordon rode out to meet him and there was some discussion about immediate surrender. Gordon showed Sheridan the note from General Lee. Both generals agreed to pull their lines back to avoid any accidents and staff officers went out to notify the commanders of the cease-fire. The firing quickly died down as the staff officers did their work, but suddenly a blast of musketry came from the left flank. Sheridan stood up and angrily demanded to know the meaning of the firing. Gordon explained that he had forgotten to send word to a brigade there. Sheridan lent him a member of his staff, Capt. Vanderbilt Allen, who, escorted by a ragged veteran of the Stonewall Brigade, carried a cease-fire order to the errant brigade. It is one of the ironies of history that a Union cavalry officer from Sheridan's staff delivered the last cease-fire order to the once proud Army of Northern Virginia. In a short time silence fell over the final battlefield.[29]

The truce was to last until 1 P.M. As the time approached, the two armies grew more uneasy. The men on the Union side had stacked arms and were lolling on the ground, some asleep and others waiting. A little after one, word circulated that the men should be ready to receive or launch an attack. There was a sense of dread among the bluecoats, and only a few troopers moved toward the stacked guns. Then, quietly and without fanfare, three men, one carrying a white flag, appeared in front of the Confederate lines on the other side of the little village.

Lee, in his best uniform, rode to the home of Wilmer McLean, the largest in the village, to await Grant's arrival. [30] Grant arrived on the scene a short time later—muddy, unshaven, and wearing a threadbare private's uniform—and rode up to Sheridan.

"How are you Sheridan?" Grant asked.

"First-rate, thank you: how are you?" cried Sheridan, with a voice and look that seemed to indicate he was having things all his own way.

"Is Lee over there?" asked Grant, pointing up the road. He had heard a rumor that Lee was near.

"Yes he is in that brick house, waiting to surrender to you," Sheridan answered.

"Well, then we'll go over," said Grant. [31]

What happened in the McLean parlor is well known.

The men of the 2nd Massachusetts watched as the generals rode back to Appomattox Courthouse. There was no cheering. They knew the war was over but, strangely, there was no overt celebration, no cheering or display. Perhaps each of the soldiers, blue and gray, realized that they were survivors. Their lives would go on; the mantle of impending death was lifted. The remembrance of the countless lost comrades must have weighed heavily on the men on both sides in that little village. In the afternoon, a few adventurous rebels hiked up the hill from their encampment to trade tobacco for food and were welcomed by their former enemies. During the evening, when the terms of the surrender were circulated around the campfires, the reaction among the Union soldiers was mixed. "We high privates don't like the idea of giving the rebels any conditions whatever," Sam Corbett wrote, "but we are willing to trust Gen. Grant and will try to think it is all right." [32]

The next morning, April 10, with the cavalry leading the way, the Army of the Potomac marched to Burkesville. Only Joshua Chamberlain, with his old brigade, remained behind to receive the surrender. As the Confederates marched up the hill to the village square to lay down their flags and arms, General Chamberlain, to his everlasting credit, ordered his brigade to present arms, the traditional military salute. It was a solemn moment and the symbolism of Chamberlain's order was not lost on the passing Confederates.

The 2nd Massachusetts stopped at Burkesville one night then moved slowly toward Petersburg, arriving there on April 20. On April 24, the regiment broke camp and started south to reinforce Sherman in North Carolina. When it reached the Dan River on the twenty-ninth, news arrived that Johnston had surrendered and the war was truly over. The regiment returned to Petersburg and on May 10 started the trek back to Washington, where the troopers participated in the Grand Review on May 23. After the review they moved to Cloud's Mill, Maryland, for a month, where they and their horses finally got some much needed rest. On June 26 they returned to Fairfax, Virginia, and remained there until they were mustered out on July 21.

According to regulations they were to be paid expenses to their home state. The Californians expected to receive enough to pay for their passage back to California, but the mustering-out officer decided that since they were part of a Massachusetts regiment, their home state was Massachusetts. By now they were used to the vagaries of the government, so they went without protest by train to Readville, where they were discharged.

Some men stayed on the East Coast but most returned to California. There was no victory parade in San Francisco. Few people even remembered that five hundred Californians had fought in the main theater of the war or that seventy of the volunteers lost their lives there. The tattered battle flags were returned and stored in the state capitol. A few years later someone put together a montage of individual photographs of sixty-one of the old veterans with the battle flag in the center. The montage is filed in the state library under "California Pioneers." The California Hundred and Battalion are not mentioned in the card files.

Appendix

Casualties

(Massachusetts recruits in italics)
(* indicates two events)

Skirmish at South Anna Bridge, Virginia, July 5, 1863

Killed/Mortally Wounded

Burdick, Joseph B., Co. A—First recorded battle death in the regiment, killed during the attack on the redoubt at the bridge.

Wounded

Ellet, Richard S., Co. A—Transferred to Mississippi Marine Brigade as a second lieutenant after recovering from his wound.

King and Queen Courthouse, July 5, 1863

Killed/Mortally Wounded

Nixon, John, Co. A—Killed by bushwhackers while at a house in King and Queen Courthouse.

Skirmish at Ashby's Gap, Virginia, July 12, 1863

Killed/Mortally Wounded

Irving, Harry P., Co. E—Shot off his horse then shot again by a rebel as he was trying to cock his pistol.
Barnes, Walter, Co. E—Native of Bloomington, Maryland.

Wounded

Brickley, Richard T.,* Co. E—Discharged June 15, 1864, because of wounds.
DeForrest, Cpl. William P., Co. E—Shot in the head and discharged September 4, 1864, because of wounds.
Hawkins, James M., bugler, Co. L—Returned to the regiment.
Joy, Maurice, Co. E—Returned to the regiment.
Moore, William H.,* Co. E—Returned to the regiment. Wounded again at Dinwiddie Courthouse.
Perry, Albert, Brigade Butcher, Co. E—Returned to the regiment.
Shaw, Sgt. Sylvanus, Co. E—Discharged June 15, 1864, because of wounds.
Smith, John, Co. E—Wounded in the head; returned to the regiment.

Captured/Died in Prison

Smith, Roswell, Co. L—Died December 14 in Richmond; he was twenty-one years old.

Vennum, Hiram, Co. E—Died December 25 in Richmond.

Captured/Escaped

Norcross, 2nd Lt. John C., Co. E—Escaped from prison in March 1865.

Captured/Exchanged

Van Vleet, DeWitt C., Co. M—Paroled at Annapolis, Maryland. Deserted from parole camp September 17, 1864.

Garrity, Thomas, Co. E—Returned to the regiment October 19, 1864.

Snicker's Gap, Virginia, July 13, 1863

Captured/Exchanged

Greenough, Henry A., Co. G—Paroled August 2, 1863, and sent to the Annapolis, Maryland, parole camp on September 24. No further record.

Skirmish at Warrenton, Virginia, July 20, 1863

Wounded

Hill, John W., Co. M—Discharged because of wounds.

Captured/Exchanged

Harvey, Charles C., Co. H—Paroled August 2, 1863; no further record.

The Ice Cream Raid, Aldie, Virginia, July 31, 1863

Killed/Mortally Wounded

Renard, Peter, Co. L—A member of Manning's detachment that attacked the captured wagons.

Little, Hazen, Co. L—Part of Manning's detachment.

Wounded

Hull, Chauncey, Co. L—Part of Manning's detachment.

Howard, Amos, Co. L—Part of Manning's detachment; returned to the regiment.

Bard, James, Co. L—Part of Manning's detachment; returned to the regiment.

Captured/Recaptured

Seagrave, Edward P.,* Co. L—A miner originally from Massachusetts, he was taken prisoner by Mosby's group after attacking with Manning and then recaptured by Colonel Lowell and returned to the regiment.

Fairfax Courthouse, Virginia, August 1, 1863

Captured

Williams, John, Co. M—According to California records he was taken prisoner while on picket duty. Massachusetts records say he deserted on December 16, 1864, at Winchester.

The Horse Raid, Fairfax/Cole's Tavern, Virginia, August 24, 1863

Killed/Mortally Wounded

McCarty, John, Co. A—One of the first men mustered into the California Hundred; was killed outright.

Varnum, Commissary Sgt. Joseph B., Co. M—Was in the act of holding a rebel by the throat and beating him over the head with an empty pistol when he was killed.

Vierick, George W., Co. A—Died of wounds September 1, 1863.

Wounded

McKenny, John W., Co. M—Returned to the regiment. Also known as McKinney.

Captured/Died in Prison

Hanson, Peter, Co. F—Was exchanged but died from the effects of his imprisonment while on the steamer *Baltic* off Hilton Head Island, South Carolina.

Captured/Exchanged

Dempsey, Cyrus, Co. A—Paroled at Annapolis, Maryland, in November 1864.

Hayford, James B., Co. M—Paroled, date unknown.

Hurley, John, Co. G—Paroled November 19, 1864.

Jenkins, Sgt. Charles M., Co. E—Paroled at Annapolis, Maryland, November 26, 1864.

Manker, William, blacksmith, Co. E—Paroled at Annapolis, Maryland, November 26, 1864.

Morris, William, Co. E—From Minersville, California; he was sent to Belle Isle Prison and paroled in April 1864.

Vienna, Virginia, October 8, 1863

Killed/Mortally Wounded

Washburn, Luman, Co. L—A thirty-five-year-old miner from California, he was wounded by guerrillas while on picket duty. Died of wounds November 14, 1864.

Fairfax Courthouse, Virginia, October 19, 1863

Captured/Died in Prison

Blanchard, Oscar, Co. E—Born in Prussia, he came to California via New Jersey; died at Andersonville Prison March 24, 1864.

Vienna, Virginia, November 23, 1864

Killed Accidentally

Wilson, Frederick, Co. L—A laborer from Canada, he enlisted in San Francisco.

Lewinsville, Virginia, December 9, 1863

Killed/Mortally Wounded

Jones, Cyrus B., Co. L—Mortally wounded in an attack by Mosby's guerrillas on his picket post; died in the Vienna hospital February 5, 1864.

Vienna, Virginia, December 18, 1863

Killed Accidentally

Bishop, 1st Sgt. William, Co. H—Details of his death are not recorded.

Wounded

Brickley, Richard T.,* Co. E—Discharged for disability after being wounded twice.

Hunter's Mill, Virginia, December 23, 1863

Wounded

Burnap, Oscar, Co. E—From American Valley in Plumas County, California. He was taken prisoner by Mosby's guerrillas during an attack on his picket post, then shot and dumped by his captors as they fled. He was subsequently discharged because of wounds.

Cooper, Seth H., Co. M—Wounded in the head during an attack on his picket post by Mosby's guerrillas. He was transferred to the Veteran Reserve Corps.

Upperville, Virginia, December 29, 1863

Wounded

McFarland, Thomas, Co. L—Wounded in hand-to-hand combat with a guerrilla that he sabered. He deserted from the hospital on May 23, 1864.

Captured/Exchanged

Hood, Cpl. John, Co. E—Captured by Mosby's guerrillas but paroled on December 31, 1864.

Difficult Creek, Virginia, January 3, 1864

Killed/Mortally Wounded

Barnes, George, Co. M—A carpenter from Marysville, California, he was shot by guerrillas while on picket duty. Died of wounds January 15, 1864.

Dranesville/Anker's Blacksmith Shop, Virginia, February 22, 1864

Killed/Mortally Wounded

Dexter, Henry, Co. M—A miner in California, he was born in Barton, Vermont.

Downey, John, Co. B—A thirty-eighty-year-old from Boston.

Ferrier, George, Co. M—A thirty-nine-year-old tanner, he could have honorably stayed in San Francisco and left the fighting to younger men.

Grover, Byron H., Co. E—He was twenty at the time of his death.

Hayden, John E. B., Co. B—Died of wounds February 29, 1865.

McCammen, J. S., Co. M—A farmer.

Miles, James, Co. B—Enlisted on December 22, 1862; one of the first members of Company B.

Powers, Richard, Co. B—A farmer.

Reed, Capt. J. Sewall, Co. A—Killed while commanding the 3rd Battalion. One of Mosby's officers, Capt. William Chapman, shot Reed in the back after he shot a German adventurer fighting with Mosby.

Spooner, Stephen, Co. B—Served with the 5th Massachusetts Infantry.

Waters, Abraham, Co. K—A blacksmith from Boston.

Wounded

Locke, Cpl. John M., Co. M—He returned to the regiment and was later promoted to sergeant.

Seccin, Cpl. Joseph, Co. M—Born in Hungary; returned to the regiment.

Wyatt, Cpl. Henry, Co. E—Returned to the regiment; later promoted to sergeant.

Captured/Escaped

Goodrich, Henry, Co. M

Captured/Died in Prison

Barnes, Newman, Co. M—Died at Andersonville Prison June 7, 1864.

Bell, William, Co. M—A trunk maker from Ireland, he died of scurvy at Andersonville Prison September 7, 1864.

Burke, Joseph, Co. M—Died of anasarca at Andersonville Prison May 21, 1864. He was twenty-seven at the time of his death.

Coffin, Alvin R., Co. M—A shoemaker from Bridgewater, Massachusetts; died at Andersonville Prison August 11, 1864.

Dexter, Jairus, Co. M—Died at Andersonville Prison July 7, 1864.

Fisher, Jackson, Co. E—Died of pneumonia at Andersonville Prison April 9, 1864.

Fuller, Andrew W., Co. G—Died at Andersonville Prison August 29, 1864.

Goodman, Samuel, Co. B—Died at Andersonville Prison August 17, 1864.

Gozzen, Herman, Co. M—A butcher from Hamburg, Germany, he died in Savannah, Georgia, in September 1864.

Hacket, Patrick, Co. M—Died of scurvy at Andersonville Prison September 9, 1864.

Hallstead, Jacob, Co. M—A carpenter from San Francisco, he died of pneumonia at Andersonville Prison March 25, 1864.

Hamblin, Edward, Co. M—Died at Andersonville Prison June 8, 1864.

Hammond, Albert O., Co. M—Died in Savannah September 16, 1864.

Harty, John G., Co. M—Born in Gusboro, Nova Scotia, he died at Andersonville Prison April 27, 1864.

Henderson, William, Co. M—Died in Millen, Georgia, October 29, 1864.

Hunt, Jesse E., Co. I—From Worcester, Massachusetts; died in Savannah, Georgia, December 18, 1864.

Hyde, Arthur L., Co. B—Died at Andersonville Prison August 9, 1864.

Jackson, William R., Co. B—A seaman from Brooklyn, New York, he died at Andersonville Prison September 10, 1864.

Jones, John, Co. M—Died of dysentery at Andersonville Prison April 18, 1864.

Kice, Thomas, Co. B—Died at Andersonville Prison May 3, 1864.

Knapp, David, Co. M—Died of diarrhea at Andersonville Prison April 14, 1864.

McDonald, Philip, Co. B—Died at Andersonville Prison April 8, 1864.

Millican, William, Co. E—A miner, he died at Andersonville Prison August 29, 1864.

Monroe, James, Co. M—Died of diarrhea at Andersonville Prison August 20, 1864.

Paris, Frank, Co. E—Originally from Quebec, he died of scurvy at Andersonville Prison August 11, 1864.

Price, Edward, Co. M—Died of diarrhea at Andersonville Prison June 15, 1864.

Rich, Charles, Co. B—Died at Andersonville Prison May 22, 1864.

Sanborn, George, Co. B—Died at Andersonville Prison September 7, 1864.

Simonsen, Anthony, Co. M—Died of scurvy at Andersonville Prison August 26, 1864.

Smith, Michael, Co. B—Died at Andersonville Prison September 1, 1864.

Spaulding, John C., Co. E—Died of diarrhea at Andersonville Prison June 19, 1864

Stevens, Thomas, Co. M—Died of typhus at Andersonville Prison July 31, 1864.

Stevenson, Cushman S., Co. B—Died in Savannah, Georgia, October 7, 1864.

Taylor, Archibald, Co. M—Died in Savannah, Georgia, in September 1864.

Weymouth, Uriah, Co. M—Died at Andersonville Prison August 15, 1864.

Captured/Deserted

Kemp, Joseph, Co. B—A twenty-one-year-old blacksmith from Roxbury, Massachusetts, he enlisted in the 10th Tennessee Infantry to escape the horrors of Andersonville Prison. Union forces captured him at Egypt Station, Mississippi, December 28, 1864. He was subsequently sent to Alton Prison in Illinois, where he enlisted in the 5th U.S. Volunteers. No further record.

Captured/Exchanged

Cain, James, Co. E—Exchanged April 30, 1865, at Annapolis, Maryland.

Crawford, Josiah, Co. E—Exchanged April 18, 1865.

Dennison, David, Co. B—Exchanged December 11, 1864, and sent home to Worcester, Massacusetts.

Folger, David J., Co. M—Released December 19, 1864, and returned to the regiment.

Hewes, Francis A., Co. M—Exchanged March 27, 1865.

Holden, Charles A., Co. M—A weaver from Lowell, his parole date is unknown. He subsequently transferred to the Veteran Reserve Corps and was mustered out on July 26, 1864.

Kelly, Thomas, Co. B—Paroled at Annapolis, Maryland, April 22, 1865.

Lawrence, Cpl. William, Co. M—Paroled February 27, 1864.

Lee, George, Co. M—Released at Jacksonville, Florida, April 25, 1865.

Manning, Capt. George, Co. M—Commanded the company during the fight; paroled at Annapolis, Maryland.

Manning, 1st Lt. William, Co. L—Wounded in the fight, he was released after Lee's surrender.

McGuire, John D., Co. B—Paroled at Annapolis, Maryland, December 16, 1864.

Mossman, Sgt. Judson, Co. E—Paroled at Annapolis, Maryland, December 26, 1864.

Osts, John, Co. E—Parole date unknown.

Pinney, Sgt. Ephraim, Co. B—Released April 29, 1865.

Turner, 1st Sgt. Levi, Co. E—Promoted to first sergeant two days before his capture; paroled October 18, 1864, and returned to the regiment.

Whitten, John, Co. B—Paroled December 25, 1864.

Wilcox, George, Co. E—Released April 22, 1865.

Wooster, Arthur J., Co. E—From Sonoma, California; paroled in November 1864 but died in Seymour, Connecticut, May 17, 1865, as a result of a disease he contracted while in prison.

Leesburg, Virginia, April 18, 1864

Killed/Mortally wounded

Goodwin, Cpl. Charles, Co. H—Died in a nearby farmhouse on April 20.

Skirmish at Rectortown, April 30, 1864

Killed/Mortally wounded

Clark, Sgt. Charles A., Co. L—Born in Mississippi, he worked as a miner in California before joining the California Battalion.

Wounded

Boggs, Daniel W., Co. L—Severely wounded but returned to the regiment.

Ferrill, Davis C., Co. L—Discharged in Washington, D.C., June 6, 1865, because of wounds.

DeMerritt, Capt. David E., Co. F—Suffered a broken leg in summer of 1863, recovered, and then had a nervous breakdown and was sent to the insane asylum in Washington, D.C. He returned to the regiment but broke down again. He was appointed acting inspector general of the brigade upon his return in December. He accidentally shot himself in the foot during this raid. He was given a disability discharge September 2, 1864.

Captured/Died in Prison

Halligan, John T., Co. F—A farmer from California, he died at Danville Prison November 25, 1864.

Little River Turnpike, Virginia, July 3, 1864

Wounded

Howard, Amos,* Co. L—A farmer born in Illinois, he was wounded while on picket duty. He later returned to the regiment.

Mouth of the Monocacy River, Maryland, July 5, 1864

Captured/Exchanged

Harbeck, Henry, Co. M—Captured while on picket duty; released April 28, 1865.

Cook, George, Co. B—Massachusetts records indicate he was taken at Rockville on this date; it seems more likely he was captured in this incident since there is no record of Confederates in Rockville on July 5.

Reports indicate two others were taken. The following men may have been taken on this date:

Duley, George, Co. B

McDonald, Michael, Co. B

Driscoll, Timothy, Co. B

Gruber, William, Co. M—Gruber would not be included in this list except for the fact that Harbeck, a fellow Co. M trooper, was captured. The usual practice was to assign men from the same company to picket duty. That appears not to have been the case in this instance.

McIntyre, Campbell, Co. B

Cobby, Thomas W., Co. E—Cobby died in parole camp December 28, 1865. He is the only Co. E man included in this list. I believe it is extremely unlikely he was one of the others taken on July 6.

Hendle, George, Co. B

Griffin, Stephen, Co. B

Fight at Mount Zion Church, Virginia, July 6, 1864

Killed/Mortally Wounded

Bumgardner, Cpl. William, Co. A—Died in a nearby farmhouse on July 22.

Dumaresq, William F., Co. K—A sailor from Jersey Island, England, he was killed just one month after joining the regiment.

Fox, Owen, Co. H—From Braintree; Chaplain Humphreys carried him to a local farmhouse where he later died.

Hanscom, Cpl. Samuel, Co. A—Joined the California Hundred December 10, 1862.

Johnson, John, Co. I—A native of Canajoharie, New York, he was killed just one month after being mustered in.

McDonald, Cpl. James, Co. F—He is buried in the old graveyard at Mount Zion Church.

Oeldrather, Charles, Co. G—A tin man from Boston.

Riordin, Patrick, Co. I—A nineteen-year-old from Marlboro.

Rollins, Charles, Co. I—A thirty-eight-year-old Canadian.

Stone, Capt. Goodrich A., Co. L—Died of wounds July 18, 1864.

Tobin, Cornelius, Co. I—A nineteen-year-old shoemaker from Marlboro, Massachusetts.

Captured/Died in Prison

Atmore, Charles, Co. A—A sailor from Boston, he died at Andersonville Prison September 26, 1864.

Bradford, Joseph L., Co. F—Wounded during the fight, he died at Andersonville Prison August 22, 1864.

Nottage, Cpl. John S., Co. F—From Ashland, he died at Andersonville Prison September 30, 1864.

Doyle, Daniel, Co. H—From Marlboro, he died at Danville Prison.

Captured/Missing

Wheeler, William H., Co. H—A nineteen-year-old farmer from Hopkinton, he disappeared while being transferred from Andersonville Prison to Millen, Georgia.

Lyons, John, Co. I—No further record after his capture.

Wounded

Beeth, Benjamin, Co. F—Later discharged because of his wounds.

Clark, Cpl. John, Co. L—Severely wounded but returned to the regiment.

Curtis, Charles, Co. F—Severely wounded.

Felch, John,* Co. L—Returned to the regiment; he was wounded again at Opequon Creek in September.

Fogg, Cpl. Nathan, Co. L—Returned to the regiment.

Logsdon, James, Co. F—Severely wounded.

Peebles, Sgt. James, Co. L—A carpenter from Kentucky, he was discharged because of his wounds.

Thomas, William, Co. G—From Brooklyn, New York.

Captured/Escaped

Rand, James, Co. K—Escaped at Charleston, South Carolina, in March 1865 as he was being transferred from Andersonville Prison.

Captured/Exchanged

Amory, 2nd Lt. Charles, Co. G

Brandon, Edward, Co. I—Released April 25, 1865.

Coleman, John, Co. K—Released May 25, 1865.

Donahue, Patrick, Co. H—Paroled February 22, 1865.

Dougherty, Daniel, Co. H—Paroled March 10, 1865.

Forbes, Maj. William, Co. B—Forced to surrender when his horse fell on him.

Kelley, John, Co. K—From Jersey City, New Jersey; paroled in February 1865 at Goldsboro, South Carolina.

Loane, Abraham, Co. A—Released April 28, 1865.

Loring, John E., Co. A—Released April 28, 1865.

Matthews, Patrick, Co. K—Sent to Vicksburg from Andersonville Prison and paroled April 22, 1865.

McGowan, John, Co. H—Paroled December 1, 1864.

Parker, George, F. Co. F—Paroled at Annapolis, Maryland, December 3, 1864.

Perkins, Freeman, Co. A—Paroled May 5, 1865.

Pratt, John H., Co. L—Paroled December 15, 1864.

Shine, Cornelius, Co. H—A currier by trade, he was paroled at Annapolis, Maryland, December 1, 1865.

Sullivan, Patrick, Co. F—A baker from Boston, he was paroled February 2, 1865.

Thaxter, Benjamin, Co. D—Paroled at Annapolis, Maryland, in December 1864, he died January 15, 1865, of diseases contracted during his imprisonment.

Walker, Edward P., Co. G—A native of Chelsea, Massachusetts.

Humphreys, Chaplain William—Was part of the group put in confinement along the waterfront at Charleston, South Carolina, in an effort to stop the bombardment of the city. He was subsequently released and rejoined the regiment.

Rockville, Maryland, July 13, 1864

Killed/Mortally Wounded

Allen, Henry E., Co. A—Died of wounds August 16 in Washington, D.C., as a result of neglect by the surgeons. He served as Colonel Lowell's orderly.

Backus, Charles, Co. K—A farmer from Nantucket Island, Massachusetts, he was twenty-two at the time of his death.

Carr, George, Co. L—A miner from San Francisco; died of wounds October 21.

Gillespie, John, Co. D—Died of wounds July 20 in Washington, D.C.

Wounded

Barenson, Abram F.,* Co. M—Returned to the regiment; was accidentally wounded at Winchester September 22.

Bayley, Cpl. John, Co. H—Discharged because of wounds.

Belmond, Charles P., Co. C—Transferred to Veteran Reserve Corps.

Cannon, Patrick, Co. C—Discharged because of wounds.

Colas, Louis, Co. G—Returned to the regiment.

Curry, William, Co. H—Returned to the regiment.

Gay, John, Co. I—Returned to the regiment.

Hall, James Co. F—Returned to the regiment.

Hart, Charles D., Co. D—Transferred to Veteran Reserve Corps.

Hill, James, Co. F—Severely wounded.

Hodson, Henry, Co. H—From Nova Scotia; died of disease while in the hospital at Alexandria, Virginia.

Johnson, George, Co. D—Discharged for disability because of his wounds.

Kelly, Edward, Co. I—Transferred to Veteran Reserve Corps.

Kercheval, Benjamin B., Co. A—Returned to the regiment.

Lowder, Francis, Co. H—Discharged for disability because of wounds.

Mashar, Phillip, Co. I—Hospitalized in Alexandria, Virginia; deserted while on a thirty-day furlough in September.

McNiff, John, Co. C—Returned to the regiment.

Minot, William H., Co. C—Discharged for disability July 13, 1865.

Nicholson, George W., Co. K—Mustered out while "absent wounded."

Plummer, George, Co. A—Returned to the regiment; commissioned a second lieutenant March 23, 1865.

Ray, William, Co. F—Discharged because of wounds.

Scott, John W., Co. A—Deserted October 22 while on furlough from the hospital.

Smith, Leonard, Co. E—Severely wounded.

Spofford, Joseph, Co. H—Was sent to Auger Hospital in Washington and later discharged because of wounds.

Stone, Joseph C., Co. K—Returned to the regiment.

Sturtevant, Rufus M., Co. K—Returned to the regiment.

Tupper, Alexander G., Co. H—Discharged May 5, 1865, because of wounds.

Wallace, Joseph, Co. C—Discharged June 14, 1865, because of wounds.

Captured/Died in Prison

Case, Daniel, Co. H—Died in Salisbury, North Carolina, December 21.

Glascott, John, Co. C—Died at Danville Prison December 13.

Marsh, William, Co. F—Died at Danville Prison February 19, 1865.

Pack, George J., Co. C—Died at Danville Prison February 2, 1865.

Captured/Escaped

Cochran, Warren, Co. F—Escaped from Andersonville Prison and walked to Tennessee.

Manchester, Luman A., Co. E—Escaped at Staunton with Samuel Rhodes and returned to the regiment August 20.

Rhodes, Samuel H., Co. E—Escaped at Staunton with Luman Manchester and returned to the regiment August 20.

Captured/Exchanged

Bampton, Robert Jr., Co. I—Released February 21, 1865.

Carr, Michael, Co. A—Paroled February 22, 1865; deserted May 28, 1865, while on furlough.

Christian, George E., Co. D—Paroled at Annapolis, Maryland, February 22, 1865.

Collins, Joseph, Co. A—Paroled February 22, 1865; deserted while on furlough.

Connealy, John, Co. C—Paroled October 18.

Cossell, Jackson, Co. F—Paroled at Annapolis, Maryland, February 22, 1865.

Downes, Frank T., Co. H—Paroled at Annapolis, Maryland, February 22, 1865.

Fisher, Milo B., Co. I—Paroled at Annapolis, Maryland, March 13, 1865.

Goulding, George W., Co. A—Paroled February 22, 1865; returned to regiment May 2, 1865.

Green, William, Co. H—Paroled at Annapolis, Maryland, February 19, 1865.

Haglan, Carl, Co. C—A shoemaker from Sweden; paroled at Annapolis, Maryland, February 22, 1865.

Howlett, James, Co. A—Paroled at Annapolis, Maryland, February 22, 1865.

Hughes, John, Co. I—Paroled February 22, 1865.

Johnson, Joseph, Co. F—Paroled at Annapolis, Maryland, October 17, 1864.

Kelly, Bernard, Co. C—Paroled at Annapolis, Maryland, February 22, 1865.

Kelly, Francis, Co. C—Paroled February 22, 1865.

Kimball, Solon D., Co. L—Paroled at Annapolis, Maryland, February 21, 1865.

McKay, James, Co. I—Paroled at Annapolis, Maryland, February 22, 1865.

McLean, Owen, Co. H—Paroled February 22, 1865.

Merriam, Jonathan, Co. A—Released March 2, 1865; discharged at Readville, Massachusetts.

Moore, Samuel, Co. H—Paroled at Annapolis, Maryland, February 20, 1865.

Morse, Charles F., Co. F—Died in Annapolis, Maryland, soon after being exchanged.

Moulton, David, Co. A—Paroled February 22, 1865.

Murphy, Cornelius, Co. A—Discharged for disability.

Partridge, James H., Co. H—Paroled February 22, 1865.

Peterson, John, Co. C—Paroled at Annapolis, Maryland, October 27.

Porter, James C., Co. A—Paroled February 22, 1865.

Pringle, William H., Co. L—Paroled at Annapolis, Maryland, February 23, 1865; died in York, Pennsylvania, April 15, 1865, from prison-related disease.

Shine, Daniel, Co. C—Exchanged in May 1865.

Slemp, John, Co. C—Paroled at Annapolis, Maryland, February 22, 1865.

Tubbs, Henry, Co. A—Returned to the regiment May 21, 1865.

Summit Station near Halltown, Virginia, August 10, 1864

Killed Accidentally

Forbes, Alexander, Co. A—Killed by the accidental discharge of a pistol.

Captured/Exchanged

Fletcher, Sgt. John, Co. A—Paroled February 22, 1865.

Mosby's wagon train attack at Berryville, Virginia, August 13, 1864

Wounded

McLean, Alfred, Co. L—The company mailman, he was shot in the thigh. McLean had suffered a disabling injury at Readville that troubled him all his life. At the time of his death in 1931 he was one of the last surviving members of the California Battalion.

Howard, Amos,* Co. L—Wounded again while returning to the regiment after recovering from the wound he received during the Ice Cream Raid.

Captured/Died in Prison

Speaight, Charles L., Co. A—Died at Danville Prison February 25, 1865.

Cedar Creek, Virginia, August 13, 1864

Captured/Exchanged

Riley, Cpl. Amos, Co. M—Captured by Confederate pickets while on a foraging expedition; exchanged in April 1865.

Winchester, Virginia, August 17, 1864

Captured/Deserted

Harmon, William, Co. K—Joined Co. F of the Confederate Foreign Legion on November 7.

Captured/Exchanged

White, William, Co. K—Paroled in Richmond February 20, 1865.
Kelley, Thomas, Co. C—Paroled February 22, 1865; deserted while on furlough June 1, 1865.
McDonald, Daniel, Co. L—Paroled March 13, 1865.
Burke, Patrick, Co. G—Released March 22, 1865.
Kelley, Michael, Co. L—Paroled February 22, 1865; returned to the regiment.
Dealing, Charles A., Co. L—A carpenter, he was paroled February 22, 1865.

Halltown, Virginia, August 20, 1864

Wounded

Bishop, Sgt. George, Co. E—Shot while on picket; discharged for disability.

Berryville, Virginia, August 21, 1864

Killed/Mortally Wounded

O'Leary, John, Co. E—From Roxbury, Massachusetts.

Wounded

Benninger, Irwin, Co. M—Discharged for disability.
Boyle, Sgt. Charles, Co. D—Returned to the regiment; also known as Callahan.
Boynton, John, Co. D—Returned to the regiment.
Grout, Cpl. Alonzo, Co. A—Discharged for disability.
McDougall, Daniel, Co. L—A native of Scotland; returned to the regiment.
O'Neil, Cpl. Patrick, Co. K—Returned to the regiment.
Rumery, Cpl. Ezra, Co. L—Returned to the regiment.
Ward, John, Co. A—Returned to the regiment.

Charlestown, Virginia, August 22, 1864

Wounded

Phillips, Capt. John, Co. C—Discharged for disability because of wounds.

Halltown, Virginia, August 24, 1864

Wounded

Leonard, Cpl. Patrick, Co. K—Returned to the regiment.

Halltown, Virginia, August 25, 1864

Killed/Mortally Wounded

Eigenbrodt, Capt. Charles, Co. E—Commanding a battalion at the time of his death; he was thirty-seven years old.

Wounded

Doyle, Sgt. John, Co. K—From Southwick, Maine.

Halltown, Virginia, August 26, 1864

Killed/Mortally Wounded

Meader, 1st Lt. Charles, Co. A—Enlisted as a sergeant; promoted to first lieutenant April 22, he was in command of Co. C at the time of his death. He listed his occupation as "traveler."

Ackerman, James, Co. A—He was one of the eight men arrested at Gloucester Point in early 1863 on Lieutenant Rumery's orders.

Wounded

Donahue, Francis, Co. H—Returned to the regiment.

Dean, Charles, Co. H—Transferred to the Veteran Reserve Corps because of his wounds.

Charlestown, Virginia, August 27, 1864

Killed/Mortally Wounded

Marden, John, Co. K—A teamster from Portsmouth, New Hampshire.

Martin, Cpl. Thomas, Co. K—Although a Californian, he enlisted in Boston and thus was not a member of the California Battalion.

Wounded

Wescott, William, Co. E—Returned to the regiment.

Captured/Exchanged

Gavin, Patrick, Co. K—Paroled October 8; deserted while on furlough February 7, 1865.

Charlestown, Virginia, August 28, 1864

Wounded

O'Connell, John, Co. F—Severely wounded during the march. His real name was Michael Walsh. He deserted from the 2nd California Volunteer Infantry April 23, 1863, to join the California Battalion.

Summit Point, Virginia, September 2, 1864

Wounded

Allen, Leonard, Co. K—Wounded in an exchange of gunfire with a Confederate scouting party.

Opequon Creek, Virginia, September 7, 1864

Killed/Mortally Wounded

Storer, John, Co. D—A cabinetmaker from Milo, Maine.
Smith, John, Co. D—Died of wounds in the hospital at Annapolis, Maryland, October 1.

Wounded

Bard, James,* Co. L—Suffered his first wounded during the Ice Cream Raid and returned to the regiment.
Turner, John, Co. F—A teamster, he was transferred to the Veteran Reserve Corps.
Shurtleff, Oscar, Co. F—Took a ball in the head but returned to duty after several months in the hospital.

Captured/Died in Prison

Small, George, Co. F—A miner from the gold country, he died at Andersonville Prison January 15, 1865.

Berryville, Virginia, September 10, 1864

Wounded

Copp, Ernest, Co. K—Accidentally wounded; discharged from the hospital in Philadelphia after the surrender at Appomattox.

Summit Point, Virginia, September 12, 1864

Killed/Mortally wounded

Dearborn, Valorus, Co. A—Shot in the head while awaiting the order to charge; died the next day.

Wounded

Munger, 2nd Lt. Lewis,* Co. F—A San Franciscan, he enlisted as corporal; returned to regiment.

Locke's Ford, Virginia, September 13, 1864

Killed/Mortally Wounded

Wilbur, Winfield S., Co. I—From Friendship, Maine; died the same day he was wounded.

Logan, Alexander, Co. D—From South Farmington, Massachusetts.

Shiffer, John S., Co. F—Died of wounds September 19 in Frederick, Maryland.

Colgan, William, Co. C—Died of wounds September 28 in Frederick, Maryland.

Wounded

McClease, Joseph, Co. I—Returned to the regiment.

Fleet, Richard, Co. C—An engineer from Falls Church, Virginia; returned to the regiment.

Morse, George W., Co. D—Discharged because of wounds.

McLaughlin, John, Co. G—Discharged at the Readville, Massachusetts, hospital because of wounds.

McKnight, Edward, Co. D—Discharged September 11, 1865, after almost a year in army hospitals.

September 17, 1864

Wounded Accidentally

McMullen, Peter, Co. K—Deserted from the hospital in Philadelphia January 2, 1865.

Winchester, Virginia, September 19, 1864

Killed/Mortally Wounded

Emerson, George, Co. I—From Derry, New Hampshire; he was twenty-one at the time of his death.

Wounded

Baldwin, 1st Lt. Josiah A., Co. L—Severely wounded, he was left in the care of a local family. He was subsequently discharged because of wounds.

Porter, Cpl. John, Co. C—A farmer from New Brunswick, he was discharged because of disability.

DeHaven, George, Co. F—A painter from Sherborn; discharged for disability June 19, 1865.

Felch, John H.,* Co. L—First wounded at Mount Zion Church; this time he was discharged because of wounds.

Gregory, Sgt. David D., Co. C—Born in Wales, he enlisted in April 1864. He returned to the regiment and later became first sergeant of Co. C.

Granville, Charles K., Co. K—Returned to the regiment.

Thompson, 2nd Lt. Edward, Co. F—Commissioned May 5, 1864; returned to the regiment.

Chadwick, Edward P., Co. F—Discharged because of wounds.

Porter, John, * Co. C—Captured and exchanged earlier in the year, he was seriously wounded at Winchester and remained in the hospital until December 9, 1865, when he was finally discharged.

Captured/Died in Prison

Bosworth, Charles, Co. C—Sent to Richmond September 27 and then to Salisbury, North Carolina, October 9. He died in Salisbury some time later.

Captured/Exchanged

Nystrom, Sgt. Charles, Co. L—Paroled October 10.

McAllister, Sgt. Henry, Co. C—Paroled at Annapolis, Maryland, February 2, 1865.

Balcolm, 2nd Lt. Darnly O., Co. F—Commissioned August 27, 1864, and transferred from Co. A.

Front Royal, Virginia, September 20, 1864

Captured/Exchanged

Moeglen, Philip, Co. M—Paroled October 8.

Luray Valley, Virginia, September 22, 1864

Killed/Mortally Wounded

Morgan, William H., Co. I—Died in Woodstock on this date; it is probable he was wounded in the Luray Valley the same day.

Wounded

Trickey, Alva W., Co. C—Discharged December 29 because of wounds.

Winchester, Virginia, September 22, 1864

Wounded Accidentally

Barenson Abram F., * Co. M—Recovered from his wound at Rockville, he returned to the regiment and was accidentally wounded.

Luray Valley, September 24, 1864

Killed/Mortally Wounded

Woodman, 2nd Lt. H. F., Co. G—Enlisted in the California Hundred and transferred to Co. G at Readville as a sergeant. The ball that hit him broke his leg, leaving an ugly wound. He was serving as Lowell's assistant adjutant general when he was wounded. He died at Mount Jackson a few days later.

Moeglen, John, Co. M—Father of Philip Moeglen, who was captured two days earlier.

Wounded

Swank, Lolma, Bugler, Co. L—Returned to the regiment.

Waynesboro, September 28, 1864

Killed/Mortally Wounded

Burns, Robert, Co. L—A laborer from San Francisco

Kingsley, Cpl. Edward, Co. L—Born in Connecticut, he became a hatter in San Francisco.

Williams, Sgt. Benjamin, Co. E—He deserted from the 4th California Volunteer Infantry to join the 2nd Massachusetts using the alias of William Butcher. The desertion charge was later dropped.

Hunter, James P., Co. L—Severely wounded, he died of disease on Christmas Eve 1864 while in the hospital at Pittsburgh, Pennsylvania.

Hurley, William, Co. I—A laborer from Salem.

Wounded

Kinnie, 1st Lt. Charles Mason, Co. L—Slightly wounded. Kinnie enlisted as a sergeant in the California Hundred. He later became a sergeant major, was commissioned a second lieutenant, and became a first lieutenant on January 25, 1864. He later became an assistant adjutant general in the Regular Army cavalry.

Wilburn, Cpl. James P., Co. M—From Sebastopol, California, he lost an arm and was given a disability discharge.

Good, Joseph, Co. G—Discharged May 11, 1865, because of wounds.

Cavanaugh, Cpl. Patrick, Co. I—Returned to the regiment.

O'Laughlin, Thomas, Co. C—Returned to the regiment.

Captured/Died in Prison

Shea, Corneille, Co. I—A teacher from New York City, he died in Salisbury, North Carolina, November 24.

Captured/Deserted

Schellinger, Franklin, Co. F—Joined the 2nd Regiment of the Confederate Foreign Legion on December 20 while a prisoner.

Captured/Escaped

Street, Pennelton, Co. M—Escaped February 5, 1865, and returned to the regiment.

Shay, Patrick, Co. C—Escaped May 9, 1865, and returned to the regiment.

Captured/Exchanged

Wolf, Louis, Co. F—Paroled, date unknown; discharged June 29, 1865, in York, Pennsylvania.

Haskell, Nathan M., Co. D—Paroled at Annapolis, Maryland, February 7, 1865.

Fisher's Hill, Virginia, October 7, 1864

Killed Accidentally

Reardon, Michael, Co. B—A harness maker from Boston.

Skirmish at Tom's Brook, Virginia, October 8, 1864

Killed/Mortally Wounded

Lawrence, Lawson J., Co. C—A farmer from Gloucester, Rhode Island.
Collins, James, Co. C—Died October 23 at the hospital in Winchester.

Wounded

Tucker, 2nd Lt. Samuel F.,* Co. L—A farmer from San Francisco, he enlisted as
    sergeant and was commissioned April 20, 1864; returned to the regiment.
Wakefield, 1st Sgt. Elhana W., Co. F—Discharged because of wounds.
Hardy, Cpl. John, Co. D—Returned to the regiment.
Lynch, Michael, Co. C—Discharged July 12, 1865, because of wounds.
Ayer, Cpl. Osborn, Co. L—Discharged because of wounds.
Conners, Cornelius, Co. D—Discharged June 19, 1865 because of wounds.
Morris, William,* Co. E—Paroled in April and returned to the regiment after be-
    ing captured August 24, 1863; returned to the regiment again after recovering
    from his wounds.

Cedar Creek, Virginia, October 19, 1864

Killed/Mortally Wounded

Beal, 1st Sgt. Merrill 1st Sergeant, Co. M—A barber by trade, he was born in
    Natick, Massachusetts.
Davis, Cpl. Asa M.,* Co. E.—Davis was slightly wounded at Fort Reno on July 10
    and had just returned to the company. His luck ran out at Cedar Creek.
Green, Stephen, Co. F—From Stoughton, Massachusetts, he enlisted in Boston
    December 31, 1863, and was sent as a replacement to one of the California
    companies. He died a few hours after being shot.
Lowell, Bvt. Brig. Gen. Charles Russell, commander, Reserve Brigade—Died of
    wounds the day after the battle.
Redman, Carl, Co. H—Born in Germany, he had only been in the regiment four
    and a half months; died of wounds November 2 in Winchester.
Rhodes, Charles, Co. C—A laborer from Boston, he was mortally wounded.
Russell, Sgt. Alvin, Co. E—A miner from the gold country, he was twenty-one at
    the time of his death.
Smith, Capt. Rufus, Co. A—Commissioned as one of the original lieutenants in
    Co. E, he commanded the company while Captain Manning was ill. He was
    promoted to captain March 1 and took command of Co. A. He was hit while
    leading the California Hundred in the first charge that morning.

Walton, William, Co. D—A saddler from St. Louis, he was among the first men to enlist in the regiment in December 1862.

Weisgerber, Stephen, Co. F—A miner from the gold country.

Wounded

Burke, Thomas A., Co. K—Deserted a month after he was wounded while on convalescent leave.

Chamberlain, Richard, Co. L—Severely wounded but recovered and returned to the regiment.

Cole, Sgt. Stephen, Co. D—Returned to the regiment.

Connel, Jeffrey, Co. H—Wounded in the left foot by shell fragments.

Crocker, Capt. Henry H., Co. E—Crocker was promoted to captain September 3, 1864.

Drought, John, Co. I—a native of New Rochelle, New York.

Hepburn, Sgt. James W., Co. E—From the gold mining town of Mokelumne Hill, California, he was discharged in March 1865. After returning to California, Hepburn was commissioned a second lieutenant in Co. A, 2nd California Cavalry, May 8, 1865, in San Francisco. He was discharged April 7, 1866.

Hussey, 2nd Lt. William, Co. C—Hussey was hit in the left shoulder. He enlisted in the California Hundred and was later commissioned and transferred to Co. C.

Kuhls, 1st Lt. Henry,* Co. L—From Nieburg, Germany, he enlisted as a private in Co. L and was soon promoted to sergeant and then commissioned a second lieutenant. Chaplain Humphreys called him an "enthusiastic, hot-blooded German."

McDonald, Sgt. Allen, Co. D—Shot in the right shoulder, he was discharged for disability. His wound bothered him for the rest of his life.

McIntosh, 2nd Lt. Isaac, Co. A—Commissioned March 3, he was rescued by Lieutenant Crocker.

Morrill, John, Co. D—Wounded in the left leg; returned to the regiment.

Roberts, Charles, Co. F—Wounded in the right thigh; he did not return to the regiment until after Appomattox.

Seagrave, Edward P.,* Co. L—He was captured by Mosby's guerrillas during the Ice Cream Raid on July 31, 1863, and subsequently recaptured by Colonel Lowell and returned to the regiment.

Sparohawk, Cpl. Jared, Co. L—He was discharged at a Philadelphia hospital because of his wounds.

Thompson, John,* Co. B—Listed his profession as soldier; only lightly wounded, he returned to the regiment and was captured less than two weeks later at Newton, Virginia.

Connel, Jeffrey, Co. H—Returned to the regiment.

Cedar Creek, Virginia, October 28, 1864

Captured/Exchanged

Foote, Charles D., Co. F—Captured by guerrillas while away from camp; exchanged at Annapolis, Maryland, February 17, 1865.

Newton, Virginia, October 28, 1864

Captured Exchanged

Thompson, John, * Co. B—The details of his capture are not known; released in January 1865.

Cedar Creek, Virginia, October 29, 1864

Captured/Exchanged

Weeks, Lewis, Co. L—Guerrillas took Weeks prisoner, perhaps with Foote; paroled at Annapolis, Maryland, February 7, 1865.

Fordham, Nathan, Co. L—A member of the band and probably one of those mentioned by Corbett; paroled February 27, 1865, he returned to the regiment May 23, 1865.

Gordonsville, Virginia, December 23, 1864

Wounded

Hardin, Cpl. James, Co. F—Returned to the regiment; also known as Harding.

Warrenton, Virginia, December 26, 1864

Captured/Exchanged

McIntyre, *William,* Co. H—Paroled February 17, 1865; returned to the regiment.

Duval, Philip, Co. H—Paroled February 22, 1865; returned to the regiment.

Gage, William, Co. H—Paroled February 22, 1865; returned to the regiment.

Mitchell's Station, Virginia, March 4, 1865

Captured/Exchanged

West, Frank, Co. M—A native of England; paroled April 12.

Curran, Timothy, Co. G—Exchange date unknown; mustered out at Annapolis, Maryland, June 5.

Murphy, Michael, Co. G—Paroled at Annapolis, Maryland, April 4; mustered out June 5.

Charlottesville, Virginia, March 5, 1865

Captured/Exchanged

Casey, George, Co. H—Paroled at Annapolis, Maryland, April 4; mustered out
June 5.

Scottsville, Virginia, March 3, 1865

Captured/Exchanged

Dugan, Thomas, Co. M—Released March 26; returned to the regiment.
Cordwell, George H., Co. B—Released March 27; returned to the regiment

Charlottesville, Virginia, March 7, 1865

Captured/Exchanged

Mulligan, William, Co. H—A native of Liverpool, England, he was paroled March
10; deserted from parole camp.

North Garden, Virginia, March 8, 1865

Captured/Exchanged

Robinson, John, Co. K—Paroled March 10; deserted from parole camp.

Frederick Hall, Virginia, March 11, 1865

Captured/Exchanged
Farrell, Felix L. C., Co. G—Paroled March 26.

Fort Union, Virginia, March 13, 1865

Captured/Exchanged
Lambert, William, Co. B—Paroled March 30.

Beaver Dam, Virginia, March 15, 1865

Captured/Exchanged
Welsh, James, Co. K—Paroled March 26.

King William County, Virginia, March 15, 1865

Captured/Exchanged

Sargent, Joseph, Co. K—Released at Aikin Landing March 26 and sent to the parole camp at Annapolis, Maryland, March 28. He went on furlough and there is
no further record.

Louisa Courthouse, Virginia, March 16, 1865

Captured/ Exchanged
Keniston, Hubbard, Co. F—Paroled March 27; mustered out at Annapolis, Maryland, June 12, 1865.

Hanover Courthouse, Virginia, March 17, 1865

Captured/Exchanged
Borman, Robert H., Co. M—Released March 20.

Concord Church, Virginia, March 17, 1865

Killed Accidentally
Roby, Charles, Co. A—Killed by a falling tree.

Columbus, Virginia, March 19, 1865

Captured/Exchanged
Taylor, Samuel, Co. L—Paroled in Richmond May 26.

White House Landing, Virginia, and March 20, 1865

Wounded
Gordon, Seth, Co. H—Slightly wounded; returned to the regiment.

White Oak Road, Virginia, March 21, 1865

Captured/Exchanged
Myers, Randolph P., Co. E—A butcher from Saint Johns, New Brunswick; paroled April 4.

White Oak Road, Virginia, March 30, 1865

Captured/Exchanged
Peel, Henry, Co. K—Paroled April 4.

Dinwiddie Courthouse, Virginia, March 31, 1865

Wounded
Tucker, Timothy, Co. M—Discharged June 15 because of wounds.
Thompson, 2nd Lt. Edward,* Co. F—Returned to the regiment after being wounded at Winchester only to be wounded again; commanded Co. B at muster out.
Moore, Cpl. William H.,* Co. E—Recovered from wound at Ashby's Gap and re-

turned to regiment; discharged June 17 from a hospital in Washington, D.C., because of this wound.

Five Forks, Virginia, April 1, 1865

Killed/Mortally Wounded

Thayer, Cpl. George F., Co. F—A miner from California.

Munger, 1st Lt. Lewis,* Co. F—Returned to the regiment after being wounded at Summit Point; killed at the head of his company while attacking enemy fortifications.

Wounded

Parker, Sgt. Arthur, Co. D—Discharged May 25 because of wounds.

Whitcomb, Cpl. Sylvester, Co. F—Severely wounded but returned to the regiment.

Field, Charles T., Co. L—Discharged June 16 in Washington, D.C., because of wounds.

Fergusen, Sgt. Thomas W., Co. H—discharged for wounds.

Tucker, 2nd Lt. Samuel F.,* Co. L—Returned to the regiment after being wounded October 8, 1864; mustered out from the hospital June 1.

Captured/Missing

Smith, James, Co. B—No further record.

Captured/Escaped

Tullock, Cpl. John, Co. G—Arrived at Annapolis, Maryland, later that month and was promoted to sergeant.

Captured/Exchanged

Kuhls, Capt. Henry,* Co. L—Returned to regiment after being wounded at Cedar Creek. He was captured while single-handedly charging enemy fortifications; released after the surrender at Appomattox.

Nottoway, Virginia, April 13, 1865

Wounded

Farren, David, Co. B—No details of this wounding; it occurred after the surrender at Appomattox.

Notes

1. Join the Cavalry!

1. California editors were frequently challenged for statements in their newspapers. One Sacramento editor avoided duels by always selecting sawed-off shotguns at twenty paces. His challengers were appalled by his choice of weapons and would wisely withdraw the challenge.

2. Arthur Quinn, *The Rivals: William Gwin, David Broderick, and the Birth of California* (New York: Crown, 1994), pp. 269–72.

3. Elijah R. Kennedy, *The Contest for California* (Boston: Houghton and Mifflin, 1912), p. 53.

4. Quinn, *The Rivals*, pp. 12–16.

5. U.S. senators were elected by the state legislature.

6. Until 1854, when a federal mint was established in California, private minters produced most gold coins.

7. Byron Farwell, *Ball's Bluff: A Small Battle and Its Long Shadow* (McLean, Va.: EPM, 1990), p. 17.

8. Ibid., pp. 158–161.

9. De Witt Clinton Thompson, "California in the Rebellion" (paper presented to the California Commandery of the Military Order of the Loyal Legion of the United States [MOLLUS], 1891), F864.T5, De Witt Clinton Thompson Papers, Bancroft Library, University of California, Berkeley.

10. Farwell, *Ball's Bluff*, p. 17.

11. In downtown San Francisco and, surprisingly in 1999, a vacant lot.

12. This guidon, along with the national flag inscribed with all of the battles of the California Hundred and Battalion and a battle standard, is on display at the state capitol in Sacramento.

13. Sam Corbett Diary, Dec. 14, 1862, BANC mss. C-F-95, Sam Corbett Papers, Bancroft Library, University of California, Berkeley (hereafter Corbett Diary).

14. The present-day name of Aspinwall is Colon.

15. Corbett Diary, Jan. 7, 1863; Richard Orton, comp., *Records of California Men in the War of the Rebellion* (Sacramento: California Adjutant General's Office, 1890). (Hereafter *CalRec.*)

16. This was before the construction of the canal across the base of Cape Cod. Steamers moving up the East Coast with passengers for Boston stopped at Stonington, thus avoiding the long and sometimes perilous route around Cape Cod.

17. *CalRec*; "City Notes," *Daily Alta Californian*, Mar. 9, 1863.

18. Corbett Diary, Feb. 6, 1863.

19. "City Notes," *Daily Alta Californian*, Jan. 25, 1863.

20. Ibid.

21. Ibid., Feb. 10, 1863.

22. Ibid., Feb. 25, 1863.

23. Quoted in ibid., Feb. 16, 1863. "Wing Oliver" appears to be a fictitious name.

24. The letters shown in parenthesis are the designations in the 2nd Massachusetts.

25. "City Notes," *Daily Alta Californian*, Mar. 23, 1863.

26. *CalRec*, p. 867.

27. "City Notes," *Daily Alta Californian*, May 30, 1863.

28. Ibid.

29. Ibid.

30. Ibid.

31. Ibid.

2. Gone for a Soldier

1. War Department, *The War of the Rebellion: Official Records of the Union and Confederate Armies* (hereafter OR and volume number), ser. III, vol. II (Washington, D.C.: Government Printing Office, 1880–1901), p. 324. All volumes cited are from ser. I unless otherwise indicated. The implication of the draft in mid-1862 is woven throughout pages 124 through 713. Note particularly the correspondence between each of the Northern governors and the War Department. Eventually, Governor Andrews delayed the draft in Massachusetts until October 15, 1862.

2. Banks to Maj. Gen. Henry W. Halleck, OR XXVI, pt. 1, pp. 699–700.

3. Sarah Forbes Hughes, ed., *John Murray Forbes, Letters and Recollections*, 2 vols. (Boston: Houghton Mifflin and Cambridge Press, 1900), pp. 2:113–17.

4. Edward W. Emerson, ed., *Life and Letters, of Charles Russell Lowell* (Port Washington, N.Y.: Kennikat, 1971), pp. 8–10.

5. Emerson, ed., *Life and Letters*, p. 13.

6. Ibid., p. 19.

7. Ibid., p. 20.

8. Patricia Faust, ed., *Historical Times Illustrated Encyclopedia of the Civil War* (hereafter HTCW) (New York: Harper and Row, 1986), p. 452.

9. Emerson, ed., *Life and Letters*, p. 20.

10. Company B Musters, *MassRec*.

11. William Lawrence, *Life of Amos S. Lawrence* (Boston and Cambridge: Houghton Mifflin and University Press of Cambridge, 1888, 1889), p. 186.

12. Ibid., p. 187.

13. Emerson, ed., *Life and Letters*, p. 31.

14. Robert G. Scott, ed., *Fallen Leaves: The Civil War Diary of Major Henry Livermore Abbott* (Kent, Ohio: Kent State University Press, 1991), p. 92.

15. Only two men from the 2nd Massachusetts were captured and returned.

16. Statistical data comp. by author from information contained in *MassRec*.

17. Twenty-three California recruits deserted within the first sixty days, a rate of only 4.6 percent (statistical data comp. by author from information contained in *MassRec*).

18. Artillery batteries were trained at instruction camps run by the federal government.

19. Emerson, ed., *Life and Letters*, p. 236.

20. Crowninshield to his mother, Feb. 18, 1863, Magnus Crowninshield Letters, Massachusetts Historical Society, Boston (hereafter Crowninshield Letters). Crowninshield, who was over 6 feet 2 inches tall and strongly built, was quite capable of knocking a man down with one blow.

21. OR II, ser. IV, p. 134.

22. Crowninshield to his mother, Mar. 23, 1863, Crowninshield Letters.

23. Corbett Diary, Mar. 28, 1863.

24. Crowninshield to his mother, Mar. 31, 1863, Crowninshield Letters.

25. *Annual Report of the Adjutant General of the Commonwealth of Massachusetts 1863* (hereafter AR followed by the year) (Boston: Adjutant General's Office, 1863), p. 933.

26. *OR* XVIII, p. 260.

27. Ibid., p. 629.

28. "Letter from the Federal Army in Virginia," *Daily Alta Californian*, June 10, 1863.

29. *OR* XVIII, p. 343.

30. "Letter from the Federal Army in Virginia," *Daily Alta Californian*, June 10, 1863.

31. *CalRec* does not mention the court-martial. It instead shows that he transferred to his old regiment, the 1st Missouri Cavalry, where he was commissioned a second lieutenant.

32. *San Francisco Call*, Sept. 16, 1863.

33. Emerson, ed., *Life and Letters*, p. 291.

34. *AR 1863*.

35. *OR* XVII, pt. 2, p. 925.

36. Ibid., pp. 793–99.

37. *Civil War Times Illustrated* (hereafter *CWTI*), Dec. 1966.

38. *OR* XXVII, pt. 2, p. 897.

39. Ibid., p. 793.

40. Corbett Diary, June 25, 1863.

41. *CWTI*, Dec. 1966.

42. *AR 1863*, p. 935.

43. Corbett Diary, June 26, 1863.

44. *CalRec*, p. 856.

45. *OR* XVII, pt. 1, pp. 837–40.

46. Corbett Diary, July 4 and 5, 1863.

47. *OR* XXVII, pt. 2, p. 852.

48. Ibid., p. 841.

49. Ibid.

50. Ibid., p. 843.

51. Judith W. McGuire, *Diary of a Southern Refugee by a Lady of Virginia* (Lincoln: University of Nebraska Press, 1995), pp. 227–28.

52. *OR* XXVII, pt. 2, p. 818.

53. *HTCW*, p. 416.

3. Gettysburg and Guerrillas

1. *OR* I, pp. 1095–98.

2. *OR* VIII, pp. 1038, 1041–42.

3. John S. Mosby, *Gray Ghost: The Memoirs of John S. Mosby* (Boston: Little, Brown, 1917; reprint, New York: Bantam, 1992), p. 37. Mosby was part of Swan's detachment, which was fifty yards behind the lines during the fight. See also *OR* II, p. 432.

4. See Mosby, *Gray Ghost*, pp. 23–24, 221; and Jeffrey D. Wert, *Mosby's Rangers* (New York: Simon and Schuster, 1990), p. 81, for Mosby's feelings about sabers.

5. Maj. John Scott, *Partisan Life with Col. John S. Mosby* (New York: Harper and Brothers, 1867), pp. 43–63.

6. *New York Times*, Mar. 11, 1863, p. 9.

7. HTCW, p. 724.

8. *Atlas to Accompany the Official Records of the Union and Confederate Armies* (hereafter OR Atlas), with a foreword by Henry Steele Commager (Washington, D.C: Government Printing Office, 1891–1895; reprint New York: Thomas Yoseloff, 1958).

9. Emerson, ed., *Life and Letters*, p. 239.

10. AR 1863, p. 936.

11. Emerson, ed., *Life and Letters*, p. 238

12. Ibid., p. 245.

13. Ibid., p. 246.

14. Ibid., p. 251.

15. Ibid., p. 252.

16. Ibid.

17. OR XXVII, pt. 3, p. 66.

18. Ibid, p.50.

19. Ibid.

20. Ibid., p. 74; AR 1863.

21. Wert, *Mosby's Rangers*, p. 87.

22. OR XXVII, pt. 3, p. 692.

23. Ibid., p. 383.

24. Ibid., pt. 1, pp. 59–60.

25. Ibid., pt. 2, p. 692.

26. Ibid., pt. 1, p. 358.

27. Ibid., pt. 3, p. 401.

28. Ibid, p. 440.

29. Emerson, ed., *Life and Letters*, p. 269.

30. Ibid.

31. The California Hundred and Battalion battle flag is inscribed with "Gettysburg" even though the unit's participation was not exactly heroic.

32. Scott, *Partisan Life*, p. 108.

33. Listed in *MassRec* as Henry P. Irvin.

34. *Daily Alta Californian*, Aug. 13, 1863; AR 1863, p. 935.

35. Janet B. Hewett, ed. *Supplement to the Official Records of the Union and Confederate Armies* (hereafter SuppOR), vol. 27, pt. 2 (Wilmington, N.C.: Broadfoot, 1996), p. 139.

36. This was Sgt. William DeForrest, who, in spite of Lowell's gloomy prognosis, managed to survive, although he never returned to the regiment. He was discharged on account of his wound in September 1863.

37. *SuppOR* 27, pt. 2, p. 139.

38. OR XXVII, pt. 1, p. 103. The only other Californians captured but not mentioned in the contemporary accounts were Dewitt Van Fleet of Company M, taken on the twelfth, and Henry Greenough of Company A, who was captured the next day at Snicker's Gap. They may have been included as stragglers. The other stragglers may have been from the New Jersey contingent.

39. George Edgar Turner, *Victory Rode the Rails: The Strategic Place of the Railroads in the Civil War*, with an introduction by Gary W. Gallagher (Reprint, Lincoln: University of Nebraska Press, 1992), p. 281.

40. OR XXVII, pt. 3, p. 706.

41. Emerson, ed., *Life and Letters*, p. 276.

42. See the Appendix for a list of the casualties.

43. Emerson, ed., *Life and Letters*, p. 278.

44. Turner, *Victory Rode the Rails*, p. 281.

45. Scott, *Partisan Life*, pp. 114–16.

46. "Our Letter from the Californians in the Massachusetts Cavalry in Service in Virginia," *Daily Alta Californian*, Oct. 4, 1863. Raymond was also known as Renard. After the war, John Viall, formerly a captain in the 5th New York Cavalry, purchased the farm where Ranard and Little were buried. He wrote the governor of Massachusetts: "They were buried here by the order and personal supervision of the lamented Lowell and here they can remain but duty to our fallen brave and especially to my brother cavalrymen prompts me to make an appeal to you for a more Christian burial for these men or that their present resting place be so marked that they shall not be at once forgotten." (Quoted in Thomas J. Evans and James M. Moyer, *Mosby's Confederacy: A Guide to the Roads and Sites of Colonel John Singleton Mosby* [Shippensburg, Pa.: White Mane, 1991], App. G.) Hazen Little's remains were moved to grave number 10305 at Arlington National Cemetery. Renard is probably at Arlington but the confusion with his name has caused his records to be lost.

47. Wert, *Mosby's Rangers*, pp. 91–92.

48. OR XXVII, pt. 2, p. 990.

49. Emerson, ed., *Life and Letters*, p. 294. Cousin John probably refers to John Forbes.

50. OR XXVII, pt. 2, p. 990.

51. Virgil Carrington Jones, *Gray Ghosts and Rebel Raiders* (New York: Henry Holt, 1956; reprint, McLean, Va.: EPM, 1984), p. 192.

4. Inglorious Warfare

1. Crownshield to his mother, Aug. 21, 1863, Crowninshield Letters.

2. "Our Letter from the Californians," Oct. 4, 1863.

3. *AR 1863*, p. 937.

4. OR XXVII, pt. 2, p. 989.

5. Emerson, ed., *Life and Letters*, p. 294; OR XXIX, pt. 1, p. 66; and *SuppOR* 27, pt. 2, p. 139.

6. OR XXIX, pt. 2, p. 26.

7. Reed's information was, of course, incorrect. Mosby never established a headquarters.

8. Scott, *Partisan Life*, p. 118.

9. OR XXIX, pt. 1, p. 68. The civilian sutlers were reported as prisoners by Mosby.

10. Ibid., p. 69.

11. "Letter from a Californian in the Massachusetts Contingent," *Daily Alta Californian*, Sept. 9, 1863. This letter was probably written by William H Moore of Company E.

12. The 35th Virginia Cavalry was part of the Laurel Brigade.

13. OR XXIX, pt. 2, pp. 53, 69.

14. Ibid., pt. 1, p. 74.

15. Emerson, *Life and Letters*, p. 298.

16. "Our Letter from the Californians," Oct. 4, 1863.

17. Sergeant Short accepted a commission as a first lieutenant in the 1st U.S. Colored Infantry. He was promoted to captain and mustered out with his regiment.

18. "Our Letter from the Californians," Oct. 4, 1863.

19. Emerson, ed., *Life and Letters*, p. 270.

20. "Our Letter from the Californians," Oct. 4, 1863.

21. Ibid.

22. OR XXIX, pt. 2, p. 652. Based on the evidence of contemporary witnesses, Mosby never made any personal gain from the activities of his guerrilla band. However, he admitted that the lure of monetary gain was the principal incentive for his men. He often eschewed difficult military targets in lieu of those where profits were certain.

23. Pierpont had been elected governor of the new state of West Virginia. His son was a member of Mosby's band.

24. Ibid., pt. 1, p. 81.

25. Ibid.

26. Ibid., pt. 2, p. 253.

27. Ibid., p. 113.

28. Ibid., p. 152.

29. *SuppOR* 27, pt. 2, p. 151.

30. Ibid., p. 132.

31. *SuppOR* 27, pt. 2, pp. 132 (Co. C), 139 (Co. F), 141 (Co. G), 144 (Co. I).

32. OR XXIX, pt. 1, p. 480.

33. Ibid., pt. 2, p. 325.

34. Shelby Foote, *The Civil War: A Narrative*, vol. 2 (New York: Vintage, 1986), pp. 792–96.

35. OR XXIX, pt. 1, p. 492.

36. Ibid., pt. 1, p. 494.

37. *SuppOR* 27, pt. 2, pp. 136–37.

38. OR XXIX, pt. 2, p. 350.

39. Ibid., pt. 1, p. 495.

40. Ibid., pt. 2, p. 392.

41. Ibid., pt. 1, p. 652.

42. Ibid.

43. Ibid., p. 658. Yankee Davis was a local Union sympathizer.

44. Corbett Diary.

45. "Letter from a Californian in the Army of the Potomac," *Daily Alta Californian*, Dec. 29, 1863. At the end of the article are the initials "T.D.B." The only soldier on the rolls with those initials is corporal, later sergeant and, even later sergeant major Thomas D. Barnestead, of Company A. Barnestead wrote several letters to the *Daily Alta Californian*. Judging from their tone he was one of those chronic complainers found in every military organization.

46. The "medical stores" were probably alcoholic spirits, thought by some to be medicinal.

47. Wert, *Mosby's Rangers*, p.108.

48. OR XXIX, pt. 1, p. 659.

49. Ibid., p. 973.

50. Both Smith and Turner were killed January 10, 1864, in an attack on Cole's Marylanders on Loudoun Heights.

51. OR XXIX, pt. 1, p. 973.

52. *MassRec* and *CalRec*.

53. "Letter from the Californians in the Army of the Potomac," *Daily Alta Californian*, Jan. 31, 1864.

54. OR XXIX, pt. 1, p. 977.

55. "Letter from the Federal Army in Virginia," *Daily Alta Californian*, June 10, 1863.

56. OR XXIX, pt. 1, p. 982.

57. Corbett Diary, Dec. 20, 1863.

58. OR XXIX, pt. 1, p. 987.

59. Ibid., p. 992

60. Ibid., pp. 994–95.

61. "Letter from the Californian Column with the Army of the Potomac," *Daily Alta California*, Jan. 31, 1864.

62. Ibid.

63. The captured courier was Cpl. John Hood of Company E. He was paroled by Mosby on December 31.

64. "Letters from the Californians in the Army of the Potomac," *Daily Alta Californian*, Mar. 22, 1864. Adams returned safely with no losses. Adams was not popular with the men. In a letter to the *Daily Alta Californian* one trooper wrote: "he has nigh well reached the climax of meanness and disgrace. By his tyrannical conduct he has lost the esteem and incurred the hatred of his men; by his habitual intemperance he has lost their respect and forfeited every claim to decency; his bad conduct on several times has caused him to be placed under arrest. Altogether he is a disgrace to California" (Feb. 14, 1864). Adams transferred to the 5th Massachusetts Cavalry on March 24, 1864.

5. The Killing Ground

1. Valorus Dearborn, *Diary, 1864* (n.p., n.d.), copy furnished to the author by a descendant of Dearborn's, Mrs. Geraldine Chase of Concord, N.H.

2. Charles Humphreys, *Field, Camp, Hospital and Prison in the Civil War, 1863–1865* (Boston: George H. Ellis, 1918), pp. 3–4.

3. Ibid., pp. 4–7.

4. Emerson, ed., *Life and Letters*, p. 445.

5. Dearborn, *Diary, 1864*, Jan. 4, 1864.

6. OR XXXIII, p. 12.

7. Dearborn, *Diary, 1864*, Jan. 24, 1864.

8. OR XXXIII, p. 388.

9. Wert, *Mosby's Rangers*, p. 139.

10. OR II, ser. IV, p. 1003.

11. OR XXXIII, 1082–83.

12. OR XXXIII, p. 1253.

13. OR III, ser. IV, p. 194.

14. Humphreys, *Field, Camp, Hospital and Prison*, pp. 20–21.

15. Corbett Diary, Feb. 7, 1864.

16. Humphreys, *Field, Camp, Hospital and Prison*, p. 21.

17. Corbett Diary, Feb. 7, 1864.

18. Ibid.

19. "Letters from the Californians," Mar 22, 1864.

20. Humphreys, *Field, Camp, Hospital and Prison*, p. 19.

21. Bell I. Wiley, *The Life of Billy Yank: The Common Soldier of the Union* (Baton Rouge: Louisiana State University Press, 1995), pp. 195–96.

22. Emerson, ed., *Life and Letters*, p. 451.

23. Wert, *Mosby's Rangers*, p. 144.

24. Dearborn, *Diary, 1864*, Feb. 22, 1864.

25. OR XXXIII, p. 159.

26. Wert, *Mosby's Rangers*, p. 146.

27. OR XXXIII, p. 159.

28. Scott, *Partisan Life*, p. 202.

29. Von Massow was the son of the chamberlain to the King of Prussia. He later became chief of cavalry in the Imperial German Army. (Mosby, *Gray Ghost*, p. 209.)

30. OR XXXIII, p. 160.

31. Scott, *Partisan Life*, p. 203.

32. Crowninshield to his mother, Feb. 27, 1864, Crowninshield Letters.

33. The second silver-and-ivory mounted pistol has never been recovered. Because it was so distinctive and unusual it probably was, and may still be, a prized family heirloom in some Virginia family.

34. OR XXXIII, p. 587; and Crowninshield to his mother, Feb. 27, 1864, Crowninshield Letters.

35. Humphreys, *Field, Camp, Hospital and Prison*, p. 15.

36. Crowninshield to his mother, Feb. 27, 1864.

37. Dearborn, *Diary, 1864*, Feb. 24, 1864.

38. OR XXXIII, pp. 591–94.

39. Dearborn, *Diary, 1864*, Feb. 24, 1864.

40. *SuppOR* 27, pt. 2, pp. 134–53.

41. *AR 1864*, p. 940.

42. Mosby, *Gray Ghost*, p. 210.

43. Dearborn, *Diary, 1864*, Mar. 12, 1864.

44. OR XXXIII, p. 714.

45. Lieutenant Sims was forced to resign because of a bad case of the piles—an uncomfortable affliction for a cavalryman

46. Dearborn, *Diary, 1864*, Apr. 4, 1864.

47. Ibid.

48. OR XXXIII, p. 836.

49. Dearborn, *Diary, 1864*, Apr. 14, 1864; and OR XXXIII, p. 875.

50. Corbett Diary, Apr. 20, 1864.

51. OR XXXIII, p. 847.

52. Humphreys, *Field, Camp, Hospital and Prison*, p. 26.

53. Ibid., 31. The casualties were all from Company H.

54. Sgt. Charles Scott of and two others from Company L were wounded. One man, John Halligan, was captured. He died in prison.

55. OR XXXIII, pp. 315–16.

56. *CalRec*, p. 861.

57. One of the wounded prisoners was John Peyton deButts. See Margaret Ann Vogtsberger, ed., *The Dulaneys of Welbourne* (Berryville, Va.: Rockbridge, 1995), p. 156. The Dulaney family home was in the heart of "Mosby's Confederacy."

58. OR XXXIII, p. 308.

59. Dearborn, *Diary, 1864*, Apr. 23, 1864. Bumgardner's wound must have been minor because he did not go to the hospital, which might have saved his life. He was killed on July 6 at Mount Zion Church.

60. Mosby, *Gray Ghost*, p. 211.

61. OR XXXVII, pt. 1, p. 691.

62. OR XXXVII, pt. 1, p. 485.

63. Ibid., p. 475.

64. Ibid., p. 485.

65. "The next morning, taking with him [Mosby] Willie Martin and Bowie, he made a reconnaissance in the vicinity of Belle Plain, and on the route fell in with a body of Federal Cavalry, by whom they were closely pursued." (Scott, *Partisan Life*, p. 222.)

66. Dearborn, *Diary*, *1864*, May 15, 1864.

67. Scott, *Partisan Life*, pp. 225–26.

68. *SuppOR* 27 and AR *1864*.

69. Dearborn, *Diary*, *1864*, June 1, 1864.

70. Ibid., and OR XXXVII, pt. 1, p. 593.

71. Dearborn, *Diary*, *1864*, June 10, 1864.

72. OR XXXVII, pt. 1, 168.

73. Ibid., pp. 168–69.

74. HTCW, p. 376.

75. Wert, *Mosby's Rangers*, p. 170.

76. Obviously Mosby was not included in Early's plans. Early bypassed Harper's Ferry.

77. Mosby, *Gray Ghost*, p. 211.

78. Scott, *Partisan Life*, p. 239.

79. John H. Alexander, *Mosby's Men* (New York: Neale, 1907), p. 79.

80. Scott, *Partisan Life*, p. 242. According to Mosby, "As this was the first occasion on which I had used artillery, the magnitude of the invasion was greatly exaggerated by the fears of the enemy, and panic and alarm spread though their territory" (OR XXXVII, pt. 1, p. 4). This is simply not true. He was probably trying to justify moving his artillery to Richmond.

81. Ibid., p. 250.

82. OR XXXVII, pt. 1, p. 34.

83. Ibid., p. 3.

84. Ibid., p. 358.

85. Ibid., pp. 358–60.

86. Scott, *Partisan Life*, p. 248.

87. Humphreys, *Field, Camp, Hospital and Prison*, pp. 101–102.

88. Ibid., pp. 108–109.

89. The graves, lined up in a row, were marked with random rocks. Recently a group of people interested in preserving Mount Zion Church and the cemetery there arranged to have standard Union army gravestones made to replace the original rocks.

90. OR XXXVII, pt. 1, p. 359.

91. Ibid., p. 4.

6. Old Jube Invades

1. Glenn H. Worthington, *Fighting for Time* (Shippensburg, Pa.: White Mane, 1985), p. 49.

2. Charles C. Osbourne, *Jubal* (Chapel Hill, N.C.: Algonquin, 1992), p. 270.

3. OR XXXVII, pt. 1, p. 108.

4. Early was delayed in Fredrick gathering a $200,000 ransom levied against the town fathers.

5. OR XXXVII, pt. 1, p. 145.

6. Ibid., pt. 2, pp. 142–45.

7. There was a shortage of officers at the remount camp, so Fry was only able to assign one officer to each company.

8. OR XXXVII, pt. 1, p. 249.

9. Ibid., p. 221.

10. Frank S. Howell, *Montgomery County (Maryland) Sentinel*, Aug. 25, 1960.

11. OR XXXVII, pt. 1, p. 166.

12. Ibid., pp. 248–49.

13. Ibid., pt. 2, p. 166.

14. Ibid., pt. 1, p. 250.

15. Ibid., p. 236; and Corbett Diary, July 11, 1864.

16. Samuel W. Backus, "Californians in the field." Historical Sketch of the organization and service of the California "Hundred" and "Battalion," 2nd Massachusetts cavalry (paper presented to the California Commandery of the MOLLUS, December 17, 1889).

17. Crocker probably encountered men from Maj. Coe Durland's detachment who identified themselves as being from the 1st New Jersey Cavalry. The 1st New Jersey was not a part of XXIII Corps.

18. OR XXXVII, pt. 2, pp. 198–203.

19. CalRec, p. 850.

20. Robert Hunt Rhodes, ed., *All for the Union: The Civil War Diary and Letters of Elisha Hunt Rhodes* (New York: Orion, 1991), p. 170.

21. Corbett Diary, July 12, 1864.

22. OR XXXVII, pt. 2, p. 201.

23. By this time Confederates on the way to the prison at Lookout Point had cut the railroad from Washington to Baltimore.

24. July 11, 1864, Emerson, ed., *Life and Letters*, p. 321. Once again Lowell just missed being hit; this news could not have been too reassuring to Josephine.

25. MassRec.

26. Regulations called for troopers to line up and count off by fours before mounting. If there was no formal count-off, numbers were assigned after the unit formed up in a column with four troopers abreast. The men in each file were designated numbers one through four from left to right. The number one man in each rank served as the guide, keeping the proper distance from the rank in front. The man on the far right of each rank—the number four—served as a horse holder when the unit dismounted. See Philip St. George Cooke, *Cavalry Tactics or Regulations for the Instruction, Formations and Movements of the Cavalry* (Washington, D.C.: War Department, 1862).

27. OR XXXVII, pt. 1, pp. 232, 244–51, 255.

28. Ibid., p. 259.

29. Ibid., p. 251. The three prisoners were stragglers taken near Offut's Crossroads.

30. Mike Fitzpatrick, "Jubal Early and the Californians," *CWTI*, May 1998.

31. Warren Cochran, *A True Story of the Civil War, 1861–1865*. LaPorte, Ind.: LaPorte County Historical Museum, n.d.

32. Emerson, ed., *Life and Letters*, pp. 40–41.

33. Howell, "A True Story of the Civil War."

34. Ibid.

35. OR XXXVII, pt. 1, p. 252, 268. For Fry's armament and resupply see ibid., pt. 2, p. 200.

36. CalRec, MassRec.

37. OR XXXVII., pt. 2, p. 280.

38. MassRec and Arlington National Cemetery records.

39. OR XXXVII, pt. 2, p. 282.

40. Ibid., pp. 278–80.

41. Ibid., pt. 1, p. 252.

42. Ibid., pt. 1, p. 267.

7. Hard Marching

1. OR XXXVII, pt. 2, p. 547.

2. Ibid., p. 332.

3. Howe had recently been sent to take command of the Harper's Ferry Military District.

4. OR XXXVII, pt. 2, pp. 316–51.

5. Rhodes, *All for the Union*, p. 171; and Corbett Diary.

6. In addition to William Ormsby there is the possibility that Pvt. Morton M. Penile of Company F may have deserted at Muddy Branch and joined Mosby.

7. OR XXXVII, pt. 1, p. 281.

8. Ibid., pt. 2, pp. 291, 353. See also Scott, *Partisan Life*, p. 251. Mosby may have avoided the train because it was guarded by about five hundred seasoned cavalrymen.

9. OR XXXVII, pt. 1, p. 249.

10. Ibid., p. 286.

11. Ibid., p. 320.

12. Ibid., pt. 2, p. 369.

13. Ibid.

14. Ibid., pt. 1, pp. 290–92.

15. Ibid., pt. 2, p. 397.

16. Ibid., p. 406.

17. See Rhodes, *All for the Union*, p. 173. Rhodes attributes this capture to Mosby. There is no mention of the captured troopers in Mosby's memoirs or any of the other memoirs by members of his band.

18. Corbett Diary, July 25, 1864.

19. OR XXXVII, pt. 2, p. 427.

20. Ibid., p. 429.

21. Ibid., p. 436.

22. Ibid., p. 455.

23. Corbett Diary, July 27, 1864.

24. OR XXXVII, pt. 2, p. 474.

25. Ibid., p. 463.

26. Ibid., p. 468.

27. Ibid., pp. 488–99.

28. Corbett Diary, July 30, 1864.

29. OR XXXVII, pt. 2, pp. 492, 449.

30. Alexander, *Mosby's Men*, pp. 99–102; but see below that some of DeLaney's men managed to escape.

31. OR XXXVII, pt. 2, pp. 496–97. The fight at Noland's Ford marked the last time the Californians would meet with Mosby's guerrillas. After the war Mosby became a Republican and campaigned for his newfound friend, presidential candidate Ulysses S. Grant, throughout Loudoun and Fairfax Counties. His espousal of the hated enemy earned him the enmity of his fellow guerrillas and there were even threats against his life. After the election Grant sent him out of harm's way by appointing him consul to Hong Kong. For a while he practiced law in San Francisco, where he once told a gathering of veterans of the California Hundred and Battalion that they were his most formidable adversaries. The old veterans, needless to say, cherished his remarks.

32. Ibid., p. 529.

33. Per Larry Rogers, sergeant major of the California Hundred reenactment group.

34. Michael J. Pauley, *Unreconstructed Rebel: The Life of General John McCausland, CSA* (Charleston, W.Va.: Pictorial Histories, 1993), pp. 54–59. The burning of Chambersburg is often cited as revenge for Hunter's raid in early 1864, which included the destruction of a number of private homes. Chambersburg was not a military target. The town, including private homes, was burned simply because the citizens could not pay the ransoms demanded. Sheridan's destruction in the Shenandoah was directed against facilities that provided food and equipment for the Confederate armies, such as mills, factories, crops, and livestock. Private homes were specifically excluded.

35. OR XXXVII, pt. 2, p. 511.

36. Ibid., p. 512.

37. Corbett Diary, July 31, 1864.

38. Wilbur Fisk, *Hard Marching Every Day*, ed. Emil and Ruth Rosenblatt (Lawrence: University Press of Kansas, 1983), pp. 246–47.

39. Pauley, *Unreconstructed Rebel*, p. 66.

8. Sheridan Takes Command

1. Part of their objection arose because Hunter was feuding with the pro-administration newspapers in West Virginia and he was accused of personally horsewhipping a Union soldier.

2. Ulysses S. Grant, *Personal Memoirs of U. S. Grant*, 2 vols. (New York: Charles L. Webster, 1885), pp. 2:317–18.

3. Bruce Catton, *A Stillness at Appomattox* (Garden City, N.Y.: Doubleday, 1954), p. 45.

4. OR XXXVII, pt. 2, p. 572.

5. Philip H. Sheridan, *Civil War Memoirs* (New York: Charles Webster, 1888; reprint, Bantam, 1991), p. 214.

6. One of Lincoln's favorite hideaways was the War Department telegraph office. It could be that this was where he saw this dispatch.

7. OR XXXVII, pt. 2, p. 582.

8. Grant, *Memoirs*, p. 2:319.

9. Ibid., p. 2:321.

10. Jeffrey D. Wert, *From Winchester to Cedar Creek: The Shenandoah Campaign of 1864* (New York: Touchstone, 1987), p. 43.

11. Two Californians, William Fair of Company M and James Miller of Company E, deserted on August 6. They were probably fed up with the constant marching.

12. OR XLIII, pt. 1, p. 710.

13. Dearborn, *Diary*, 1864, Aug. 7, 1864.

14. Dearborn and Corbett Diaries, Aug. 7, 1864.

15. Corbett Diary, Aug. 8, 1864.

16. Custer, who briefly commanded a division after Gettysburg, was resentful of Wilson's promotion to divisional command, and called him "That upstart ass." Wilson turned out to be one of the war's outstanding cavalry leaders (Wert, *From Winchester to Cedar Creek*).

17. Sheridan, *Memoirs*, p. 219.

18. OR XLIII, pt. 1, p. 486.

19. Edward J. Stackpole, *Sheridan in the Shenandoah: Jubal Early's Nemesis* (Harrisburg, Pa.: Stackpole, 1961), pp. 403–404.

20. Emerson, ed., *Life and Letters*, p. 312. Emphasis in original.

21. This brigade was the only frontline command delegated to guarding trains.

22. OR XLIII, pt. 1, pp. 740–50.

23. Ibid., p. 730.

24. Dearborn, *Diary, 1864,* Aug. 10, 1864.

25. Corbett Diary, Aug. 10, 1864.

26. OR XLIII, pt. 1, p. 42.

27. Dearborn, *Diary, 1864,* Aug. 11, 1864.

28. Corbett Diary, Aug. 12, 1864; and OR XLIII, pt. 1, p. 422.

29. Corbett Diary, Aug. 13, 1864.

30. OR XLIII, pt. 1, p. 799.

31. Ibid. p. 775.

32. OR XLIII, pt. 1, p. 783.

33. Ibid., p. 634.

34. Scott, *Partisan Life,* p. 276.

35. The Reserve Brigade consisted of the 1st U.S. Cavalry, the 2nd U.S. Cavalry, the 6th Pennsylvania, the 1st New York Dragoons, and the 2nd Rhode Island—all commanded by Col. Alfred Gibbs of the 1st New York Dragoons.

36. OR XLIII, pt. 1, p. 632.

37. The 144th Ohio was mustered in in May. It fought at the Monocacy, losing thirty men killed and about a hundred captured before Mosby's attack on Sheridan's supply wagons.

38. See also Dennis E. Frye, "I Resolved to Play a Bold Game," in *Struggle for the Shenandoah,* ed. Gary W. Gallagher (Kent, Ohio: Kent State University Press, 1991), pp. 107–26, for a full discussion of Mosby's ineffectiveness in the 1864 Shenandoah Valley campaign.

39. Civil War records from the National Archives, Washington, D.C., and family history.

40. Sheridan, *Memoirs,* pp. 226–27; and Wert, *From Winchester to Cedar Creek,* pp. 35–38.

41. Sheridan, *Memoirs,* p. 228; and OR XLIII, pt. 1, pp. 801, 811.

42. Sheridan, *Memoirs,* p. 228–29; and OR XLIII, pt. 1, p. 816.

43. OR XLIII, pt. 1, pp. 57–58.

44. Sheridan, *Memoirs,* p. 229.

45. OR XLIII, pt. 1, p. 795; Dearborn, *Diary, 1864,* Aug. 16, 1864.

46. OR XLIII, pt. 1, p. 19.

47. Ibid., p. 822.

48. Ibid., p. 811.

49. Dearborn, *Diary, 1864,* Aug. 17, 1864.

50. Corbett Diary, Aug. 17, 1864.

51. Dearborn, *Diary, 1864,* Aug. 17, 1864; and Corbett Diary, Aug. 17, 1864.

52. Emerson, ed., *Life and Letters,* p. 324.

53. Ibid., p. 48.

54. Corbett Diary, Aug. 17, 1864.

55. Emerson, ed., *Life and Letters,* p. 324.

56. Wert, *Mosby's Rangers,* p. 195.

57. Ibid., p. 490.

9. Opequon Creek and Fisher's Hill

1. William J. Miller, "Demons that Day," *Civil War,* Dec. 1996.

2. Ibid. See also Scott, *Partisan Life,* pp. 280–82.

3. Miller, "Demons That Day."

4. Ibid.

5. Corbett Diary, Aug. 20, 1864.

6. Dearborn, *Diary, 1864,* Aug. 20, 1864.

7. Ibid.

8. Ibid.

9. Lowell to his wife, Emerson, ed., *Life and Letters*. The 2nd Massachusetts lost twenty-two men during the period August 10–24.

10. Ibid., p. 326.

11. Eigenbrodt, a native of San Francisco, was the last of the original California captains. He was the senior captain in the regiment and in command of a battalion at the time of his death.

12. Corbett Diary, Aug. 25, 1864.

13. Emerson, ed., *Life and Letters*, p. 51.

14. OR XLII pt. 1, p. 486. The 15th South Carolina was in Kershaw's division.

15. *MassRec*.

16. Corbett Diary, Aug. 27, 1864.

17. *CalRec*, p. 476.

18. Dearborn, *Diary, 1864*, Aug. 29, 1864.

19. Corbett Diary, Aug. 30, 1864.

20. OR XLII pt. 1, p. 486.

21. Emerson, ed., *Life and Letters*, p. 334.

22. Corbett Diary, Sept. 6, 1864.

23. Ibid.

24. Ibid., Sept. 8, 1864.

25. The 1st, 2nd, 5th, and 6th U.S. Cavalry Regiments were in Brig. Gen. John Buford's command that delayed Lee's army long enough for Meade to deploy the Army of the Potomac on the first day at Gettysburg. For the 2nd Massachusetts to be brigaded with them was a measure of the esteem Sheridan had for the regiment and Colonel Lowell.

26. Emerson, ed., *Life and Letters*, Sept. 8, 1864, p 337.

27. Ibid. Sept. 9, 1864, p. 337.

28. Two Californians, Pvt. Benjamin F. Hoxsies of Company L and Sgt. Lemuel McCarty of Company F, became part of this very select group in December 1864. They served with Sheridan throughout the rest of the war.

29. Sheridan, *Memoirs*, pp. 239–40.

30. Corbett Diary, Sept. 9, 1864.

31. Emerson, ed., *Life and Letters*, p. 345.

32. OR XLIII, pt. 1, p. 95. Early commanded the Army of the Shenandoah, which included his II Corps and Breckinridge's troops. Breckinridge was commander of the Department of Southwest Virginia, and he returned to on September 17. In the early stages of the 1864 Shenandoah Valley campaign, and on the date of the attack described here, Breckinridge commanded two divisions—his own, led by Wharton, and Gordon's division (formerly Early's division). Accordingly, throughout OR XLIII Sheridan and other Union leaders refer to "Breckinridge's Corps."

33. *CalRec* and *MassRec*.

34. Grant, *Memoirs*, p. 1:327.

35. Ibid., p. 1:328.

36. OR XLIII, pt. 1, p. 811.

37. For some unknown reason the VI Corps's wagons were not left in accordance with Sheridan's orders. The road running through the hills from Berryville to Winchester was very narrow and there was no room to pull wagons out of the way for advancing infantry. As a result, Crook's VIII Corps was held up getting into position.

38. Stackpole, *Sheridan in the Shenandoah*, p. 220.

39. Ibid., p. 228.

40. Crowninshield to his mother, Oct. 2, 1864, Crowninshield Letters. Crowninshield is incorrect with regard to casualties. See Appendix.

41. Emerson, ed., *Life and Letters*, p. 348.

42. Stackpole, *Sheridan in the Valley*, pp. 230–31.

43. Quoted in Robert Underwood Johnson and Clarence Clough Buel, eds., *Battles and Leaders of the Civil War*, Grant-Lee ed., 8 vols. (New York: Century, 1884–1887), vol. 4, pt. 2, p. 510.

44. Lt. Gen. Jubal Anderson Early, CSA, *Autobiographical Sketch and Narrative of the War Between the States* (Reprint, New York: Konecky and Konecky, 1994), pp. 426–27.

45. *MassRec* and *CalRec*. See Corbett Diary for the regard the enlisted men had for Baldwin.

46. *OR* XLIII, pt. 1, p. 428.

47. Corbett Diary, Sept. 21, 1864.

48. *OR* XLIII, pt. 1, p. 428.

49. Corbett Diary, Sept. 21, 1864.

50. Wert, *Mosby's Rangers*, p. 212.

51. Scott, *Partisan Life*, p. 318.

52. Wert, *Mosby's Rangers*, p. 212.

53. A docent at the Confederate Museum at Front Royal whose great, great grandfather had been in Mosby's band told the author that only one guerrilla had shot McMaster. According to her, the killer was a known hothead. When asked for the name she refused to respond in spite of urgings. So, even today, the locals still protect and nurture the Mosby band!

54. Scott, *Partisan Life*, p. 319.

55. Wert, *Mosby's Rangers*, p. 214.

56. *OR* XLIII, pt. 1, p. 490.

57. Scott, *Partisan Life*, p. 320.

58. Wert, *Mosby's Rangers*, p. 216.

59. Ibid., p. 215.

60. At this point in the war Mosby did not have a headquarters in the normal sense. Overby and Carter could not answer because there was no answer.

61. Wert, *Mosby's Rangers*, pp. 217–18.

62. Crowninshield to his mother, Oct. 2, 1864, Crowninshield Letters.

63. Corbett Diary, Sept. 23, 1864.

10. "A Crow Will Have to Carry His Own Provisions"

1. *OR* XLIII, pt. 1, p. 48.

2. Stackpole, *Sheridan in the Shenandoah*, p. 251.

3. *OR* XLIII, pt. 1, p. 26.

4. Ibid., p. 27.

5. Sheridan, *Memoirs*, p. 256.

6. *OR* XLIII, pt. 1, p. 429; and Corbett Diary, Sept. 25, 1864.

7. Emerson, ed., *Life and Letters*, p. 349.

8. *CalRec*, p. 856.

9. Sheridan, *Memoirs*, pp. 257–58.

10. John B. Gordon, *Reminiscences of the Civil War* (New York: Charles Scribner's Sons,

1904), p. 331. General Early delivered this gun to Sheridan at Cedar Creek; the Reserve Brigade captured it.

11. Sheridan, *Memoirs*, p. 260; and OR XLIII, pt. 1, p. 441.

12. See OR XLIII, pt. 1, p. 50.

13. Corbett Diary, Sept. 27, 1864. The price of boots was about three to four times what it was in the North.

14. Emerson, ed., *Life and Letters*, p. 350.

15. For a complete listing see OR XLIII, pt. 1, p. 436.

16. Ibid., pt. 2, p. 218.

17. Emerson, ed., *Life and Letters*, p. 351.

18. Corbett Diary, Sept. 28, 1864.

19. Stackpole, *Sheridan in the Shenandoah*, p. 264.

20. Emerson, ed., *Life and Letters*, p. 352. The sergeant was never identified by Colonel Lowell.

21. Southern Historical Papers, courtesy of Earl E. Meese of the Waynesboro Historical Society, who found this article in the Virginia Historical Society Museum in Richmond.

22. OR XLIII, pt. 1, p. 491.

23. Corbett Diary, Sept. 30, 1864.

24. Special Orders No. 44 dated September 30, 1864, ORXXXXIII pt. 2, pg. 218.

25. OR XL, pt. 2, p. 168.

26. OR XLIII, pt. 2, p. 153.

27. Ibid., p. 174.

28. OR XLIII, pt. 2, p. 249.

29. Ibid., pt. 1, pp. 815, 873, 944, 949; and pt. 2, pp. 115, 116, 146, 263, 264.

30. Corbett Diary, Oct. 3, 1864.

31. OR XLIII, pt. 2, p. 217.

32. The word *scouts* was used interchangeably with spy during the Civil War. Today the three men would be classified as spies. If they had been captured by Union troops they would have been instantly hanged.

33. Johnson and Buel, eds., *Battles and Leaders*, vol. 4, pt. 2, p. 525.

34. Sheridan, *Memoirs*, p. 261; and HTCW, p. 485.

35. OR XLIII, p. 217.

36. Houses were supposed to be left alone; hopefully Corbett was wrong.

37. Corbett Diary, Oct. 5, 1864.

38. The destruction was not as complete as some have described. In some areas farmers continued to send tithes of their crops to Confederate authorities. See John R. Hildebrand, ed., *A Mennonite Journal, 1862–1865: A Father's Account of the Civil War in the Shenandoah Valley* (Shippensburg, Pa.: Burd Street, 1996) for a view from a Shenandoah farmer's perspective.

11. The Woodstock Races

1. Millard K. and Dean M. Bushong, *Fightin' Tom Rosser, CSA* (Shippensburg, Pa.: Beidel, 1983), pp. 59–60.

2. Ibid., p. 116.

3. Corbett Diary.

4. Lowell to his wife, Oct. 9, 1864, Emerson, *Life and Letters*. Pvt. Frank Enos was Lowell's orderly.

5. Quoted in Horace Porter, *Campaigning with Grant* (New York: Century, 1897; reprint, New York: Bantam Books, 1991).

6. OR XLIII, pt. 1, p. 447.

7. Emerson, ed., *Life and Letters*, p. 470.

8. OR XLIII, pt. 1, pp. 446–47.

9. Corbett Diary, Oct. 10, 1864.

10. OR XLIII, pt. 1, p. 431.

11. Stackpole, *Sheridan in the Valley*, p. 272.

12. OR XLIII, pt. 1, p. 559.

13. Union troopers who lost a horse in combat were generally regarded as heroes and often got a week or so of rest at a remount camp in the rear.

14. OR XLIII, pt. 1, p. 492; and Corbett Diary, Oct. 11, 1864.

15. Mosby attacked the railhead several times. In one raid he derailed a supply train, forcing VI Corps to detour toward Ashby's Gap.

16. Sheridan, *Memoirs*, p. 267.

17. OR XLIII, pt. 1, p. 492.

18. Corbett Diary, Oct. 12, 1865. General Merritt was very popular with the troops.

19. OR XLIII, pt. 2, p. 340.

20. Ibid., p. 339.

21. Ibid., p. 345.

22. Ibid., p. 355.

23. Sheridan, *Memoirs*, p. 268.

24. National Trust now owns Belle Grove Plantation and it is open to visitors. The field where the brigade camped is directly to the north of the main house.

25. Corbett Diary, Oct. 18, 1864.

26. Sheridan, *Memoirs*, p. 269.

27. Ibid.

28. OR XLIII, pt. 2, p. 389.

29. Ibid.

30. Sheridan, *Memoirs*, p. 270.

31. OR XLIII, pt. 2, p. 390.

32. The general topography has changed very little in the past 130 years even though only a portion of the battlefield is protected by The Cedar Creek Battlefield Trust.

33. Capt. William N. McDonald, *A History of the Laurel Brigade*, ed. Bushrod C. Washington (Baltimore: Mrs. Kate McDonald, 1907), pp. 308–309.

34. Emerson, ed. *Life and Letters*, p. 363.

35. OR XLIII, pt. 2, p. 561; ibid., pt. 1, p. 580.

12. Sabers at Cedar Creek

1. Corbett Diary, Oct. 18, 1864; and Charles Henry Veil, *The Memoirs of Charles Henry Veil: A Soldier's Recollections of the Civil War and the Arizona Territory*, ed. Herman J. Viola (New York: Orion, 1993), p. 55.

2. James H. Kidd, *A Cavalryman with Custer* (New York: Sentinel Press, 1908; reprint, New York: Bantam, 1991), p. 301.

3. Emerson, ed., *Life and Letters*, p. 357.

4. Corbett Diary, Oct. 18, 1864.

5. Humphreys, *Field, Camp, Hospital and Prison*, p. 169.

6. Corbett Diary, Oct. 19, 1864; and Joseph W. A. Whitehorne, *The Battle of Cedar Creek* (Strasburg, Va.: The Wayside Museum of American History and Arts, 1987), p. 21.

7. Humphreys, *Field, Camp, Hospital and Prison*, p. 169 and OR XLIII, p. 492.

8. Kidd, *Cavalryman with Custer*, p. 303.

9. Thomas A. Lewis, *The Guns of Cedar Creek* (New York: Dell, 1988), p. 248.

10. Kidd, *Cavalryman with Custer*, p. 304.

11. The column probably followed Hite Chapel Road to the rear of the VI Corps but in front of the remnants of XIX Corps.

12. Kidd, *Cavalryman with Custer*, p. 305.

13. Ibid., p. 306.

14. Whitehorne, *Battle of Cedar Creek*, p. 22.

15. Johnson and Buel, eds., *Battles and Leaders*, vol. 4, pt. 2, p. 518.

16. Emerson, ed., *Life and Letters*, p. 63.

17. This was the same George Getty who took part in the expeditions against the South Anna bridges.

18. The stone walls, some bearing pockmarks from bullets, are still there today.

19. OR XLIII, pt. 1, p. 478.

20. Ibid., p. 478.

21. Colonel Moore was arrested after the battle. However, a court of inquiry did not charge him and he was released on November 10, 1864 (OR XLIII, pt. 2, p. 595).

22. Hussey, who enlisted in the California Hundred, was commissioned in July 1864.

23. Devin's report is in OR XLIII, pt. 1, p. 479.

24. Emerson, ed., *Life and Letters*, p. 64.

25. Ibid., p. 63.

26. Gordon, *Reminiscences of the Civil War*, p. 341.

27. Ibid., p. 344.

28. OR XLIII, pt. 1, p. 562.

29. Sheridan, *Memoirs*, p. 273.

30. Ibid., p. 274.

31. "Sheridan's Ride" by Thomas Buchanan Reade was required reading for years after the war.

32. Sheridan's horse "Reinzi" was presented to him by the officers of the 2nd Michigan Cavalry in Reinzi, Mississippi. He rode Reinzi in nearly every engagement he participated in during the war. After the ride to Cedar Creek the horse was renamed "Winchester." Winchester died in 1878 and his body was mounted and presented to Sheridan. Later it was donated to the Smithsonian Institution, where it is on display in the Hall of Armed Forces History.

33. Lewis, *Guns of Cedar Creek*, p. 266.

34. Ibid., p. 269–70.

35. OR XLIII, pt. 1, p. 450.

36. Corbett Diary, Oct. 19, 1864.

37. Lewis, *Guns of Cedar Creek*, pp. 271–72.

38. Col. Benjamin W. Crowninshield, "Cedar Creek," in *The Battle of Cedar Creek and the Recaptured Guns* (Reprint, Gaithersburg, Md.: Olde Soldier Books, 1987). There appears to have been no love lost between the Crowninshield cousins. After the battle, Benjamin sold his horse to Caspar at an inflated price. Caspar wrote of the exchange: "I am very well mounted now—I bought a horse from Ben C which I like very much. Ben bought him some time ago & gave 100 dollars for him. He charged me 250 for him—the horse was worth the

money but I felt that if I had been leaving the service & had a horse that I did not wish to take home & Ben had wanted him I should have been only too glad to have given him to Ben as a present however I suppose in this world it is 'each man for himself & damn all favors.'"

39. Emerson, ed., *Life and Letters*, p. 64.

40. Sheridan, *Memoirs*, p. 279.

41. Camp Downey was at present-day East 12th Street and 17th Avenue, overlooking Lake Merritt.

42. Richard K. Tibbals, "Thirty Years Later," *CWTI*, Apr. 1986.

43. Ibid.

44. Kidd, *Cavalryman with Custer*, p. 311.

45. This is an inside joke. The Confederates had captured most of the guns being used against Merritt's division earlier in the morning. Merritt is tweaking VIII and XIX Corps artillerymen for losing their guns.

46. OR XLIII, pt. 1.

47. See OR XLIII, pt. 1, p. 434, for Torbert's report. Merritt's report is on p. 450. See also Kidd, *Cavalryman with Custer*, p. 461.

48. OR XLIII, pt. 1, p. 523.

49. Sheridan, *Memoirs*, p. 281.

50. Emerson, ed., *Life and Letters*, p. 65.

51. Kidd, *Cavalryman with Custer*, p. 311.

52. Sheridan says in his memoirs that Gibbs succeeded Lowell. However, the OR clearly states that Crowninshield took over, as does Crowninshield. See Crowninshield Letters, Oct. 21, 1864; and OR XLIII, pt. 1, p. 161.

53. Sheridan, *Memoirs*, p. 281.

54. Lewis, *Guns of Cedar Creek*, p. 234.

55. Sheridan, *Memoirs*, p. 280.

56. OR XLIII, pt. 1, p. 524.

57. Crowninshield Letters (emphasis added).

58. Kidd, *Cavalryman with Custer*, p. 312.

59. OR XLIII, pt. 1, p. 525.

60. Kidd, *Cavalryman with Custer*, p. 312.

61. Lewis, *Guns of Cedar Creek*, p. 303. For Custer's outlandish remarks, see ibid., p. 310.

62. Both of these buildings are still in existence. The house where Lowell died is privately owned and not open to the public. The old inn, built in the eighteenth century, is well worth a visit. Someone recently placed a monument in the inn's garden commemorating Lowell's death.

63. Thanks to Dr. R. LaPorta, trauma surgeon, for the probable diagnosis. Lowell's chances of survival would have been uncertain even with today's surgical techniques.

64. This note is not included in his published letters, and rightly so.

65. Emerson, ed., *Life and Letters*, p. 67.

66. Crowninshield to his mother, Oct. 21, 1864, Crowninshield Letters.

67. Emerson, ed., *Life and Letters*, p. 68.

68. *Harper's Weekly*, Nov. 12, 1864.

69. In 1863 Tucson, Arizona Territory, was occupied by the 1st California Cavalry, part of the "California Column." On August 29, 1866, the post was made permanent and renamed Camp Lowell (later Fort Lowell). It was a military post until 1891, when it was transferred to the Interior Department. Remains of the old fort, now within Tucson's city limits, have

been partially restored. See Robert Frazer, *Forts of the West* (Norman: University of Oklahoma Press, 1965).

70. OR XLIII, pt. 1, p. 136.

71. Ibid., pp. 526–27.

72. Douglas Southall Freeman, *Lee's Lieutenants: A Study in Command*, vol. 3, *Gettysburg to Appomattox* (New York: Charles Scribner's Sons, 1944), pp. 609–10.

13. Burning "Mosby's Confederacy"

1. OR XLIII, pt. 1, p. 451.

2. Corbett Diary, Oct. 22, 1864.

3. Humphreys was among the Union officers imprisoned in Charleston by Confederate authorities in an attempt to alleviate the Union bombardment.

4. Corbett Diary, Nov. 1, 1864.

5. OR XLIII, pt.1, pp. 529–30.

6. Corbett Diary, Nov. 5, 1864.

7. OR XLIII, pt. 2, p. 910.

8. Ibid., p. 920. Pvt. Oscar Burnap, shot in the face and crippled for life while a prisoner of Mosby, might have had different thoughts on Mosby's treatment of prisoners.

9. "Letters from the Californians," Mar. 22, 1864.

10. Corbett Diary, Nov. 8, 1864.

11. Ibid.

12. Mobberly was the leader of a small guerrilla band in the lower Shenandoah Valley. He was *not* part of Mosby's band or any other regularly constituted Ranger group. He frequently committed robbery, attacked isolated pickets, raided into Maryland, and was generally considered an outlaw. A $500 reward was placed on his head and he and his band eventually were exterminated.

13. Corbett Diary, Nov. 11, 1864.

14. OR XLIII, pt. 2, p. 604.

15. Ibid., pp. 611, 624, 630.

16. Ibid., p. 604.

17. OR XLIII, pt. 2, p. 639.

18. Corbett Diary, Nov. 19, 1864.

19. OR XLIII, pt. 2, p. 650.

20. Ibid.

21. "Letters from the Californians," Mar 22, 1864.

22. Corbett Diary, Nov. 15, 1864.

23. Ibid.

24. Sheridan, *Memoirs*, p. 286.

25. OR XLIII, pt. 2, p. 671.

26. Ibid., p. 670.

27. Ibid., p. 687.

28. Ibid., pp. 688, 689.

29. Ibid., p. 731.

30. Ibid., p. 685; and Wert, *Mosby's Rangers*, p. 261.

31. OR XLIII, pt. 2, p. 701.

32. Ibid., p. 721.

33. Quoted in Wert, *Mosby's Rangers*, p. 262.

34. Corbett Diary, Dec. 3, 1864.

35. OR XLVI, pt. 1, p. 673.

36. Ibid., pp. 653–63.

37. These numbers were about double Early's available force.

38. OR XLIII, pt. 2, p. 669.

39. Ibid., p. 740.

40. OR XLVI, pt. 1, see pp. 668–740, 936.

41. Corbett Diary, Dec. 14, 1864.

42. OR XLVIII, pt. 2, p. 743.

43. Ibid., p. 919.

44. Ibid., p. 778.

45. Ibid., p. 780.

46. Ibid., p. 785

47. Ibid., p. 800.

48. Ibid., p. 802.

49. Corbett Diary, Dec. 19, 1864.

50. OR XLIII, pt. 1, p. 39.

51. Ibid., pt. 2, p. 675.

52. Ibid., p. 677.

53. McDonald, *History of the Laurel Brigade*, p. 333.

54. Humphreys, *Field, Camp, Hospital and Prison*, p. 195.

55. Ibid., pp. 195–98.

56. OR XLIII, pt. 1, p. 678.

57. *CalRec*. Hardin managed to get back safely, then later deserted from Cloud's Mill.

58. OR XLIII, pt. 1, p. 678.

59. Ibid.

60. Humphreys, *Field, Camp, Hospital and Prison*, p. 199.

61. Ibid., p. 200.

62. OR XLIII, pt. 1, p. 97.

63. This was probably Sgt. John T. Barker of the 25th New York Cavalry, who disappeared on December 29 near Kernstown. There is no further record of Barker; guerrillas presumably killed him.

64. Daniel Sutherland, *Seasons of War: The Ordeal of a Confederate Community, 1861–1865* (New York: Free Press, 1995), p. 370.

65. OR XLIII, pt. 2, pp. 677–79.

14. Virginia Mud

1. OR XLVI, pt. 2, p. 27.

2. Corbett Diary, Jan. 4, 1865.

3. OR XLVI, pt. 2, p. 27. This of course meant that the troops managed to "capture" enough local building material to build their winter quarters and stables.

4. Ibid., p. 36.

5. Ibid., p. 56.

6. Ibid., p. 125.

7. OR XLVI, pt. 2, p. 323.

8. *CWTI*, Feb. 1969; and Penny Coleman, *Spies!: Women in the Civil War* (Cincinnati: Betterway, 1992), p. 81.

9. OR XLVI, pt. 2, p. 356.

10. Ibid., p. 656.

11. They died at: Danville, N.C.—10; Florence, S.C.—1; Savannah, Ga.—6; Richmond, Va.—2; Salisbury, N.C.—4; Millen, Ga.—1; Andersonville, Ga.—36. Of the 264 men captured, 60 died in prison, 3 deserted, 11 escaped, 185 were exchanged, and 5 were missing (data compiled by author using information in *CalRec* and *MassRec*).

12. Robert E. Denney, *Civil War Prisons and Escapes: A Day-by-Day Chronicle* (New York: Sterling, 1993), p. 361.

13. OR XLVI, pt. 2, p. 701.

14. Ibid., pp. 711, 713.

15. Corbett Diary, Feb. 26, 1865.

16. OR XLVI, pt. 1, p. 485.

17. Ibid., p. 475.

18. Sheridan, *Memoirs*, p. 293.

19. OR XLVI, pt. 1, p. 485.

20. Ibid.

21. Ibid., p. 489.

22. OR XLVI, pt. 1, pp. 515–16.

23. Ibid. p. 476.

24. Corbett Diary, Mar. 2, 1865.

25. The railroad, the target of Sheridan's advance, runs east to west from Rockfish Gap through Waynesboro and then Fisherville, across Christian's Creek to Staunton, and on through the Appalachians.

26. The ridge is now an upscale residential area.

27. OR *Atlas*, plate 71–4.

28. OR XLVI, pt. 1, p. 502.

29. OR XLVI, pt. 1, p. 503; Early, *Memoirs*, pp. 387–89.

30. Ibid.

31. See OR XLVI, pt. 2, p. 509, for a list of battle flags taken by Custer at Waynesboro.

32. Bushong and Bushong, *Fightin' Tom Rosser*, pp. 168–69.

33. OR XLVI, pt. 1, p. 528.

34. Ibid., pp. 528–29.

35. Ibid., p. 912. Sixty-five officers and 1,333 men arrived at Stephenson's Depot, including 30 men and 4 officers captured along the way.

36. In retrospect it seems that the Reserve Brigade troopers were becoming demolition experts.

37. Veil, *Memoirs*, p. 58. Charles Veil was on General Gibbs's staff.

38. OR XLVI, pt. 1, p. 500; Corbett Diary, Mar. 3, 1865.

39. Sheridan *Memoirs*, p. 296.

40. OR XLVI, pt. 1, p. 486.

41. Ibid., p. 490.

42. Corbett Diary, Mar. 4, 1865.

43. Ibid., Mar. 5, 1865.

44. AR 1865, p. 632.

45. Frederick Quant Diary, Mar. 6, 1865, Banc Film 2095, Bancroft Library, University of California, Berkeley (hereafter Quant Diary); OR XLVI, pt. 1, p. 486.

46. Duguidsville is now, sadly, called Bent Creek.

47. There were at least three New Markets in the Virginia of 1865.

48. Quant Diary, Mar. 6, 1865.

49. OR XLVI, pt. 1, p. 500.

50. AR 1865, p. 632.

51. Quant and Corbett Diaries, Mar. 7, 1865.

52. The 6th Pennsylvania, normally part of the Reserve Brigade, was marching under General Merritt's direct orders.

53. James Longstreet, *From Manassas to Appomattox: Memoirs of the Civil War in America* (Philadelphia: Lippincott, 1896; reprint, Secaucus, N.J.: Blue and Grey Press, 1984), p. 591.

54. Sheridan, *Memoirs*, p. 297.

55. OR XLVI, pt. 1, p. 491.

56. Corbett Diary, Mar. 8, 1865.

57. Ibid.

58. Today Howardsville is only a post office and general store. The sole addition is a gasoline pump. The country is still a backwater area and has changed only a little from what it was during the war. It is worth a day's drive to meander down the little country lanes paralleling the river—it is a trip back in time.

59. OR XLVI, pt. 1, p. 500.

60. Ibid., p. 498.

61. Sheridan, *Memoirs*, p. 298.

62. Corbett Diary, Mar. 11, 1865.

63. At the time Campbell was only nineteen years old. He stayed in the army after the war, serving as a scout. Rowland became a prominent lawyer in Pittsburgh.

64. Porter, *Campaigning with Grant*, pp. 397–99.

65. OR XLVI, pt. 1, p. 492.

66. Sheridan, *Memoirs*, p. 298.

67. OR XLVI, pt. 1, pp. 492, 500.

68. AR 1865, p. 632.

69. No prisoners were taken, so Maxwell was not aware that he was facing veteran Confederate troops.

70. OR XLVI, pt. 1, pp. 493, 496, 501.

71. Ibid., pt. 3, p. 36.

72. Ibid., pt. 1, p. 501; Corbett Diary, Mar. 17, 1865.

73. Longstreet, *From Manassas to Appomattox*, p. 591.

74. Ibid., p. 591.

75. OR XLVI, pt. 3, p. 58.

76. Ibid., pt. 1, p. 334.

77. OR XLVI, pt. 1, pp. 496, 499, 501, 507.

78. Ibid., pt. 3, p. 51.

15. Dinwiddie Co urthouse

1. OR XLVI, pt.3, pp. 35–68.

2. Corbett Diary.

3. Alfred H. Guernsey and Henry M. Alden, *Harper's Pictorial History of the Civil War* (New York: Fairfax, 1995), p. 158.

4. OR XLVI, pt. 3, Pp. 160–65.

5. Ibid., p. 192.

6. Grant, *Memoirs*, p. 2:437.

7. OR XLVI, pt. 1, p. 50.

8. Grant, *Memoirs*, pp. 2:437–38.

9. Sheridan, *Memoirs*, p. 306.

10. Ibid., pp. 306–307; and OR XLVI, pt. 3, p. 234.

11. Sheridan, *Memoirs*, p. 310.

12. OR XLVI, pt. 1, pp. 1101–16.

13. The six companies of the 6th Pennsylvania, normally part of the Reserve Brigade, were assigned to Sheridan's headquarters.

14. OR XLVI, pt. 3, p. 389.

15. Ibid.

16. Ibid., pt. 1, p. 55.

17. Ibid., pp. 1101, 1127.

18. Sheridan, *Memoirs*, p. 311.

19. OR XLVI, pt. 1, p. 797.

20. Sheridan *Memoirs*, p. 311.

21. OR XLVI, pt. 1, p. 1102.

22. OR *Atlas*, plate 94, nos. 8 and 9.

23. OR XLVI, pt. 1, p. 1287; Longstreet, *From Manassas to Appomattox*, p. 596.

24. Ibid., pt. 3, p. 389.

25. Ibid., pt. 1, p. 803.

26. Ibid., p. 804.

27. Clifford Dowdey's *Lee* (Boston: Little, Brown, 1965), p. 535.

28. Ibid., p. 325.

29. Sheridan, *Memoirs*, pp. 314–15.

30. Grant, *Memoirs*, p. 2:438. Grant describes this meeting out of chronological order. The key phrase that establishes the timeframe is at the beginning of the paragraph reading: "One day, after the movement I am about to describe had commenced, . . ." on the next page. He starts the description of the movement with the words, "Finally the 29th of March came . . ." Thus, the meeting took place on March 30.

31. Sheridan, *Memoirs*, p. 315.

32. Ibid., pp. 314–15.

33. Humphreys, *Field, Camp, Hospital and Prison*, pp. 234–35.

34. OR XLVI, pt. 1, pp. 1102, 1116, 1122, 1127.

35. Ibid., pt. 3, p. 325.

36. Sheridan, *Memoirs*, p. 315.

37. Chamberlain, *Passing of the Armies*, p. 48; OR XLVI, pt. 1, p. 1299.

38. OR XLVI, pt. 1, p. 1122.

39. Porter, *Campaigning with Grant*, p. 432.

40. The Reserve Brigade had about 500 men, Gregg and Smith about 2,200, and Custer about 2,000, for a total of 4,700. Two of Devin's brigades and one of Crook's were not part of this fight. In addition, one should remember that when the unit was fighting dismounted, a quarter of the men would be in the rear with the horses.

41. The numbers shown here for Sheridan's troops are those in his reports and the returns in OR XLVI, pt. 3, p. 391. The Confederate numbers are from Dowdey, *Lee*, pp. 533–34.

42. OR XLVI, pt. 1, p. 1110.

16. The Five Forks Shad Bake

1. OR XLVI, pt. 1, p. 1111.

2. Ibid., p. 419.

3. Ibid., p. 869.

4. Ibid., p. 1299.

5. SuppOR 8, The Warren Court of Inquiry, pp. 469, 475, 476.

6. OR XLVI, pt. 1, p. 1104.

7. Ibid., p. 838.

8. Ibid., p. 879.

9. Ibid., p. 880.

10. Gibbs was sick this day, so orders went straight from Sheridan and Merritt to Colonel Crowninshield. See SuppOR 8, p. 818.

11. SuppOR 8, pp. 817–18.

12. OR XLVI, pt. 1, p. 1124.

13. SuppOR 8, pp. 1502, 1503.

14. These horses were probably from Devin's division, which was directly north of the Gravelly Run Church road.

15. Joshua Lawrence Chamberlain, The Passing of the Armies (New York: Bantam, 1993), p. 92.

16. Ibid., p. 96.

17. A full left wheel—90 degrees—would have put the division in a correct alignment to march past the Confederate line.

18. OR XLVI, pt. 1, p. 1124.

19. SuppOR 8, p. 1504.

20. Henry A. Chambers, The Civil War Diary of Captain Henry A. Chambers: Fredericksburg to Appomattox, ed. T. H. Pierce (Wendell, N.C.: Broadfoot's Bookmark, 1983), p. 257.

21. Bushong and Bushong, Fightin' Tom Rosser, p. 172.

22. Ibid., p. 173.

23. Chamberlain, Passing of the Armies, p. 104.

24. Ibid., p. 107.

25. Warren finally got a court of inquiry in 1879 and after two years was partially exonerated. Unfortunately, the findings were of no comfort. Warren died a bitter and angry man on August 8, 1882, three months before the findings were published.

26. Corse later reported that the cavalry to his front had made only a few ineffectual demonstrations during the afternoon. Custer's division was in front.

27. Dowdey, Lee, p. 537.

28. SuppOR 8, p. 1499.

29. OR XLVI, p. 1124.

30. Ibid., pt. 1, p. 1128.

31. CalRec and MassRec.

32. OR XLVI, pt. 1, p. 1264.

33. CWTI, May 1966; and Mosby, Gray Ghost, pp. 299–300.

34. OR XLVI, pt. 1, p. 1124.

35. Ibid., pp. 1124, 1128; Corbett Diary.

36. The OR Atlas calls this road the River Road because it paralleled the Appomattox between the river and the Namozine Road (Plate 74-6).

37. Sweat House Creek is west of Deep Creek. It joins Deep Creek just before the outlet to the Appomattox.

38. This is probably at the crossing near Bridgeforth's Mill.

39. OR XLVI, p. 1119.

40. Dowdey, *Lee*, p. 547.

41. Ibid., p. 548.

42. Ibid., p. 552; OR XLVI, pt. 1, p. 1107.

43. OR XLVI, pt. 1, p. 1124.

44. Corbett Diary, April 4, 1865.

45. OR XLVI, pt. 1, pp. 1119, 1124, 1128.

46. Corbett Diary, April 4, 1865.

47. OR XLVI, pt. 1, pp. 1119, 1132.

48. Sheridan, *Memoirs*, p. 335.

49. OR XLVI, pt. 1, p. 905.

50. Ibid., pp. 681, 839.

51. Dowdey, *Lee*, p. 533.

17. Road Block at Appomattox

1. OR XLVI 1 p. 1107.

2. Ibid., p. 1294.

3. Ibid., p. 1295.

4. Francis H. Kennedy, ed., *The Civil War Battlefield Guide* (Boston: Houghton Mifflin, 1990), p. 281.

5. OR XLVI, pt. 1, pp. 1126, 1128; *Civil War Battlefield Guide*, pp. 278–81.

6. Dowdey, *Lee*, p. 563.

7. Corbett Diary, April 5, 1865.

8. Dowdey, *Lee*, p. 564.

9. Ibid., p. 565.

10. OR XLVI, pt. 1, p. 1109.

11. Grant, *Memoirs*, p. 2:626.

12. Ibid.

13. Ibid., p. 2:479.

14. OR XLVI, pt. 1, p. 1126.

15. Ibid., p. 1132.

16. Corbett Diary, Apr. 8, 1865.

17. OR XLVI, pt. 1, pp. 1126, 1128.

18. Corbett Diary, Apr. 9, 1865.

19. Grant, *Memoirs*, p. 2:485.

20. OR XLVI, pt. 1, p. 1109.

21. Dowdey, *Lee*, p. 572.

22. Corbett Diary, Apr. 9, 1865.

23. Dowdey, *Lee*, p. 574.

24. Grant, *Memoirs*, p. 2:483.

25. Dowdey, *Lee*, p. 574; Grant, *Memoirs*, p. 2:628.

26. Dowdey, *Lee*, p. 574.

27. Gordon, *Reminiscences*, pp. 439–40.

28. Longstreet, *From Manassas to Appomattox*, p. 627.

29. Gordon, *Reminiscences*, pp. 440–41.

30. Ironically, McLean had owned a farm and house at the site of the war's first major battle—the First Battle of Bull Run—and moved to Appomattox to get out of the war zone.

31. Porter, *Campaigning with Grant*, p. 324.

32. Corbett Diary, Apr. 10, 1865.

Bibliography

Unpublished Materials

Bancroft Library, University of California. Berkeley.
    De Witt Clinton Thompson Papers
    Frederick Quant Diary
    Sam Corbett Papers
Magnus Crowninshield Papers. Massachusetts Historical Society. Boston.
Valorus Dearborn Diary. Privately printed and provided by Mrs. Geraldine Chase of Concord, N.H.

Newspapers and Periodicals

Civil War Times Illustrated
Daily Alta Californian
Harper's Weekly—reprints published 1961 through 1965
Montgomery County (Maryland) Sentinel
New York Times
San Francisco Call

Books

Adjutant General of the Commonwealth of Massachusetts. *Massachusetts Soldiers, Sailors and Marines in the Civil War*. 8 vols. Boston: Norwood Press, 1931.

Alexander, John H. *Mosby's Men*. New York: Neale, 1907.

Annual Report of the Adjutant General of the Commonwealth of Massachusetts. 3 vols. Boston: Adjutant General's Office, 1863–1865.

Atlas to Accompany the Official Records of the Union and Confederate Armies. Foreword by Henry Steele Commager. Washington, D.C.: Government Printing Office, 1895. Reprint, New York: Thomas Yoseloff, 1958.

Bushong, Millard K., and Dean M. *Fightin' Tom Rosser, CSA*. Shippensburg, Pa.: Beidel, 1983.

Catton, Bruce. *A Stillness at Appomattox*. Garden City, N.Y.: Doubleday, 1954.

Chamberlain, Joshua Lawrence. *The Passing of the Armies*. New York: G. P. Putnam's Sons, 1915. Reprint, New York: Bantam, 1993.

Chambers, Henry A. *Diary of Captain Henry Chambers*. Edited by T. H. Pierce. Wendell, N.C.: Broadfoot's Bookmark, 1983.

Cochran, Warren. *A True Story of the Civil War, 1861–1865*. LaPorte, Ind.: LaPorte County Historical Museum, n.d.

Coleman, Penny. *Spies!: Women in the Civil War*. Cincinnati: Betterway, 1992.

Cooke, Philip St. George. *Cavalry Tactics or Regulations for the Instruction, Formations and Movements of the Cavalry*. Washington, D.C.: War Department, 1862.

Cooling, Benjamin Franklin. *Jubal Early's Raid on Washington, 1864*. Baltimore: Nautical and Aviation, 1989.

Dearborn, Valorus. *Diary, 1864*. n.p., n.d. Copy provided by Mrs. Geraldine Chase of Concord, N.H.

Denney, Robert E. *Civil War Prisons and Escapes: A Day-by-Day Chronicle*. New York: Sterling, 1993.

Dowdey, Clifford. *Lee*. Boston: Little, Brown, 1965.

Early, Jubal A. *Lieutenant General Jubal Anderson Early, C.S.A.: Autobiographical Sketch and Narrative of the War Between the States*. Philadelphia: J. B. Lippincott, 1912. Reprint, New York: Konecky and Konecky, 1994.

Emerson, Edward W. *Life and Letters of Charles Russell Lowell*. Port Washington, N.Y.: Kennikat, 1971.

Evans, Thomas J., and James M. Moyer. *Mosby's Confederacy: A Guide to the Roads and Sites of Colonel John Singleton Mosby*. Shippensburg, Pa.: White Mane, 1991.

Farwell, Byron. *Ball's Bluff: A Small Battle and Its Long Shadow*. McLean, Va.: EPM, 1990.

Faust, Patricia, ed. *Historical Times Illustrated Encyclopedia of the Civil War*. New York: Harper and Row, 1986.

Fisk, Wilbur. *Hard Marching Every Day*. Edited by Emil and Ruth Rosenblatt. Lawrence: University Press of Kansas, 1983.

Foote, Shelby. *The Civil War: A Narrative*. 3 vols. New York: Vintage, 1986.

Frazer, Robert. *Forts of the West*. Norman: University of Oklahoma Press, 1965.

Freeman, Douglas Southall. *Lee's Lieutenants: A Study in Command*. Vol. 3. *Gettysburg to Appomattox*. New York: Charles Scribner's Sons, 1944.

Gallagher, Gary, ed. *Extracts of Letters of Major General Bryan Grimes to his Wife*. Wilmington, N.C.: Broadfoot, 1986.

———, ed. *Struggle for the Shenandoah: Essays on the 1864 Valley Campaign*. Kent, Ohio: Kent State University Press, 1991.

Gordon, John B. *Reminiscences of the Civil War*. New York: Charles Scribner's Sons, 1904.

Grant, Ulysses S. *Personal Memoirs of U. S. Grant*. 2 vols. New York: Charles L. Webster, 1885.

Guernsey, Alfred H., and Henry M. Alden. *Harper's Pictorial History of the Civil War*. New York: Fairfax, 1995.

Hewett, Janet B. ed. *Supplement to the Official Records of the Union and Confederate Armies*. 100 vols. Wilmington, N.C.: Broadfoot, 1996–1998.

Hildebrand, John R., ed. *A Mennonite Journal, 1862–1865: A Father's Account of the Civil War in the Shenandoah Valley*. Shippensburg, Pa.: Burd Street, 1996.

Hughes, Sarah Forbes, ed. *John Murray Forbes: Letters and Recollections*. 2 vols. Boston: Houghton Mifflin and Cambridge Press, 1900.

Humphreys, Charles A. *Field, Camp, Hospital and Prison in the Civil War, 1863–1865*. Boston: George H. Ellis, 1918.

Johnson, Robert Underwood, and Clarence Clough Buel, eds. *Battles and Leaders of the Civil War, Grant-Lee Edition*. 8 vols. New York: Century, 1884–1887.

Jones, Virgil Carrington. *Gray Ghosts and Rebel Raiders*. New York: Henry Holt, 1956. Reprint, McLean, Va.: EPM, 1984.

———. *Ranger Mosby*. Chapel Hill: University of North Carolina Press, 1944. Reprint, McLean, Va.: EPM, 1972.

Kennedy, Elijah R. *The Contest for California*. Boston: Houghton Mifflin, 1912.

Kennedy, Frances H., ed. *The Civil War Battlefield Guide*. Boston: Houghton Mifflin, 1990.

Kidd, James H. A Cavalryman with Custer. New York: Sentinel Press, 1908. Reprint, New York: Bantam, 1991.

Lawrence, William. Life of Amos S. Lawrence. Boston and Cambridge: Houghton Mifflin and University Press of Cambridge, 1888, 1889.

Lewis, Thomas A. The Guns of Cedar Creek. New York: Dell, 1988.

Longstreet, James. From Manassas to Appomattox: Memoirs of the Civil War in America. Philadelphia: Lippincott, 1896. Reprint, Secaucus, N.J.: Blue and Grey, 1984.

McDonald, Capt. William N. A History of the Laurel Brigade. Edited by Bushrod C. Washington. Baltimore: Mrs. Kate McDonald, 1907.

McGuire, Judith W. Diary of a Southern Refugee by a Lady of Virginia. Lincoln: University of Nebraska Press, 1995.

Miller, Frances T., ed. The Photographic History of the Civil War. 10 vols. New York: Review of Reviews, 1911.

Mosby, John S. Gray Ghost: The Civil War Memoirs of Colonel John S. Mosby. Boston: Little, Brown, 1917. Reprint, New York: Bantam, 1992.

Orton, Richard, comp. Records of California Men in the War of the Rebellion. Sacramento: California Adjutant General's Office, 1890.

Osborne, Charles C. Jubal: The Life and Times of General Jubal A. Early, CSA. Chapel Hill, N.C.: Algonquin, 1992.

Pauley, Michael J. Unreconstructed Rebel: The Life of General John McCausland, CSA. Charleston, W.Va.: Pictorial Histories, 1993.

Pickett, LaSalle Corbell. The Heart of a Soldier: As Revealed in the Intimate Letters of General George E. Pickett, C.S.A. New York: Seth Moyle, 1913. Reprint, Gettysburg, Pa.: Stan Clark, 1995.

Porter, Horace. Campaigning with Grant. New York: Century, 1897. Reprint, New York: Bantam, 1991.

Quinn, Arthur. The Rivals: William Gwin, David Broderick and the Birth of California. New York: Crown, 1994.

Rhodes, Robert Hunt, ed. All for the Union: The Civil War Diary and Letters of Elisha Hunt Rhodes. New York: Orion, 1991.

Scott, Maj. John. Partisan Life with Col. John S. Mosby. New York: Harper and Brothers, 1867.

Scott, Robert G, ed. Fallen Leaves: The Civil War Diary of Major Henry Livermore Abbott. Kent, Ohio: Kent State University Press, 1991.

Sheridan, Philip H. Civil War Memoirs. New York: Charles Webster, 1888. Reprint, New York: Bantam, 1991.

Slade, A. D. A. T. A. Torbert, Southern Gentleman in Blue. Dayton, Ohio: Morningside House, 1992.

Stackpole, Edward J. Sheridan in the Shenandoah: Jubal Early's Nemesis. Harrisburg, Pa.: Stackpole, 1961.

Stephens, Robert Grier Jr., ed. Intrepid Warrior: Clement Anselm Evans, Confederate General from Georgia: Life, Letters, and Diaries of the War Years. Dayton, Ohio: Morningside House, 1992.

Stevens, Gen. Hazard. The Battle of Cedar Creek and the Captured Guns. Reprint, Gaithersburg, Md.: Olde Soldier Books, 1987.

Sutherland, Daniel. Seasons of War: The Ordeal of a Confederate Community, 1861–1865. New York: Free Press, 1995.

Turner, George Edgar. Victory Rode the Rails: The Strategic Place of the Railroads in the Civil

War. With an introduction by Gary W. Gallagher. Reprint, Lincoln: University of Nebraska Press, 1992.

Veil, Charles Henry. *The Memoirs of Charles Henry Veil: A Soldier's Recollections of the Civil War and the Arizona Territory*. Edited by Herman J. Viola. New York: Orion, 1993.

Vogtsberger, Margaret Ann, ed. *The Dulaneys of Welbourne*. Berryville, Va.: Rockbridge, 1995.

War Department. *The War of the Rebellion: A Compilation of the Official Records of the Union and Confederate Armies*. 128 vols. Washington, D.C.: U.S. Government Printing Office, 1880–1901.

Warner, Ezra J. *Generals in Blue: Lives of the Union Commanders*. Baton Rouge: Louisiana State University Press, 1995.

Wert, Jeffrey D. *Mosby's Rangers*. New York: Simon and Schuster, 1990.

———. *From Winchester to Cedar Creek*. New York: Touchstone, 1987.

Whitehorne, Joseph W. A. *The Battle of Cedar Creek*. Strasburg, Va.: Wayside Museum of American History and Arts, 1987.

Wiley, Bell Irvin. *The Life of Billy Yank: The Common Soldier of the Union*. Baton Rouge: Louisiana State University Press, 1997.

Woodward, Harold R. *Defender of the Valley: Brigadier General John Daniel Imboden, CSA*. Berryville, Va.: Rockbridge, 1996.

Worthington, Glenn H. *Fighting for Time*. Shippensburg, Pa.: White Mane, 1985.

Index

Page numbers in *italics* refer to illustrations.

200–201, 319n62; as disciplinarian, 17–18; early years of, 14–15; engaged to Josephine Shaw, 17; Halleck countermands Hooker's orders, 42; joins McClellan's staff, 16; marries Josephine Shaw, 61; meets with Hooker, 41; meets with Stanton, 37–38; military ambitions of, 16–17; at Opequon Creek, 138; ordered to Vienna, 59; patrols against Mosby, 61–65; praised by Auger, 76–77; proposes sutler escort, 54; pursues Mosby, 39, 43–45; pursues White, 54–55; recruitment efforts of, 17–18; on Reed's abilities, 23; at Rockville, 95–100; shot at Cedar Creek, 195–96; at Tennallytown, 91–95; war-weariness of, 148

Lowell, James Jackson, 6, 16
Luray Valley, 119, 140–41, 291, 292
Lynch, Michael, 293
Lynchburg, 80–81
Lyons, John, 283

Mackenzie, Maj. Gen. Ranald S., 240, 264, 268–69
Maddox, Samuel, 110
Manassas Gap Railroad, 121, 149–50
Manchester, Luman A., 98, 285
Manker, William, 277
Manning, Capt. George A., 11, 72, 178, 281
Manning, Lt. William C., 11, 72, 281
Marden, John, 132, 288
Marsh, William, 285
Martin, Cpl. Thomas, 132, 289
Maryland, Southern, 34–35, 36
Mashar, Phillip, 285
Massachusetts, soldier quotas of, 5, 6, 10, 14
Massanutten Mountain, 119
Massow, Baron Robert von, 71–72
Matthews, Patrick, 284
Maxwell, Lt. Col. George R., 234, 323n69
McAllister, Sgt. Henry, 291
McCammen, J. S., 279
McCarty, John, 55–56, 277
McCarty, Sgt. Lemuel, 314n28
McCausland, Brig. Gen. John, 112–13, 312n34
McClease, Joseph, 290
McClellan, Gen. George B., 16, 203
McCook, Maj. Gen. Alexander McD., 92, 93
McDonald, Sgt. Allen, 294
McDonald, Daniel, 287
McDonald, Cpl. James, 85, 283
McDonald, Michael, 282
McDonald, Philip, 280

McDougall, Daniel, 288
McFarland, Thomas, 65, 278
McGowan, John, 284
McGuire, John D., 281
McIntosh, Lt. Isaac, 294
McIntyre, Campbell, 282
McIntyre, William, 295
McKay, Cpl. James, 176, 286
McKendry, Capt. Archibald, 6, 9, 177
McKenny, John W., 277
McKnight, Edward, 290
McLaughlin, John, 290
McLean, Alfred, 125, 287
McLean, Cpl. Alfred A., 12
McLean, Owen, 286
McLean, Wilmer, 273, 327n30
McMasters, Lt. Charles, 141–42, 315n53
McMillan, Brig. Gen. James, 198
McMullen, Peter, 290
McNiff, John, 285
Meade, Maj. Gen. George G., 42, 59, 73, 154, 242
Meader, 1st Lt. Charles, 132, 288
Meigs, Lt. John, 118, 151
Meigs, Brig. Gen. Montgomery C., 93, 95
Melville, Herman, 75
Merriam, Jonathan, 286
Merritt, Sgt. Gilbert R., 12, 163
Merritt, Brig. Gen. Wesley, 182; at Cedar Creek, 194, 201–202, 204, 319n45; commands 1st Division, 117; destroys guerilla support, 209; at Five Forks, 265; at Milford Creek, 145; named Chief of Cavalry, 222
Merry, Sgt. Thomas, 51–52
Mickey, John, 56
Miles, James, 279
Miller, James, 312n11
Millican, William, 280
Minot, William H., 285
Mitchell's Station, 296
Mobberly, Capt. John W., 207, 320n12
Moeglen, John, 292
Moeglen, Philip, 291
Monocacy River, 82–83, 88–89, 282
Monroe, James, 280
Montjoy, Capt. R. P., 207
Moore, Col. Alpheus, 187, 318n21
Moore, Samuel, 286
Moore, Cpl. William H., 248, 275, 298
Morgan, William H., 291
Morrill, John, 294

A descendant of a pioneer family that came to San Francisco in 1848, **James McLean** graduated from the University of California in 1956. While serving in the Korean War he became interested in the Civil War when a Navy librarian suggested he read Bruce Catton's trilogy on the Army of the Potomac. McLean started collecting volumes of the Official Records and any other books he could find relating to that conflict. When his brother, the family genealogist, told him they had a great-great-uncle who fought in the Civil War, he discovered the California Hundred and Battalion in the *Official Records*. He retired in 1993 to devote more time to writing the history of those units. This book is a culmination of that twenty-year effort.